The Whiskey Rebellion

THE WHISKEY REBELLION

Frontier Epilogue to the American Revolution

Thomas P. Slaughter

New York   Oxford
OXFORD UNIVERSITY PRESS
1986

Oxford University Press

Oxford   New York   Toronto
Delhi   Bombay   Calcutta   Madras   Karachi
Petaling Jaya   Singapore   Hong Kong   Tokyo
Nairobi   Dar es Salaam   Cape Town
Melbourne   Auckland

and associated companies in
Beirut   Berlin   Ibadan   Nicosia

Published by Oxford University Press, Inc.,
200 Madison Avenue, New York, New York 10016

Oxford is the registered trademark of Oxford University Press

Library of Congress Cataloging-in-Publication Data
Slaughter, Thomas P. (Thomas Paul)
The Whiskey Rebellion.
Bibliography: p.   Includes index.
1. Whiskey Insurrection, 1794.   2. Pennsylvania—
History—Insurrection of 1794.   I. Title.
E315.S59   1986   973.4'3   85-30975
ISBN 0-19-503899-1

Printed in the United States of America

This book is dedicated to the memory of
Wesley Frank Craven and Warren I. Susman.

CONTENTS

The Whiskey Rebellion

INTRODUCTION

AT DAYBREAK on July 16, 1794, about fifty men armed with rifles and clubs marched to the house of John Neville, regional supervisor for collection of the federal excise tax in western Pennsylvania. They demanded that Neville resign his position and turn over to them all records associated with collection of the tax on domestically distilled spirits. He refused. Shots were fired. In the ensuing battle five of the attackers fell wounded. One of them later died. Neville and his slaves, who together had defended the premises from secure positions inside the house, suffered no casualties. The mob dispersed.

The following day a crowd of between 400 and 800 locals returned to the scene. This time Neville protected his home with the help of the slaves and eleven soldiers from Fort Pitt. Again the two sides exchanged fire. Neville escaped under cover of a thicket. One or two of the aggressors fell dead. One soldier may have died, three or four were wounded, and two deserted during the course of battle. The remaining guards surrendered after the mob torched the house and outbuildings. The mansion, barns, slave quarters, and most storage bins burned to the ground.

The Whiskey Rebellion, as it is traditionally known and studied, had begun. Before it was over, some 7000 western Pennsylvanians advanced against the town of Pittsburgh, threatened its residents, feigned an attack on Fort Pitt and the federal arsenal there, banished seven members of the community, and destroyed the property of several others. Violence spread to western Maryland, where a Hagerstown crowd joined in, raised liberty poles, and began a march on the arsenal at Frederick. At about the same time, sympathetic "friends of liberty" arose in Carlisle, Pennsylvania, and back-country regions of Virginia and Kentucky. Reports reached the federal government in Philadelphia that the western country was ablaze and that rebels were negotiating with representatives of Great Britain and Spain, two of the nation's most formidable European competitors, for aid in a frontier-wide separatist movement. In response, President Washington nationalized 12,950 militiamen from New Jersey, Pennsylvania, Maryland, and Virginia—an army approximating in size the Continental force that followed him during the Revolution—and personally led the "Watermelon Army" west to shatter the insurgency.

3

This book grows from a desire to understand better the consequences of the ongoing inter-regional confrontation that culminated in the Whiskey Rebellion. The story of that crisis, as it is retold here, focuses on the Rebellion as a climactic event in the process of political and social change that provoked and sustained the War for Independence. Conflict was at the heart of the Revolution, and conflict among Americans was at least as important a part of the story as cooperation against a common enemy. In the aftermath of the violent international struggle that virtually ended in 1781, conflict remained the body and soul of American politics through the end of the century. Politics became, in the words of historian John Howe, a "deadly business" because its practitioners shared an inflated vision of the stakes and a waning tolerance for opposition.[1] Political change from 1780 through 1800—the victory of particular politicians, ideologies, and interests—was not understood by many participants as progressive, inevitable, or consistent with the principles of the Revolution. Our retelling of these stories should not, therefore, imply or assert a consensus among contemporaries.

To reduce an entire era or experience to economic interest, class, regionalism, and power also distorts the picture, however. Ideas are not mere rationalizations for actions. Thoughts precede, incorporate, and explain political acts to those who commit them. There is no accurate version of reality that isolates thought from action, that fails to see the relationship between common and conflicting ideas and the realities of individual and group behavior. There is, as Gordon Wood once wrote, a connection between rhetoric and reality, and our understanding of the past is clearest when we plumb the depths of that relationship.[2] The Whiskey Rebellion illustrates some of the bonds among society, politics, regionalism, ideology, and conflict during the Revolutionary era. In retrospect, it seems something of a violent epilogue to the confrontations that racked the nation during that tumultuous period.

A host of contexts shaped conflict within American society during the two decades after 1780. The intense rhetoric of debates and the violent exploits on both sides of the excise question exposed some of those fundamental cleavages. Many disparate issues focused on the taxation conflicts of 1791 through 1794. Among the most significant were the relation between representation and just taxation in a republic, the tensions between eastern mercantile and western agricultural regions, debates over the rights and duties of citizens, the place of protest in a republican society, international competition for North America, the problem of western lands, policies on westward expansion, independent statehood movements, Indian warfare, the relationship between federal and state governments, and navigation of the Mississippi River. All of these issues and others fueled the fires of partisanship, contributing to the failure of the political process and the resort to arms in 1794.

The story of the Whiskey Rebellion is an oft-told tale. Local historians have recounted its drama time and again to illumine and defend the deeds of liberty-loving ancestors and local heroes. Descendants of the rebels' local enemies and ideological heirs of Federalist leaders have responded in kind with vituperative assaults on the character, the politics, the intelligence, and the integrity of the rebels and historians who have sympathized with their cause. As a result, we have no comprehensive account of the Rebellion. Instead, we have local histories of events as they appeared to western Pennsylvanians, and political narratives of the Washington administration's response to disorder in the three frontier counties.[3]

The only modern book-length treatment, Leland D. Baldwin's *Whiskey Rebels* (1939), recounted the story well from the rebels' point of view.[4] Baldwin relied heavily on the insightful, but personal, contemporary accounts of Hugh Henry Brackenridge and William Findley. He was unable to exploit the full resources of the Library of Congress and the National Archives that document the federal government's perspective. Although Baldwin (and subsequent local historians) examined documents in Pittsburgh carefully and with much success, he lacked access to the manuscripts scattered from Ottawa south to Hartford, New York, Newark, Trenton, Philadelphia, Harrisburg, Baltimore, Annapolis, Richmond, Louisville, Raleigh, Durham, and Nashville that reveal the national dimensions of excise-tax resistance. These collections would have convinced him, as they have me, that the Rebellion was not confined to western Pennsylvania, but was a frontier-wide movement that tells us much about our national history. British, French, and Spanish manuscripts would have shown him that it was an event of international significance as well.

The Rebellion once attracted the attention of historians who disputed its meaning, but who agreed that it was significant. Four books, scores of articles, and countless references in historical texts appeared during the half-century after the episode. The single largest example of armed resistance to a law of the United States between the ratification of the Constitution and the Civil War was once deemed a major historical event. The War between the States, and the Union's survival of even that awesome challenge, altered historical perspectives, though. Historians came to discount anachronistically the opinions of those who, like Chief Justice John Marshall, lived through the Whiskey Rebellion and believed it a dire threat to the Republic, the most important incident of the nation's first quarter-century under the Constitution. The survival of the Union for 200 years has led some historians to dismiss the Rebellion as "duck soup" or "almost charmingly benign." During this century, excluding my efforts, only Baldwin's monograph, one collection of essays, and one doctoral dissertation on the Rebellion have appeared. Compared with the fifty years following the event, few articles on the

Rebellion have been published since the Civil War. Modern textbooks often fail even to mention it, and few allow it much space.[5]

This book challenges the reigning assessment and seeks to restore the Whiskey Rebellion to its former place in our history. One key to even modest success in this enterprise involves pushing the frontier to center stage in the drama of early American politics, where contemporaries knew but historians have often forgotten that it belongs. It is also essential to explore the contexts surrounding the Rebellion—ideological, social, political, and personal—in order to assess the perceptions of opponents. Only then can we hope to measure and weigh the meaning of events to those who lived through them. Such an agenda does not eschew interpretation, and this book certainly has a point of view; it does demand engagement of all sides even, or especially, when the author lacks equal sympathy for all the actors in his historical theater.

These goals help explain the organization as well as the content of what follows. The book is divided into three parts —context, chronology, and consequence. Part One is devoted to long-range contexts extending in some cases before the mid-eighteenth century. These five chapters address ideological, inter-regional, local, and personal perspectives on issues that produced conflict for decades, and in some cases for centuries. They are portrayed here primarily, but not exclusively, from a western vantage point. Until we sketch the broad landscape of political life that included fissures between Americans, we cannot begin to comprehend why people again took up arms over the issue of internal taxes, the deteriorating nature of East-West relations during the 1780s, and the distinctive temper of life on the frontier; we cannot possibly fathom the nature and degree of conflict that emerged between 1791 and 1795 over what has seemed to many historians a rather insignificant tariff on domestically distilled spirits.

Part Two—chronology—picks up the story in 1790, with the first proposals for a national excise on liquor, and carries it through the first six months of 1794. These five chapters attempt to weave the complex web of domestic and international affairs in a way that places the Rebellion within the chronological fabric of other events. More fully than in Part One, eastern nationalist perspectives are integrated with the alternative visions of frontiersmen. Chapters Six through Ten try to illumine some of the reasons why political discourse became less of a dialogue and more of a shouting match, ultimately waged with guns, over the course of the 1790s. They seek to recapture some of the horror, the panic, and the violence that was eighteenth-century life, but which has disappeared from many histories of the era.

The three chapters that constitute Part Three of the book—consequence—explore the culmination of events described in the first two parts. One chapter details events of the Rebellion itself. Another considers the federal government's decision in August 1794 to crush anti-excise resistance by force of arms, and the manner in which the plan was formulated. The final chapter covers the spreading violence outside western Pennsylvania and the dramatic march of federal troops from their respective points of origin in New Jersey, Pennsylvania, Maryland, and Virginia.

Implicit in the interpretation of all three parts is the belief that early Americans were not philosophers isolated from the competing strains of power, self-interest, and practical politics. Ideology was a critical ingredient of their behavior, and they were not purely rational men and women, immune to fear and the tensions of social strife. We do them a disservice and diminish their credibility—and ultimately their accomplishments—by ignoring or obscuring their humanity in all of its guises.

Partly to reinforce these points about the relationship between rational and emotional components of action, chapters are presented in two parts. Each one is introduced by a vignette designed to illustrate a critical episode in people's lives: the slaughter of peaceful Christian Indians, for example, introduces one chapter to portray as vividly as possible the nature of violence on the frontier; the massacre of one white woman's family and her kidnapping by Indians begins another to show the sort of fear, horror, and depression that constantly afflicted settlers; and Philadelphia's yellow fever epidemic precedes a third chapter to help visualize the strains that affected officials living there in 1793 and 1794.

These are the sorts of primary events that served as filters or background for all others. The rational and irrational politics of the 1790s makes more sense when we view it in light of these fundamental experiences that shaped everything else that people thought and did. Violence, fear, illness, poverty, mourning, and other forms of emotional and physical distress were also causal factors in politics, as well as the more commonly acknowledged and more easily recognizable ones discussed elsewhere in the book. The opening vignette in each chapter is then followed by the substantive text as described above.

Artistic concerns also dictate arrangement of the story of the Whiskey Rebellion into three parts. Historians have recently become concerned anew with our audiences. The "scientific" history of recent decades has exacted a heavy price in the number of readers who can understand and who are interested in our work. The call for revival of narrative techniques in response to the limitations of social science history, both as science and literature, has provoked fierce debate in public forums and more widely in private seminars and discussions among historians. Even those who agree about the necessity of writing for wider audiences, however, are not calling for a return to the nineteenth century. The task ahead is to approximate to the best of our abilities the storytelling talents of previous eras, and to wed literary strategies to the analytical requirements of the modern historical profession.[6]

By separating out, to some degree, analysis from narrative—context from chronology and consequence—perhaps the story of political conflict in post-Revolutionary America can be retold with much of its innate drama intact, while still making a contribution to historical knowledge. Perhaps this book can present one example of what the new narrative history might look like at the same time that it seeks to understand the meanings of the Whiskey Rebellion for those who lived through it.

PART ONE: CONTEXT

He wanted to know the history of the country. He had a college textbook, a big thick one. Years later, showing it to me, he prodded it with his finger, and said, "I durn near memorized every durn word in it. I could name you every date." Then he prodded it again, this time contemptuously, and said, "And the fellow who wrote it didn't know a God-damned thing. About how things were. He didn't know a thing. I bet things were just as they are now. A lot of folks wrassling round."

Robert Penn Warren, All the King's Men.

*manner as to disfigure" it, and then paraded Graham back and forth
across the three frontier counties in which he was supposed to collect
the excise. Celebrants gaily but purposefully forced Graham to trudge
through the mud to stills he had intended to visit in his official capacity,
halting at each for a raucous ceremony and a "treat" of alcohol. At each
stop they insulted Graham further and forced him to participate in the
festivities. Now whiskey distillers in the region were accomplices to the
crowd action. There could be few witnesses other than Graham against
his tormentors, and the communal commitment to "liberty and no excise," reaffirmed at every stop, was reinforced by the drunken good time
shared by all. Not surprisingly, then, names of participants never emerged from the wilderness. Perpetrators of what an unsympathetic chronicler of the event termed the "most audacious and accomplished piece
of outrageous and unprovoked insult that was ever offered to a government" were never prosecuted.[1]*

Excise TAXES and excise collectors had never been popular in
Anglo-America or in Great Britain. As early as 1610 members of the
British Parliament expressed their fear that "interior" or "inland"
duties—what some Americans later called "internal" taxes—might become a general practice. Traditionally, British taxes had been collected
on land and on foreign goods at the port of arrival. Excises (a term
synonymous with interior or inland taxes) on domestic productions and
trade were a known and feared Continental innovation in state finance.[2]

After repulsing another Crown attempt to impose inland taxes in
1626, Parliament itself levied the first English excises in 1643 to help
finance its army during the Civil War. These taxes on beer, ale, cider,
and perry were extended the following year to salt, beef, rabbits, and
pigeons. Opposition was immediate, violent, and persisted in some regions for over a century thereafter. Riots and "tumults" in different parts
of the kingdom during 1647 forced Parliament to exempt beer consumed
by the poor and to repeal taxes on beef and salt. Butchers had rioted
against the excise on their product; a mob burned down the London
excise house during the 1650s; and the taxes on an ever-lengthening list
of products remained uncollectable in some regions of the nation well
into the nineteenth century. In 1686 a collector at Cumberland reported
that "whenever any endeavour is made to gauge the drink brewed . . .
riots are daily committed on the officers by the inhabitants. . . . Sheriff's
officers refuse to execute the processes for fear of their lives." In 1789
excises on alcoholic beverages were still not enforceable in the region
between Chester and Flint because local justices refused to charge miscreants for such crimes.[3]

Resistance was always greatest in Scotland, Ireland, Wales, and the
outlying rural parts of England. In some areas the costs of collection
exceeded the revenue realized from the tax. Seven years of protracted

Chapter One

THE TAX MAN COMETH

People sometimes act out their ideologies and perceived self-interests with their feet or their fists, or both. Such was the case in April 1786 when word got around western Pennsylvania that a state excise officer named William Graham had dared to appear in Washington County. Locals had heard that the excise man was asserting his authority to collect taxes on distilled beverages in the three southwestern counties of the state, and they meant to teach him a lesson. During the night a man disguised as Beelzebub confronted Graham in his lodgings and announced that the tax man was to be handed over "for torment to a legion of devils . . . waiting outside." Somehow Graham escaped his nocturnal visitors, but the next day he was again confronted by a black-faced crowd that wanted to see him damned, at least figuratively, and perhaps literally. The mob approached the tax man in what he rightly interpreted as a menacing manner. Graham drew his pistols in self-defense, but wisely refrained from firing. Although he might have injured or killed several of the frontiersmen, the collector would certainly have sealed his own fate as well.

Members of the mob seized Graham's pistols and broke them into pieces before his astonished eyes. Others grabbed his official papers and shared in the joy of tearing the documents to shreds. Then they ordered the excise man to stomp the scraps of paper and the dismantled weapons into the muddy road. To the crowd's amusement, he complied. Next they told Graham to curse himself. He did. They demanded that Graham curse his commission of office and the politicians who gave it to him. Again the tax collector obeyed the frontier mob.

The crowd still was not content that the tax man, the excise, and state authority had met with sufficient humiliation. So, they cut the hair off one side of Graham's head. They braided the other half in an unsightly and mocking manner, cut a hole in the cock of his hat, and fixed it sideways on his head with the pig-tail protruding from the hole. Then the mob exposed Graham to what were perhaps lewd "marks of ignominy." He submitted to all of this passively, probably hoping to survive with the least possible violence to his person, property, and pride.

Unfortunately for the tax collector, communal sport with him as victim was not yet over. Indeed, the mob also dressed his horse "in such a resistance to the excise swept Scotland following the Union in 1707. In 1776, some 126 people in northern Wales were convicted of crimes against the excise laws, but the fines were uncollectable and the sentences unenforceable. The commissioner of excise in the region believed that he would need "a small military force" to collect the tax on spirits. Tax men were attacked in their homes, beaten up, horsewhipped, robbed on the highway, and killed on duty. One had his nose cut off; another was dragged out of bed and murdered in front of his family.[4]

Administration was always more efficient, less violent, and less corrupt in the immediate environs of London. Indeed, despite continuing pockets of resistance, the excise surpassed the land tax and customs duties to become the single most lucrative source of government income between the years 1713 and 1799. For much of that period it constituted over 40 percent of all Treasury receipts; in 1733 it produced 55 percent of the revenue. Thus, when Englishmen fought over interior taxes, there was much more than theory, ideology, or prejudice at stake. The excise quickly became the heart of the revenue system in an age when wars and administrative centralization put unprecedented strains on the empire's fiscal resources.[5]

From the beginning, the excise was politically divisive and fissured Parliament along Court versus Country lines, with rural backbenchers opposing the tax in principle and in practice as morally offensive, politically dangerous, and economically devastating to farmers and small producers. During the seventeenth century, opponents denounced the excise as "the Devil's remedy" and the "high road to slavery." It was condemned because "the clamor, charge, and other inconveniences of the excise of native commodities is far more than the profit thereof," and because it caused a price-rise during an era of relatively stable prices and wages. Some writers portrayed inland taxes as bulwarks of the standing armies that were, on occasion, used to collect them. Andrew Marvell found the tax detestable because:

> Excise, a monster worse than e'er before
> Frighted the midwife, and the mother tore.
> A thousand hands she has, a thousand eyes,
> Breaks into shops, and into cellars pries;
> With hundred rows of teeth the shark exceeds,
> And on all trades, like Casawar, she feeds. . . .
> She stalks all day in streets, conceal'd from sight,
> And flies like bats with leathern wings by night;
> She wastes the country, and on cities preys.[6]

Never, within memory, had the poor, the propertyless, and the disenfranchised been taxed for support of the government. The excise seemed at the time a landmark in the history of British political theory and practice. Tax collectors were acquiring the authority to search a man's home without a warrant, and to prosecute a crime outside the regular system of courts and appeals. Subjects denounced this assault on British liberties. None could remember when taxes had reached so deeply into the pockets of British subjects or extended to the everyday lives of so many. Riots against the tax, and violence against excise men, testified to the reluctance of the poor to accept their new civic responsibilities. These interior taxes seemed to agrarian landowners a grave threat to the liberty, the property, and the tranquility of the nation. As the system of excise grew, its opponents lamented the corruption of its officers, its discrimination against rural patterns of production and trade, and its prejudice in favor of large manufacturers. By the eighteenth century the nation seemed on the verge of a "general excise," a system that taxed every item of domestic production and consumption.[7]

Excises were supported by those who favored a powerful national government: politicians from urban areas and those who represented the interests of international merchants. Efficient tax collection was a necessity for strong central control, and this tax with its bevy of collectors bought patronage for Court politicians, extended the government's reach farther and deeper into the nation, and provided some relief from increased import duties for those engaged in the trade. Large distillers of alcoholic beverages actually favored an excise on their products because of its prejudice in favor of efficient production. They helped write and revise legislation; during the seventeenth century they were also responsible for collecting the tax. London concerns used this power to wrest control over appointments of tax collectors away from local gentry and to drive small commercial and home distillers out of business.[8]

Advocates of inland duties favored them over import tariffs because they were easier to administer than other taxes, because they were collected from a comparatively small group of producers or traders, and because they were reasonably "sure" levies, less affected by wars, piracy, and other vicissitudes of international trade. Interior taxes thus seemed to some "the most proper ways and means to support the government in a long war." Supporters argued that the excise was the "most equal and indifferent levy that can be laid upon the people." It was a "voluntary" tax in the sense that people controlled how much they paid by how much they consumed. Theory, propounded by Thomas Hobbes among others, argued that consumption was a fair measure of wealth or capacity to pay, thus making excises the "least prejudicial" of taxes. Advocates of the excise also sometimes adopted a moral reformist tone, arguing that it was good policy to tax people's vices and might actually result in more temperate consumption of evils such as spirits and tobacco. Such arguments were not intended, of course, to justify the excises on soap, salt, coal, meat, candles, and other "necessities."[9]

All the issues that divided Britons over inland taxes came together in 1733, when Sir Robert Walpole recommended stricter enforcement measures and reviving the excise on salt. Walpole's "excise scheme" fell victim to the grandest display of public opposition to a proposed law during the eighteenth century. It produced the following year the most bitter and, from the perspective of the government, the most dangerous Parliamentary elections between the years 1714 and 1830. The excise crisis resulted in the most striking example in its time of a minister's being coerced by popular opinion, and Walpole's defeat on this issue effectively made it impossible to extend the excise system further for the rest of the century.[10]

Supporters of the government were genuinely surprised by the size and fury of popular unrest over the tax. They were shocked to find crowds burning Walpole and the Queen in effigy to the shouts of "No excise, no wooden shoes!" Court politicians were overwhelmed by the greatest advertising campaign devoted to a political issue that the nation had ever seen. They were engulfed by the greatest deluge of petitions and instructions from constituents that had ever flooded Parliament. Many were frightened and appalled by the riots throughout the country and personally intimidated by London mobs that seemed to threaten the very houses of lords and commons.

Walpole anticipated the usual flurry of opposition from the rural members, and might have predicted the posturing of the always excitable London mob. He saw his proposals as important tinkering with an established system, but not as novel impositions. He expressed worry over the frauds that enabled ignoble producers to evade the existing inland duties and thus reduce the revenue by a significant but incalculable sum. He proposed the additional tax on salt as "the most equal and the most general . . . the most just, and the least burdensome" method for raising additional revenue. In so doing, the minister sought to make his bureaucratic apparatus more efficient and to relieve somewhat the burden of the land tax on property owners. For the latter he might even have expected gratitude from the rural patriarchs who sat in Parliament.[11]

Instead, Walpole's plan struck a sensitive ideological nerve in the general populace that the political opposition sought to exploit for its own partisan purposes. The proposal was denounced in Parliament as "a most fatal stroke to the liberties of my country." The traditional fears of "swarms of tax gatherers," standing armies, "arbitrary laws of excise," and the threat posed by enhanced patronage power in the hands of government all had their Cassandras on the floor of the house. William Pulteney argued that the excise "breathes nothing but the principles of the most arbitrary and most tyrannical governments that have been established in Europe." He complained of the "oppressive and vexatious powers" of excise officers and the "cruel oppressions" that some of them already inflicted on the populace. He denounced the excise as a "badge of slavery" and Walpole's proposal as "a downright plan for arbitrary power." The tax gatherers seemed actually to threaten Parliament itself

by intimidating voters who attempted to cast ballots against the gaugers'
political patrons. [12]

These themes were then amplified in the popular press. Beginning on
October 28, 1732, and continuing for eight weeks thereafter, the *Craftsman* elaborated in bloody detail the calamities portended by the excise.
Standing armies and interior taxes seemed to its authors to go hand-in-
hand:

> For as a large army cannot be supported under our present circumstances
> of debts and expenses without burdensome taxes . . . so it is evident from
> history that a general excise can never be established without a standing
> army to support it; and in these two points consist the most terrible ideas
> which we can possibly form to ourselves of arbitrary government.

Poverty and slavery seemed the inevitable consequences of such a system. The homes of Englishmen, their pocketbooks, and even the bodies
of their wives and daughters would be ravished under the arbitrary
powers of excise men to search and seize without warrants. The very
word "excise" carried an "odious sound and a very disagreeable idea
annexed to it," but it did not matter to opponents "whether such impositions are called excises, inland duties, or any other name," for in the end
they all amounted to the same threat. Such was not true for other taxes
collected in other ways—such as import duties and land taxes. The issue
was not paying taxes versus paying none, at least for the partisan writers
and politicians of the era, but rather the particular dangers posed by
interior taxes. And, indeed, increases in other forms of taxation provoked grumbling, but nothing even approaching the scale of opposition
to the excise. [13]

The excise crisis of 1733 was a critical moment in the history of opposition to internal taxes. Popular instincts against the excise took on a life
of their own once acted out with unprecedented success in the streets of
city and town. Opposition to the tax was articulated with clarity and
force by masters of the printed word, and sung in ditties that echoed for
decades among the less literate masses. In one sense, it matters little
whether the opposition pamphleteers were sincere in their predictions
of doom, since they were neither the creators nor the passive receptors
of the canon they inscribed. Their basic intuitions were shared by those
who revolted against excises for almost a century before the radical
Whigs wrote, and by Scots, Irish, and Welsh peasants of their own day
who never read or heard the fine words of the eighteenth-century
Commonwealthmen. [14]

Publication of the opposition pamphlets was also an event of immense
significance in its own right. The ideas and even the very words of the
pamphleteers served for the rest of the century, on both sides of the
Atlantic, as facilitators of protest against ideologically repulsive excises.
They functioned as rallying cries that helped unite the oral and written

cultures of opposition to centrally imposed internal taxes. When Lord Bute proposed a cider tax in 1763—justified, he thought, by the need for increased revenues to pay war debts, the desirability of greater efficiency in collection of taxes, and in the name of equity to all tax-payers—he was drowned by the same tidal wave of protests that had overwhelmed Walpole.[15]

In America, when a proposed liquor excise bill appeared before the Massachusetts legislature during 1754, the same themes, the same fears, and the same language of resistance surfaced on the streets and in the popular press. Again some feared that an excise tax would "deprive us of part of our liberty," that a military force would prove necessary to crush the unrest provoked by the law, and that the consequences would include "destruction of a free constitution and the support of arbitrary power." The excise was again portrayed as an entering wedge of despotism, an assault on the liberties of Englishmen, and a threat to the homes and families of every citizen. "When the excise man's deputy comes," an opposition pamphleteer again predicted, "if he likes the poor man's wife, he will not like his account, [and] will not agree with him or acquit him." Poverty, tyranny, violence, and slavery appeared again on the political horizon.[16]

Thus, even before colonists and Parliament confronted each other over the issue of taxation, the instincts of opposition to centrally imposed internal taxes and a language in which to articulate those fears were available weapons honed by decades of political warfare. It would take the Stamp Act crisis of 1765 to begin uniting the physical, oral, and written traditions of opposition to internal taxes in America. It would take time and some measure of creativity to shape that ideology in conformity with uniquely American perspectives and conditions. Ultimately, in America just as in Great Britain, internal taxes would unite in opposition those who opposed paying any tax to support a remote central government with those who resisted paying only this one sort of levy.[17]

The term "internal tax" was itself something of an American invention, at least in the way colonists used it. When Parliament met in the early months of 1766 to discuss the Stamp Act rebellion in the colonies, its members focused first on the "strange language" of American arguments against the tax. Most British politicians could not even understand what the colonists were talking about.[18]

William Pitt tried to explain. According to Pitt, Americans believed that "the House had no right to lay an internal tax upon America, that country not being represented" in Parliament. Another speaker emphasized the same point when he observed that "the Americans think that the imposition of internal taxes ought to be confined to their own Assembly." They believed "this law unjust in its original," because it was constitutionally novel. No previous act of Parliament had "laid an internal tax, at least no internal tax which can so fairly be called so as this act." According to their British interpretors, the colonists maintained that sovereignty was constitutionally divided between Parliament and their local Assemblies. They held that internal taxes could be levied justly only by local, representative institutions—not by a remote Parliament in which they were not represented.[19]

Some M.P.s were still not sure they comprehended the American position or that it made any sense. "I cannot understand the difference between external and internal taxes," George Grenville asserted in response to Pitt's explanation. William Blackstone and Lord Mansfield, the two reigning experts on such matters, could find no such distinction in law, either common or statute. Blackstone also denied that under British law "the right of imposing taxes arises from representation." Lord North apparently understood, but rejected, the constitutional argument offered by the colonists. He noted that "in point of right there is no difference [between internal and external taxes]; in point of operation there certainly is: external might not go further, internal might."[20]

What some Americans had done, to the utter confusion of most members of Parliament, was take a commonplace operational distinction between internal and external taxes, invest it with ideological significance similar, but not identical, to that traditionally expressed by British opponents of excise taxes, and turn it into a constitutional argument with its own unique terminology. The ideological distinction so novel to Parliament's ears was apparently a commonplace in the colonies. In 1764, even before the Stamp Act rebellion, Thomas Hutchinson, lieutenant-governor of Massachusetts, informed a Connecticut correspondent that "your distinction between duties upon trade and internal taxes agrees with . . . the opinion of most people here."[21]

There is no reason to question his assessment. American witnesses called before Parliament in 1766 told its members the same thing. Testimony from residents of Massachusetts, Rhode Island, New York, Pennsylvania, and Virginia agreed; they testified that crowds, newspapers, pamphlets, politicians, and private citizens in each of these colonies "make the distinction between internal and external duties." It was the understanding of most American witnesses, even those who did not share the sentiment, that colonists opposed the Stamp Act because it was an internal tax, that they would predictably resist any other internal tax, but that there was less danger of violent protest against external taxes, at least on ideological grounds.[22]

Just as in the case of British opposition to excises, Americans expressed their disdain in song, poetry, prose, and mob violence. Crowds throughout the colonies assaulted the persons and property of men associated with the act. Protestors also wrote, sang, and shouted their contempt for internal taxes. On August 29, 1765, for example, a crowd paraded through the streets of Newport, Rhode Island, and constructed

a gallows for the effigy of a "stamp man." On one of the gallows posts
they hung a copy of a ditty heard on the streets of colonial towns that
summer. The pertinent stanza read as follows:

> Those blessings our fathers obtain'd by their blood,
> We are justly oblig'd as their sons to make good;
> All internal taxes let us then nobly spurn,
> These effigies first—next the stamp paper burn.

The language of the ideological distinction between internal and external
taxes had penetrated beyond the intellectually rarefied world of pamphlet literature. We might even surmise, as Hutchinson and others did,
that crowds mouthing such words had some understanding of their
meaning. Those who sang this song apparently shared a hatred of the
Stamp Act. They expressed a disdain for internal taxes of all sorts and
saw them as threats to the liberties hard-won by their ancestors. They
were also, it appears, distinguishing between two types of taxes and
making an ideological argument against only one.[23]

At the heart of this distinction were theories about the relation between representation and freedom, about the constitutional necessity for
dividing sovereignty between Parliament and colonial legislatures, and
about the role played by taxes in all of these theories. As Benjamin
Franklin defined the terms for Parliament, an American theory of representation lay at the center of the dispute. "I think the difference [be-
tween internal and external taxation] is very great," Franklin testified.
"An external tax is a duty laid on commodities imported; that duty is
added to the first cost, and other charges on the commodity, and when
it is offered to sale, makes a part of the price. If the people do not like it
at that price, they refuse it; they are not obliged to pay it. But an
internal tax is forced from the people without their consent, if not laid
by their own representatives."[24]

A majority of the Massachusetts General Court had advanced this
same theory of representation in a November 1764 petition to Parliament. The legislature pointed out in this official communication that the
colonies "have always judged by their representatives both of the way
and manner in which internal taxes should be raised within their respective governments." According to this argument, garnering the consent of
the people through their chosen representatives was a necessary precondition for the just exaction of internal taxes. Colonists differed about
what it would take to represent them adequately, but Stamp Act resisters, with few exceptions, could agree that Americans were not represented in Parliament. In other words, they did not accept the notion of
virtual representation.[25]

While American opponents of the Stamp Act concurred that there was
a necessary link between representation and authority to assess internal
taxes, they disagreed profoundly about what constituted adequate repre-

sentation for the task. Some maintained that tensions between the colonies and Britain would be eased by acceptance of M.P.s elected by
colonists. "If you choose to tax us," Franklin wrote to Richard Jackson,
"give us members in your legislature, and let us be one people."[26]

Others were not so sanguine: the geographical remoteness of Parliament would always, under any conceivable electoral arrangement, deny
them adequate representation for the purpose of assessing internal
taxes. Thomas Fitch, for example, thought the colonies were "subordinate jurisdictions or governments which by distance are so separated
from Great Britain that they are not and cannot be represented in
Parliament." According to Stephen Hopkins, the colonies were "at so
great a distance from England" that Parliament could never truly know
American conditions and could not become sufficiently representative to
levy internal taxes.[27]

During the 1760s this ideological quarrel among Americans had little
impact on the organization of intercolonial opposition to Great Britain. It
was not the sort of issue that would prevent Fitch and Franklin—or
others who had different standards of representation—from uniting
against Parliament and its internal stamp tax. By either standard, colonists were not represented in Parliament. After the American Revolution,
however, this would be precisely the sort of issue that fissured domestic
politics and promoted conflict over taxes levied by the new national
government.

The terms of another potential ideological clash were also defined during the 1760s but submerged on an intercolonial or national level beneath
other concerns until the 1780s. Some Americans contended during the
1760s that sovereignty could be divided between Parliament and colonial
assemblies, but not shared—that divided sovereignty in fact described
traditional relationships within the empire. Those who embraced this
critical distinction separated authority over internal from authority over
external taxes. Writing before the Stamp Act revolt, Richard Bland
pointed out that Virginians were "in every instance . . . of our EXTERNAL
government . . . subject to the authority of the British Parliament, but in
no others." Since Bland maintained that colonial legislatures had exclusive right "to legislate matters relating to their INTERNAL government," it
seemed to him that "any tax respecting our INTERNAL polity which may
hereafter be imposed on us by act of Parliament is arbitrary . . . and may
be opposed." The Connecticut legislature drew the line dividing sovereignty in the same place, as revealed in the title to its 1764 pamphlet:
*Reasons Why the British Colonies in America Should Not Be Charged
with Internal Taxes*. Thomas Hutchinson, at least, thought that most
people in his acquaintance agreed.[28]

Even before the Stamp Act it seemed clear to Franklin that "two
distinct jurisdictions or powers of taxing cannot well subsist together in
the same country. They will confound and obstruct each other." He

reasoned that sovereignty could be divided between different levels of government, but that authority over internal and external taxes, for example, could not be shared. In the case of the North American colonies, which were an ocean away from Parliament, the division of authority over taxation was traditional, practical, and necessary. "When any tax for America is proposed in your Parliament," Franklin wrote, "how are you to know that we are not already taxed as much as we can bear? If a tax is proposed with us, how dare we venture to lay it, as the next ship perhaps may bring us an account of some heavy tax imposed by you." Franklin, Bland, and the Massachusetts General Court in its 1764 petition all argued that this traditional arrangement of divided sovereignty should continue as long as the colonies were not represented in Parliament.[29]

Some Americans rejected this vision of divided sovereignty in 1765, as others would for relations between the states and federal government during the 1780s and 1790s. James Otis, for example, denied any limitation on Parliament's authority. He believed that "the Parliament of Great Britain has a just and equitable right, power, and authority *to impose taxes on the colonies, internal and external, on lands as well as on trade.*" Even in dissent, however, Otis communicated in the language of America's popular protest; those, like Otis, who denied the validity of the ideological distinction in 1765 recognized its vitality and thus legitimized the terms of its argument. Rhode Island physician Thomas Moffatt did not like it, but he read the distinction "in the newspapers." William Kelly, of New York, did not understand it, but he knew colonists made "a distinction between internal taxes and some others which I did not quite comprehend." Virginia merchant James Balfour reported that "the distinction between internal and external duties" was common in his colony, and his fellow Virginian George Mercer agreed that "the Stamp Act being an internal tax was one of the great objections to it."[30]

Those Americans who embraced an ideology imbued with distinctions between internal and external taxes shared a range of fears similar to those expressed by opponents of Walpole's excise. Theirs were embellishments of radical Whig horrors conjured for the education of a public at risk of losing its liberty. "It is seldom," wrote a contributor to the *Boston Evening-Post* in reference to the Stamp Act, "indeed very seldom, that any people have had more at stake than we at present have." "The Parliament of Great Britain have no right to level an internal tax upon the colonies," another writer stormed. Some Americans believed that when Parliament sought "to establish stamp duties and other internal taxes" for the colonies, it threatened to reduce Americans to "the miserable condition of slaves." Linking the issue of representation to his fears, Stephen Hopkins argued that a legislature too remote to appreciate American conditions and interests could not possibly "determine with confidence on matters far above their reach." In all likelihood, such policy would compel colonists "to go naked in this cold country" or else clothe themselves in animal skins. Property, civilization, even the physical survival of the colonists seemed at risk. Expanded jurisdiction for admiralty courts to enforce the new tax would inflict cruel punishments—in costs, time, and anxiety—even on those found innocent of charges. Remote, unrepresentative legislatures and remote, inaccessible courts of law threatened colonial prosperity. Local legislative bodies and local courts knew local conditions. They could, therefore, better dispense justice and more equitably assess internal taxes.[31]

The British justification of the Stamp Act as necessary to raise funds for American defense seemed to Hopkins similarly fallacious: "To take the money of the Americans . . . and lay it up for their defense a thousand leagues distance from them when the enemies they have to fear are in their own neighborhood, hath not the greatest probability of friendship or prudence." Again, Hopkins was expressing a localist argument and fears. He would leave laws, justice, and even defense (despite its external connotations) to those who knew local conditions from experience. Since circumstances varied widely among the colonies, each, according to Hopkins, should administer its own affairs; otherwise, central authority would threaten the property and hence the freedom of colonists. "They who have no property," Hopkins concluded, "can have no freedom, but indeed are reduced to the most abject slavery."[32]

Some Americans did not endorse the concept of divided sovereignty in the 1760s. They disagreed with other Americans and with the British about the meaning of "representation," and the disagreement was already an important ideological quarrel. Their American opponents demanded division of authority over internal and external taxes between local and central governments and denied in principle the right of a central government to tax their property. By "taxes" they may have meant "internal taxes," but by "representation" American localists did not mean sending several delegates hundreds of miles to be outvoted by politicians with interests alien to theirs.

The riots stopped with repeal of the Stamp Act. There were few protests against the Revenue Act of 1766, a blatant revenue-raising measure but an external one. Efforts to organize intercolonial resistance to the Townshend duties after 1767 were divisive and far less successful than the Stamp Act protests. Never again before the Revolutionary War would Americans—outside of Boston—achieve the same sort of unanimity against British taxes that they enjoyed during Stamp Act resistance. And that was due at least in part to Parliament's de facto respect for the constitutional distinction colonists had made during the 1760s. In the absence of the ideological dimension of internal taxation, it was clearly difficult to unite Americans of diverse economic interests against British external taxes. It would take the presence of British soldiers in Boston after 1768, "customs racketeering," and the Coercive Acts to reignite the localist fires fueled by the Stamp Act.[33]

The principle of divided sovereignty—of divided authority over internal and external taxes—was not abandoned during the 1770s. Since the concept was never challenged, there was no perceived need to articulate or defend it. Americans did not reach a consensus over this principle during those years. They still disagreed about the validity of divided sovereignty as a description of the British constitution and as an eternal verity for political society. When the issue of Parliament's authority emerged in the first Continental Congress, according to John Adams, "some were for a flat denial of all authority; others for denying the power of taxation only; some for denying internal, but admitting external, taxation." In other words, Americans still differed about the ideological significance of internal taxes and about the localist description of divided sovereignty within the empire. But this dispute was a secondary issue of intercolonial affairs in 1774, one that could again be ignored as Americans united to confront more pressing threats to their liberties.[34]

When they established their own central government under the Articles of Confederation, however, Americans reserved all tax-making authority to the states. Because the Continental Congress possessed no independent power over taxes, the latent disagreement over divided sovereignty never became a divisive issue within that body, at least from a localist perspective. Granted, when the impost seemed a genuine possibility, some in Congress insisted that the states retain control over collectors. This certainly was a variant of fears about tax collectors appointed by remote central governments; but Congress, with its circumscribed powers, never posed the same sort of threat as Parliament. Given the fate of the much less ideologically controversial impost, it is unimaginable that the states would have approved any internal tax.[35]

When delegates gathered to reorganize the central government in 1787, the voices of those who cared deeply about divided sovereignty and the ideological distinction between internal and external taxes were not heard. The Constitution proposed by the Philadelphia convention granted a national congress the unlimited "power to lay and collect taxes, duties, imposts, and excises." The document thus gave the central government taxing authority in both internal and external realms as defined during the 1760s. The Constitution also denied the states power to act independently in the external sphere; it reserved for the central government exclusive control over customs duties, regulation of interstate trade, international treaties, and other portions of the parliamentary sovereignty that colonists acknowledged in the 1760s. The taxing authority of the proposed national government would be no less, and was certainly designed to be even greater, than anything attempted by the British government during the 1760s and 1770s.[36]

Localists—now pejoratively termed Antifederalists by proponents of

the Constitution—discovered and passionately denounced parallels between British claims in the 1760s and powers granted by the document
to the central government. Most shocking of all was the renunciation of
local control over internal taxes so soon after the war to secure such
rights from Great Britain. A Pennsylvania writer had not forgotten the
"glorious struggle" with Britain; he was appalled that the proposed national Congress would be "vested with every species of *internal* taxation," and he feared that the collection of such taxes would be enforced
by that bane of all radical Whigs, "the standing army."[37]

This anonymous author and others believed, as some colonists had in
the 1760s, that "there is a strong distinction between external and internal taxes." William Goudy of North Carolina feared that the taxation
clause of the proposed Constitution "will totally destroy our liberties."
He and the majority of North Carolina's ratifying convention thought
Article 1, section 8 should be amended to substitute a quota system for
authority to lay internal taxes. Only if the quota remained unfilled by
the states should the national congress be permitted to enact excises and
other internal taxes.[38]

Antifederalists shared a more precise understanding of what they
meant by external and internal taxes than colonists had during the
1760s. The "Federal Farmer" saw clear differences between the two
sorts of taxes. "External taxes," he wrote, "are import duties, which are
laid on imported goods; they may usually be collected in a few seaport
towns, and of a few individuals, though ultimately paid by the consumer; a few officers can collect them, and they can be carried no higher
than trade will bear, or smuggling permit—that in the very nature of
commerce, bounds are set to them." For these reasons—the natural and
fixed limitations on the amounts assessed, the few places where the
taxes could be collected, the few officers employed in collection, and the
limitation of taxes to items produced by foreigners—he believed that
external taxes might be assessed legitimately and collected by a republican central government.[39]

Taxes laid on property, produce, manufactures, and commerce were
different matters. Antifederalists thought that only the states should act
in these realms. "Internal taxes," the "Federal Farmer" observed, "as
poll and land taxes, excises, duties on all written instruments, etc. may
fix themselves on every person and species of property in the community; they may be carried to any lengths, and in proportion as they are
extended, numerous officers must be employed to assess them, and to
enforce the collection of them." Others agreed that the result must be a
proliferation of taxes on every species of property in order to keep the
collectors engaged, and that the resulting "disorder and general dissatis-
faction" with the national government would ultimately provoke violent
suppression by a national army.[40]

Others foresaw a similar result for the system proposed in the Constitution. The new government would immediately lay excise and other "internal taxes upon your lands, your goods, your chattels, as well as your persons at their sovereign pleasure," and "the produce of these several funds shall be appropriated to the use of the United States, and collected by their own officers, armed with a military force, if a civil aid should not prove sufficient." First would come a raft of internal tax laws; then tax collectors would follow shortly behind. "The tax-gatherers will be sent," warned Joseph McDowall of North Carolina, "and our property will be wrested out of our hands." "If the tax-gatherers come upon us," he predicted, "they will, like the locusts of old, destroy us." But not all citizens would submit to such oppression. In some regions, at least, the locusts McDowall warned of would be met by armed men determined to defend their hard-won liberties. Robert Livingston of New York thought the result must be either abdication of duties and office by the tax collectors or "an internal war."[41]

This civil war was perhaps what localists feared most from the internal taxing power of the proposed central government. Patrick Henry warned: "Look at the part which speaks of excises, and you will recollect that those who are to collect excises and duties are to be aided by military force. . . . Suppose an excise man will demand leave to enter your cellar, or house, by virtue of his office; perhaps he may call on the militia to enable him to go." These were the same fears voiced for over a century by British opponents of the excise. Americans had not yielded to such intrusions in the past, and they would not do so now.[42]

Lack of knowledge about, and sympathy for, the conditions and views of many regions would make the national legislature the wrong institution to enact internal taxes. As in 1765, it was hardly certain that the whole people could ever be represented in a national Congress. Since only experience would tell, localists believed that powers of internal taxation must be reserved to the states, at least for the time being. "If a proper representation be impracticable," reasoned the "Federal Farmer," "then we shall see this power resting in the states, where it at present ought to be, and not inconsiderately given up." For now, it was at least clear that the legislative branch of the central government would have "but very little democracy in it." Compared with the states, then, the federal government would be freer to ignore the desires of a large portion of the citizenry and would possess the financial and military might to enforce its will—to the possible extinction of the states and individual liberty.[43]

Pennsylvania Antifederalists could not trust the system embodied in the Constitution, or the sort of men who would run it, with internal taxing power under any circumstances. The Constitution seemed almost to ensure a wave of economic repression and political violence. To them it appeared that the "same force that may be employed to compel obedience to good laws, might and probably would be used to wrest from the people their constitutional liberties." They predicted use of state militias "to enforce the collection of the most oppressive taxes"; they imagined the marching of Pennsylvania militiamen to New England or Virginia to "quell an insurrection occasioned by the most galling oppression." Ultimately, they believed, the death of state governments would follow adoption of this Constitution with its authority to levy internal taxes and raise armies to enforce the laws. Patrick Henry prophesied that "your rich, snug, fine, fat, federal offices—the number of collectors of taxes and excises will outnumber any thing from the states." He foresaw these excise men grazing the states clean, leaving nothing but a consolidated national government behind.[44]

For Antifederalists, then, the issues and the stakes had changed little from the 1760s. The constitutional conflict over internal and external taxation had at least as much meaning for Americans in 1787 as in 1765. In both cases some saw the reservation of internal taxation to the colonies/states as crucial to the survival of liberty. In each case they predicted violent conflict and consequent loss of liberty as the likely results of granting the central government authority to assess internal taxes. It made little difference that the central government after 1787 would be managed by elected Americans rather than British politicians over whom they had virtually no influence. The problems of representation remained largely the same. Whether elected or not, men who shared no sympathy for the needs of some regions could not represent all their constituents' interests adequately to tax them. In 1787 as in 1765, some believed that internal taxing authority must be left to local representatives who lived among their electors and knew their wants and needs. Under the proposed system this would not be possible. Each congressman would represent as many as 30,000 people, and districts would grow even larger. A senator from Philadelphia, Boston, or Charleston, for example, could never truly appreciate or represent the unique problems and needs of frontiersmen.

Furthermore, as a matter of logic and political theory, those who opposed the Constitution strongly resisted the idea that two sovereign governmental bodies could coexist, share concurrent jurisdiction, cooperate, and survive. They believed that sovereignty could be divided but not shared. To give both the national government and the states authority to lay internal taxes was to decree the virtual death of the states. The larger and stronger government would inevitably overwhelm the states with taxes, tax collectors, and, if necessary, soldiers to enforce its laws. In the face of such might, states would be compelled to repeal tax laws or simply leave an overburdened populace alone and not collect taxes at all. In the end, the states would either fade to shadows or be violently annihilated by a national army. However the end came, the fate of the citizen, the state, and the nation would ultimately be the same. Discontent, resistance, repression, violence, tyranny, and death would be the short and brutal history of the American republic.

As subsequent events showed, the Antifederalists were only partially correct in their predictions. The state governments were not annihilated, of course, nor did they glide out of existence. The national government did not dissolve in a cauldron of tyranny and anarchy. On the other hand, the nationalists' assurances—which localists interpreted as promises—that a direct excise would only be a tax of last resort proved false. One of the earliest fiscal measures of the new Congress was the whiskey excise of 1791. The opposition was also correct in predicting that passage of internal taxes by a remote central government would bring the nation to the brink of an "internal war."

The Pennsylvania militia would not march to New England or Virginia to "quell an insurrection occasioned by the most galling oppression." The militias of Pennsylvania, New Jersey, Maryland, and Virginia would hike west, however, to suppress an excise-tax revolt on the other side of the Appalachian Mountains in 1794. The Whiskey Rebellion would result from precisely the sorts of tensions feared by British opponents of excises since the seventeenth century and by American opponents of centrally imposed internal taxes in 1765 and 1787–88.

Chapter Two

THE QUEST FOR FRONTIER AUTONOMY

The summer of 1764 brought both an end to the Great War for the Empire and the beginning of yet another conflagration on Pennsylvania's frontier. Still reeling from years of warfare with their French and Indian enemies, settlers now faced another bloody wave of Indian incursions in Pontiac's War. Neither the empire nor the colony's eastern-based government provided succor or protection for those living on the fringes of civilization, and Indian forays now actually pushed back the edge of settlement hundreds of miles. Carlisle, a small town about one-third of the way across the colony, "was become the barrier, not a single [white] individual being beyond it," as frontiersmen abandoned their homes for the comparative safety of cis-Appalachian life.

Frustrated by their inability to inflict punishment on their Indian enemies, and bitter over the colony's refusal to provide any aid, a band of Scots-Irish frontiersmen lashed out in an easterly direction against the only Indians they could find. The settlers were furious that the colony provided food, clothing, and protection for "Moravian" or Christianized Indians living around Lancaster, but no relief for white refugees. They were enraged by rumors that the "peaceful" Indians funneled supplies and perhaps information to the warriors who rampaged unchecked in the western country.

At dawn on December 15, fifty-seven armed settlers descended on the village at Conestoga Manor, where a group of about twenty Indians lived under the government's protection. Brandishing firelocks, short-swords, and hatchets, the whites quickly dispatched the three Indian men, two women, and one boy they found at home. The ancient Chief Shehaes was chopped to pieces in his bed. All the victims were scalped and their bodies mangled. The huts were then set on fire with the bodies inside, and the avenging frontiersmen dispersed after a search for the other villagers and a brief celebration of their victory.

Lancaster officials feared for the lives of those Conestoga Indians who had escaped the massacre and decided to collect them in the county workhouse for their protection. White frontiersmen heard of this plan, and another band of about fifty men attacked the workhouse on Decem-

ber 27. When the sixteen unarmed Indians realized their fate, "they divided into their little families, the children clinging to their parents. They [the adults] fell on their knees, protested their innocence, declared their love to the English, and that, in their whole lives, they had never done them injury." Still in the posture of prayer, each man, woman, and child was hacked to death. The murderers then mounted their horses, "huzzaed their triumph, as if they had gained a victory, and rode off— unmolested!" Despite the attempts of authorities, no one was ever apprehended for this crime. No witnesses could be found to testify against the frontiersmen who publicly bragged about their identity as "Paxton Boys" for the rest of their lives.

Colony officials in Philadelphia were outraged by the two massacres, but, as usual, their edicts had no effect in the West. The government did make provisions to move other peaceful Indians back East, and even tried, unsuccessfully, to export some to New York. The fury of the frontiersmen against all Indians and the colony had not abated. Reports reached Philadelphia early in the new year that "some thousands" of pioneers were marching toward the city intent on eliminating the remaining Conestoga Indians and pressing their other demands on the legislature. Ultimately, only two hundred arrived; and a promise to consider their petitions brought a close to the Paxton affair.

The colony then ignored the petitions, refusing to consider back-country requests for an increased representation in the legislature, protection against Indian foes, tax relief, assistance for the dispossessed, stipends for veterans of Indian wars, and local trials for Indian-related offenses. Eastern officials continued to dismiss western demands on grounds of self-interest and moral revulsion at the violence of settlers. Interregional relations remained, as they would for decades, at an impasse among people with alien perspectives, cultures, interests, and ideologies. Indians went on acting as rogue pawns in the chess game of intracolonial politics.[1]

IF THE PASSAGE of time accomplished anything during the two decades after the Paxton riots, it heightened inter-regional tensions. The frailty of existence and the violence of everyday life continued to make frontiersmen different from easterners, and contributed to the alien perspectives of the two districts. The cultures and interests of East and West were so contrary during those years that both sides predicted violent conflict; and internal taxation and Indians were not the only issues that brought the colonies and then the United States to the brink of civil war.

During the 1780s many, if not most, Americans believed that the nation would inevitably divide in two. As a foreign traveler remarked in 1781, the possibility of "a separation of the federal union into *two parts*, at no distant day. . . . was a matter of frequent discussion . . . and seemed to be an opinion that was daily gaining ground." Some predicted that the country would split into northern and southern halves. Others foresaw eastern and western nations separated by the mountains that formed a convenient north-south line and defined the beginning of the frontier. Many people anticipated this probability with glee. Others lived in horror of the consequences threatened by secession of the West.[2]

Eastern predictions of western intrigues for separation arose from educated appraisals of geographic and economic realities, from knowledge and rumors about machinations on the frontier, and from inter-regional prejudices. Nationalists melded fact and suspicion into a highly negative vision of the more locally oriented frontiersmen. Timothy Pickering, for example, could be surprised by little evil that westerners might attempt since they were "the least worthy subjects in the United States. They are little less savage than the Indians." Tobias Lear's prophecy in 1787 that "within fifteen years the inhabitants to the westward of the Alleghany will be a separate, independent people," derived partly from a common bias against the foreigners then settling on the frontier and also from his understanding of geography and the economics of trade.[3]

Violent confrontation was not inevitable. Initially many westerners envisioned themselves creating new states in the American confederacy. They believed that independence would help resolve the injustices of their relations with eastern-based governments. As states, frontier areas would gain greater economic and political autonomy. They would have a louder voice in Congress and enjoy more influence on policy decisions, especially those relating to taxation, trade, land, Indians, and the negotiations with Spain for navigation of the Mississippi River.

The resistance of seaboard politicians to pleas for autonomy, however, eventually led increasing numbers of frontiersmen to consider other options, including union with Spain or even reunion with Great Britain. Westerners were exasperated by the apparent unwillingness of the Continental Congress to push their demands in negotiations with Great Britain and Spain, and by the nation's inability to provide them protection against their "savage" foes. As early as 1783 George Mason was predicting that continued neglect of the westerners' needs would "occasion another war in less than seven years." Only two years later there was a Mississippi crisis. War between the United States and Spain or among Americans over navigation of the river seemed possible. By 1786, widespread economic distress heightened frustrations resulting from the failure of statehood petitions and anxiety over the insincere or impotent attempts of the national government to secure navigation rights from Spain.[4]

With each confrontation during the 1780s the gulf between frontier and more settled regions seemed to grow. By 1790 the chasm appeared to many on both sides to be wider than ever before. None of the issues had been resolved. The potential for violent conflict had never seemed greater. In fact, the 1780s eroded the patience of opposing groups and thereby diminished the potential for peaceful resolution of inter-regional differences.

Frontier movements for autonomy traveled through three distinct stages from the beginning of the Revolution through adoption of the federal Constitution. The first two are discussed in this chapter, the third in Chapter Three. In the first stage—roughly from 1775 through 1780—some settlers remained loyally tied both to the individual state governments under whose authority they fell, while all regions of the frontier expressed a desire to become members of the national confederacy. Watauga and Maine exhibited no wish for statehood. Vermont, Westsylvania, and Transylvania all displayed heartfelt support for the Continental Congress and recognized the authority of that body to determine their fates as independent entities.

New Hampshire, Massachusetts, New York, Pennsylvania, Virginia, and North Carolina—the states from which the proposed districts would be carved—rejected these petitions out-of-hand. The arguments were never seriously considered, and the grievances were dismissed as ravings of fanatics and anarchists. At best, state officials reasoned, signers of frontier petitions were well-intentioned but ignorant and deluded farmers. They simply had been misled by the fanatics and anarchists. The problem of the West, some easterners believed, was one of education or, if need be, suppression of nonacculturated immigrants.

In the second stage of frontier independence movements—from about 1780 through 1785—petitioners became frustrated by the state governments. It was now clear to many westerners that a clash of economic interest and power rather than a debate over Revolutionary principles would determine their fate. Support from the Continental Congress seemed to be their only hope. But even the commitment of Congress to the principles of the Declaration of Independence was now suspect in light of inaction by that body on previous statehood petitions. Frontiersmen still had faith, however—faith in the Revolution, faith in Congress, and faith in their interpretation of the Revolutionary creed and its application to their own cases. Settlers in Vermont, western Pennsylvania, Virginia, and North Carolina, although frustrated, continued to bombard Congress with remonstrances. They still considered themselves patriots and active supporters of the Revolution. Not until 1785, when a third stage began in the relations between western and eastern Americans, would frontiersmen reassess their loyalty to a united nation.

Stage One: c.1775–1780

When the rhetoric of liberty, freedom, and self-determination began to circulate throughout America during the Revolutionary era, westerners thought of applying it in ways far different from those intended by eastern pamphleteers. Every argument about lack of representation, unfairness of tax burdens, insensitivity to local conditions, lack of protection, and inadequacy of courts and civil police applied on the frontier even more than in the East. But frontiersmen thought that the answers to their common grievances lay just as much in separation from the remote eastern colonies to which they were attached as from the distant island-nation of George III.

These were not new problems, of course, nor were frontier perceptions of injustice born of the Revolutionary ferment. Strains between seaboard governments and back-country settlers began in the seventeenth century, with Bacon's Rebellion in Virginia only the best known of numerous armed confrontations between those at the center and peripheries of colonial life. The Paxton riots in eighteenth-century Pennsylvania and the Regulator movements of Revolutionary North and South Carolina were only the latest in a series of frontier protests against the perceived inadequacies of East-West relations.[5]

The Revolution seemed to provide an occasion, and a language, for resolving the perennial complaints of wilderness life. Settlers believed that easterners would now welcome their petitions with open arms. They imagined the task at hand was simply to phrase their petitions in a form and manner of expression convincing to proto-Lockeian Whigs—in other words that they needed merely to reconstruct a convincing model of the Declaration of Independence and the states or Continental Congress would graciously succumb to the logic of their demands. Over the years they would discover themselves naïve, but in the context of the 1770s their expectations were not absurd.

As early as September 1775, for example, Transylvanians petitioned the Continental Congress for recognition as the fourteenth colony. These people, living in what eventually became part of Kentucky, "having their hearts warmed with the same noble spirit that animates the united colonies," wished to share in the struggle for liberty against Great Britain. The petition came at an inopportune moment for Congress. Since the existing colonies had themselves just petitioned George III for redress of a whole range of grievances, there seemed to be some "impropriety in embarrassing our reconciliation with anything new, and the taking under our protection a body of people who have acted in defiance of the King's proclamations." Transylvania existed without British sanction and in contravention of the Proclamation Line of 1763. To encourage such an enterprise would, Congress believed, undermine the credibility of their statements of loyalty to the Crown and would "be looked upon as a confirmation of that independent spirit with which we are daily reproached." John Adams denounced the Transylvanians as unduly "charged with republican notions and utopian schemes." Thomas Jefferson, on the other hand, found their requests reasonable and believed it to the advantage of Virginia that a "free government" prospered on its borders. Jefferson was in a minority on this question, however, and the petition was dismissed. Through the decisive intervention of Virginia, the "infant colony" did not survive the war.[6]

The Continental Congress unwittingly encouraged other frontier applications for statehood by recommending in the spring of 1776 that all colonies "where no government sufficient to the exigencies of their affairs have been hitherto established . . . adopt such government as shall, in the opinion of the representatives of the people, best conduce to the happiness and safety of their constituents in particular and America in general." In the summer of 1776, inspired by self-interest, the Continental Congress, and the Declaration of Independence, people in the border region claimed by Pennsylvania and Virginia proclaimed their independence from both states. Announcing that they had "imbibed the highest and most extensive ideas of liberty," these people declared that they could "with difficulty submit to being annexed to or subjected by . . . any one of those provinces, much less the being partitioned or parcelled out among them." It seemed clear to the hopeful founding fathers of the state of Westsylvania, from the Revolutionary principles ringing loudly in their ears, that "no country or people can be either rich, flourishing, happy or free . . . whilst annexed to or dependent on any province, whose seat of government is . . . four or five hundred miles distant, and separated by a vast, extensive and almost impassible tract of mountains, by nature itself formed and pointed out as a boundary between this country and those below it."[7]

The summer of 1776 found settlers in the Watauga region of North Carolina in a similar mood. These people in what later became eastern Tennessee were so remote from the tremors shaking the colonies that "reports of the present unhappy differences between Great Britain and America" initially reached them only as rumors from far-away places. Once aware of the serious nature of the conflict and the principles upon which it was based, however, they decided to cast their lot with the colonies, declare their independence from Britain, and join the confederacy of states. By unanimous consent of the people, the Wataugans established a committee that resolved in convention "to adhere strictly to the rules and orders of the Continental Congress," and to bear their "full proportion of the continental expense." They desired only the right of self-government, sanction for the establishment of courts, and legal validation of their deeds and leases from the Indians. Initially they sought not even separation from North Carolina, but annexation "in such manner as may enable us to share in the glorious cause of liberty, enforce our laws, and in every respect become the best members of society."[8]

By 1780 numerous petitions for independent statehood had circulated in the frontier regions from Vermont to the Carolinas. Unfortunately for the ideals and ambitions of frontiersmen, and for the tranquility of the new nation, no state holding claims to western lands readily succumbed to the petitions of backwoods patriots. New York, New Hampshire, and the Continental Congress refused, for example, to recognize the independence of Vermont during the 1770s and 1780s. Ironically, to deny the right of representatives from twenty-eight Vermont towns to convene and adopt their own constitution in 1777, eastern republicans would have to ignore, reject, or reformulate their own ideology which recognized the inalienable right of people "to alter or abolish" political relations and "to institute a new government." Generally, they chose to ignore the contradictions, seldom directly confronting the implications of Revolutionary rhetoric for frontier realities. They also had to reject implicitly their own encouragement of such actions in the Continental Congress's letters to the people of Quebec, in its recommendations to form states, and in the Declaration of Independence.[9]

Indeed, it was in specific response to the Declaration that citizens of the New Hampshire Grants region began the process of establishing an independent government. In their "Declaration and Petition" to Congress of January 1777 the Vermonters explained that "when the declaration of the honorable the Continental Congress, of the fourth of July last past, reached your petitioners, they communicated it throughout the whole of their district; and being properly apprised of the proposed meeting, delegates from the several counties and towns in the district did meet . . . for the purpose of forming themselves into a distinct and separate state." Confident that they were acting within their rights as described in the Declaration of Independence and assured of the support of the Continental Congress, which had, after all, seemed to encourage such actions, a convention of Vermont citizens drafted and endorsed their constitution on July 2, 1777. Laboring in the best spirit of a blossoming American constitutionalism, the Vermonters declared their right to establish a government rooted in "the authority of the people" gathered "in general convention, for the express purpose of forming such a government."[10]

Vermonters modeled their proposals on the Pennsylvania constitution of 1776, but the Continental Congress rejected them nonetheless. Delegates apparently believed that Congress's best interests lay in maintaining harmony between New York and New Hampshire, which had rival claims to Vermont, rather than in endorsing the principles upon which Congress was established. As historian Peter Onuf has observed, however, to reject the Vermont petitions for statehood "American revolutionaries were thus compelled to develop a counterrevolutionary argument against the independence of frontier regions from the original thirteen states."[11]

From an eastern perspective, authority to create new governments in the Revolutionary situation derived essentially from two sources. One was the natural right of self-determination. Simply put, the argument proclaimed that the freedom of people to govern themselves legitimized the creation of both the new nation and new states within that nation. The natural rights theory appealed to westerners as well as easterners during the Revolution, and became the primary ideological justification for frontier independence movements. The original thirteen states also claimed legitimacy based on their status as successors to the colonial governments. According to this doctrine, the states succeeded the colonies that long antedated the Revolution, and their authority derived from powers granted by kings and Parliament.

Initially, these two theories seemed compatible and mutually reinforcing. When frontiersmen in Vermont and elsewhere coopted the natural law argument as a rationale for separation from the original thirteen states, however, easterners elevated the succession doctrine to a position of higher law. The notion that succession provided authority superior to natural law appears particularly odd for the period during and after a Revolution against the legitimating source of the claim; and the eastern argument seemed ideologically impoverished to westerners at the time. It fit compatibly, though, with practical economic, military, and political concerns of eastern elites, and with the hierarchical ideology of those who sought an ordered settlement of the frontier. It was sincerely embraced by Revolutionary leaders who feared a scission of the nation, anarchy on the frontier, and an undermining of public policy toward the Indians as well as distribution of western lands.[12]

The initial stage of frontier petitioning was now drawing to a close. By 1780 no state had acknowledged the justice of frontier pleas for either redress of grievances or independent statehood. Many backwoodsmen now believed that state officials sought to deny them the fruits of independence—to exclude them from the "all men" of the Declaration of Independence. They thought the Continental Congress most likely to sanction their quest for autonomy. Loyalty to the states had certainly declined in all remote rural areas. But neither faith in the principles of the Revolution nor trust in the Continental Congress as the arbiter and defender of those principles had diminished. Congress thus became the focus of frontier hopes.

During 1780, Congress began negotiations with Spain on the greatest single grievance of settlers from Pennsylvania south —restricted navigation of the Mississippi River. News of instructions to minister John Jay heartened these people and contributed to their vision of the national government as sympathetic to western demands. Congress's mandate to Jay included securing "some convenient port or ports below the thirty-first degree of north latitude on the Mississippi River for all merchant vessels, goods, wares, and merchandises belonging to the inhabitants of these states." What the westerners did not know in the early months of 1780 was that Spain had no intention of negotiating this demand and that Jay immediately abandoned the Mississippi question in order to pursue the fundamental wartime purposes of his mission. He requested

and received permission to ignore his instruction on the navigation issue. The economic needs of the West were secondary to the national
cause of independence. It seemed unreasonable to Jay, and to most
members of Congress, to jeopardize the possibilities for speedy resolution of the war in the name of demands that could be negotiated at a
later date. From an eastern perspective, it was impossible to "justify
protracting the war, and hazarding the event of it for the sake of . . .
retaining the navigation of the Mississippi which we should not want this
age, and of which we might probably acquire a partial use with the
consent of Spain."[13]

Knowledge of such priorities did not, in the short run, diminish the
dedication of frontier areas to the Revolution or undermine settlers'
trust in the Continental Congress. Few westerners doubted the sincerity or questioned the integrity of national leaders. Fewer still considered
options proferred by Canadian officials at least as early as 1780. In that
year Frederick Haldimand, Captain General and Governor of the Province of Quebec, tried to lure frontiersmen to renounce the rebellious
colonies and reunite under the protection of the British monarch. "Being informed," Haldimand proclaimed from Canada, "of the distressed
situation in which the inhabitants of the back settlements bordering on
Canada are, and being well assured that very many of them, wearied out
with the oppression and tyranny under which they have groaned for
some time, are desirous of returning to their allegiance, and of enjoying
the blessings of peace and good order, I therefore promise such of them,
(without exception) as will surrender themselves . . . a safe and commo-
dious retreat." Despite evidence that their resources and interests were
being sacrificed for the defense of other regions, few northwesterners
accepted Haldimand's offer. The western country as a unit remained
loyal to the Revolutionary cause despite hardships, grievances, and lack
of assistance from the state and national governments.[14]

Stage Two: c.1780–1785

During the 1780s other frontier independence movements met with
rebuffs similar to those given Vermont, Watauga, and Westsylvania.
Nonetheless, settlers continued their appeals for some measure of autonomy throughout the period. Increasingly, however, pleas for recognition, representation, and redress of grievances became more strident,
and options considered by westerners were less patriotic than before.

Rejection of the Westsylvania petition, for example, did not kill desires for a new state. The same grievances that provoked the initial
request continued to plague western Pennsylvanians. They still felt
abused by unfair taxes, lack of protection from Indians, uncertain boundaries, allotment of the region's best lands to speculators, and lack of
accessible markets for their produce. Easterners continued to label their

protests the work of cranks and fanatics. "This country is just like other parts of the world," Assemblyman Thomas Scott asserted. "Let a petition be formed to burn the church and some signers may be got to it." The state assembly's response—a propaganda campaign designed to "bring over the deluded to a proper sense of their duty"—only aggravated tensions between the two regions. Although the state's position was couched in the language of justice and patriotism, the real issue was the economic interests of eastern speculators in western lands, who packed more clout in the assembly than frontiersmen. In the face of such a hard political fact, no true dialogue on western grievances could begin. The state would not entertain notions that might threaten to tear "their dearly earned property" from politically powerful easterners.[15]

A similar inter-regional battle was being fought at the same time in North Carolina. In 1776 the Wataugans were content to request only representation in the state legislature and establishment of courts in their region. By 1784, when delegates from the same area met in convention, only total independence from the state would satisfy them. They were embittered by eight years of rejection. One man rose, took from his pocket a copy of the Declaration of Independence, and angrily recounted the unfulfilled promises of its drafters. He then described parallels between the principles and grievances of the Declaration and those of frontiersmen. On the heels of this inspirational speech another delegate moved to declare the three western counties independent from North Carolina. Thus was born the short-lived state of Franklin.[16]

Under pressure from the governors of Virginia and North Carolina, Congress rejected the Franklin appeals and returned to North Carolina the frontier lands ceded to it by that state. The governors convinced members of Congress that, once sanctioned, statehood movements would spread to the border regions of other states. Congress's rejection of the statehood pleas of frontiersmen successfully fragmented the independence movement in Franklin, but at the price of increased tensions and greater loss of western loyalty, thereby strengthening the hand of foreign governments with ambitions on the frontier.[17]

Again, as in the cases of Watauga, Westsylvania, and Vermont, Congress was subject to countervailing stresses. These included the need to maintain good relations among the established states, the wishes of its most powerful constituents and members, the fear of setting precedents for fragmentation of the republic, and, on the other side, the principles under which it had fought the Revolution and justified its own existence. Again, the interests of eastern speculators in western lands had priority over those of backwoods farmers. The governor of North Carolina, for example, argued that the size of eastern investments and potential incomes at stake for his state were too immense to permit cession of the West. He realized that, "no doubt we are railed for want of generosity . . . [but] I can venture to say that there will be no cession of any land worthy of acceptance." To miss such a lucrative opportunity for the sake of "some vile agrarian law" seemed absurd to the governor.[18]

Settlers in the "eastern country" districts of Maine acted out this same pattern of frustrated petitioning to their parent state of Massachusetts during the first half of the decade. Although they had many grievances, most settlers remained loyal to the state in 1780 when they endorsed its new constitution. By 1785, however, clergymen, physicians, lawyers, and farmers had joined together to convince fellow citizens of the necessity for independent statehood. During the intervening five years, they had become convinced, just as those in other frontier regions, that they would never realize the promise of the Revolution while appended to another state.

Their complaints, as well as the pattern of petitioning and rejection, conformed to those of other frontier separatists. In their second convention, held in January 1786, leaders of the Maine independence movement compiled a list of these grievances. The litany included the insensitivity of the Massachusetts legislature to Maine's unique needs; the complexity of the remote state government; the expense for Maine citizens pursuing their political interests; the inaccessibility of state courts; under-representation in the legislature; the unfairness of the "present mode of taxation" to their region; the discriminatory operation of trade regulations; and, in sum, the "inconvenient, expensive, and grievous" nature of all dealings with the state. In light of these problems and the unresponsiveness of Massachusetts to pleas for redress, delegates to the September 1786 convention saw independent statehood as the best solution.[19]

Farmers in western Massachusetts also sought reform throughout the Revolutionary era. In town meetings, county conventions, and petitions emanating from these gatherings, rural protesters pleaded their case before the deaf ears of cosmopolitan politicians. Through the mid-1780s, however, many westerners still had faith in the state government and sought reform by nonviolent means.

Between 1780 and 1785 the Massachusetts convention movement was at its height. Demands voiced by petitioners were the classic ones of frontier peoples—lowering of government salaries, wider publication of laws, reduction of taxes and shifting of the tax burden from land to commerce, passage of tender laws, repeal of the state excise tax, court reform, heavier luxury taxes, moving the capital west from Boston, and establishment of local registrars and judges of probate. Over time the conventions moved from rather conservative suggestions about fiscal reform to more radical demands for judicial and political change. The nature of requests reflected the distance, expense, and complexity of dealing with a geographically remote government. They also mirrored the unique economy of the western region compared with the East. Most petitioners were subsistence farmers specializing in flax, lumber, and livestock production in addition to practicing general agriculture. And most of them were apparently debtors.[20]

Although they had been slow to adopt the cause of Sam Adams and the Boston Whigs, once westerners embraced the Revolution's principles they did so quite literally and with an undiminishing fervor not matched to the east. Throughout the 1780s these rural republicans continued to insist that the ideals espoused against Great Britain should apply at home. The Berkshire convention movement began in opposition to British courts and slipped quickly into protests against the equally discriminatory practices of the Massachusetts government. In 1778 the Berkshire constitutionalists voted by a six-to-one margin against opening the common pleas courts where debt cases were heard. By 1781 petitioners were pleading the special case of frontier conditions. The farmers requested tax relief because they were "destitute of money" and already burdened by the cultivation of "a hard and barren soil, particularly unfavorable to grain of every kind." The state excise tax also provoked ideological howls from the wilderness. "We esteem it a matter of great grievance," a Hadley convention announced, "that *excise* should be paid on any articles of consumption in a free republic."[21]

Their petitions were not favorably received in Boston. Easterners condemned even the methods of protest used by the farmers. According to merchant David Sewell, "these conventions of counties are seeds of sedition [that] ought always to be opposed." A "Citizen" wrote to the *Worcester Magazine* that such meetings were "treasonable to the state" and the proposed remedies of the petitions were simply "measures to defraud their own and public creditors." The irony of such reactions to their pleas for redress was not lost on the westerners. Parallels to the colonies' petitioning of Great Britain seemed obvious to the rural New England patriots. It was the state's rejection of this parallel that a "Freeman" caricatured in the *Worcester Magazine*: "When we had other rulers, committees and conventions of the people were lawful—they were then necessary; but since I *myself* became a ruler, they cease to be lawful—the people have no right to examine my conduct."[22]

Simultaneous with the convention and petitioning campaigns of 1780–86, sporadic violence demonstrated the frustration of a minority with economic conditions, courts, and taxes. Violence was endemic to the western counties, but with the exception of the Northampton riots associated with Samuel Ely, these actions were on a small scale and easily suppressed by local officials. Most were locally oriented and found a few irate farmers brutalizing a tax collector or "rescuing" a neighbor's property from sheriff's sale. Some Grotonians, for example, attacked a tax man in October 1781. On September 24, 1782, eight Berkshire County citizens freed a pair of oxen from the constable who had confiscated the animals from their debtor-owner. During 1783 Worcester County crowds terrorized a tax collector and attempted to prevent an execution sale. On

May 20, 1783, sixty men armed with bludgeons tried to keep county judges from entering the Springfield courthouse. In each case, however, local officials were able to raise posses that quelled the disturbances.

Such violence was not yet endorsed by large numbers of rural citizens. What is significant here is the unfolding pattern of protest and alienation. The grievances and methods of those in western Massachusetts conformed strikingly with those of trans-Appalachian frontiersmen. Also notable is how much the responses of seaboard-based New England governments resembled those of other states with aggrieved western settlers.[23]

The Continental Congress also continued to disregard frontier conditions in its negotiations with Spain during the 1780s. Despite its willingness to forgo claims to navigation rights on the Mississippi, no treaty had been signed with Spain during the Revolution. By 1783 Spain had not formally recognized the United States, nor had the Mississippi question been resolved. And it was during the first half of the decade that western suspicions of Congress's sincerity in the negotiations grew. During this same period the first serious rumblings of western discontent with the national government could be heard.

As early as 1779 the French minister to the United States, Conrad Alexandre Gerard, reported that Congress was not totally committed to securing navigation of the Mississippi from Spain. France, like Spain, wished Great Britain to lose the colonies, but nonetheless feared strong and expansive American settlements along the Mississippi River. Gerard was, therefore, quite pleased to find that representatives from the nine states north of the Potomac had no real interest in development of the Southwest or navigation of the Mississippi. Furthermore, many of the delegates, including the influential Samuel Adams and Gouverneur Morris, actively opposed rapid settlement of frontier regions. Morris believed that if the way were cleared for the frontiersmen to trade in New Orleans, the day would rapidly approach when westerners would claim their independence or come to dominate the East. He predicted that the United States would incur enormous expenses to keep settlers subject to the national government and that perpetual war would result between East and West.[24]

Many southerners also advocated slow, centrally controlled westward expansion. It was a union of northerners and southerners that implemented the eastern-oriented Land Ordinance of 1785, the Indian Ordinance of 1786, and the Northwest Ordinance of 1787. The same partnership of Tidewater elites and northern nationalists supported the new Constitution. And, some westerners predicted, ratification of the Constitution meant the persistence of a conservative policy toward westward expansion and continued foot-dragging in negotiations for navigation of the Mississippi. Residents of Charleston, South Carolina, for example, publicly opposed attempts to negotiate navigation rights from Spain.

Edward Rutledge wrote from that city in 1786 that "the subject of the western waters I found was in the possession of many of our people on my arrival. . . . the majority of those with whom I have conversed, believe we should be benefited by a limited cession of it to Spain, or rather a cession of it for a limited time." Virginian Richard Henry Lee concurred with the views of other eastern nationalists, including George Washington, when he wrote that "if this navigation could be opened and the benefits be such as are chimerically supposed, it must in its consequences depopulate and ruin the old states."[25]

When Don Diego de Gardoqui, the Spanish minister, arrived in New York in 1785, he too was pleased to find numerous "men of judgment" in Congress who were persuaded that free navigation of the Mississippi was not a desirable object for America. Among the men most opposed to this possibility was John Jay, now Secretary for Foreign Affairs, who was commissioned by Congress to begin anew formal diplomatic and trade negotiations with the Spanish plenipotentiary. Both Jay and Gardoqui understood that it would be dangerous for their nations formally to abandon negotiations on the Mississippi question. As Gardoqui put it in a letter to the Viceroy of Mexico, "I leave it to the superior talent of your excellency to infer how well it would be for us to avoid the vexations of such a naturally robust people [i.e., the American frontiersmen], trained to war and accustomed to the last degree to greatest hardships, as was duly proven when England lost the flower of her troops at the hands of a few naked colonists without military discipline."[26]

Jay's duplicitous dealings, which were contrary to his instructions and the official position of Congress, were bound to leak out and exacerbate distrust among delegates—and they did. By late 1785 Jay's abandonment of the navigation demand was known even to those who opposed the maneuver. Jay was biding his time, hoping to wait until the situation was politically right to request from Congress an alteration in his instructions. On May 29, 1786, Jay believed the moment had come and he formally requested permission to negotiate a commercial treaty and forgo any efforts to secure navigation rights on the Mississippi. But Jay was wrong in his estimation of the political mood, and his application precipitated what one historian has called "the most serious issue that agitated the Continental Congress during its five years of peace-time history."[27]

Debates on Jay's instructions monopolized the energies of Congress throughout the summer of 1786. During the month of August, Rufus King described delegates as still "warmly interested in the question, which is considered as very important by the speculators in the western lands." For his part, King stood with the speculators in support of Jay because "should we embarrass ourselves in the attempts of imprudent men to navigate the Mississippi below the northern boundary of Florida, we can expect no favors from the Spanish government." Others thought

that it was militarily foolish as well as economically and politically disad-
vantageous for the United States to demand navigation as a precondition
for a commercial treaty with Spain. Arthur St. Clair argued that Congress should agree to Jay's request since it would merely require forbearance for a term of years of a right that the United States did not
have the power to assert. Such an agreement *would* check the settlement of the western country, and St. Clair saw that as one of its greatest
advantages. The nation was too thinly populated, he believed, and government was already having difficulty keeping pace with the advance of
frontiersmen. Ultimately, Congress voted seven to five in favor of Jay,
Spain, and the speculators by altering Jay's instructions as he had requested. It was clear, however, that the necessary nine states could
never by marshaled to ratify any treaty that might result from those
directions.[28]

The perceived betrayal of the West on the Mississippi question served
to alienate some within Congress and others outside that body. Jay's
actions helped fuel boiling rumors about conspiracies to suppress agricultural regions and dismember the Union. James Monroe saw a link
between two dastardly plots. "Certain it is," Monroe wrote in August
1787, "that committees are held in this town of eastern men and others
of the state upon the subject of a dismemberment of the states east of
the Hudson from the Union and the erection of them into a separate
government. . . . The object in the occlusion of the Mississippi on the
part of these people . . . is to break up so far as this will do it, the
settlements on the western waters, prevent any in future, and thereby
keep the states southward as they now are." The men "of a private kind"
who gave birth to this scheme of disunion described by Monroe were,
he thought, aiming to weaken what would become the southern of the
two nations by denying it a strong frontier. Keeping the Mississippi
closed to trade was thus at the heart of the scheme. According to Monroe, Jay and his party intended to pursue the issue "as far as possible
either as the means of throwing the western people and territory without the government of the United States and keeping the weight of
population and government here, or of dismembering the government
itself, for the purpose of a separate confederacy. There can be no other
object than one of these."[29]

Madison, Jefferson, and others outside Congress also predicted disunion if the navigation demand was abandoned. Jefferson feared that
"the act which abandons the navigation of the Mississippi is an act of
separation between the eastern and western country. It is a relinquishment of five parts out of eight of the territory of the United States. . . .
If they [i.e., westerners] declare themselves a separate people, we are
incapable of a single effort to retain them." Those who voiced suspicion
of Jay's motives, and foresaw dire consequences, were certainly correct
to believe that the American negotiator saw no advantage in securing

navigation of the Mississippi. Surely, too, Jay thought that the "western country will one day give us trouble" and that the time was quickly approaching when the interests of all might be served by secession of the West. There is no evidence, however, to document a connection between Jay's beliefs, his actions, and a conspiracy to foment rebellion in the West. But conspiracy theories are not always based on concrete evidence, and distrust is often bred in suspicion rather than hard facts. Whatever the intentions of those who opposed free navigation, the reluctance of the national government to secure this western demand contributed directly to separation movements on the frontier. Whatever the evidence for theories that some easterners intended to ignore or work actively against the perceived interests of the West, rumors of such attitudes had their effect in the alienation of "the men of the western waters" from the national government.[30]

The British recognized these sectional rifts within American society, and their official policy reflected the knowledge. They would just watch and wait for a while before getting involved in American domestic affairs. Inaction seemed the most effective plan. At any moment, southwest Virginia, western Pennsylvania, or Vermont might separate from the United States. British officials predicted that union with Canada would be a likely consequence in each case. Active interference in these regions, they believed as late as 1789, might prove costly and counter-productive.

British policy on relinquishment of frontier forts partly reflected this sort of thinking. Although they intended to hand over the forts in 1783, neither Lord Sydney nor Lord North remained in office long enough to execute the policy. By the time the political waters had calmed, petitions of English and Canadian fur traders, concern about commitments to Indian allies, anger at American vindictiveness against returned loyalists, and confidence in the imminent disintegration of the United States combined to make the British reluctant to move quickly to implement the treaty that ended the Revolution. Such precipitate action as returning the forts could only serve to strengthen the tottering confederacy and, in the event of an American civil war, might prove unnecessary anyway.[31]

By the same token, intrigues with frontier separatists might only encourage the bickering colonists to reunite against a common British enemy. Better to let them fight among themselves. As early as October 1783, Frederick Haldimand, Governor General of Quebec, reported to North that he had rebuffed several "persons of influence" from Vermont who had visited him and appeared to solicit annexation of their region by Canada. He discouraged them completely, told the men that he could not interfere, and that he had orders to do his best to conciliate the affections of citizens in Canada and the United States.[32]

His superiors thought that Haldimand had gone too far by dismissing the separatists. They informed him that it was not British policy to

interfere "openly" in such movements, but it "would be difficult to
refuse to take them under our protection should they determine to
become subjects of Great Britain." Do not give them arms or money
before they succeed, but by all means let them know that they would be
welcomed under the protection of the Crown after they had seceded.
Haldimand was to use his discretion but take no overt action before
informing the home government. And, indeed, it appears that few
tempting opportunities for interference presented themselves to Canadian governors before 1786.[33]

By then the time was ripe for another shift in inter-regional relations.
Westerners were frustrated in their attempts to secure redress of grievances or independence from the states. They had tried and failed over a
period of years to gain, by their measure, a fair hearing in Congress for
their discontents. Many believed by 1786 that Congress was not making
a serious effort to secure navigation of the Mississippi from Spain. They
knew that the American negotiator opposed acquisition of that right and
sought to limit settlement of the frontier. Some now suspected a wider
conspiracy among easterners to debilitate the western economy permanently and among New Englanders to dismember the Union. Together,
years of political frustration, chronic economic turmoil, and mounting
evidence of eastern disaffection from the principles of the American
Revolution were undermining western loyalty to the nation. As yet, few
had taken action on these perceptions, but they were more attentive to
schemes and schemers, and more sensitive to perceived eastern injustices than frontiersmen had been ten or even five years before.

From an eastern nationalist perspective, the situation appeared quite
different. Social order seemed more at risk than political liberty.
Anarchy, more than tyranny, appeared the gravest threat to the nation's
survival. In this light, the "epidemic . . . spirit of making new states"
portended disorder, disunion, and disaster. "If every district so disposed
may for themselves decide that they are not within the claim of the
thirteen states," argued a New Hampshire assembly, "we may soon have
ten hundred states, all free and independent." From such fragmentation
of the nation, others contended, nothing but "anarchy can be expected
to ensue." In sum, nationalists asserted that "the idea of making separate states is generally reprobated as product[ive] of the worst evils [to]
the Confederacy."[34]

It seemed that for every frontier separatist who believed that "the
people alone have an incontestible, unalienable, and indefeasible right
to institute governments, and to reform, alter, or totally change the
same," there was a nationalist who countered that a jurisdiction lacked
the "right totally to disengage itself from its constitutional connections,
and set up a separate government." "The constitution is *equally
binding*," such friends of order argued, "in all its parts, on *every subject*
[and] if one article is broke, the *whole is dissolved*—and anarchy and

confusion the consequence." Neither perspective was "right," and neither was "wrong." Each made sense given the experiences, interests, and ideology of its adherents. Problems came not from the incorrectness, insincerity, or immorality of one side or the other, but from the devotion of both sides to principles and self-interests that by 1786 led many to anticipate "the horrors of a civil war."[35]

Chapter Three

SECTIONAL STRIFE

Massy White was born in Somerset County, New Jersey, on March 18, 1770. After the war for Independence, her father, Edward White, acquired rights to land in western Pennsylvania for his service with the Continental Army, and the family moved to this undeveloped property near Redstone Old Fort (later called Brownsville) on the banks of the Monongahela River. There Massy met John Harbison and, when she was seventeen, married him against her father's wishes. Some time in 1789 the Harbisons moved to the headwaters of Chartier's Creek, in Allegheny County. They lived about twenty-five miles from Pittsburgh, the nearest town, but within 200 yards of Reed's Block House, a well-guarded military establishment. Massy's husband was a scout for the army.

One night, when Massy's husband was away from home, two other scouts lodged in the Harbison's cabin. The men rose shortly before dawn and left the hut, leaving the door unsecured. Mrs. Harbison and her three children were still fast asleep. They awoke when a pair of Indians pulled Massy, by her feet, from the bed. The house was full of Indians armed with guns and tomahawks. Massy's first impulses were to embrace her infant and then grab a second petticoat to put on over the thin one she had on. An Indian tore the slip from her hands as part of his booty, while his companions ravaged the house for other items of interest.

Massy tried to alert soldiers in the fort, but she was captured, gagged, and claimed by a warrior as his squaw. Several Indians asserted the same right before one enforced his possession with an impressive display of ferocity. A group then attacked the blockhouse—killing one soldier and wounding another—while the rest began their escape.

The Indians pushed Massy along in front of them with the infant still in her arms and her five-year-old son at her side. The three-year-old stood by the fire crying bitterly. The warriors attempted to drag the boy along but he refused and began to wail pitifully. In response an Indian picked up the youngster by his feet and swung him against the door-frame, splattering blood, skull fragments, and brains on the ground. The Indians scalped the boy, stabbed him repeatedly, and only then abandoned the corpse.

Massy screamed and fell into a swoon at the sight of her butchered child. Her captors raised her from the ground and slapped her about the head and face until she regained consciousness. They then marched off with Massy, her infant, and her other son in tow. Later, the Indians would also murder the five-year-old. The child sobbed continuously; his mother believed that he was mourning his dead brother. Fearful that the youngster's crying would lead to their capture by white soldiers, two Indians took the boy aside, tomahawked, and scalped him. Again, Massy fell to the ground, senseless, with the infant still in her arms.

Eventually Massy Harbison escaped to tell the tale of her captivity. She recounted in horrid detail the murders of her children at the hands of thirty-two Indians, two of whom were white men painted and garbed as savages. She recognized several of the warriors—two she knew to be Senecas and two Munsees—as frequent travelers in the area. She reported on life among her captors, and her escape and six-day flight. Finally, she was united with her husband, with whom she moved to Bull Creek in 1794 and disappeared from the historical record.[1]

IN THE YEARS after 1785, frontiersmen continued to suffer under the same conditions as during the previous two decades, and they remained incensed by under-representation in state legislatures and lack of state assistance in meliorating the conditions of wilderness life. But during this third stage of East-West relations the loyalty of many settlers to national unity became truly weak. Fears of disloyalty that were once only a chimera of eastern politicians now had a basis in the inter-regional tensions these same men had helped to foment. Even after 1790, when the immediate threat of a Spanish conspiracy and the violence of Shays's Rebellion had passed, nationalists had good reasons to suspect that the trauma was not yet over. They had cause to anticipate with dread the disintegration of the republic.

By the fall of 1786, no grievance of western Massachusetts farmers had been resolved. No condition burdening the region had improved. It seemed to the rural villagers that the Boston-based state government had no intention of resolving inequities in the economic relations between city and country. To them it appeared that the state was just as insensitive to their needs as Great Britain had been to the grievances of its North American colonies. Many had grown weary of fruitless protest over the last ten years. Calling themselves "Regulators," they abandoned written remonstrances and launched armed assaults on the state courts.

The cycle of protest in western Massachusetts had, as on the Appalachian frontier, reached a final stage. The era of loyalty to existing governments was over. Outright rebellion in the names of liberty and justice now ruled the day. As these rural people knew well, the canon of Whig political philosophy dictated resistance to tyranny by every means.

When conventions of the people and their petitions failed to impress rulers with the need for change, the aggrieved had not only the right but the duty to resist oppression by force, to take the weapons of change into their own hands and destroy and institutional chains that bound them. The Shaysites, as the rural rebels came to be known, would not shun their duty. They would not relinquish their rights as free men to rulers in Boston any more than they had to those in London ten years before. They would, as they saw it, defend their liberties at any price.

By December 1786 about 9000 men had taken up arms against the state. Over one-quarter of the adult male population of rural New England was prepared to revolt. Most were from small villages rather than market towns. Overwhelmingly they came from the west. Over half of the Shaysites called themselves yeomen or husbandmen and lived on small tracts of land. A sizable minority (over 20 percent) were landless and termed themselves agricultural laborers. About one-third and most of the officers had fought in the Revolution. They were not wealthy men, and many were poor by any measure. They were not well educated by Boston standards, but had learned the lessons of Revolutionary politics.[2]

The cosmopolitan politicians of Boston had a different point of view. To the easterners, the farmers appeared to be "a party of madmen" who were conducting "a formidable rebellion against reason, the principle of all government." The official portrayal of Shaysites as "knaves," "thieves," and "madmen" hardly served to establish a dialogue between the two sides, nor was it intended to contribute to peaceful settlement of the conflict. On the contrary, the common eastern vision of rural protestors as anarchists and levellers made repression an absolute duty. Otherwise, the day would quickly come when "private property will fall with them and lie wholly at the mercy of the most idle, vicious, and disorderly set of men in the community."[3]

Political leaders finally responded to the protests by launching armed reprisals in the winter of 1786–87. As Fisher Ames saw it, the state responded in the only rational way possible to avoid a wholesale return of New England to barbarism. Many New Englanders believed that the Shaysites represented an international threat as well. "Our eternal foes are still at work," a contributor to the *Massachusetts Centinel* remarked. "They are making use of every method in their power," he continued, "to interrupt our tranquility, and sow the seeds of discord and dissension." And there is evidence that by 1787 the Canadian governor, Lord Dorchester, was not above some unofficial meddling in American affairs. On February 24, 1787, five leaders of the Shaysite resistance arrived in Quebec. They met with Dorchester and requested arms and ammunition. According to spies for the Massachusetts government, Dorchester promised to help the rebels through Britain's Indian ally, Chief Joseph Brant. The insurgents were impressed by Dorchester's hospitality and apparent sympathy for their cause. But no help ever arrived; British officials had apparently encouraged the insurgents and perhaps even misled them to expect economic and military aid. If so, it was either an irresponsible miscalculation or a cruel hoax. In any case, one can only speculate about what might have happened if Great Britain had been more forthcoming with support for the rebels. One can only hypothesize about the possible results had an effective leader emerged from the Shaysites to unite and focus the disparate protests of settlers in Maine, Vermont, New Hampshire, and Massachusetts.[4]

Shays's Rebellion had a calming effect on Maine's independence movement. Moderates in the conventions apparently lost their nerve in the face of the Rebellion and refused to press their demands while the state of Massachusetts was under siege. Some took the position that 1786–87 "was by no means a proper time to seek relief—the western part of the Commonwealth, from real or pretended grievances, were but a step from anarchy—that we should but add to the confusion—that conventions at all times were dangerous things, and always so considered by the General Court." In vain, more daring members protested that "if we were really injured, as had been acknowledged, any time was a proper time to obtain relief . . . that the General Court termed conventions dangerous assemblies was not disputed—so did the Parliament of Great Britain once pronounce our General Courts. . . . If we were injured, it mattered not by whom, whether by the government of Britain or of Massachusetts, in either case duty to ourselves required immediate exertion."[5]

Calls to action were not heeded. The September 1786 convention lasted only two days. Between then and January 1787, opposition to separation gained more strength. A note from the town of Machias explained its unwillingness to send delegates to the January convention: "While our political and pecuniary affairs labor under such complicated embarrassments, we think it unwise and unkind farther to perplex the departments of our administration." Only thirty-two of the ninety-three towns had responded. Of these, twenty-four favored and eight opposed separation, with a total of 618 of 970 votes in favor of secession. Unlike independence movements in other frontier regions, Maine's died with nary a whimper in 1787, only to be reborn during the next decade.[6]

Vermonters, on the other hand, pressed forward with negotiations in Canada and Great Britain with no diminution of fervor. As a result of repeated efforts during 1786 and 1787, they secured increased trading privileges with Canada. But their ambitions had now clearly grown. In 1788 Ethan Allen presented Canadian officials with another memorial, this time seeking both greater trading concessions and a promise to supply arms in the event of a Vermont rebellion against the United States. Vermont's petitions to Congress were getting no action and leaders of the region's independence movement had apparently decided to explore other avenues simultaneously in their quest for autonomy. Allen claimed in the memorial to have the loyalty of 15,000 men who were willing to resist aggression by the United States and any efforts to subjugate Vermont. Both Lord Dorchester and Lord Sydney delayed making any response.[7]

Impatient with their slim record of success in appeals to Canada, and having reached a point of high frustration with the United States, the Allens decided to go straight to Britain for some decisive action. At Whitehall on May 4, 1789, Levi Allen presented a memorial to Lord Sydney that the British interpreted as requesting a great deal more than commercial privileges. "The locality of Vermont," Allen's petition read, "as well as the disposition of its inhabitants, renders its connection with Canada the most natural as well as the most advantageous of any." The memorial elaborated no further on this point, but went on to request commercial privileges that Britain had already granted to the citizens of Vermont.[8]

Unfortunately for Allen, Great Britain became embroiled in the Nootka Sound controversy before it took any action on his requests, and was especially reluctant to offend the United States while preparing for war with Spain. Perhaps as a result of this international crisis, the British response to Allen's petition was far from what he and his fellow separatists desired. It appeared to Britain that "a commercial intercourse is already opened between the province of Quebec and the state of Vermont . . . upon as extensive a plan as the people of Vermont seem to have wished." Since Allen must be fully aware of this fact, the Privy Council concluded, "it is reasonable to infer that he has some other object in view besides the establishing a free commerce between the countries, and that he has probably received secret instructions for this purpose."[9]

It is clear from this same document that the Council recogized the potential of the situation. Although at the present time it might not be "politically prudent . . . to risk giving offense to the United States," as a matter of long-term policy it would certainly "be to the benefit of this country to prevent Vermont and Kentucky, and all other settlements now forming on the interior parts of the great continent of North America, from becoming dependent on the government of the United States." The geography of the region west of the mountains alone dictated a closer connection with either British Canada or Spanish Louisiana than with the United States. Two practical avenues of commerce lay open to the settlers— north through Lake Champlain and the St. Lawrence River to Montreal or south down the Mississippi to New Orleans. Difficulties negotiating the southern route with Spain should, if the British played their cards right, make the northern passage "much the most convenient."[10]

The Vermont petitioners appeared also to be seeking formal union with Canada. Their expression of this desire in Levi Allen's memorial remained cryptic, however, as it must before Britain was forthcoming with its own position. It would be foolish for the Allens to say too much at an early stage, especially since they were simultaneously pursuing similar negotiations with the United States. Whichever government moved first with an agreement to recognize their independence would secure the loyalty of Vermont's leaders.[11]

Things were different on the southwest frontier during the latter half of the 1780s. There, encouragement and some measure of support were offered by Spain to leaders of separatist movements. In Franklin and Kentucky there was no shortage of leaders for such schemes. Thus, in the Southwest, the desire for independence was just as strong as in rural New England, but the possibility for success was greater.

The state of Franklin had exercised sovereignty over the three western counties of North Carolina throughout the first half of 1786. In August of that year, however, a schismatic group, encouraged by the parent-state, held elections for the North Carolina legislature. From then through 1788 the two parties vied for control of the western counties. The result was civil strife. Two conflicting sets of laws were passed, two county courts met, two competing militias called men to arms, and two different authorities levied taxes on the frontiersmen.

Rather than securing greater freedom, justice, and equitable taxation, as the founders of Franklin had hoped, they were now confronted by a hopelessly confused system and near-anarchy. A visitor to the state in 1787 reported that "politics in this part of the country run high. You hear in almost every collection of people frequent declarations— 'Whorah for North Carolina!'—and others in the same manner for the state of Franklin. . . . God only knows where this confusion will end. I fear it ends in blood." By 1788 conflict had resulted in bloodshed. Many now believed that neither North Carolina nor the United States would concede the right of Franklinites to independence within the national government. By rewarding loyal frontiersmen with power, political office, and recognition, the state of North Carolina continued to exploit the divisions in local politics. Without a united effort, the fledgling district had no hope for securing recognition from the United States.[12]

For Spanish minister Diego de Gardoqui the secession movement in the Southwest came at an auspicious time. He was now convinced that no amount of Spanish gold, craftily spent among members of the American government, would have the effects desired by Spain. Gifts of a prized ass to President Washington, a stallion to John Jay, and a cash "loan" to Colonel Henry Lee had brought little discernible return. Franklin provided an ideal occasion to try his hand at another sort of intrigue. Shortly after he learned of John Sevier's revolt against the state of North Carolina, Gardoqui dispatched an emissary to test the waters for a Franklin-Spanish alliance. Gardoqui instructed Dr. John White to make secret proposals on behalf of Spain and to act in concert with Don

Estevan Miro, Governor of Louisiana, in his efforts to secure the loyalty
of the disaffected frontiersmen. According to White, "Gardoqui gave me
letters to the chief men of that district with instructions to assure them
that if they wished to put themselves under the protection of Spain and
favor her interests they should be protected in their civil and political
government." The two conditions set by Spain for its assistance were
that the political office-holders of Franklin take an oath of allegiance to
the King of Spain and that the state's inhabitants renounce fealty to any
other sovereign. "They have eagerly accepted these conditions," White
reported to Miro, "and the Spanish minister [Gardoqui] has referred me
to your favor, patronage, and assistance to facilitate my operations."[13]

Sevier confirmed White's report in a letter to Gardoqui during September 1788. "The people of this country have come to realize truly
upon what part of the world and upon what nation depend their future
happiness and security," Franklin's governor assured the Spanish minister, "and they readily infer that the interest and prosperity of it depend
entirely upon the protection and liberality of your government." All that
he needed from Spain, Sevier pleaded, was a loan of a "few thousand
pounds [and] such other military assistance as your understanding
deems it necessary and convenient to supply us with."[14]

Still, it was the Mississippi question that remained at the heart of
Franklin's ambitions. Indeed, Charles Robertson predicted, "we cannot
long remain in our present state, and if the British *or any commercial
nation who may be in the possession of the mouth of the Mississippi* would
furnish us with trade, and receive our produce there cannot be a doubt
but the people on the west side of the Appalachian Mountains will open
their eyes to their real interest." But Spain, not Britain, controlled the
mouth of the Mississippi, and the leaders of Franklin's independence
movement would even aver loyalty to a Catholic monarch rather than
remain within the American confederacy under existing conditions.[15]

Unfortunately for the frontier rebels, promises were all they received
from Spain at this time. The intentions of Gardoqui and Miro were
apparently sincere, and they acted within the bounds of instructions
from Spain. As with the governors of British Canada, however, communications were delayed, overt actions required authorization at the highest level, and the wheels of bureaucracy ground ever so slowly. The
Spanish vacillated in response to European events. And nothing happened. As late as September 1789, Robertson and his followers awaited
the promised assistance. In expectation of Spanish aid, they held
another convention and delegates insisted again on separation from
North Carolina. In such a condition, Robertson wrote, "unprotected, we
are to be obedient to the new Congress of the United States; but we
cannot but wish for a more interesting connection. The United States
afford us no protection. . . . For my own part, I conceive highly of the
advantages of your government."[16]

The Franklinites could not remain in limbo forever. They had made their point to North Carolina, and fears of Spanish intrigues, loss of revenue-raising land, and hostile neighbors on the frontier contributed to the parent state's more conciliatory attitude in 1789. The westerners were now even more frustrated by the Spanish than they had been by North Carolina and the Continental Congress. Spain had missed an opportunity to wrest one section of the frontier from the United States. Sevier accepted his election to the North Carolina legislature. During this session the assembly again ceded the western counties to the federal government. This was an encouraging sign to the westerners who saw it as a first step toward independent statehood. It would at least keep them under the sovereignty of the United States for the time being.

The new national Congress accepted the cession and established a territorial form of government in the region. The President named Sevier Brigadier General for the Southwest Territory. Although Sevier was not appointed governor, as many in the region had hoped, the military office at least demonstrated the good will of the national government. Independent statehood was not immediately forthcoming, but settlers were now confident that it would be soon. The Mississippi question remained unsettled, however, and the westerners were far less sanguine about the eventual resolution of this, their most pressing demand. Until both statehood and navigation of the Mississippi were secured for the people of Franklin, their ties to the United States would remain weak, their loyalty to the nation shallow, their susceptibility to schemes designed to achieve these goals always a possibility.

In a similar fashion, the federal government forestalled another potentially disruptive frontier independence movement with the Northwest Ordinance of 1787. The Ordinance gave courts, a body of law, and a government under the authority of national officials to the Ohio region. The government thus brought unruly settlers under marginal control with promises of protection against Indians, and independent statehood at a later date. Such reasonableness would at least prevent the wholesale defection of the region during the immediate future.[17]

The situation in Kentucky was more volatile than in the Northwest, however, precisely because the central government made no move to alleviate the settlers' gravest concerns. By 1786 Kentuckians were convinced, just as the Franklinites were, that Congress intended to concede Spain's claim to exclusive navigation of the Mississippi. Rumors of Jay's machinations had taken root in fertile frontier soil. Some settlers were "greatly alarmed" and "thrown into utmost consternation and distress" by such reports. Petitioners expressed this alarm to the Virginia Assembly in the hopes that the state would understand their plight and make heroic efforts to secure the privilege of navigation for the westerners. According to the Kentucky memorialists, "treaties of commerce have heretofore been formed even between the most despotic powers for

reciprocal advantages in the commercial intercourse between their respective subjects and dominions, but never have they before heard of a
project being proposed, much less a treaty formed which shut the doors
of commerce to one part of a community and deprived it of its natural
rights for the benefit of the others." They would not tolerate such "subversive and abhorrent" actions, ones that were so obviously contrary to
their rights, interests, and the constitutions of the state and federal
governments.[18]

Conventions of Kentuckians had met as early as December 1784. The
purposes of that convention and the one of August 1785 were similar.
Delegates sought statehood and membership in the confederacy. There
is no evidence that members of these conventions contemplated secession from the nation at that time. In any case, it seems certain that a
large majority of delegates, and most of the people they represented,
remained loyal to the Union.

In places, the tone of the convention's rhetoric was high. The delegates modeled their final report on the Declaration of Independence and
proclaimed Virginia's land tax and the necessity of delivering payment to
the remote state capital "equally subversive of justice as any of the
statutes of the British Parliament that impelled the good people to
arms." But even as late as their fifth convention in September 1786,
Kentucky delegates made their plea for independence conditional on the
agreement of the Continental Congress to accept them as the fourteenth
state. By 1787, however, there was evidence of mounting frustration, at
least among some Kentuckians. On July 21 of that year Harry Innes, a
prominent local attorney and politician, informed Virginia Governor Edmund Randolph about his assessment of Kentucky's mood. "The Indians
have been very troublesome on our frontiers," Innes wrote, "and still
continue to molest us, from which circumstance I am decidedly of opinion that this western country will, in a few years, revolt from the Union
and endeavor to erect an independent government; for under the present system, we can not exert our strength, neither does Congress seem
disposed to protect us."[19]

The Mississippi question constituted a grievance of equal weight with
Kentuckians. During March 1787, in response to a circular emanating
from "a committee of correspondence in the western part of Pennsylvania," Kentucky delegates met yet again at Danville. This time they
considered with alarm the report that John Jay had proposed a cession to
Spain of navigation rights on the Mississippi for twenty-five or thirty
years. Some called for yet another convention in May for the purpose of
"convincing Congress that the inhabitants of the western country are
united in the opposition and consider themselves entitled to all the
privileges of freemen, and those blessings procured by the Revolution,
and will not tamely submit to an act of oppression which would tend to a
deprivation of our just rights and privileges."[20]

The atmosphere had clearly changed in the West. Settlers were no longer willing to "tamely submit" to Congressional disregard of their rights and needs. Kentuckians openly considered secession from the Union. Spain, too, was now receptive to more radical schemes on the frontier. And James Wilkinson was prepared to unite the ambitions of Kentucky, Spain, and himself.

On his own initiative, Wilkinson embarked on a personal and political trade mission to New Orleans in August 1787. Ignoring the Spanish prohibition of such ventures, he took the chance that rules might be bent or broken if the bait was sufficiently tempting. According to Wilkinson, he and his fellow Kentuckians were motivated by the overwhelming need to secure a transportation route for their produce. The Mississippi to New Orleans or other water routes north to Canada were the only logical alternatives. The Spanish officials should see that it was to their disadvantage for American settlers to forge strong trade links with British Canada. Moreover, Spain might deny the frontiersmen navigation rights for a time, but it would not be possible for Spain to "permanently resist the claim to the *navigation of the Mississippi* of the already powerful and increasing American settlements west of the Appalachian Mountains." Denying his request could only result in driving the Kentuckians into the arms of Great Britain, thus making Louisiana and Mexico less secure. The carrot of profits from a commercial connection and the stick of a possible union with Spain's European enemy seemed to Wilkinson irresistible incentives for Spanish accession to his demands. The Kentuckians were ready, he announced, to open negotiations with Spain "for our admission *to her protection as subjects*."[21]

Miro forwarded the memorial to Spain, but not until November 1788 did the Supreme Council of State record its verdict on Wilkinson's requests. Immigration of the disillusioned Americans into Spanish territories was to be encouraged. The Spanish would provide Wilkinson with remuneration for his attempts to dismember the United States. Kentuckians would pay only a 15 percent duty on goods shipped via the Mississippi to New Orleans rather than the 25 percent levied on others enjoying this privilege. Finally, the Kentuckians "should not be suffered to lose hope that in case of success they would be admitted" as subjects of the Spanish monarch.[22]

Wilkinson responded to the news of these decisions with a second memorial. The situation had changed dramatically. By taking well over a year to respond to his enquiries, Spain had perhaps lost the opportunity to gain Kentucky for the Empire. When he wrote his first memorial, the national government of the United States "was weak, confused, and divided, powerless to manage or to regulate the propensities of the smallest district." Now the United States had a new central government, one that "although untried and of doubtful success, has inspired people in general with the loftiest hopes."[23]

As a result, the independence movement in Kentucky splintered. The long silence of the Spanish and the revitalization of the American government had "led to apprehensions among various prominent men already gained over to our party, because without any response from Spain we could not expose ourselves, ignorant as to whether or not she would sustain us, to the risk of entanglement with the Congress." These reasons, in addition to new prospects for British support, would make Wilkinson's task of winning Kentucky for Spain more difficult. But he still might succeed if the Spanish delivered more than promises. Already he had invested much of his personal fortune in Spain's behalf. Money and speed were the essence of the problem. Great Britain was already interested, and the United States Congress had it within its power "to win the affection of the westerners." Wilkinson believed that "the discordant and irreconcilable interests of the two sections of the country absolutely prevent their real connection," but that "the moment is critical" for action. Delay would only play into the hands of Spain's enemies.[24]

In retrospect, it appears that secession of Kentucky from the Union was less likely in 1789 than it had been just a year or two earlier. Wilkinson had made his play at the July 1788 Danville convention and failed. The proposition was hotly debated in Kentucky newspapers, but feelings were warm on both sides of the issue. The moment for action had passed, at least temporarily. The United States government had contributed as much as Spanish inaction to undermining Wilkinson's plans. "[President George] Washington has begun to operate on the chief heads of this district," he lamented. Several of Wilkinson's fellow conspirators and some of the most influential men of the district had accepted national posts. Harry Innes was now a judge; George Nicholas a district attorney; and others were on the national payroll as well. All was not lost, however, according to Wilkinson: "I know that Harry Innes is friendly to Spain and hostile to Congress, and I am authorized to say that he would much prefer receiving a pension from New Orleans than from New York." "Liberal donations" would be necessary to wrest these influential men from the talons of the new American government.[25]

Miro was shocked by this abrupt turn-around in affairs. He had anticipated the possibility of negative repercussions from granting navigation to Kentuckians for a fee, but he "never imagined that the effects would be so sudden, and that the large number of influential men [friendly to Spain] . . . would have entirely vanished." Spanish intrigues on the frontier were not to end, however. A pension for Wilkinson was recommended to ensure his loyalty and continued reports. And Miro engaged another spy to watch Wilkinson. Next time an occasion presented itself, the Spanish would be better prepared to exploit their advantages.[26]

In Kentucky, just as in Franklin and the Northwest Territory, the American government enjoyed some success in quashing the immediate potential for violent and permanent disaffection from the Union. Although the major concerns of settlers in these regions—protection against Indians and navigation of the Mississippi—still remained, in each case the future looked more promising in 1789 than it had in 1786. This was not true for the inhabitants of Vermont, Maine, or western Pennsylvania. Residents of each region had some—as in the cases of Vermont and Maine—or all—in western Pennsylvania—of the grievances of other frontier areas. Fewer people in these regions shared the optimism of Ohioans, Kentuckians, and Franklinites.

Western Pennsylvanians had fared worst of all during the 1780s. Their economy had declined precipitously. Indians still rampaged unchecked by any military force. Even more of the region's best lands were now in the hands of eastern speculators. There seemed no promise of new markets for the region's produce. And the national and state governments appeared not even to entertain the notion of an independent Westsylvania. No promises had been made to the Pennsylvania frontiersmen. No hope had been extended for redress of their grievances. Anyone who bothered to notice could have perceived the creation of a truly desperate populace, a growing body of frustrated men with little to lose. But, from the perspective of Philadelphia, the problem of frontier unrest appeared quite different.

The nation had weathered two potentially devastating episodes—Shays's Rebellion and the Franklin secession movement—in recent years. President Washington had good reasons to suspect the loyalty of settlers in Maine, western Pennsylvania, and Kentucky as well. He also knew something of Spanish and British intrigues on the frontier and assumed the worst.

Few friends of the national government believed that the crisis had passed. Virginia and federal officials were frightened, for example, by the potential disloyalty of the Kentuckians. Washington was "greatly alarmed" by news from the western country. Others believed that frontier plans were "pregnant with . . . much mischief to America." Nationalist politicians warned that the country must remain constantly on guard against domestic and foreign intrigues. Henry Lee feared that "the contagion will spread and may reach Virginia." Another Federalist predicted that the "seeds of dissension" sown in New England and Pennsylvania "will not end without a civil war." To Thomas Marshall, the political situation in the western country seemed "critical." "It appears plain to me," he wrote to Washington, "that the offers of Lord Dorchester, as well as those of Spain, are founded on a supposition that it is a fact that we [i.e., Kentucky] are about to separate from the Union." Dorchester's assessment was very similar to that of friends of the American nation. "The politics of the western country are verging fast to a crisis," reported the Canadian Governor General, "and must speedily eventuate in an appeal to the patronage of Spain or Britain."[97]

From the East, as from Quebec, London, New Orleans, or Madrid, it was difficult to discern differences among the conditions and attitudes of frontier settlers. To the President, it seemed a question of rampant disloyalty, unwarranted demands, irresponsible actions, and little recipiocation from the west in return for the efforts and expenditures of the national government. The nation was doing its best, in Washington's eyes, to put down the Indian threat. It was actively considering the statehood applications of Kentucky and Vermont. It had made provisions for the eventual admission of the Northwest and Southwest territories to the Union. The western Pennsylvanians were another case. Washington knew the region, and he knew the people. He personally opposed creation of an independent Westsylvania. He was doing his utmost to bring improved transportation for commerce to the region by the construction of canals. These efforts would have to suffice. It was all the East could spare and more than the West had a right to expect. As the President saw it, there was little room left for compromise. And, in retrospect, the President's belief that disloyalty in the West constituted a major threat to the nation was reasonable in light of information available to him.

New state movements in the years following the Revolution should have startled no one. Those who desired independence and local control acted in the spirit of the Revolutionary era. Certainly the British were not surprised, and no doubt they took some satisfaction from the disillusionment of frontier peoples with their new national government. The *Gentlemen's Magazine* had offered an explanation for the actions of Franklin's founders in 1785. The reason according to the London periodical, was that "the people of the western counties found themselves grievously taxed for the support of government without enjoying the blessings of it." The irony of this explanation, so recently after American riots against British taxes, was not lost on English readers.[28]

Some saw the establishment of Franklin as a hopeful sign of an imminent trend in the new nation. Another Briton, for example, wrote that "we are in daily expectation of hearing of a coalition between them [i.e., Franklinites] and the Vermonters and New Hampshire Grants, who are also disaffected; and it is a matter of doubt whether the balance of power would not be in their favor, even against the United States, if matters should come to an open rupture, as there are a great many over the whole continent quite tired of their independence." Such possibilities certainly did exist, precisely because westerners were disappointed by the reluctance of the United States to encourage independence movements on the frontier. Many were not pleased with the practice of republican rule. By the latter half of the 1780s, many were willing to seek other avenues to reach the promises of Revolutionary rhetoric.[29]

In light of these trends, Great Britain's secret agent "P. A.," or "P. Allaire," as he sometimes signed his dispatches, advised his employers that the time for caution on the frontier had ended. Writing from New York in August 1790, this spy argued that 5000 to 7000 men from the western country would join the British in a military venture to conquer Spanish Florida if, in return, they were guaranteed free navigation of the Mississippi River to New Orleans. "Take the Floridas," P.A. advised. "Open a free navigation of the Missisippi for the western inhabitants, and you bind that country and its inhabitants forever in spite of Congress, or all the world, for without the Mississippi, its fruitfulness is useless; a few frigates and 2000 men would retake it in three weeks and if proper means were made use of I would engage for a sufficient number to assist." It would take an investment of no more than 2000 men and a few ships on the part of Britain and "you may rest assured that an equal number from the western territory will join you, not by order, consent, or approbation of the United States, but by those who acknowledge allegiance to NONE."[30]

P.A. reported that the western country did not recognize the authority of the United States. It was an independent entity ready and able to act in any way its residents saw fit. He described the settlers as "men, hardy, inured to fatigue and danger, expert marksmen who live by hunting and who have for these last five years lived constantly in the western woods and who are as constantly attacking and attacked by the Indians. These men . . . are equal to any 5000 sent from Europe: they want the free navigation of the river, they want the lands along the river, and above all they want employment, being most of them destitute of clothes and money." Just send him £2000, 2000 men, and one British officer and in return Britain would have the Floridas and the loyalty of the entire frontier. It would be "a second India." Britain would "command the granary of America" and, ultimately, Mexico and Peru as well.[31]

Eastern politicians had also perceived a pattern to frontier unrest. They noticed the connections between demands from Maine to Franklin, and thought they diagnosed causes in the characters of men like James Wilkinson and the ambitions of Great Britain and Spain to dismember the nation. They were right about the ambitions of Wilkinson, Britain, and Spain. They were wrong to label these the "causes" of frontier unrest.

Changing attitudes toward the French Revolution during the 1790s would also help eastern nationalists to explain the causes of political violence among what they identified as a frontier rabble of foreign anarchists. Cosmopolitan officials failed to take seriously the political philosophy articulated by frontier peoples, even though it was modeled on ideas published by American Revolutionaries. Nationalists believed that they had won an intellectual argument over the principles of radical constitutionalism, or even coopted it, in 1788. The task for the 1790s, these men believed, would be to enforce their victory, not to modify or compromise its potential. They would defend the "fixed principles" of the Constitution.

To many settlers these eastern politicians seemed unbending in their pursuit of Atlantic mercantile interests against those of western agriculturalists. No compromise appeared imminent. No dialogue on Revolution principles ever began. No indication of eastern awakening to the desperate economic state of the frontier emerged. Ignorance, indifference, economic self-interest, and a commitment to ordered settlement of the West all contributed to national policies that enraged frontiersmen. Coincidence, luck, bureaucratic bungling, and personal miscalculation had saved the United States from all but two major outbreaks of political violence during the 1780s. But unless new policies secured navigation of the Mississippi, assisted in defense of the frontier, established more equitable methods of taxation, developed alternative methods and routes of trade to the frontier, and recognized the independent statehood of frontier peoples, the potential for violence would increase, not diminish over time. Unless mercantilist politicians acknowledged the validity of ideological principles emblazoned on the frontier intellect from the time of the Stamp Act crisis, no dialogue over the fundamentals of republican rule could begin. Many easterners had changed the way they thought about representation, taxation, and republican rule. Many westerners had not. Taxation was always a touchy issue with eighteenth-century Americans. But to impose a taxation crisis on top of inter-regional stress would simply fuel the sparking embers of East-West conflict.

Chapter Four

LICE, LABOR, AND LANDSCAPE

Abraham Russ lived about twenty-two miles from Pittsburgh on the banks of the Allegheny River, some two miles above the mouth of Bull Creek in western Pennsylvania. Towards evening on March 22, 1791 the extended Russ family was preparing for dinner when seven Indians walked into the settlers' cabin. The Indians left their rifles at the door in a well-known token of friendship and requested to dine with the white frontiersmen. The family welcomed their guests, perhaps more out of fear than hospitality. John Dary, a thirteen-year-old boy, suspected the worst and left the house to hide in the woods while the Indians supped.

When the Indians had finished their meal, one of them rose and stood squarely against the door to prevent members of the household from leaving. The other Indians rose as well and began methodically to butcher and scalp their hosts. They disposed of four men, one old woman, and six children in this manner.

Mrs. Dary, sister of Russ, witnessed the death of her mother and her child. An Indian lifted the eighteen-month-old infant by its feet and dashed the child's brains out against the skull of old Mrs. Russ. Thus with one horrid blow both were dispatched. In the panic of witnessing such a sight Mrs. Dary literally dismembered part of the frail cabin and escaped through the wall. Three of her daughters, a sister-in-law, and three nieces followed. Agnes Clark and two of her children also escaped in this manner, as did Catherine Cutright, who had lost both husband and son in the massacre.

These women and children ran to the river, where their screams brought Levi Johnson from a mile and a half away. He shuttled the living across the river in his canoe while the Indians were plundering and setting fire to the cabin. Seventeen persons thus fled into the night. Once across the river, the survivors ran nine miles in the cold to a place of shelter. Two boys who had escaped separately hid in the woods near the cabin for three days before venturing forth.

News of the carnage traveled fast over the countryside. Families from miles around packed their belongings and moved to a defensible location at James Paul's farm on Pine Run. About seventy or eighty women and

children gathered there by morning. The men erected a blockhouse
where everyone lived together throughout the summer. The men also
pursued the Indians, but to no avail. Several enlisted for six months'
service with General Arthur St. Clair to fight the Indians as well.[1]

T HIS, THEN, WAS the western country. It was wild and very violent. It was a place where humans prided themselves on their inhumanity and gouged out each other's eyes in recreational contests. The frontier had a logic of its own and brooked no instruction from the East.
Inhabitants cared little for outsiders. They were independent actors on
the American scene, beyond the pale of some eastern values and many
eastern laws.[2]

The western country was, perhaps most of all, a place of conflict.
Violence between Indians and whites was already legendary on the
frontier, and hostile interaction among the frontiersmen was even more
common. Here at the headwaters of the Ohio, there was much evidence
of past conflict among men of European descent. Remains of the French
Fort Duquesne were still visible in the 1780s. A protective ditch,
mounds of earth, and bastions remained, but were long grown over with
grass and pastured by cattle. Pittsburgh itself was conquering the
groundworks in the decade after the Revolution as townsmen erected
houses on the site. Grant's Hill, a decisive battleground of the Seven
Years War, still bore the marks of conflict. Grant and 800 Highland
Scottish troops met defeat here at the hands of French and Indian
enemies. Weather-whitened bones and rusted implements of war were
still to be found on the hill during the 1780s. Nor had Anglo-Americans
buried their dead on Braddock's Field, where "men's bodies [were]
lying around as thick as the leaves do on the ground; for they are so
thick that one lies on top of another for about a half-mile in length, and
about one hundred yards in breadth." Only visitors seemed appalled by
the physical remains and the vermin that fed upon them. Children
played amongst the carnage, apparently without suffering any pangs of
revulsion.[3]

Paradox as well as conflict scarred the land, the people, and the
history of the region. Geography formed the heart of the western country's character, and paradox marked the center of its topographical face.
The western country lay at the crossroads of European wars for the
continent. It stood at the military and geographical center of English
and French contests for North America. It was isolated, though, from
the population centers of the English colonies—now American states—
by the Appalachian chain of mountains. Pittsburgh sat at the very spot
where the tributary systems of the Allegheny and Monongahela rivers
converged and formed the Ohio to become part of the vast effluent
empire of the Mississippi River. And yet settlers had no obvious market
or easy route of trade, partly because the lower Mississippi was con-

trolled by Spain. A final example of paradox found settlers living on
some of the richest agricultural soils known to North America, amid the
most abundant game any had ever seen, but barely surviving long
winters from lack of food, shelter, and appropriate clothing.

The mountains and rivers were grand, but they were also fierce. The
harsh seasonal change from fall to winter was both welcomed for its
respite from intense summer work and feared for the toll of human and
animal life taken by the brutal cold. Similarly, the joy of spring was
often tempered by the floods and muddy thaws that exacted a grievous
price in lives and labor.

Such harsh extremes deeply influenced patterns of thought and action on
the frontier. It is tempting to equate raging rivers, wild fluctuations of
temperature, and awesome mountains with common character traits
among the people who inhabited the wilderness, and such reductionism
has provided the grist for several historiographic mills. But it is difficult to
demonstrate the causal linkage between phenomena of geography and
climate and those of personality and ideology. It is even hard to decide, for
example, whether the salient feature of western country geography was the
formidable Appalachian peaks that isolated the region from the East or the
passes that cut between the mountains and served as sluices for the immigrants and armies cascading through them into the wilderness.[4]

Both mountains and passes shaped the region's history. An obsessive
love for personal liberty and a rabid intolerance for cultural, racial, and
ideational difference prospered simultaneously and in blunt contradiction among the region's inhabitants. During the 1780s, outsiders who
visited the western country perhaps saw the extremes and contradictions
most clearly. They observed the paradoxes of character and climate, and
in so doing revealed as much about themselves as they did about the
region they visited. Some expressed eloquently the link between the
people who inhabited the wilderness and the environment visitors saw
as a cause for the character of frontier life. It was a commonplace in
travelers' literature that civilization had degenerated on the frontier in
response to harsh conditions. Less common were those accounts that
portrayed frontiersmen as uniquely blessed in character and health as a
result of their pristine surroundings.[5]

All agreed that climbing through the mountains was perilous. "The
roads are so steep," wrote a woman traveler in 1787, "that the horses
seem ready to fall backwards." Once past the mountain peaks, however,
the people, their habitat, and their way of life seemed to most travelers
as low-fallen as the mountains were high. Irreligiosity, immorality, and
dirtiness struck most visitors and some residents as the dominant traits
of Pittsburgh life. During the 1780s, Virginian Arthur Lee found "not a
priest of any persuasion, nor church, nor chapel, so that they are likely
to be damned, without *the benefit of clergy*." John Wilkins agreed that
"there appeared to be no signs of religion among the people," and it

seemed to him that "the Presbyterian ministers were afraid to come to the place lest they should be mocked or mistreated."[6]

Other vices of frontier life were even more repulsive to some eastern visitors. John Wilkins observed that "all sorts of wickedness was carried on to excess, and there was no appearance of morality or regular order." William Winans confirmed Wilkins's opinion in greater specificity. "The whole society was, with very few exceptions, about as wicked as fallen human beings can be on this side of utter perdition. Female seduction was frequent, quarreling and fighting decidedly customary—drunkenness almost universal, and therefore scarcely a matter of reproach." David McClure found that "the inhabitants of this place are very dissipated." He abhorred the settlers for thinking themselves "beyond the arm of government and freed from the restraining influence of religion." To his horror, many of the local Indians kept a squaw, "and some of them a white woman," as mistresses. Religiously, according to Winans, men met every Sunday, not for church services, but "to drink, to settle their differences, and to try their manhood in personal conflict. And many were the black eyes and bitten members which were the fruits of these hebdomadal reunions of the neighborhood."[7]

And then there was the filth, not just of the mind and soul, but of the persons, homes, blankets, and clothing of frontier people. Easterners were often shocked and were usually appalled by the living conditions. After days of arduous journey through nearly impenetrable mountains and over inadequate roads, travelers longed for shelter from the elements. Some westerners were quite friendly and eager to share their food, housing, and blankets. Mary Dewees's experience was not unusual. She thought that the day of travel had been unduly harsh, but "this night our difficulties [really] began: we were obliged to put up at a cabin at the foot of the hill, perhaps a dozen logs upon one another, with a few slabs for a roof, and the earth for a floor, and a wooden chimney constituted this extraordinary ordinary. The people [were] very kind but amazing[ly] dirty. There was between twenty and thirty of us; all lay on the floor, except Mr. Rees, the children and your Maria, who by our dress or address or perhaps both, were favored with a bed, and I assure you that we thought ourselves lucky to escape being fleaed alive."[8]

Inhabitants struck one visitor as "a parcel of abandoned wretches," who lived "like so many pigs in a sty." Another described settlers as "the scum of nature." And many had examples of interpersonal violence as well as filth to report. One was appalled that a man horsewhipped, then fatally shot another who had kicked his dog while trying to break up a dog fight. Others remarked with horror on the number of one-eyed men, victims of eye-gouging, who resided on the frontier. The amount of whiskey consumed, and the uninhibited violence of those under its influence, apparently transcended anything that easterners had ever witnessed or imagined.[9]

For most frontiersmen, life was very hard during the 1780s by any standard. For most it got worse over the decade. In 1780 more than one-third of western Pennsylvania's population was landless. Over the next fifteen years the proportion of landowners declined, until 60 percent in some townships were without land. By the mid-1790s landholdings of the average taxpayer had fallen substantially, and in Fayette County a majority of inhabitants were landless. Most settlers were living at a bare subsistence level and conditions were getting worse.[10]

While most property-owners were losing ground during the 1780s and 1790s, a small number of men actually consolidated and increased their holdings. The bottom 10 percent of taxpayers was falling from ownership of 2 percent to 1 percent of the region's land as the top decile increased its possession from about 26 to 35 percent by the mid-1790s. Nothing like the mythical classless frontier society ever existed in the western country. Upper and lower classes locked in place, and opportunities for upward mobility were becoming increasingly limited. By the 1790s the percentage of wealth controlled by the lowest decile of the population had dropped to zero in several western townships. About one-quarter of the taxable male population became "croppers," laborers who farmed the land of others and paid their rent in crops.[11]

Most of the great landowners who profited from the consolidation of wealth in the western counties were outsiders. Few of the great residential landholders of the 1780s were able to hold their ground against eastern speculators. Nearly 75 percent of the largest landholders lost property and their positions in the hierarchy of wealth by the 1790s. Nearly 90 percent took no part in the great land-grab of the period. In Washington County, the number of absentee landowners increased over the decade from 280 to 366. And even more significantly, the proportion of land owned by absentees increased over the decade as well. Literary evidence suggests that nonresidents also monopolized the most fertile property in the region.[12]

An unprecedented growth in population hit the western country simultaneous with this process of stratification, and the two phenomena were no doubt closely related. The free population of western Pennsylvania increased about threefold—from about 33,000 to 95,000—from the end of the Revolution to the turn of the century. Between 1783 and 1790 the population of the state's three western counties grew by approximately 87 percent. Roughly the same number of immigrants arrived each year through the 1790s as well. During this same period the state as a whole experienced growth of about 40 percent; by comparison, then, the western country was growing much faster.[13]

The great population influx had actually begun as early as 1770 in the western country. George Croghan, resident trader and land agent for George Washington, wrote on October 2, 1770, that "last year, I am sure, there were between four and five thousand [new settlers], and all this spring and summer the roads have been lined with wagons moving to the Ohio." By the summer of 1771 there were about 10,000 families in the region. By 1774 the population had probably reached 30,000. Residents began discouraging friends and relatives from following them. In 1773, a Scottish immigrant wrote home that "much of the fine land on the Ohio and Mississippi will be quickly taken up." He perceived that the area was already overcrowded with people who wanted, but could not obtain, their own land.[14]

Population growth came in spurts rather than in a constant stream before the end of the Revolution. From the outbreak of Dunmore's War in 1774 through 1782 the region suffered almost continuous assaults by Indians. Reports of these incursions discouraged potential immigrants at least temporarily and even led many settlers to abandon their homes for the comparative safety of other regions during the Revolution. The town of Bedford, for example, was home to about one hundred families before the hostilities, but only twenty during the war. Since casualty figures were nowhere near this high, it seems clear that people were sometimes leaving the frontier even more quickly than others were arriving. In 1778 a traveler was struck by "the sight of so many deserted houses along the glades, on the doors of which was written, either with chalk or coal, 'good people, avoid this road, for the Indians are out murdering us'."[15]

The 1790 federal census provides some information on the size and ethnic background of the region's populace. About 37 percent were of English origin or descent, 7 percent had Welsh names, 17 percent were Scottish, 19 percent Irish, and 12 percent were German. The ethnic heritage of the remaining 8 percent cannot be determined. The various immigrant groups were not evenly distributed among the western counties. Germans, for example, were the largest single nationality to settle in Bedford County. Non-English settlers predominated in all the western counties, but most strongly in Westmoreland and Bedford. Those of English origin or ancestry comprised 47 percent of Fayette and 43 percent in Allegheny and Washington counties.[16]

The statistics on land-ownership and population growth reveal a society in extreme social and economic turmoil. They describe a place where poverty was the standard in 1780 and where living conditions declined over the next fifteen years. The tiny mud-floored and often chimneyless cabin was the common abode of these pioneers, and outside the towns these flea- and lice-infested hovels sprouted up at an increasing rate over time. The percentage of rural landowners declined by about 59 percent over the same period. Wealth became concentrated in the hands of fewer men residing in the West, while absentee-owners from the East enhanced their holdings. A majority of residents experienced a sharp decline in all economic categories even as they pushed back the edge of the wilderness.

Settlers perceived, as well as experienced, their collective decline in standard of living. The downward trend was relative not only to their own absolute level of subsistence but also to the lifestyles of a small group of men, most of them newcomers, who resided in the region. The increasing wealth of faceless absentee landlords who controlled the best lands of the region was also obvious. Resentment grew over time as the pattern of loss and gain became apparent to even the humblest, most ill-educated of the frontiersmen. By the 1790s the western counties faced the potentially explosive combination of a disgruntled rural proletariat ruled by a very small number of comparatively wealthy overlords. Immigrants were also frustrated by the disparity between their inflated expectations for life in America and the harsh realities of frontier experience. By the 1790s common laborers and artisans, many of them disenfranchised, were the typical settlers in some townships.[17]

Over the same time, the richest citizens grew considerably wealthier, owned a greater percentage of the land, and monopolized the overwhelming number of public offices in the region. Thirty-six men dominated the political life of Fayette and Washington counties. Twenty-six of them were among the wealthiest 10 percent of the region's populace. Five were the richest men in their townships. And 69 percent of these political leaders bucked the trend of economic decline in the region by increasing their landholdings. John Neville, for example, managed to increase his 1781 holdings of 1000 acres while the median landowner was losing a significant part of his 100-acre farm. At a time when the average western Pennsylvanian did not even own one cow and one horse, Neville possessed ten horses, sixteen head of cattle, and twenty-three sheep in addition to his eighteen slaves and his political office as regional inspector of the federal excise tax on distilled spirits.[18]

County sheriffs, the actual enforcers of law, were among the wealthiest 10 percent of the population. This was an apparent conspiracy of wealth, law, and power that bred resentment among a portion of the citizenry. These visible manifestations of inequality were resented by tenant-farmers, who resisted a tax structure based upon items of domestic production rather than on land. Common people perceived that government—as embodied in these men—conspired against them. Such perceptions led those at the bottom to reason in class terms, to equate easterners with wealth, power, and absentee landlordism, and to see local enforcers of eastern laws as self-interested lackeys of eastern elites.[19]

People had traveled west for land and in the naïve hope of securing, if not quick wealth, at least economic autonomy. Many had read—or had read to them—propaganda tracts circulated by speculators in eastern cities, in Britain, or in Europe. Gilbert Imlay's pamphlet was typical of this genre. It neglected to mention the Indian wars. It ignored the harshness of living conditions for the poor, misrepresented the potential for upward mobility, and lied about the weather and the terrain. "Large

tracts of land lay all along the banks of . . . [the Monongahela], from
the Old Fort to Pittsburgh, which are capable of being made into extensive and luxuriant meadow ground," Imlay wrote in 1792. This was true,
but he neglected to inform his readership that the best land in this
stretch was owned by speculators who sought only tenants to clear trees.
Imlay described a heavenly place where coal lay on the surface of the
earth for the picking, where vast open plains promised to become "the
most valuable grazing country in all America," and where the great
tributary systems of the region provided transportation of crops to market in a pleasant, fast, and profitable fashion. Again, half-truths. The
Mississippi was sometimes closed to American trade by the Spanish and
at other times taxed, so there were few profitable markets downstream.
Others had long ago engrossed the luxuriant lands he described and,
banking on the potential they too espied, would not sell them at any
reasonable price, nor on credit. Resident overseers were well armed and
did not look kindly on those who tried to pluck coal from their employers' property.[20]

Propaganda tracts also misrepresented conditions for trade. "Every
article [of local production] has sold extremely well," Imlay wrote.
"Every kind of grain, fibrous plants, cotton, fruits, vegetables, and all
sorts of provisions" were easily grown and sold to settlers in Ohio and
Kentucky. "Linen and woollen cloths, leather, and hats . . . are manufactured with considerable success," he reported. The inundations of the
major rivers were predictable, limited to several months of the year, and
productive for the farmers and traders. Indeed, those who believed any
of this tale had reason to expect a lifetime of health, wealth, and peace.
In Imlay's western country, the young led a grand life of dancing and
courting. The older people were wise seers who devoted their evenings
to discussing politics, art, and science.[21]

The truth was not so pleasant. Reality struck those who arrived with
such unreasonable expectations very hard. John May, for example, had
heard or read some of the promotional literature. In 1789 he invested in
a trading venture designed to capitalize on the wealth of the western
country described therein. He arrived at the frontier during May, timing his journey well to avoid the worst and enjoy the best weather the
region's promoters said it had to offer. When he reached Pittsburgh on
May 26, this entrepreneur was shocked to find "money affairs here at a
low ebb. Everybody [was] unwilling to part with money, but very anx-
ious to get it." He was confronting a situation unknown in the metropolitan East. There was such a dearth of cash that the Pittsburgh region
subsisted on a barter economy. If he were to trade at all here, May
would have to barter his goods for crops and transport them back over
the mountainous terrain he had just traveled with such great difficulty
and a lighter load.[22]

May found accommodations in private houses despicable. He lodged on the twenty-seventh of the month at a ramshackle log cabin. It thundered and rained throughout the night. The roof leaked, the walls rattled, and the ground was hard and infested with insects. He "slept but little and rose the first chance." "The confusion crazes me," May wrote of his short stay in Pittsburgh. Life was too different, too rough, and "much too promiscuous" for his taste. "Such a port as this," he wrote in his diary, "[is] worse than the stormy seas." But he could not leave. The rains had washed out the roads. "Such a wild goose chase as I have been on!," May lamented. He had visited Summerell's, Redstone, Elizabeth's Town, Fort Pitt, Greensburg, and the Laurel Mountain region without selling a thing. "Would to God I was out of this business and so far on my way home," he despaired.[23]

What food May could buy made him nauseous. The people he communed with were rude, ignorant, dirty—not at all the gay young blades and wise old men the propagandists had led him to expect. He felt "surrounded with devils." Until the roads were cleared, May had to stay in a cabin at the foot of the Laurel Mountain. "Not a house within five miles," he complained, "except a little cabin. Our inmates are all Dutch [i.e., German] excepting the beasts. She who was mistress is dead. The old man, a daughter of eighteen, two hired women a little older, three hired men, a number of children, besides a bear and five dogs make up our bedlam." Only later would May realize that he lodged with one of the more prosperous families in the region.[24]

May calculated his costs for transporting merchandise from Baltimore at a phenomenal £74.7.10. And there was no place to go. Thwarted by the weather—a tornado had now knocked down trees and strewn them "a thousand ways, in the most confused manner"—by the unexpected poverty of the region, and by the dearth of specie in the West, May suffered emotionally and financially. He settled with the wagoners for what they were due, stored his remaining goods in an abandoned cabin, and struck out for home. "The best we can expect," he feared, "will be to save ourselves, probably we shall fall short of even that."[25]

Other commentators were also struck by the overall poverty of the region and by the level of destitution suffered by the western poor. The standard for these impressionistic comparisons was the East—Philadelphia, Baltimore, New York, and the rural stretches east of the Appalachian chain. But what distinguished the West from the East was not the distribution of wealth among its populace or the fact that conditions were getting worse for the poor.[26]

Three factors in this portrait do stand out, however, as unique by comparison with the East. First, the total economic pie from which the frontier poor were receiving an increasingly thinner slice was itself much smaller than back East. Hence, in the West, the poor were more impoverished by absolute standards than their urban counterparts during the 1780s and 1790s. The contrast was striking to eastern visitors who had

never seen white men living in such destitution. Second, the expectations of the back-country poor were in greater conflict with the realities
of their lives than was the case for the needy in eastern cities. Many
westerners had left the cities with the belief that life would be materially
better in the West, if not easier. They had braved the wilderness to
acquire their own land, and instead they were as a group considerably
poorer and they now had to suffer Indian attacks and much harsher
living conditions. To find after such traumas that their chances of ever
owning land, of ever escaping the grasp of landlords, was even more
remote than in the East, was especially devastating. Finally, and even
more frustrating, was the absence of the very landlords on whom they
could focus their wrath. Unlike in the East, a high and growing percentage of the rentier class was invisible to its tenants. There were fewer
opportunities to negotiate grievances or to engage personally in the
reciprocal relationships associated with dependency. Their expectations
had been raised, their realities lowered, and the perpetrators—as they
saw it—of their condition were mere names on leases and ejectment
suits. Here were people "much disappointed in getting land," a disgruntled populace waiting for a spark to ignite and aim their rage.[27]

By the 1790s the western country's inhabitants also divided among
themselves for reasons other than stratification of wealth and political
power. Small towns now dotted the landscape and although none exceeded 400 residents there was a marked difference between the styles
of farm and town life. Pittsburgh, the largest of these villages, boasted a
population of 376 in the 1790 census. By 1796 there were nine towns in
Fayette and eight in Washington County. The identifiable occupational
groups in these new urban centers were artisans (16 percent), merchants
(4 percent), professionals (3 percent), and "dependent classes" (43 percent). On the average, town residents were even poorer than their rural
counterparts. Propertyless ex-slaves, laborers, servants, widows, and
other dependent poor composed the single largest identifiable group of
townsmen. A man such as the merchant Benjamin Wells, who became
an excise collector during the 1790s and ranked among the wealthiest of
the region's inhabitants, was a notable exception to this rule of western
life.[28]

The vast majority of poverty-stricken people in the western country
were not town-dwellers, however. Whether they owned land, most
frontiersmen sought to scratch a living from the environment in which
they lived. The agricultural revolution sweeping Britain in the eighteenth century had yet to reach these humble farmers. They knew little
of crop rotation, nor were they able to fertilize the soil with manure
from their wandering cattle. With the exception of Indian corn, their
crops were those of medieval England—wheat, oats, barley, rye, buck-
wheat, flax, and hemp. Their ploughs showed no improvement over
those of ancient Romans. Moldboards were straight and made of wood.

The new curved moldboards that Thomas Jefferson and others were experimenting with had not yet arrived in western Pennsylvania. Harrowing was done by dragging thornbushes across the fields. Farmers planted corn "Indian fashion," scattering seeds over unploughed land. Results, not surprisingly, were often disappointing or downright disastrous. Some years the squirrels and birds seemed to harvest more than the husbandmen. Indians, panthers, wolves, and bears threatened crops as well. Frosts came as early as the third week in September and spoiled harvests. Floods sometimes came in March and April, ruining the ground for planting.[29]

The soils of the West were so rich that some crops, such as wheat, often prospered despite the primitive methods of the planters. These periodic excesses, the scarcity of hard cash in the West, and the growing non-agricultural population of the region, created a barter economy. Merchants advertised their ready acceptance of "cash or country produce" for merchandise. A 1786 newspaper advertisement, for example, listed the acceptable commodities for barter. "Cash, flour, whiskey, beef, pork, bacon, wheat, rye, oats, corn, ashes, candlewick, tallow, etc., etc.," would all suffice for exchange. Ginseng, snakeroot, skins, furs, and "country linen" were also common commodities of frontier marketing. It was unfortunate that trader John May had not heard about this aspect of western life before he made his disastrous trek from Boston.[30]

The desire to fill local needs and discover a profitable commodity for inter-regional exchange led farmers to distill their grains into whiskey. In Washington County, for example, there were about 500 stills by 1790, one for every ten families. The capacity of most stills was less than 100 gallons and provided little more than was necessary for home consumption. The average distiller could turn his own surplus grain plus perhaps that of a few neighbors into a potable necessity and a commodity for which there was at least some market.[31]

Even with the benefits of rich soils and large quantities of local whiskey to numb settlers against the cold, the work, the fleas, and the prospects for annihilation by Indians, life in the western country was a delicate balance between dearth and excess. Settlers lived both physically and psychologically at the edge of subsistence. Any year the frosts and snows might come too early or too fiercely. Any spring the thaws could come too late, or in a torrent of water and mud that was even more devastating. And even when the weather was relatively cooperative, there were always the unpredictable attacks of Indians or wild beasts on human and animal life. Almost everyone knew somebody who had lost a wife to the Indians, or a child to a panther or bear. Widows could attest to the rage of the Monongahela at floodtide, the torture of seeing one's spouse succumb to a burning fever, or the horror of witnessing the murder and scalping of a loved one.

No one helped the frontiersmen at these times of hardship. No one sent food or medicine from Philadelphia to save the children. No eastern armies succeeded in crushing the Indians once and for all. No resources came from the state government to repair the roads or build new routes to far-away markets for the fruits of their labor. The frontiersmen were alone and resigned to it. They were a fiercely independent people who accepted the labor, the lice, and the landscape of the wilderness with a stoic, often stuporous, fortitude. In return, they demanded total liberty to fight the Indians whenever and however they wanted, to trade in markets wherever they could be found, and to spend the meager profits of their labors as they saw fit.

Such a bargain could not be struck with the new national government organizing at Philadelphia in 1790. No longer would westerners be free to treat taxes and collectors as they wished. No longer could they expect to deny rents to landlords without legal consequences. No longer could they exist outside the pale of eastern laws and eastern law enforcers, as had been their practice for decades prior to ratification of the Constitution.

Western countrymen had avoided contact with governments almost entirely during the 1760s. Border disputes between Virginia and Pennsylvania had erupted into a local war during the 1770s and resulted in refusal to pay taxes to either state. Although land taxes produced state revenues in the region during the 1780s, Pennsylvania's excise on whiskey was a dead letter in the West. When ratification of the national Constitution appeared certain in the summer of 1788, Westmoreland County residents felt threatened by the new system and established a committee of correspondence to explain their reasons for opposition to the document. They suggested amendments that would restore local control over domestic concerns. They objected to the Constitution's lack of specific protection of individual rights, and they expressed traditional fears about its power to levy internal taxes and maintain a standing army. Finally, they denounced the remoteness of the new institutions and the inadequate representation they would have there. The perspective of these pioneers was different from those who wrote and voted to ratify the Constitution, but similar to that of colonists who had opposed the Stamp Act. They had much in common with Englishmen who had resisted the intrusion of a national government empowered to collect excises and otherwise usurp local rights and control. And they shared with other Antifederalists a range of fears and disregard for central authority insufficiently representative to protect their liberties and interests.[32]

Frontiersmen did not yet know for sure that liberty from central authority had ended. They did not perceive that they no longer had the freedom to nullify laws passed by geographically remote legislatures in which they were, by their measure, underrepresented. They would soon find out, however, that even while the Indians rampaged in the wilderness, while adequate markets were still denied them, and while internal improvements were far from reaching the frontier, westerners were still expected to pay the price of multiple governments beyond their influence and their finances. The facts of power, if not the logic of political theory, would dictate their participation in the new government of the United States. The price of this involuntary membership was rising, even as many westerners' ability to finance membership in the new political order declined. The frontiersmen had learned their lessons about political liberty during the Revolution, now they would learn about political power.

Settlers did not totally lack respect for law, but some acts of the eastern legislatures seemed especially unjust from a wilderness perspective. The Pennsylvania whiskey excise of 1783 was, for example, the only act passed by the state legislature since the Revolution to evoke "general disapprobation [and] universal abhorrence and detestation" among the frontiersmen. Not all officials of the state government met the kind of brutal treatment reserved for excise collectors who appeared in the territory. Settlers found something uniquely egregious about this particular type of law and its methods of enforcement.[33]

In 1790, petitioners from Westmoreland County tried to explain the unusual circumstances of frontier life that led to the necessity of repealing this tax. They did not deny that part of their opposition stemmed from local addiction to "spiritous liquors," but this was not what made their case unique. "Independent of habit," the petitioners argued, "we find that the moderate use of spirits is essentially necessary in several branches of our agriculture." In a region where labor was exceedingly scarce, only the free use of alcoholic beverages could secure the steady engagement of agricultural laborers. Workmen demanded frequent and liberal draughts of liquor and would simply move on when denied their ration. It was to fill this sort of need that stills were erected in the first place. Commercial sale of the beverage was only a secondary function of distillation. To tax whiskey at the point of production was, therefore, an untoward burden in the West because much liquor was never sold, and the quantities that reached local markets seldom brought much cash.[34]

Whiskey was an item of barter like grain or milk or cattle. Where could the frontiersmen secure the cash necessary to pay this tax? "With as much propriety," the petitioners reasoned, "duty might be laid on the rye we feed to our horses, the bread we eat ourselves, or any other article manufactured from the products of our own farms." They realized that the unfairness of the tax in the West was difficult for easterners, "whom Providence has placed under the meridian rays of commercial influence," to understand. But the western country's economy was so different from the East's that taxes on domestic productions created unbearable burdens. When such a tax was payable in cash at the point of production, the injustice was effectively doubled.[35]

Ultimately, the state legislature saw the light. Excises were abhorrent to many citizens on political, cultural, and economic grounds. They were difficult, indeed often unprofitable to collect, and the federal government was considering moving into this area of taxation in the near future anyway. Better to repeal the obnoxious tax in the face of such problems. Some frontiersmen were ecstatic. They believed that they had won a great victory in the halls of government. Their resistance to the excise, their refusal to pay, their petitions, and their assaults on excise collectors had proved effective. Liberty had triumphed and they had successfully made their case to eastern politicians.[36]

Of course, the frontiersmen were wrong. Their methods were, if anything, counterproductive to their cause. In truth, eastern politicians thought little and cared less about the desires of the pioneers. Few troubled themselves to read and even fewer to understand the numerous petitions from chronically discontented farmers who refused to pay their share of government expenses. The people had representatives. They lived in a democratic republic and could vote in elections. Under the circumstances such petitions were clearly extralegal and, in the eyes of eastern nationalists perhaps even illegal, a seditious remnant of days gone by.

Westerners saw a positive relationship, however, between their actions and repeal of the state excise. In similar circumstances they would try the same tactics and expect the same results. For the time being perhaps it was best that the two regions failed to comprehend the breadth and depth of their disagreements. In the long run, though, the gulf of understanding and sympathy between East and West could produce only conflict.

Chapter Five

GEORGE WASHINGTON AND THE WESTERN COUNTRY

The Pittsburgh militia was frustrated and angry in March 1782. Each year its members organized an expedition into the Ohio country to subdue hostile Indians, but seldom found the warriors who periodically swept down upon their homes. Even less frequently were they able to exact revenge for such acts as the recent murder and impaling of a woman and child. Many understood the popular biblical allusion that portrayed all Indians as Canaanites. If the analogy were apt, it was their duty as Christians to wipe the heathens from the face of the earth and redeem the promised land for God's chosen race.

But what about the "Moravian" Indians on the Muskingum River? They were Christians and Indians. They dressed like white men, wore their hair like the white settlers, were an agricultural people, appeared pacific, intermarried with whites, and seemed to live moral lives. All the more reason to be suspicious, the frontiersmen reasoned. No doubt the missionized Indians were merely advance parties—spies—for the murderous savages who inhabited the wilderness. When it came to a contest of loyalties, the frontiersmen believed, you could always count on an Indian—Christian or heathen—to side with his racial brethren.

Word of the militia's intentions to act on this line of thinking reached the Christian Indians at Gnadenhutten in early March. The Indians discredited the information. White men were their friends, co-religionists, and brothers in the eyes of God. Indian warriors supported by the British were the white men's real enemies. If the militia was marching toward the Muskingum, it must be to rest among friends before a more arduous journey into the Ohio Country.

On March 6 a party of about 160 whites appeared on the trail to Gnadenhutten. About a mile from the town they spotted a lone Indian walking toward them. They fired several shots at Joseph Shabosh, who fell to the ground with a broken arm. Shabosh did not try to escape, still assuming that the party had mistaken him for someone else. He told the men that he was the son of a white man, the missionary John Shabosh; that he was one of the Christian Indians living in the nearby village; and that he was their friend. Finally, Shabosh realized that the attack was

75

no mistake. He begged for his life. A number of the whites seized young Shabosh and chopped him to pieces. Joseph's brother-in-law watched the entire episode from about 150 yards away, had time to warn the village of its danger, but fell into a state of shock and hid himself in the forest throughout the day and night.

Another Indian who may have witnessed the scene was murdered in his canoe. The militia moved on. Most of the Indians—men and women— were working in the cornfields. The whites hailed the laborers as their friends and brothers, told the Indians that they came to save them from the dangerous Indian allies of Great Britain, and to move them closer to their friends at Pittsburgh. The Indians were still not suspicious. They left their work and walked with the white men into the village. There the whites told the Indians to pack their belongings for the journey. A number of the frontiersmen moved on to the town of Salem, where they prepared the Indians of that town for the same trek to Pittsburgh. All were to rendezvous at Gnadenhutten. The Indians of both villages freely gave up their arms—guns, axes, and knives—to their "protectors."

Once all the Indians of both villages had gathered at Gnadenhutten the trap was sprung. No longer did the militiamen commend the Indians as good Christian people. No longer were the Indians promised better homes, more teachers, and attractive churches nearer to their white friends. Now the militia called them "warriors," not Christians. Now the white men accused them of stealing all the horses found in the villages; contended that all their axes belonged to white people; and insisted that pewter basins and bowls, tea-kettles, cups and saucers, and pots found among their effects were stolen property as well. How did the whites know these items were pilfered? Someone had branded the horses with initials, a practice unknown to Indians. The axes had names written on them and Indians did not write on axes. Indians used wooden bowls and spoons, not pewter. In other words, the militiamen used all signs of the Indians' acculturation to a white world as evidence of their "Indianness"—their barbarity, duplicity, and general depravity. The fact that the Indians appeared more "civilized" by Anglo-American standards than the settlers themselves was an irony that perhaps had a profound inspirational effect upon the horror that followed. Clearly, the whites felt that racial characteristics transcended cultural or religious integration.

The visitors announced their intentions to kill their Indian hosts. All Indians must die so the whites could claim the land and material goods that they believed were rightfully theirs. No amount of pleading could alter this logic. The Indians—about forty-two men, twenty women, and thirty-four children—became resigned to their fate and asked for a slight reprieve to prepare their souls. Their captors granted the request and the Indians knelt down and joined together in communal prayers. The whites withdrew to consider the manner of execution. Some suggested burning the Indians alive in their homes. Others favored death by scalping. A final group expressed some doubt about the enterprise. Perhaps it would be wiser to take the Indians as prisoners or even to let them go.

When the militiamen returned with their verdict, one of death by bludgeoning and scalping, the Indians were singing hymns. The whites separated their victims into two groups—men in one, women and children in the other—and led them to the huts or "slaughterhouses" where they would die. In no case did the captives resist. One woman named Christiana fell to her knees before the militia captain and begged for her life. He assured her that the situation was out of his control. The others went to their deaths, bound in pairs, without a word of protest. Christian education had prepared these devout people to suffer martyrdom passively.

A man named Abraham was the first to fall at the blow of a cooper's mallet found in the execution hut. The first woman to die was Judith, an elderly widow. The same pioneer who felled Abraham dealt apparent death-blows to about thirteen others before his arms wearied. All ninety-six Indians were scalped, many while they were still alive. Frenzied whites mangled some bodies with hatchets.

Of the approximately one hundred people in the two villages only four survived. One was John, the man who witnessed the murder of Joseph Shabosh and hid in the woods. An eight-year-old boy named Benjamin was adopted by a member of the militia. Two other youths escaped from their executioners. Thomas was about fifteen years of age and was, therefore, brought to the men's execution hut. He was beaten on the head, scalped, and left for dead. Regaining consciousness, he feigned death and thus narrowly avoided the executioners who returned to admire their handiwork. At dusk he crept over the dead bodies to the door of the hut and then into the forest. Another boy escaped from the women's execution hut by raising a plank used as a trap-door and hiding in the cellar. He waited there, amid the blood streaming through the floor, until dark, when he left his hiding place and climbed through a window in the hut. Another youth, who was with him in the cellar, could not fit through the window and was burned alive the next morning when the militia set fire to the "slaughterhouses." The two escaped boys saved the village of Schoenbrunn by warning the inhabitants of impending doom before the militia arrived.

Some of the dead Indians had been among those protected by the Pennsylvania government from the Paxton Boys during 1763 and 1764. Some of the militiamen participating in the massacre had been Paxton Boys. Later, others would be Whiskey Rebels as well. Not everyone in the region endorsed the slaughter of peaceful Christian Indians, but there was little protest. The force of communal values endorsing these events was too strong to resist. Indeed, no apologies for the massacre ever emerged from the West. Reports of the murders scandalized some

eastern politicians, but the perpetrators were never punished. Laws of
the states and nation certainly did not extend to the protection of Indi-
ans on the frontier, at least not in 1782.[1]

EVEN THOSE EASTERNERS who had experienced the trials of
wilderness living found it difficult to sympathize with the perspectives,
the culture, and the violence of frontiersmen. Knowledge of back country conditions and settlers bred contempt more often than empathy
among those who witnessed but did not share the pioneer spirit.
George Washington knew the western country and its people as well as
any nonresident of his day. He had witnessed the harshness and the
beauty of its environment first-hand in a series of visits that spanned
decades. He had participated in the violence that left bodies strewn
across Braddock's Field. And he had explored, surveyed, mapped, and
contrived to own some of the best of its rich soil. As President his
opinions would be crucial to relations between the two regions; and for
this reason alone, the history of Washington's relationship with the western country is an essential context for the story told here. It takes on
additional significance, though, because Washington's role in events surrounding the Whiskey Rebellion has seemed an enigma to historians
sympathetic to the rebel point of view. His anger, militarism, and apparent vindictiveness in relations with the frontiersmen have struck Washington's political and historiographic foes as eccentric contrasts to his
legendary demeanor under fire. Fascinating in its own right, and largely
untold, the story of Washington's frontier experiences helps to illumine
the consistent pattern of his decisions as President and adds to our
understanding of this heroic figure as a very human being.[2]

Washington was obsessed with the frontier. No President's life before
Andrew Jackson's was so shaped by the wilderness. No President, including Jackson, received more of his education from the forest and less
from formal schooling. Even Jackson and Lincoln studied law, while
Washington never imbibed more than the rudimentary instruction of
primary grades. Quite literally, the western country—what is today
northwestern Virginia, West Virginia, Kentucky, western Pennsylvania,
and southeastern Ohio—was the first President's classroom. It was there
that he studied his professions of surveying and war-making. There he
learned to lead men, to espy and speculate in promising land, to plan
and execute military strategy, to dun tenants, and to bully squatters on
his property. From these youthful experiences Washington formed last-
ing opinions about the back-country's significance for the survival of
British North America. As President, he perceived that the fate of his
personal finances, the nation, and indeed the world were inextricably
bound to the frontier; and he interpreted threats to the West as menaces
to them all.

Washington's wilderness education began in 1748, when he was sixteen years old; and the lessons of this first trek impressed indelible prejudices on his young mind. The journey he took west with a friend and a team of surveyors was supposed to be a lark for the young man. Washington found it mostly a trial, however, and complained bitterly in his journal about the rain, mud, insects, and people he encountered. He learned the tribulations of wilderness travel during spring rains; he learned to avoid lice-infested bedding and hostels; and he learned that the transportation route to the western country from Virginia was over "the worst road that was ever trod by man or beast." He met his first Indian war party (complete with an enemy's scalp), saw his first war dance, and ate his first meal without the amenities of table, linens, and silverware. None of this appealed to him. Finally, Washington encountered his first frontier settlers and found them, to his disgust, "as ignorant a set of people as the Indians."[3]

To the young traveler with a full month of wilderness living under his belt, the frontier seemed a lice-ridden place of rotten, muddy roads; wild war-making and head-scalping Indians; abundant in large and tasty game, but inhabited by white settlers no more civilized than their aboriginal neighbors. Washington found himself unhappily "amongst a parcel of barbarians and an uncouth set of people." He described the living habits of the frontiersmen as comparable to those of "dogs or cats." The weather and insects forced him to abandon more civilized practices and sleep as the denizens, in his clothes "like a Negro."[4]

Despite his antipathy to the western country's inhabitants, Washington was drawn to its environs time and again. The lure was land, and the growth of Washington's affinity to the West was linked to his accumulation of frontier real estate. Upon the death of his older brother Lawrence in 1752, the young Virginian inherited an interest in the 500,000-acre Ohio Company grant and received a commission in the Virginia militia. The warrior's legacy gave the younger Washington a personal stake in the western country's future and an opportunity to defend it.

The militia office brought Washington his second occasion to travel west. As the ambassador of Virginia's Governor Dinwiddie, he embarked on October 31, 1753, with the famous warning letter to French commander Joncaire at Venango. Washington accomplished his errand, but the French, not surprisingly, refused the British command to abandon disputed wilderness territory. The trip did enable him to experience the frontier again, and with a shrewder eye for the region's developmental potential. The environment and its inhabitants were even less hospitable than during his first journey, and they greeted Washington with several life-threatening situations. "Excessive rains and vast quantity of snow," swollen rivers and streams, and assaults by "French" Indians reinforced his earlier opinions. The weather and the denizens seemed equally savage to the young militiaman.[5]

The land was another matter. He already owned some, and he became enamored of other tracts during this trek. The area near the confluence of the Allegheny and Monongahela rivers—the future site of Pittsburgh—attracted him particularly. Well-timbered bottom land with rich alluvial soil most struck his fancy and was duly noted in the journal for future reference.[6]

Patriotism, military ardor, and his increasing financial stake in the international conflict for the western country brought Washington back for years of military service in the Great War for the Empire. It was a war that he personally started with the assassination or combat killing (depending upon one's French-Canadian or Anglo-American point of view) of Jumonville. It was a wartime experience that increased the centrality of the western country to all that Washington held dear.[7]

Motives are always difficult to weigh, and Washington's are no exception. He was certainly motivated by a passionate martial spirit. At this time of his life, he wished "for nothing more earnestly than to attain a small degree of knowledge in the military art." He revelled in the excitement of combat, as his famous testimony to the symphonic quality of gunfire attests. "I heard the bullets whistle," Washington proclaimed, "and, believe me, there is something charming in the sound." He clearly indulged his quest for honor, refusing a commission that insulted his sense of social rank, then accepting a more suitable office of command even though it was unofficial and without pay.[8]

Patriotic fervor also contributed to Washington's growing commitment to the western country. In 1754 he informed Governor Horatio Sharpe of Maryland that "the glowing zeal I owe my country" was influencing his concern for the frontier. It was patriotism, he wrote, that led him to lament the "lethargy we have fallen into," and to attempt to arouse "the heroic spirit of every freeborn Englishman to attest the rights and privileges of our King (if we don't consult the benefit of ourselves) and rescue from the invasion of a usurping enemy our Majesty's property, his dignity, and land."[9]

It was not only patriotic zeal and military ardor, however, that motivated Washington's risk of life and fortune on the frontier. Indeed, according to his own testimony, the two alone would not have been enough to impel him to the wilderness time and again. This same passage from his letter to Governor Sharpe gives a clue to Washington's other ambitions. He was also inspired in the period before the Revolution by what he termed "the benefit of ourselves." Washington believed that no other motive or combination of motives alone could compel men to the howling wilderness of his experience without the critical one of personal gain. "What inducements have men to explore uninhabited wilds," he reasoned, "but the prospect of getting good lands?" "Would any man," he asked, "waste his time, expose his fortune, nay, life, in such a search, if he was not to share the good and the bad with those that came after him? Surely no!"[10]

According to Washington, then, it was at least partly the quest for material gain that led him to invest time, money, and his life on the frontier. When he engaged Jumonville, defended Fort Necessity, and accompanied Braddock into the general's last battle, it was with an eye toward ultimate personal profit. When bullets passed through his clothing, when enemies shot horses out from under him, and when he suffered an excruciating "bloody flux," Washington took it all in stride partly because he hoped that compensation awaited him at war's end. He endured the heat, insects, rain, mud, snow, and swollen rivers of the western country. He fought its Indians, commanded its indolent settlers in battle, and tolerated the multitude of inconveniences that came with uncivilized life. After all this he meant to reap his fair reward. And Washington was not a man easily denied his vision of justice.

During the 1760s and 1770s Washington mounted a campaign for land on the frontier more impressive than any he ever executed as a general—and more successful. He had an acquisitive genius and was a ruthless exploiter of advantage. Governor Dinwiddie had offered a 200,000-acre bounty to encourage enlistments for the war. After the fighting ended, however, it took some persuasion to convince the House of Burgesses to finance the governor's promise. By the time that the militia's leader—George Washington—got around to petitioning and persuading the new governor and House of Burgesses to deliver on the bounty, he had accumulated claims to more than 20,000 of those frontier acres for himself. Between the years 1754 and 1769 Washington purchased rights from soldiers too poor, too cynical, or too naïve to bank on the word of an ex-governor. Some gladly surrendered their apparently ephemeral claims; others declined Washington's offers of £10 for each 2000 acres. Some men suspected that he labored disingenuously in behalf of the grantees in order to force them into capitulation to his offers. Why, they asked in retrospect, did it take their commander a decade and a half to draw up the petition and exert his influence within the House of Burgesses? Some men even refused to sell to Washington, while agreeing to identical terms offered by others. So Washington took his investment scheme underground and engaged his brother Charles to find out "(in a joking way, rather than in earnest, at first)" what value the militiamen put on their rights. Once he had cajoled this information from the men, Charles was to purchase 15,000 acres in his own name. "Do not," George insisted, "let it be known that I have any concern therein." If the truth were known, prices would rise, resentment would rekindle, and the scheme for vast acquisitions would founder on the shoals of Washington's unpopularity with the men.[11]

Once Washington succeeded, the grant materialized during the next session of the assembly. There is no evidence to substantiate the militiamen's accusations that the timing was more than a coincidence, but it is clear that Washington lied about the openness of his accumulation of rights. There is no doubt that some of his comrades-in-arms were furious at him for his machinations. He broke a Virginia law limiting the size of surveyed tracts. Contrary to another law he secured an additional personal grant of 5000 acres. He engrossed the best soil for himself at the expense of fellow officers and men who trusted their commander to make a fair survey and distribution. The whole process was not, as Washington averred, "a lottery only."[12]

The Virginian's lust for frontier soil did not end here, though. In 1773 he was still charting claims and entreating a western Pennsylvania agent to scout out more land "that you would increase my quantity to fifteen, twenty, or twenty-five thousand acres" in that district alone. Eventually, Washington would own over 63,000 acres of trans-Appalachia, becoming one of the largest absentee landlords the western country knew during his day. Settlers who based their counter-claims on deeds or on proto-Lockeian arguments of superior right to ground they tilled, both fell before Washington's assaults. Indians, the laws of Pennsylvania, and edicts by the monarch of the British Empire proved mere annoyances crushed by the superior force of Washington's determination to own ever more land.[13]

Washington's methods for acquiring frontier acreage were machine-like in their efficiency. The process began with either a personal sighting or a report by one of his agents engaged for the purpose. William Crawford filled the role ably in western Pennsylvania in the years before his death at the hands of irate Indians in 1782. "Look me out a tract of about 1,500, 2,000, or more acres in your neighborhood," Washington instructed Crawford in 1767. "It will be easy for you to conceive that ordinary, or even middling land, would never answer my purpose or expectation," Washington continued. "A tract to please me must be rich . . . and if possible good and level." Crawford found Washington many such plots over the years.[14]

The next step after identification was for the agent to travel to the Pennsylvania land registry office at Carlisle. There Crawford sought out Colonel Armstrong, a friend of Washington's, who helped circumvent the colony's laws. Washington knew that acts regulating speculation limited the amount of land that could be registered, but he suggested a plan to break those laws. He informed Crawford that "Pennsylvania customs will not admit so large a quantity of land as I require, to be entered together . . . [but] this may possibly be evaded by making several entries to the same amount." In other words, disguise the single claim as several smaller, but coincidentally contiguous, claims as a way of negating the law's intent. Colonel Armstrong was amenable and the property was duly registered.[15]

The Proclamation Line of 1763 might also have proved a barrier to Washington's plans. Again, however, he saw the edict designed to protect Indian land from encroachment merely as an inconvenience to be overcome. He instructed Crawford, therefore, to move quickly "in attempting to secure some of the most valuable lands in the King's part which I think may be accomplished after a while notwithstanding the proclamation that restrains it at present and prohibits the settling of them at all." No king, no Indians, no colonial assembly would keep Washington from his desire "to secure a good deal of land."[16]

The process of acquiring frontier real estate did not end with the establishment of unassailable legal rights to the ground. Always, there were squatters, recalcitrant tenants, and other intruders to reckon with. When Doctor John Brisco, for example, made clear his intention to settle on an undeveloped plot in the Ohio Valley wilderness, he received a scathing rebuke from hundreds of miles away. Washington had heard of Brisco's plans, consulted his maps, and realized that he (Washington) wanted the acreage in question for himself. He then dashed off a note to Brisco expressing the personal wound this knowledge gave him and a stubborn resolve to resist such infamy with all his energies. Washington could prove by the testimony of witnesses that he had visited the spot in November 1770 and expressed a desire to possess it. Technical difficulties (i.e., laws) had prohibited him from staking the claim, but he still intended to do so "(not withstanding any improvement you either have, or make upon it)." "I have judged it expedient to serve you with this notice thereof . . . ," he threatened Brisco, "and assure you at the same time, that I am determined not to relinquish my right to this tract, which contains 587 acres, and which I am ready to pay for at any time, till I have at least spent the full value of the land in support of my claim."[17]

Brisco succumbed and abandoned the land, buildings, and improvements he had made in the interval. But still, Washington was not to enjoy this particular tract unchallenged. After Brisco moved out, one Michael Cresap settled in. Again, Washington angrily dashed off a note to the intruder, stating that he found it "a little hard . . . that I cannot be allowed to hold this bottom (which is but a small one) in peace and quietness 'till a legal right can be obtained, which I always have been and still am ready to pay for, as soon as I know what office to apply." Cresap, himself a speculator who resided in the region, was not cowed by Washington's threats. A year later Washington was still complaining about his inability to throw Cresap off the land.[18]

The same problem plagued Washington on other tracts. The locals had little respect for the rights of absentee owners. He lost a 3000-acre parcel to rival claimants who simply moved in and took over his unoccupied lands on Chartier's and Racoon creeks. From Washington's perspective the situation was most unjust. The land was his by rights of grant or purchase, discovery, surveying, and registry. His tracts were marked clearly and Crawford warned people off, when he found them, before they began to settle and improve the plots. But often these frontiersmen either did not understand or did not care about the legal rights of owners who neither lived on nor developed the land. These settlers apparently embraced a proto-Lockeian vision of ownership that saw labor and use as the critical ingredients of rightful possession.[19]

The right kind of people simply were not settling on the frontier. Until order was brought to the Fort Pitt region, upright citizen-businessmen had little hope for enforcing their legal rights. Neither the laws of colonial governments in Philadelphia and Williamsburg nor the edicts of the empire's London bureaucrats had much force in the western country. Washington himself had prospered from his ability to evade the intentions of both Great Britain's Proclamation Line and Pennsylvania's and Virginia's land speculation laws. Once these "legal" ends were achieved, however, Washington and other like-minded entrepreneurs saw no inconsistency in branding intruding settlers as outlaws or in seeking strong government to enforce their claims. It would be a while, however, before the forces of order would emerge victorious in the western country. It would take both an American Revolution and a revolution in American government to achieve those ends. In the interim, landlords would just have to muddle through as best they could.[20]

The Revolution caused Washington to abandon temporarily his quest for wealth in frontier real estate. The war was also a propitious event for Washington's land dealings, though, because a royal injunction negating his frontier claims (and others like them) was overturned by the Virginia legislature in 1778. Victory thus ensured the "legality" of his frontier acquisitions. At war's end, enforcement of the law became Washington's main concern, and soon after his return to private life he embarked on a trip to the wilderness to enforce his claims. The particular dispute that he sought to resolve during this journey concerned lands on Miller's Run, a branch of Chartier's Creek, in Washington County, Pennsylvania.[21]

Washington's estimation of the settlers' worth had not risen since the 1740s. Irritation and sarcasm mark his September 19 entry, when, "being Sunday, and the people living on my land, *apparently* very religious, it was thought best to postpone going among them till tomorrow." The next day, the group of Scottish settlers at Miller's Run attempted to negotiate with the Revolutionary hero. They wished to purchase the acreage from him rather than dispute the claim in court. Washington was not interested. He listened, apparently impatiently, to their pleas. They described in detail the hardships they had endured, the religious principles that had brought them to the frontier, and their determination to stay on the land they had cleared and cultivated.[22]

Washington responded with an offer of 999-year leases or sale over three years with interest. They had little money, but would agree to his price, even though they thought it very high, if Washington would extend the period for payment and forgo the interest. He refused. Washington was angered by their determination to fight for the land in court.

Such people usually backed down when threatened with a lawsuit. He replied "with dignity and some warmth, asserting that they had been forewarned by his agent, and the nature of his claim fully made known; that there could be no doubt of its validity, and rising from his seat and holding a red silk handkerchief by one corner, he said, 'Gentlemen, I will have this land just as surely as I now have this handkerchief'."[23]

Washington engaged Thomas Smith, a Carlisle, Pennsylvania attorney, to bring suits in ejectment against the Scottish settlers. Smith thought he contended with more than a small band of poverty-stricken immigrants. Indeed, the suit became, according to the lawyer, a local political issue. "I . . . have the strong and fomented prejudices of party to contend with," Smith wrote, "and I have some reason to believe that a good deal of art and management were used before the people were prevailed with to stand the ejectments."[24]

Under the circumstances, Washington and Smith thought themselves unlikely to get favorable decisions from a local court. Regional prejudices and party fervor could be partially ameliorated, however, by filing suit in the friendlier Pennsylvania Supreme Court. The state justices, it could be expected, would not be prejudiced against the suit as Washington County justices probably were. They would undoubtedly make out a less hostile jury list. And they were likely to rule more favorably on points of law, if only because they knew the law better than their local counterparts. The court heard arguments during October 1786. In each case the jury returned a verdict favorable to Washington and one that he was able to enforce.[25]

It was clearly a victory for Washington, but not one without a price. Speculators were never popular in the region. Washington and other absentee landlords monopolized much of the area's best land while local farmers labored to scratch a living from what remained. Washington owned thousands of acres and did not even farm or live on them, although he tried to hide these facts by having his agent build dummy dwellings on the tracts. It just did not seem right to the local people. As a consequence, Washington and other speculators were rapidly becoming the most despised men in the western country. His suit against the Miller's Run Scots exacerbated the local image of Washington as a rapacious speculator and grasping landlord. Over time he would become even less popular in the Pennsylvania county that bore his name.[26]

Nonetheless, by the time he left the region for home in 1784, Washington was in a reflective mood. He was, of course, disappointed by his inability to rescue his lands from resident "land jobbers and speculators." He was satisfied by the recovery of his property from the incompetent or purposefully dishonest management of his overseer. And he was "well pleased" by his success in securing facts about the area and settlers. He had not visited the region for fourteen years and had relied on the testimony of others. Now he had first-hand knowledge "coming at

the temper and disposition of the western inhabitants and making reflections thereon, which otherwise must have been as wild, incoher[en]t,
and perhaps as foreign from the truth, as the inconsistencies of the
reports which I had received even from those to whom most credit
seemed due, generally were."[27]

Back home in Virginia, Washington ruminated over the lack of industry among western Pennsylvanians. The richness of the soil and absence
of markets for their products left them content to produce no more than
they could consume. The solution was clearly to establish better routes
of communication and trade with the West: "Extend the inland navigation as far as it can be done with convenience and show them by this
means how easy it is to bring the produce of their lands to our markets,
and see how astonishingly our exports will be increased and these states
benefitted in a commercial point of view."[28]

Initially, Washington's interest in developing water routes to the West
had been almost entirely personal and profit-oriented. The canals themselves, through tolls, would produce income for investors. Commercial
traffic would bring prosperity to Virginia entrepôts such as Alexandria
and to new towns that would spring up along the trade route. And, far
from least, when access to the western country became easier, the value
of its land would increase substantially. As the claimant to tens of thousands of acres in the region, Washington kept this potentiality very
much in mind.

The particular measure Washington sought during the 1780s was in-
corporation of the Potomac Company by the state of Virginia, which he
secured on January 5, 1785. His success in this venture brought to a
close ten years of efforts to procure the sufferance of Maryland and
Virginia for this canal venture. The Annapolis Convention of 1786 was
arranged in no small part through the labors of Washington and fellow
investors. It met precisely to solve the kinds of problems confronting
interstate commercial projects of this sort.[29]

At about the same time, and even more importantly, the political
necessity for closer union between East and West struck Washington.
"No well informed mind need be told," he wrote, "that the flanks and
rear of the united territory are possessed by other powers, and formidable ones too. . . . For what ties let me ask, should we have upon those
people . . . if the Spaniards on their right, or Great Britain on their left,
instead of throwing stumbling blocks in their way as they now do,
should invite their trade and seek alliances with them?" This was no
paranoid dream, no unlikely hallucination Washington beheld. He
knew, first-hand, the weakness of the tether that bound the frontiersmen to the government. "The western settlers . . . ," Washington observed, "stand as it were on a pivet—the touch of a feather would almost
incline them any way." These people were mostly foreigners, and even
those who were not failed to embrace passionately the patriotic cause

that united the American states. Living as they did at a subsistence level, these people could not be trusted, could not be depended upon to defend the frontier from the depredations of England and Spain. And, Washington believed, were the West to fall, the rest would soon follow. Without the frontier buffer against foreigners and Indians, the commercial and political decline of the nation would proceed apace.[30]

The solution to this problem lay near at hand, according to Washington. What bound people together was not political abstractions or philosophical ideals. Pecuniary interests would dictate the future course of the western country. The certain means to link the commercial welfare of West with East lay not in building better roads to Philadelphia, although that would work at great expense and to the sacrifice of Virginia's commercial interests. The future prosperity of the United States, Virginia, the frontier, and George Washington would come with the extensions of navigable waterways—canals—from the Potomac straight through to the Monongahela. These thoughts were not new to Washington in 1784. As early as August 1754 he had begun to explore the potential for water routes to the West. By the 1780s, however, he saw the political necessity for internal improvements as transcending the commercial significance of such developments. Although the profit of investors was an "immense object" of Washington's endeavors, the threat of national disintegration now weighed even more heavily on his mind.[31]

The menace of frontier secession seemed so great and the costs so high that every obstacle must be placed in the path of western autonomy. Indeed, of all the threats to the nation's survival, Washington thought none more severe than the back-country's independence. "I confess to you candidly," he wrote to James McHenry, "that I can forsee no evil greater than disunion." With the stakes so high, and the completion of commercial routes from the East so far in the future, Washington believed other, more negative steps, must also be taken to ensure the westerners' loyalty. To several officials Washington expressed his view that opening the Mississippi River to American trade should not be an immediate goal of negotiations with Spain. "The navigation of the Mississippi," he wrote, "*at this time* ought to be no object with us. On the contrary, until we have a little time allowed to open and make easy the ways between the Atlantic states and the western territory, the obstruction had better remain. There is nothing which binds one country or one state to another but interest."[32]

The immediate needs of western settlers for markets must be sacrificed to the long-term benefits of eastern merchants, eastern canal investors, eastern speculators in western lands, and, of course, the nation itself. If government officials followed the path Washington outlined, which they did, western farmers would pay the price of American union, while eastern investors profited from the restricted markets for western produce. The western country would remain, even more than the colonies had been in the British empire, economic captives of remote commercial and political overlords.

Frontiersmen, who thought the central government was actively seeking Spanish concessions on Mississippi navigation, only slowly came to view political relations with the East in such a light. First, they would seek to work within the commercial and political systems dictated by more powerful eastern elites. They would first try changes in their methods of marketing surplus grain—distilling it into a more portable and potable commodity—and petitioning for resolution of grievances through normal channels. When their alternative marketing method, too, was threatened by the whiskey excise of 1791, while the Mississippi still remained closed to their trade and Indians still threatened their lives, the potential for inter-regional conflict increased dramatically. Washington's personal relationship with the western country, his vision of the region and its people, and his actions as President contributed to the confrontation.

By 1789, then, when Washington became President, his unique relationship with the western country was entering its fifth decade. He had learned of mud, lice, and "barbarians" on his first western trip in 1748. He had come to appreciate the beauty and value of western lands from his brother, his own travels, and investments in every major land scheme that passed his way. He knew intimately and sought to exploit efforts of the Ohio Company of Virginia, the Mississippi Company, and the Vandalia Colony fiasco. He had weathered the elements, French attacks, and Indian arrows. He was charmed by the whistle of bullets, had horses shot out from under him, and his clothing riddled with near misses. He had mapped, surveyed, purchased, and plotted to acquire approximately 58,000 acres beyond the Appalachian Mountains. He claimed 4695 acres in southwestern Pennsylvania alone. He had struggled and clawed in person, in letters, and in court for the ground. And, he had invested much of his money, many of his adult years, and an immense amount of energy to develop commercial water routes to the West.[33]

Obviously, the western country was personally very important to Washington. He also now saw it as perhaps *the* most crucial element in the survival of the United States. As a buffer against England, Spain, and hostile Indians it was a vital component of the nation's defense. As a potential market and source of farm products it would become an essential ingredient of the nation's economy. This subtle but significant evolution in Washington's attitudes toward the frontier by the 1780s left two things unchanged. His elevation of the western country to the highest priority of national affairs did not alter his disdain for its inhabitants, as subsequent events would demonstrate; nor did his accession to the presidency end his quest for capital gain. Indeed, Washington now sought to use the influence of his office in the same ways that he had always exploited personal connections in behalf of business enterprises. "I am now about [to] give you a little trouble on my private account," the President informed a political appointee. His mixture of public and private affairs included solicitation of a customs collector's aid in selling some tobacco and wheat, an attempt to convince the commissioners of the District of Columbia to purchase rocks from his quarry, and the enlistment of a U. S. Senator to sell land in western Pennsylvania. Given this fluid relationship between Washington's public and private concerns, what biographer James Thomas Flexner has termed a "careless" attitude toward the propriety of such behavior, we should not be shocked by the realization that public policy decisions were affected by perhaps unconscious or unexamined motives of a private nature. Flexner recognized that Washington had "a personal economic stake" in the outcome of the Whiskey Rebellion; and there is evidence, which is discussed in Chapter Seven, that the President's private experiences influenced his public decisions about how to handle anti-excise unrest.[34]

Washington's attitude alone does not explain the single largest armed confrontation among American citizens between the Revolution and the Civil War, or comprehend the range of issues that provoked resistance to federal law in the frontier region of every state from Pennsylvania south to Georgia. President Washington's prejudices, financial interests, hostile relations, and perceptions of the frontier's importance for America's survival do tell us much, however, about his personality, his motives, and his role in the inter-regional conflicts that racked America during the 1780s and 1790s.[35]

PART TWO: CHRONOLOGY

For West is where we all plan to go some day. It is where you go
when the land gives out and the old-field pines encroach. It is
where you go when you get the letter saying: *Flee, all is discovered*.
It is where you go when you look down at the blade in your hand
and see the blood on it. It is where you go when you are told that
you are a bubble on the tide of empire. It is where you go when you
hear that that's gold in them-thar hills. It is where you go to grow
up with the country. It is where you go to spend your old age. Or it
is just where you go.

Robert Penn Warren, *All the King's Men*.

Chapter Six

INDIANS AND THE EXCISE

The Reverend John Corbley, his wife, and five children lived in Muddy Creek, Pennsylvania, in the environs of Pittsburgh, during the early 1790s. One Sunday morning the family set out on the mile-long hike from their home to the local meeting house. Corbley meandered some distance behind the others, deep in meditation about his forthcoming sermon. The minister was stunned from this reverie by the shrieks of his wife and children, who were under assault by a band of Indians. He first considered trying to beat back the attackers with a stick that he found on the ground. The futility of such heroics was obvious to him, however, so Corbley ran for his own life with one warrior in hot pursuit. Other Indians snatched the infant from his wife's arms, dismembered, and scalped it. Then they shot and scalped Corbley's wife, and hatcheted and scalped his six-year-old son and four-year-old daughter.

About ten minutes later, when he thought it was safe, Corbley returned to the scene and discovered the aftermath of the massacre. Two other daughters survived the assault, but they were "mangled to a shocking degree." He took some relief from the recovery of the two girls, although their tomahawk-scarred faces and scalped heads served as disturbing reminders to Corbley and his neighbors of the losses and terror they all had endured.[1]

FROM A FRONTIER perspective, all other issues were secondary to the Indian war. The threat posed by hostile natives to the lives and meager resources of settlers was the central fact of western experience. Like the Corbleys, other frontier whites lived in fear, and with visible reminders of the tenuousness of their existence. To them, the link between Indian depredations and federal taxes seemed obvious, although to us, as to eastern nationalists at the time, the relationship may appear obscure.

Frontiersmen saw themselves as the most beleaguered of citizens and worthy of an exemption from additional burdens. The region's fragile economy and local traditions of ideological opposition to internal taxes also contributed to hostile reception of excise-tax collectors. Settlers' conviction that the West was under-represented in the national government, however erroneous the perception may have been, added to feelings of persecution. And the national government's inability to defeat the Indians or secure free navigation of the Mississippi River left them reluctant to pay for a central government that delivered no visible services. These issues were connected in the minds of westerners, but at the heart of them all was the relation between the central government's impotency and its demands for internal taxes.

Indian depredations were frighteningly common in the Ohio Valley during the years before 1795. Between 1783 and 1790 natives killed, wounded, or took prisoner an estimated 1,500 whites and stole about 2,000 horses. Massacres were widely reported in the East to the goriest last detail. Seldom did a week pass without some account of horror in the West. Massacres of peaceful Indians were no less brutal, and were also repulsive to easterners. About the same time as the Corbleys' travail, a party of frontiersmen swooped down upon some friendly Indians who had gathered on the west side of Beaver Creek in Allegheny County for the purposes of trade. The settlers murdered three men and one woman and "committed divers other acts of violence and plunder." Futilely, Governor Mifflin of Pennsylvania offered a $1,000 reward for the capture of perpetrators of this frontier atrocity.[2]

The national government devoted almost five-sixths of its operating budget to war in the West during the years from 1790 to 1796—a total of $5,000,000. The state governments of Pennsylvania and Virginia contributed money, materials, and men toward western tranquility as well.[3]

Brigadier General Josiah Harmar's expedition against the Miami Indians in late 1790 was the first fruit of this national assault on the native tribes. It took months to assemble 1,500 militiamen from Pennsylvania and Kentucky to supplement the small contingent of national troops, and when they arrived, the militia were physically ill-fit for duty and poorly supplied. Officers told Harmar that "they had no idea of there being half the number of bad arms in the whole district of Kentucky as was then in the hands of their men." The Pennsylvanians "were worse armed," some of them carrying no weapons at all. The two states had apparently aimed at only technical compliance with the request for troops and thus had sent "a great many hardly able to bear arms, such as old, infirm men, and young boys . . . there were a great number of them substitutes who probably had never fired a gun." The militia would serve only as dead weight on a sluggish army, consumers of victuals that were already in short supply. These were the soldiers who marched toward the Miami River in October 1790. This was the formula for disaster ahead.[4]

On October 18 a contingent of the Kentucky militia happened upon about one hundred Indians. Many of the whites never fired a shot. Some dropped their weapons and ran off at the first Indian war whoop and never stopped running until they reached the Ohio River. The remaining regular soldiers suffered catastrophic losses. A force of 400 regulars and militia under Major Wyllys met a similar fate. On the same day they encountered a party of fewer than one hundred Indians. When the militia ran off, Wyllys and most of the regulars were killed.[5]

It was an expensive and humiliating debacle. It was the first time United States troops had faced Indians of the Northwest in pitched battle. Previously, the Indians respected and feared the regular soldiers who pierced the wilderness silence with loud drums and louder cannons. This was no longer true. Life in the western country was less safe for white settlers after Harmar's campaign than it had been before, and relations between eastern Americans and frontiersmen were now worse as well. The national government blamed frontier militia for the defeat. Westerners blamed the central government for incompetent defense of the frontier. In one sense it matters little who was right in the dispute because everyone acted, nonetheless, on his own interpretation of events.

And as if things were not bad enough, from a frontier perspective, the national government then enacted an excise tax on the single most significant item of frontier trade. On top of the squalor, in response to pleas for deliverance from savage foes, the government heaped an ideologically, culturally, and economically repulsive tax on the very people least able and least willing to suffer the imposition. Or that, at least, is how people in the western country understood the whiskey excise of 1791.

Despite the long history of opposition to internal taxes, despite the widely shared prejudice against excise—that "hateful tax levied upon commodities"—a bill came before Congress on May 5, 1790, to lay a duty on spirits distilled within the United States. The act was a logical outgrowth of Secretary of the Treasury Alexander Hamilton's report on public credit presented to Congress earlier in the year. Once assumption of state debts was agreed upon, a method of repaying them inevitably followed.[6]

The plan for meeting revenue needs through new duties on imported and domestically distilled spirits met rough treatment in Congress. The bill was first defeated in the House by a slim margin of five votes (31–26). It was then reintroduced with a motion to strike the excise clause. This version fell by a wider margin (35–19). Finally, the original act went down by a handy 35-to-23 vote on June 21. Few comments survive in the recorded debates to indicate the nature of opposition, but it seems odd that the motion to stike the offensive excise clause was defeated by a wider margin than the unamended version. It appears strange that the act fell by a mere five votes on the first reading and then twelve votes on the final consideration. Apparently, motives unrelated to the politics of taxation were also involved.[7]

Supporters of the tax bill were not despondent over its failure during the first session of Congress. Indeed, Hamilton, Tench Coxe, and Fisher

Ames were confident that the excise and import taxes on liquor would be adopted next time around. In order to secure the necessary Pennsylvania votes for assumption of state debts—a measure dear to the hearts of New Englanders—it had to be separated from the funding issue. "In short," Ames reported, "it was becoming probable that the whole would be postponed to the next session." At the same time, "the negative upon the ways and means [of paying the debts], by opening the eyes of the advocates of the funding to a sense of their danger, really contributes to the security of the provision for public credit." This was the nature of the political deal struck to secure passage of at least part of Hamilton's program. Ames admitted that it was a rather "paradoxical" method of conducting public business, but a practical one.[8]

At the same time, the scheme of Pennsylvanian and southern politicians to move the capital first to Philadelphia and then to the Potomac was also involved in the calculations. "To do this," Ames predicted, "and at the same time reject the assumption [of state debts], is such an outrage on the feelings of the eastern [i.e., New England] people, as I persuade myself they dare not commit." Ames and his New England colleagues saw, therefore, "strong indications of assent to assumption" and indulged "a very confident hope of success" in the funding measures during the next session.[9]

Hamilton renewed the quest for a whiskey excise in his December 1790 report on public credit. He calculated a probable shortfall of $826,624.73 in revenue necessary to sustain the national debt. The proposed taxes on domestic and imported spirits would realize about $975,000, thus more than meeting the government's needs. Of this, Hamilton estimated, the excise would provide approximately $270,000.[10]

The proposed method of raising revenue was identical to the measures introduced during the previous session of Congress. Despite the earlier defeat, the Secretary offered three reasons for his adherence to the recommendations. Hamilton believed that the negative votes of the past spring were not prompted by opposition to the taxes themselves, but by "collateral considerations"—apparently those political concerns mentioned by Fisher Ames. Since these problems were now overcome, Hamilton felt confident that the tax bill would find a more receptive audience in Congress. Furthermore, he could conceive of no substitute system "equally conducive to the ease and interest of the community." And, finally, the "efficacy and productiveness" of the proposed measures would be apparent to all friends of the government who read his report.[11]

Hamilton also anticipated several probable lines of opposition to the excise provisions and offered counter-arguments to potential critics. Traditionally, excises were resisted because they were oppressive, because of the summary jurisdiction invested in the tax men, and because of collectors' authority to enter and search private residences indiscriminately.

The proposed system suffered from none of these defects. According to Hamilton, any revenue laws that were so constructed "as to involve a lax and defective execution, are instruments of oppression." This law would be efficiently administered. Under the proposed act, collectors had no summary jurisdiction; the accused retained rights of trial by jury. Finally, the discretionary power of searching was "restricted to those places which the dealers themselves shall designate . . . as the depositories of the articles on which the duties are to be laid."[12]

Other options, including a land tax or higher import duties, would not suffice, according to Hamilton. Land taxes must be reserved for occasions "more directly affecting the public safety." Potentially taxable land, houses, and commercial buildings were an important revenue reserve for the nation. By leaving this source of funds untapped, the nation would reap great benefits among its international creditors. Likewise, the ability to resort to such a tax-base at a later date would be "conducive to the tranquility of the public mind, in respect to external danger, and will really operate as a powerful guarantee of peace." Higher import taxes could not be levied, according to Hamilton, "without contravening the sense of the body of the merchants." Because of the support that the mercantile community had thus far displayed toward the national government, "there will be perceived to exist the most solid reasons against lightly passing the bounds which coincide with their impressions of what is reasonable and proper."[13]

Finally, for the stable fiscal management of the national government's affairs, Hamilton thought it necessary to promote a balanced fund of revenue sources. The government was now entirely dependent on "external" taxes. Such reliance was dangerous in light of "the vicissitudes of the continuance or interruption of foreign commerce." The nation would be far better advised to depend upon "a variety of different funds formed by the union of internal and external objects."[14]

Back in 1788, Hamilton had sought to dispel fears of national excise taxes under the proposed Constitution. In *Federalist* XII, he argued that the nation must long rely on external taxes to finance the debt and fund the government. Excises must at least be "confined within a narrow compass." The main reason he predicted a circumscription of internal taxes was "that the genius of the people will ill brook the inquisitive and peremptory spirit of excise laws." By 1791 he had either forgotten his analysis of America's "genius," changed his mind, or did not care. Historians disagree heatedly about Hamilton's motives in 1788 and 1791.[15]

Whatever Hamilton's reasons—and we really cannot discern them from surviving documents—the proposed excise did raise a storm of controversy within and without Congress during early 1791. On January 22 the Pennsylvania assembly instructed the state's senators to oppose a national excise. The legislature resolved that "any proceeding on the part of the United States tending to the collection of revenue by means of excise, [is] established on principles subversive of peace, liberty, and the rights of citizens." The Assembly knew of no existing public emergency that would "warrant the adoption of any species of taxation which shall violate those rights which are the basis of our government, and which would exhibit the singular spectacle of a nation resolutely oppressing the oppressed of others in order to enslave itself."[16]

The state legislators also ruminated over the unfortunate ideological change that had apparently swept the halls of national politics since 1775. In that year a Congress composed of many of the same men now in power—including George Washington—attempted to rouse the inhabitants of Quebec to join their struggle against Great Britain. In a resolution of the Continental Congress they had argued that Britain " 'subjected you [i.e., Quebec] to the impositions of excise, *the borrower of all free states,* thus wresting your property from you by *the most odious of taxes'.*" What had changed, the Pennsylvanians asked? Nothing that they could perceive had altered in the nature of taxation, representation, or national circumstances. For the federal government to enact such a tax was just as much an abomination as was the perfidious claim of Great Britain to such authority. The legislators knew that the Constitution granted Congress the power to levy such an internal tax, but little did they suspect, "that in a time of profound peace with every foreign nation, when the blessings of liberty were expected to flow through our land, there would be selected from amongst those powers the most odious amongst them, which we conceived could never be called into operation but in the most pressing emergency, when every other source should have failed and sunk beneath the public demand."[17]

Within Congress a lively opposition surfaced as well. Senator William Maclay, for example, was quite proud that "so much independence has been manifested by the yeomanry of Pennsylvania. Indeed, I am fully satisfied that if a spirit of this kind was not manifested from some quarter or another our liberties would soon be swallowed up." Maclay was himself suspicious of Hamilton's motives. Most taxes, among right-thinking men, arose from necessity. In this case, however, it seemed that "the difficulty is to find a plausible pretext for extending the arm of taxation . . . and the reigning party seem to consider themselves as wanting in duty if the fiscal rent-roll should fall short of the royal revenues of England." Maclay, as others, thought "war and bloodshed . . . the most likely consequence of all of this." The legislature of Pennsylvania "had been obliged to wink at the violation of her excise laws in the western part of the state ever since the Revolution." But Maclay believed that Hamilton and the national government would not be so flexible. The Secretary of the Treasury would force the issue even though "nothing short of a permanent military force could effect it." If a standing army, internal war, and annihilation of the state governments were their end, Maclay believed supporters of the Hamiltonian system well on the road to success.[18]

John Sevier, once President of Franklin and now Congressman from North Carolina, was equally opposed to the excise proposal. He too was quite certain that the tax could not be collected in frontier areas; and he recognized and shared the ideological and economic prejudices against this tax. But he was much less chagrined than Maclay at the probable meaning of its passage for western settlers in his state. Even if it passed Congress, Sevier trusted that the excise "will not reach us." He apparently believed that the citizens of North Carolina's three western counties could ignore the law with impunity. In light of this assumption, Sevier was actually "of [the] opinion, should the excise bill be passed, we [i.e., residents of North Carolina's western frontier] shall derive great benefits from it; (proviso) we can keep clear ourselves, as it would have a direct tendency to encourage emigration into our country, and enable us to sell the production of our own distilleries lower than our neighbors." In other words, the act would give people in regions beyond the reach of federal law a competitive advantage against the more settled areas that were accessible to the arm of central enforcement. [19]

The House debates found opposition taking several lines. Most who spoke against the tax bill could agree that an excise was "odious, unequal, unpopular, and oppressive." They thought this was particularly true in the South and in the more rural or frontier regions of other states as well. Citizens in these areas had "no breweries or orchards to furnish a substitute for spirituous liquors, hence they become a necessary article." One Congressman cited a Reverend Morse (presumably Jedediah), who had declared grog "a necessary article of drink in the southern states." [20]

In addition to Pennsylvania, the legislatures of Maryland, Virginia, North Carolina, and Georgia voiced their opposition to such a tax. In these states, argued several members of Congress, an excise on whiskey would operate unequally, and "deprive the mass of the people of almost the only luxury they enjoy." Such a law would also "convulse the government . . . [and] let loose a swarm of harpies, who, under the denominations of revenue officers, will range through the country, prying into every man's house and affairs, and like a Macedonian phalanx bear down all before them." Soon, the opposition argued, "the time will come when a shirt will not be washed without an excise." [21]

Others struck at the law on other grounds. A duty on imported molasses, one argued, would provide a comparable revenue more efficiently and not raise any of the sensitive ideological or inter-regional issues of the proposed excise. Some favored an increase of the impost or even a land tax over the excise. A few believed that Hamilton had intentionally underestimated the probable revenue from existing duties on imported teas and wines. Finally, someone noted that the proposed bill granted discretionary power to the President on the matters of salary and appointment of collectors. This observation touched the perennially sensitive fear of executive power, with the tyrannical tendencies threatened by such wholesale grants of authority. Some thought the nation would be served better by a congressional investigation of the issues raised by Hamilton's report and his proposed taxes. At present they had no basis for evaluating his figures, and no alternative plan. The appropriate response, they believed, was to postpone, study, and reconsider.[22]

The excise also had support from outside the halls of state. Friends of the tax, just as those who opposed it, offered both economic and moral arguments to defend their position. Public creditors and merchants who specialized in foreign imports expressed a pecuniary self-interest in the bill. No one, on either side, wanted to be gored by the national government's fiscal bull. Social reformers, who had no obvious economic stake in the tax, defended it on grounds that carried as much moral weight for them as the ideological critique of internal taxes did for foes of the tax. The heart of moral support for the excise came from those concerned about the harmful effects of drink on the physical and mental well-being of the nation's imbibers. A contributor to a Philadelphia newspaper believed that if mothers, wives, and sisters could be enfranchised for just this one vote (he was no enlightened philosopher of women's rights), the tax would be supported by an overwhelming margin of the nation's population. For himself, "when I behold reason the boasted preeminence of man over the beast—expunged as it were by the excessive draughts of this poisonous fluid; and when I reflect upon the melancholy consequences of intoxication, I am ready to wish (if it could be collected) that 100 percent duty was laid upon it."[23]

Hamilton had attempted to tap this potential wellspring of support in his December 1790 report on public credit. And he succeeded in getting the endorsement of the respected Philadelphia College of Physicians. These medical doctors and teachers enthusiastically supported his efforts to reform the "morals and manners" of whiskey consumers. The physicians offered their combined professional opinion that "a great proportion of the most obstinate, painful, and mortal disorders which affect the human body are produced by distilled spirits." The doctors expressed no doubt that a plague or other pestilential disorder threatening thousands of persons would bring the most vigorous actions of government. They saw "no just cause why the more certain and extensive ravages of distilled spirits upon human life should not be guarded against with corresponding vigilance and exertions."[24]

Opponents of the excise in Congress were outraged at the physicians' "interference." They believed that these medical men had no business instructing Congress how to perform its duties, and no right telling the American people how to conduct their lives. Congressman Jackson of Georgia argued that this sort of advice, if heeded, could quickly get out of hand. Next thing they knew, House members would be told by the doctors to legislate against mushrooms; and "they might petition Con-

gress to pass a law interdicting the use of ketchup because some ignorant persons had been poisoned by eating mushrooms."[25]

Proponents of the excise offered a similar indictment of the Pennsylvania assembly's "interference" in the business of Congress. Fisher Ames
thought it "awkward" that a measure would be debated in two legislatures at once. "Is this not anarchy?" he asked. Another writer expected
that the assemblymen would soon pass a resolution " 'that Congress
might go home, as the Pennsylvanians were (in their own opinion) competent to do their business for them.' " Critics leveled the same sort of
harangue against North Carolina's assembly for instructing its Senators
against the excise. If such practices continued, it was evident to some
that "the business of legislation must stand still," and that the country
would "revert to its former state of anarchy and imbecility."[26]

Some friends of the excise adopted an interpretation of national-state
relations reminiscent of the Constitution's opponents. They endorsed
the Antifederalist argument that "the state governments [are] competitors for power with the legislature of the Union." They believed that
the different governments were locked in a battle for survival that only
one could win. "Is it not evident," asked one writer, "that such a state
of things will lead to struggles that must in the end prove fatal to
either one or the other of these establishments?" Fisher Ames thought
the battle was imminent, that "the state governments seem to beat
their drums, and prepare to attack us." He believed the national government had "many advantages over them," and that "the superiority
of the one to the other will be brought to the test." This was exactly
the turn of events predicted and most feared by Patrick Henry and
other critics of the Constitution in 1787. Ames did not fear the battle;
he relished it. Hamilton may have agreed with Ames's perspective, but
Washington probably did not. Articulation of this bellicose attitude
drew the lines starkly within Congress and throughout the press. It
fired the worst suspicions of those who already distrusted national officials and institutions.[27]

Defenders of the revenue bill responded to critics in several other
ways as well. Some denied outright that it was an excise at all. Others
argued that it harbored none of the defects of such measures. Samuel
Livermore of New Hampshire thought the term "excise" had been "very
improperly applied on the present occasion, for the duty cannot be said
to be an excise." Excises were unequal taxes and this was not. This duty
would fall equally on rich and poor. This was a "mere duty of impost,"
according to the Congressman. The debates suggest that Livermore's
semantic distinction had no persuasive power. Opponents noted how
carefully the act's drafters refrained from using the word excise in the
text of the bill and in discussions, but they saw it as a dishonest trick
designed to forestall criticism.[28]

Others agreed with Livermore, however, that the usual criticisms of excises did not apply to this tax. "It is the part of meanness," argued a contributor to the *Connecticut Courant,* "of a tale-bearer, and disturber of the peace, to deal in blind hints, and cautious slander, which the law will not take hold of." Congressman Theodore Sedgwick of Massachusetts agreed that "in framing the present bill, great attention has been paid to prevent its being attended with those qualities which, in other countries, rendered taxation by excise justly obnoxious to popular resentment." Indeed, another supporter of the act believed that the opposition had merely applied "a string of terms, without any meaning in respect to the subject under debate."[29]

Some arguments avoided the ideological questions raised by excises and emphasized the need for fiscal responsibility. In the face of the huge deficits described by Hamilton, Congress had to take swift action to repay the nation's debts. Congressman John Laurance of New York referred his colleagues to Hamilton's report. "If this deficiency exists," Laurance argued, and he saw no reason to doubt it, "and if the United States are bound to make provision for the debts they have assumed to pay, the duties contemplated by the bill appear the most obvious for the government to recur to." Virginia Congressman William B. Giles thought the necessity for these taxes "was abundantly apparent" from Hamilton's report. He also argued the "expediency" of the proposed mode of taxation. Thomas Fitzsimons of Pennsylvania agreed that Hamilton had not overestimated the potential deficit. Indeed, he contended that "the deficiency would be much larger than the sum mentioned." And even if the excise did produce a surplus, "there are objects to which it can be applied highly beneficial to the United States."[30]

Furthermore, some Congressmen contended that the excise was fully consistent with American "principles of liberty." And not only was the tax necessary for the fiscal solvency of the government, not only was it the most expedient mode designed to meet the nation's needs, but "the great body of the people" thought this the best way to meet the problem. Contrary to what critics were saying, Congressman Livermore perceived the excise "agreeable to the people—they will consider it as drinking down the national debt." Outside of Congress, he had "not found a single individual who has objected to it." It was members of Congress and the Pennsylvania Assembly, some maintained, who endeavored "to promote jealousy and distrust" among the people for their own political ends. Thus far, "the good sense of the people . . . [had] prevented them from imbibing a restless spirit of complaint from the oft repeated, the groundless jealousies and apprehensions of more than eagle-eyed politicians, so it is to be hoped they will not in future be seduced to change the solid blessings of the government for the positive miseries of discord and sedition [just] because some persons say they are averse to measures that have never been tried."[31]

Whatever the opposition's motives, friends of the excise believed that dissent weakened the nation. These attempts "to excite the people to destroy" the government were "more injurious to our wealth than the Hessian fly in our wheat-fields." While the insect attacked only one grain, "anarchy and civil discord spare nothing. The insect takes the seed—violence would seize the crop." The criticisms were all "prejudices and suspicions" with no real foundation in fact. It seemed likely, therefore, that the opposition planned to thwart the government at every turn regardless of the measures proposed by the administration.[32]

Friends and foes of the excise parted company on several fundamental issues. Opponents of the measure argued that the present case was comparable to pre-Revolutionary taxation controversies. Supporters of the excise disagreed. In their opinion, equation of the present bill with the British excise in Quebec was an act of willful deception by opponents of Hamilton's fiscal program. There was no sense in which the events of 1765 or 1775 resembled the issues in 1791. "It may be justly observed," according to a writer in the *General Advertiser*, "that there exists some difference in bearing a burden imposed by a government in which we had no participation, and in paying a tax laid by our immediate representatives, and for the support of a government of our own choice."[33]

Supporters of the excise believed that Shays's Rebellion was the parallel case. One writer reasoned that, "as soon as the county convention in Massachusetts in 1786 began to vote the measures of the government [as] grievances, that state was shaken to its center. It is turning the principle of life into a pestilence; it is arming the right hand against the left." Now the Pennsylvania legislature was doing the same thing, and doing it hypocritically since the state still enforced its own excise on spirits even as it criticized the national government for considering a similar tax. The true issue was not the threat to liberty posed by an excise tax, but the threat to order raised by irresponsible and hypocritical enemies of the national government.[34]

The charges and insinuations were exaggerated and personally insulting. Neither side credited the other with honest motives or consistent patterns of belief. Each accused the other of disloyalty. Friends of the excise blasted its opponents for disregarding the political and social stability of the nation. They branded opponents as sore losers, as unrehabilitated Antifederalists, as hypocrites who grasped at any ideological straw to attack the government, even when their own behavior was inconsistent with the principles they espoused. With similar volume and heat, foes of the excise berated its supporters for disloyalty to the principles of the Revolution, for masking their financially self-interested designs with conjured figures and dishonest predictions of economic and social decline. They accused their opponents of cynically elevating the principles of order and defense of the Constitution above those of liberty and equality.

One need not adopt a similarly partisan stance to interpret the sources of conflict. Most activists for and against the excise were no doubt sincere men who did not sympathetically understand their opponents' arguments. The friends and foes of the national government were displaying signs of what Marshall Smelser has described as "social paranoia." The excise debate was an early example of the fierce passions, the hatred, fear, anger, and suspicion of the Federalist era. But this does not entirely explain the nature of disagreement over the excise before it was adopted by Congress. Clearly, the Pennsylvania Assembly, for example, did not see itself as hypocritical for decrying a national excise while harboring a state one. To understand the state legislators' self-perceived consistency, one must recall the debates over "internal" and "external" taxation in 1765 and 1787. The argument then and in the years following 1791 would be that "internal" taxes were justly enacted only by the most local, most representative bodies of government. Some men could and did defend the justice of raising such taxes at the state level. Others—further along the political spectrum that ranged from monarchical to democratic tendencies—believed that even the state legislatures were too remote from some constituencies to legislate internal taxes.[35]

Supporters of Hamilton's program did not share this localist ideology. Few supporters of the excise took localism very seriously. In the years following adoption of the excise, however, others continued to adhere to a localist perspective and would explain their beliefs in public forums. Some would also defend their right to live in a political society supporting those views. It was a consistent, not a hypocritical, view of the political world. It was part of an ideology that reached back to long-honored Anglo-American traditions, and it was credible to some who opposed the Stamp Act in 1765 and to the Antifederalists of 1787. Opponents of Hamilton's program in 1790 and 1791 did not denounce all taxes. There was no outcry of similar magnitude against the external levy on imported spirits. It was only the excise provision of the revenue act—the internal tax—that aroused fervid opposition.

This is not to argue, however, that pecuniary self-interest was not a dynamic part of the taxation debate. Those areas of rural and frontier America most economically dependent on whiskey distillation were, of course, the same regions most opposed to an excise on domestically produced liquor. The regions of the nation where land taxes or higher import duties would have been most burdensome, and where distillation was less economically significant, defended the excise and the government's efforts to collect it. But life and the excise question are both more complex than that. A constellation of overlapping and sometimes contradictory spurs and brakes would contribute to an excise crisis in the years ahead. Those regions where the dominant ideology was localist *and* where the economic interests of many people dictated opposition to the excise would be the places to expect the strongest resistance to

collection of the tax. Although much of the South leaned toward localism, not all southerners had an economic stake in the excise debate. On
the frontier, however, the two motives—economic and ideological—
combined with other frustrations of western life to create, in the excise,
a truly volatile issue.

Conflict over this tax was marked by both economic and ideological
clashes, and the two were mutually supporting. Two different visions of
a just political world shot past each other in a semblance of debate. The
interests of divergent regional economies brooked no compromise. Until
an inter-regionally integrated economy, a national ideology, and a spirit
of compromise emerged, national politics would continue to display all
the signs of dysfunction apparent in the excise controversy. Until the
voices of rural America were heard and heeded, public policy would
reflect the interests of a geographic minority of the nation. From a
western perspective, such an impasse was unacceptable and appeared to
threaten the survival of both the Union and the principles upon which it
was established.

The tax bill, including the excise provision, passed Congress easily
before the session's end in March 1791. Opponents of the excise within
Congress included virtually all the men who could be considered representatives of frontier districts. They were joined by four others who had
previous records of localist sympathy. It was truly a regional vote, but
not only in the North-South sense that historians have generally as-
cribed to the excise battle. Congressional opposition came from every
state outside New England. Almost unanimously, representatives of urban mercantile districts supported the bill.[36]

After the fact, proponents of the excise observed that it was necessary
to raise funds for frontier defense. Foes of the tax did not believe it.
They argued that this *ex post facto* rationalization was only designed to
temper western resistance. Since virtually no one raised the issue of
paying for Indian wars during debates on the excise, perhaps enemies of
the bill were correct to question the motives of their political opponents.
In any event, administration attempts to crush hostile tribes in the
western country continued during 1791 under the leadership of General
Arthur St. Clair, while frontiersmen remained unsatisfied with the government's efforts and unconvinced that the excise served their best
interests.

Again, as during Harmar's expedition, militia accompanying regular
soldiers on their western journey was composed largely of substitutes for
draftees, the flotsam of frontier communities. Many were recent arrivals
to North America; some were ill-equipped for life in the forest, fell into
a virtual state of shock at the sight of an Indian, and barely knew the
butt of a rifle from the barrel. But this was an expected problem to
General St. Clair, one to be worked around or through. It would also be
an excuse if the expedition failed. Easterners could point to the militia

and aver that the frontiersmen were a worthless lot, incapable of self-defense despite the best efforts of eastern soldiers and no matter how much eastern money was siphoned off to Indian wars.

This time, westerners had a credible excuse if plans went awry. They could blame rapacious eastern merchants for the problems of the campaign. Under the best of circumstances it would not have been an easy expedition. Secretary of War Henry Knox had called for construction of forts at thirty- to forty-mile intervals stretching from the Ohio deep into the heart of Indian territory. But "fatal mismanagements and neglects" by the quartermaster general and suppliers of military stores committed the army to a hopeless venture. Tents, knapsacks, camp kettles, cartridge boxes, and pack-saddles were woefully deficient in quantity and quality. The saddles, for example, arrived after the army had departed. Transportation costs therefore made them twice as expensive as the same items purchased at Fort Pitt. And most of them were useless anyway. They were too large for the horses owned by the army and improperly constructed for wilderness use. Much of the powder, when it finally arrived, was unfit for firing. Money for the purchase of supplies arrived months after St. Clair had been forced to scrounge for goods on credit. Two traveling forges, necessary for shoeing horses and repairing weapons, reached Fort Washington without the essential anvils. Over 675 guns came two months late, and most of them were inoperable. By October 12 the army had three days' supply of flour remaining, and that only because the soldiers were marching on one-fourth to one-half rations.[37]

President Washington had bestowed words of warning on St. Clair before the army's departure in April. "As an old soldier," Washington advised, "as one whose early life was particularly engaged in Indian warfare, I feel myself competent to counsel. General St. Clair, in three words, beware of surprise . . . again and again, General, beware of surprise." By November 4, St. Clair was seriously ill, so responsibility for heeding the President's warning fell to another. The army, too, was weak and much of it sick. The soldiers *were* surprised, and many of them were killed.[38]

There were about 1400 men in camp when, about a half-hour before sunrise, the Indians pounced. Within a few minutes the entire camp was surrounded and the militia ran, many without firing a shot. St. Clair's losses were even greater than those remembered by Washington from Braddock's defeat thirty-six years earlier. Indeed, St. Clair's army lost 913 men, sixty-eight of them officers, making it the greatest defeat ever inflicted by Indians on a white force in North America. If the Indians had systematically pursued the fleeing troops, rather than remaining behind to torture the wounded and plunder the camp, losses would have been even greater. The most telling eyewitness account was that of the defeated commander himself. "The retreat," St. Clair reported to

Knox, "was, in fact, a flight. The camp and artillery was abandoned. . . .
But the most disgraceful part of the business is that the greatest part of
the men threw away their arms . . . even after pursuit . . . had ceased.
I found the road strewn with them for many miles. . . . The route continued to Fort Jefferson, twenty-nine miles, which was reached a little
after sun-setting."[39]

Ultimately the contractors were cleared of criminal misconduct in
supplying St. Clair's army. The militia was blamed for getting the
powder wet, for example, and for damaging rifles and other supplies by
ignorant or willful mishandling and lack of care. Other problems were
written off, at least in part, to the vagaries of transportation and communication over hundreds of miles. "The want of discipline and experience
in the troops" was deemed more instrumental in the defeat than the lack
of functioning arms and sufficient rations.[40]

Eastern politicians may have been convinced by this attribution of
causes in defeat. Frontiersmen were not. They felt that the militia had
been led irresponsibly into the wilderness to die, and it seemed to them
that eastern merchants caused the failure. Congressional inquiries convinced at least some westerners, not of the merchants' innocence but of
a conspiracy between government and the plyers of illicit trade. And all
settlers in the western country slept less soundly in the wake of St.
Clair's defeat.

Successive petitions from western Pennsylvania revealed the "apprehensions" of frontiersmen and their "defenseless situation, having
neither garrison, arms, or ammunition in case of attack from the Indians." Defense now absorbed even more of their time, energies, manpower, and paltry wealth than it had before adoption of the Constitution. They reaped no discernible benefits from their relations with the
new national government; life had become even harsher on the frontier
since the inauguration of President Washington. Not surprisingly, then,
in light of frontier perceptions of the region's collective plight, secession
and union with Great Britain or Spain again seemed a plausible
alternative.[41]

From a European perspective, the defeats of Harmar and St. Clair
were gratifying. The British believed that their interests lay in peace
between the Indians and the United States, but not at the price of
American conquest of the Northwest tribes. These military expeditions
seemed to threaten Britain's economic and political relations with the
Indians and brought American soldiers dangerously close to British frontier forts. Britain also retained an interest in fomenting discord between
the United States and its frontier. As during the 1780s, this desire was
not backed by consistent policy. But Vermont and Kentucky were still
the regions most actively cultivated by British officials, and Levi Allen
remained the major British informant on Vermont affairs. His commission by the governor and assembly of Vermont in 1789 seemed to indi-

cate a continued official capacity, but Allen had not lived in Vermont for years. Ethan Allen, Levi's brother and prime political contact, was now dead, and Allen's party had lost the most recent election for governor. Both Allen and the British officials who relied on his authority were shocked, therefore, when the United States offered independent statehood in 1791, and chagrined when the Vermonters accepted the long-sought invitation.[42]

The United States also offered, and Kentucky accepted, independent statehood in 1791. British aims to keep Americans from forging a larger and stronger union were thus dealt two blows in the same year. The possibility of *united* defection of the frontier now seemed less likely than in 1790. The nation's competitors for North America—Great Britain and Spain—would no doubt continue to foment back-country disloyalty, but the efforts of each seemed at low ebb, at least for the moment.

Nonetheless, unrest on the frontier was still rampant, and the Indians remained a grave problem. Free navigation of the Mississippi was unavailable, the British forts in the Northwest were still a threat, and the economic status of most frontiersmen was deteriorating. For western settlers outside of Vermont and Kentucky nothing had been accomplished during 1791, and even to settlers in the fourteenth and fifteenth states, their new status delivered promise, but not redemption, from the commercial and political ills affecting western societies. Relations between West and East were still strained, although less in some frontier regions than others, and everyone believed that if the potential for statehood was not realized, the Union was likely to split.[43]

Little hope for the future inspired western Pennsylvanians at year's end. No realistic possibility for independent statehood existed. Indians remained a constant menace. Economic conditions were declining for many in the region. And on top of it all, the new national excise now threatened the only viable cash product of the western country's meager existence. The lowliest of western inhabitants felt oppressed, and some of the middling sort shared their views. Many, however, were too poor, too weak, too beaten to move. Few imagined that conditions were better elsewhere. False promises had brought them to the frontier and they would not be duped again.

Chapter Seven

ASSEMBLY AND PROCLAMATION

During the fall of 1791 an apparently well-bred and educated young man by the name of Robert Wilson appeared in western Pennsylvania. At first he claimed to be a schoolteacher in search of employment. Being "somewhat deranged in his understanding," Wilson also suffered the delusion that he was an excise man charged to travel the United States enquiring whether distillers conformed to the new law.

The fellow's vociferous claims to association with the tax soon resulted in an assault by a band of locals. The assailants pulled Wilson from his bed, marched him five miles to a blacksmith's shop, then stripped him naked and heated a bar of iron in the forge. They next demanded that Wilson renounce his office. When he refused, proclaiming that he would not resign even if they tortured or threatened to murder him, the attackers applied the burning rod to several parts of his body. Wilson begged only for his underwear, but refused to recant his oath of office—an oath he never took for an office he never held. The men knocked him down, burned his clothes to ashes, "beat and abused him severely, and burnt him with a hot iron, both behind and before, for he was an excise man." Then they tarred and feathered him, and left him naked in the forest. Wilson lived to recount his ordeal to a sympathetic sheriff and a judge. His injuries were described by one witness as more horrible than any he had ever seen, "sufficient to make human nature shudder at the idea of having such barbarians in a country that ought to be civilized." By the time that several of the perpetrators identified by Wilson came to trial, the deranged schoolmaster had wandered away from the area and they were released for lack of evidence.[1]

PETITIONS FROM THROUGHOUT the frontier had asked the national government to reject Alexander Hamilton's proposed excise in 1790 and 1791. Petitioners had argued that such an internal tax posed a threat to liberty and to their local economies. Citizens in the western counties of Pennsylvania had also described the extra burden presented by the tax during the Indian war. To fight off barbarous savages with one hand and rapacious tax-gatherers with the other would be a hardship even for these hardy pioneers, inured though they were against trauma and suffering. Kentucky and North Carolina petitioners shared this perception and also noted that the unfair burden of an excise on distilled spirits would in effect be redoubled until free navigation of the Mississippi was secured for citizens of their regions.

Nonetheless, the excise had been adopted even as Indians rampaged through the western country, and while settlers remained unable to find a profitable outlet for the produce of their agricultural labors. As many frontiersmen interpreted events, the government was prepared to drain what little specie entered their region by means of an ideologically offensive excise on top of the other ordeals. It was more than these isolated and independent-minded people could bear. According to William Findley, "the people [of western Pennsylvania] anticipated their experiencing peculiar hardships from the excise." The Indian war, the poverty of many, and the lack of specie in the region made the potential burden of the tax seem brutal. These were not new arguments, according to Findley. He had heard them expressed against the state excise from the time of his arrival in the western country. The arguments "arose from their situation, and the simplest person feeling their force, knew how to use them."[2]

Some frontiersmen now aimed for repeal. Earlier petitions had been strictly private affairs in the sense that they represented the views only of those who signed them. Frontier republicans now took another step in the evolution of excise protest. They sought electoral validation for anti-excise remonstrances by calling extralegal assemblies that claimed to embody the "sense of the people" throughout the region. This, they hoped, would constitute a more credible statement of opposition. Public meetings on the excise ought to enhance the organizational base of the protests as well. The process was necessarily complex, cumbersome, and slow to evolve. But that was one of the prices paid for republican defense of liberty, and it was also important to give the national government opportunity to respond at each stage of the protest. Only by treading this time-worn path could the actions of frontier delegates be sanctioned by the local interpretation of republican theory.

On July 27, 1791, for example, interested persons met at Redstone–Old Fort (Brownsville), in southwestern Pennsylvania, to consider how next to proceed against the excise. The loathsome tax had been adopted despite the earlier protests. Many believed that their needs had been ignored yet again by a remote central government overly influenced by wealthy eastern merchants, speculators in western lands and public securities, and other "moneyed-men." No offices of inspection had yet been opened in the western country, but nonetheless, "the people in the region were in great consternation." Threats to liberty were no less disturbing than the reality they heralded. Paranoid, perhaps, but these American Whigs were acting no differently from those of 1765 and 1776.

To these men, the issues raised by the excise seemed precisely analogous to those of the Stamp Act.[3]

These westerners were concerned that their protests appear credible to eastern elites. Their goal was to effect change through reasoned, albeit extralegal, demands for redress. The meeting chose Edward Cook to preside. He was highly respected in the community, and he was certainly not a radical. In fact, Cook had been one of the region's most vocal advocates for ratification of the national Constitution. This was no gathering of rabid Antifederalists, no coven of demonic anarchists as Alexander Hamilton would later aver. Neither was this meeting a "cause" of unrest. It was not the work of "demagogues," as the Treasury Secretary suggested. It could be described more fairly as a spontaneous rising of moderates concerned for their liberties, worried about their financial interests, but as yet determined to work peacefully to secure their political ends. Those who attended this assembly seemed hopeful that they could convince their neighbors to abjure violence. Many of those present gave vent to their anxieties about the excise law and the hardships it would impose. Even so, no one challenged the legality of Congress's actions; on the contrary, "the Constitutional authority of Congress to enact it [i.e., the excise] was asserted." The majority acknowledged Congress's power to tax, but sought to convince it to repeal the law. No minority voiced disagreement.[4]

The gathering was also deeply concerned with process. A majority of the participants believed that it was necessary to survey public opinion and elect representatives to an assembly of the people. The traditionally accepted methods for discerning the voice of the people in constituent assemblies was not to be ignored. They wanted their actions to appear republican in their own eyes, in the eyes of their neighbors, and, if possible, in the eyes of those eastern politicians who had adopted the excise. These frontiersmen were not democrats, but neither were the eastern elites they wished to convince. Large numbers of local people were excluded at this stage by gender, racial, and minimum-property limitations on the franchise. This was an assemblage of republicans and required a consensual decision reached by "responsible" members of the community.

Since the Redstone meeting had no claim to representativeness, the July assembly recommended a more authoritative convention. The several counties in the region would elect delegates—three from each elective district. These delegates, in turn, were to collect "the sense of the people in each county" on the excise question. The three representatives would be selected by the county delegation to form a committee. This committee was to prepare a statement of its constituents' views and present them to a subsequent meeting at Pittsburgh in early September.[5]

Washington County elected representatives who met on August 27, according to the Redstone assembly's directions. The county delegates chose three of their number to meet with those elected by Fayette, Allegheny, and Westmoreland, "to express the sentiments of the people of those counties in an address to Congress, in relation to the excise law and other grievances." The phrase "other grievances" was later interpreted by federal officials as early evidence of subversive intentions. The mention of "other grievances" also led Neville Craig, a local opponent of the proceedings, "to a strong suspicion that some at least of the leaders were not influenced by a mere desire to get rid of the tax on whiskey, some of them were perhaps secretly hostile to the existing form of government."[6]

Delegates to the Pittsburgh assembly of September 7, 1791 did have "other grievances." They decried the "exorbitant salaries of officers" [i.e., officials] in the national government, "the unreasonable interest of the public debt," and congressional refusal to make "discriminations between the original holders of public securities and the transferees." To these western Pennsylvanians, it seemed "contrary to the interest and happiness of these states being subversive of industry by common means, where men seem to make fortunes by the fortuitous concurrence of circumstances, rather than by economic, virtuous, and useful employment." Still greater an evil, it seemed to this western populace, was "the constituting a capital of nearly eighty millions of dollars in the hands of a few persons who may influence those occasionally in power to evade the Constitution." This had already occurred with the establishment of a national bank. Nonetheless, delegates saw the excise as the gravest threat to the liberties of the nation, the most abominable legislative act of the young national government. "More especially," they declared, "we bear testimony to what is a base offspring of the funding system, the excise law of Congress."[7]

The excise constituted a unique threat because it embodied in one law so many evils. The law was "deservedly obnoxious to the feelings and interests of the people in general," because it infringed liberty, was discriminatory against a particular region of the nation, expensive to collect, and "liable to much abuse." It operated against one domestic manufacture and not those of other areas; it was "insulting to the feelings of the people to have their vessels marked, houses painted and ransacked, [and] to be subject to informers." The act produced a bad precedent by "tending to introduce the excise laws of Great Britain and of countries where the liberty, property, and even the morals of the people are sported with."[8]

The delegates resolved, therefore, that the law discouraged agriculture, fell most heavily on newly settled areas, "especially upon the western parts of the United States," and was particularly discriminatory against citizens of the "laborious and poorer class," who were the consumers of cheap, domestically produced alcoholic beverages. As policy, the taxing of the natural produce of the soil and especially commodities manufactured from that produce, seemed unjust to these rural people. It set an anti-agricultural precedent by taxing grain, especially rye, "and there can be no solid reason for taxing it more than any article of the growth of the United States."[9]

There is no evidence supporting Neville Craig's or Alexander Hamilton's description of this meeting as intentionally subversive of the government. They were wrong to portray it as the work of die-hard Antifederalists, if by that term they meant those who opposed adoption of the national Constitution in 1787 or men who sought the destruction of the existing form of government in 1791. Some delegates certainly had been Antifederalists in 1787. Some members of the assemblies may have favored secession from the East in 1791, but, if so, they never expressed those sentiments, nor did they "control" the meetings. In this case, William Findley's version of events conforms better to surviving evidence. He claimed that the meetings were "intended to promote submission, and not opposition, to the law." That appears likely. Community leaders argued for compliance, petition, and patience. They were trying to channel opposition into nonviolent modes of action. They failed, as witnessed by the treatment of the deluded Robert Wilson.[10]

On September 11, 1791, sixteen men assaulted a real excise collector named Robert Johnson in Washington County. They were disguised in women's clothes and cut off Johnson's hair, tarred and feathered him, stole his horse, and left him in the forest in a "mortifying and painful situation." Johnson recognized two of the "women" and convinced a local judge to issue warrants for their arrest. The responsibility for serving the warrants fell on a deputy marshal who feared for his life if he tried to fulfill this duty. Rather than risk his own neck, the marshal hired a cattle drover named John Connor to deliver the documents. Connor, apparently an illiterate, did not comprehend the nature of his task. For his efforts Connor was whipped, tarred and feathered, robbed of his horse and money, and left tied to a tree for over five hours by supporters of the accused.[11]

Protest against the excise law was thus proceeding simultaneously along two paths in western Pennsylvania. The Redstone and Pittsburgh meetings of July and September 1791 found some men organizing and attempting to channel anger into extralegal, but peaceful methods of dissent. The public gathering, the constituent assembly, and the petition were their preferred tactics. In these elected bodies, community leaders who opposed the excise could articulate the ideological, political, economic, and social reasons for resisting this internal tax. Others could blow off steam, harmlessly, in a public forum. The region's views might then be communicated to Congress in a fashion most likely to convince the cosmopolitan elites who formed its majority.

Others in the community were less patient and less peaceful in their methods. The brutalizing of Johnson, Connor, and Wilson during the fall of 1791 was not sanctioned or led by the same men who were at the forefront of the petition movement. Edward Cook, John Cannon, Hugh Brackenridge, William Findley, and Albert Gallatin—men whose names would be forever linked with the region's opposition to the excise— certainly had no role in the more violent episodes. The two move- ments—peaceful and violent—were largely unrelated in membership and were not mutually supportive during 1791 and 1792. Violence oc- curred *despite* the best efforts of most delegates who met at Redstone and Pittsburgh in the summer of 1791.

Federal officials, however, did not perceive a distinction between the two movements. They imagined that the organizers of the assemblies were fomenters rather than mediators of frontier unrest. They held the "respectable citizens" of the region responsible for stirring up the rabble. They never did credit the self-perception of frontier elites, who congratu- lated themselves for diminishing the frequency, the degree, and the spread of violence. The unsympathetic response of government officials was partly based on lack of knowledge, partly on prejudices against those who lived in the West, and partly on the information they were supplied by John Neville, Neville Craig, and other informants on the scene.

Neville reported in the fall of 1791 that those associated with the assembly and petition movement in western Pennsylvania were really ambitious politicians "fishing for a place in Congress." He worried that "while the matter lay in the hands of the rabble I did not think that it would grow to any height, but since it has been taken up by so many of what we call the leading men, it begins to look somewhat serious." As regional inspector of the excise, Neville came quickly to fear for his life, and he imagined a conspiracy between his elite opponents in local poli- tics and the "rabble" who threatened violence to those associated with the tax. He was alarmed, alienated from political moderates in the re- gion, isolated, and prone to exaggeration. He was also proud, stubborn, confident, and dedicated to the responsibilities of his office. What he needed, Neville advised in late 1791, was an armed force to help him collect the tax.[12]

No one tried to enforce the excise in western Pennsylvania during the winter, spring, or early summer of 1792. Quiet therefore prevailed. Although the tax had been law for almost a year and a half, no revenues reached Philadelphia from the western Pennsylvania survey. In August 1792, however, it appeared that the excise might soon come to the western country. Neville was beginning to set up shop, although he was finding it difficult to establish an office in Washington County. No one would rent him space. Finally, an ad in the *Pittsburgh Gazette* produced a landlord named William Faulkner, a newcomer to the area and an army officer. The inspector then took out another advertisement in the *Gazette* announcing that he was prepared to register stills at the Faulkner residence.[13]

Friends had warned Neville that this was a dangerous enterprise. Faulkner received his warning from a less amiable band of "Indians." Several days after the ad appeared about twenty men, colorfully hued in their version of war-paint, arrived at the address listed in the *Gazette*. They began at once to break down the entries to Faulkner's home. Peter Myers, a soldier in Faulkner's command, was in the house. He yelled down from an upstairs window to the intruders. If they wanted to get in, he would be glad to open the door. This he did, and the "Indians" rampaged through the residence, turning over bedding and furniture in a frenzy of frustrated searching for the owner of the house. Their goal, as some expressed it to Myers, was to shave the head of Faulkner and tar and feather him. Some even threatened to remove one of his limbs, others to kill the captain as retribution for his sufferance of the excise. Fortunately for Faulkner, neither he nor any member of his family was at home.[14]

The crowd next considered burning down the house, but decided against it because of the danger to buildings nearby. Finally, they contented themselves with a less destructive warning to the owner. They shot holes through the sign on the front of the house and left the dwelling with shot in the ceiling of every room. Later, a crowd confronted Faulkner as he rode across the countryside searching for deserters from his command. The people denounced him for renting his house to Neville. Someone drew a knife. The mob threatened to tar and feather Faulkner and reduce his house to ashes. To avoid these consequences he must swear to prevent the office of inspection from operating out of his residence. Faulkner complied and kept his word.[15]

Neville thought it unlikely that he could find another office in Washington County. "I shall be obliged," he wrote George Clymer, "to desist from further attempts to fulfill the law." The conscious imitators of Boston Tea Party "Indians" certainly had cause to rejoice. They had good reason to believe that they had won another victory for the cause of liberty.[16]

Again, as in 1791, not all efforts to nullify the excise law were violent. A notice in the *Pittsburgh Gazette* on July 21, 1792, called for another meeting of local residents to decide the next steps in their protest. Since Congress had not removed "the numerous evils" of which they had complained in their September 1791 petition, the author(s) of the advertisement recommended that inhabitants of the western counties meet again "to deliberate on the most advisable means of obtaining redress." Twenty-four delegates gathered over the two-day period of August 21 and 22 and affixed their names to a broadside which they then posted throughout the region. John Cannon was chosen to chair the meeting. He, like Edward Cooke, who presided over the 1791 assembly, was no radical. He had supported adoption of the national Constitution; he was one of the largest landowners in the region; he was the founder of

Cannonsburg, Pennsylvania; and he was George Washington's land
agent in the western country. Again, as in 1791, this was not a meeting
of "frontier rabble." It was a gathering of highly respected members of
the community, designed to direct peaceful opposition to a law that
provoked unrest on the frontier.[17]

The assembled delegates labored "STRONGLY with a sense of the fatal
consequences that must attend an excise." They were "convinced that a
tax upon liquors which are the common drink of a nation operates in
proportion to the number and not to the wealth of the people, and of
course is unjust in itself, and oppressive upon the poor." They had
learned the lessons taught by other excises in other countries "that internal taxes upon consumption, from their very nature, never can effectually
be carried into operation without vesting the officers appointed to collect
them with powers most dangerous to the civil right of freemen, and must
in the end destroy the liberties of every country in which they are introduced." To the remote western counties in particular, "the late excise law
of Congress, from the present circumstances of our agriculture, our want
of markets, and the scarcity of a circulating medium, will bring immediate
distress and ruin." The delegates thought it their duty, because of these
objections, to persist in their remonstrances to Congress and to pursue
"every other legal measure that may obstruct the operation of the law,
until we are able to obtain its total repeal."[18]

Both the tone and substance of this resolution were stronger, more
insistent, more desperate than the pleas of earlier years. Delegates were
now prepared to augment their petition drive with "every other legal
measure" they could conceive. Committees of correspondence modeled
on their Revolutionary predecessors were established to coordinate actions among the western Pennsylvania counties and to communicate
with "any committees of a similar nature that may be appointed in other
parts of the United States, and also, if found necessary, to call together
either general meetings of the people in their respective counties, or
conferences of the several committees."[19]

Finally, delegates to the 1792 meeting resolved to treat those members of their communities who cooperated with enforcers of the tax as
social pariahs. "In the future," they decided, "we will consider such
persons as unworthy of our friendship, have no intercourse or dealings
with them, withdraw from them every assistance, and withold all the
comforts of life which depend upon those duties that as men and fellow
citizens we owe to each other, and upon all occasions treat them with
the contempt they deserve." The delegates requested that their fellow
citizens join them in ostracizing those who accepted offices, otherwise
supported, or even complied with, the excise.[20]

In the face of what they perceived as ignorance and regional prejudice
on the part of the national government, these westerners were becoming radicalized. They had moved from private petitions, to public assem-

blies, and now, to ostracism of those reluctant to join the community in
tax resistance. It was a pattern familiar to all who remembered the
evolution of protest in Revolutionary America. It was a serious business
when viewed from either side of the Appalachian chain. And the physical violence displayed by the "Indians" at Captain Faulkner's house, in
its symbols, its methods, and its effects, contributed as well to the
familiar portrait of challenge to authority.

There is no evidence that the western Pennsylvania protests were part
of an independence movement during 1791 and 1792. Some eastern
politicians, however, thought otherwise. They remembered the Revolution and its more anarchistic dimensions with profound disdain. They
recalled the threats to national union posed by frontier independence
movements during the 1780s, and episodes in western Massachusetts,
Kentucky, and Franklin with horror. The case at hand seemed strikingly
similar. Some easterners interpreted every petition, every assembly,
and every act of violence as British politicians had in the 1760s and
1770s. Each was seen as a thinly disguised challenge to the very roots of
authority and order. They were wrong to see rebellion at every turn,
but that is hindsight. It now seems clear that the very act of interpreting
protest as sedition contributed a necessary element to creating the disenchantment, frustration, and anger necessary for it to become just
that—a challenge to the principles of government and membership in
the burgeoning American empire. Just as in 1765 and 1776, political
leaders and their opposition made mutually self-fulfilling prophecies.

Perhaps if the western Pennsylvanians had been alone in their resistance to the tax, protests would have seemed less threatening to the
government. During 1791 and 1792, however, the petitions, assemblies,
and violence against the excise were widespread. The frontier of every
state south of New York experienced unrest. In the degree and kind of
protest there was little to mark western Pennsylvania as unique.

The law was a dead letter in Kentucky, where no one would pay, no
one would dare to collect, and no sheriff would try to enforce the excise.
Not a penny in whiskey taxes reached the national government from this
frontier state. Whiskey was also smuggled into the region from western
Pennsylvania. According to Thomas Marshall, inspector of the Kentucky
survey, "the people of Monongahela have sent down large quantities of
spirits to Kentucky and the northwest side of the Ohio . . . The importers of that liquor have sold it as low as one quarter of a dollar per
gallon, which is much lower than it can be afforded, provided the excise
is paid. The prevailing opinion is that the whiskey is smuggled off leaving the duty unpaid." Despite evidence of defiance, however, government officials could find no one to prosecute excise evaders in Kentucky
as late as 1794. "There is not a gentleman of the law in the country,"
reported supervisor of collection Edward Carrington, "who, for the fees
usually paid . . . would . . . conduct . . . prosecutions."[21]

The excise inspector for Virginia's Northwest survey had no revenues to show for his labors either. In the central part of the state, distillers in Augusta entered into an association against the excise "until we can petition for redress or repeal [the tax] by force." In the tidewater and long-settled regions of Virginia, enforcement came off with fewer hitches. Only on the frontier was resistance widespread and effective.[22]

The situation was similar in North Carolina. Little opposition manifested itself in the coastal areas, with the exception of a brief period of recalcitrance in the most northern seacoast survey. In the fifth or western survey, however, "menaces . . . [to] the property of the officers and strong dispositions to violence . . . appeared." The excise inspector of the western region resigned because of harassment. Whiskey was also being smuggled out of this district, which had once been the state of Franklin, without paying the tax. This was precisely the competitive advantage John Sevier wanted for North Carolina's western counties when Congress considered the law. Attempts to enforce the excise in these frontier counties provoked only violence. For example, when one collector requested permission to gauge a farmer's still, the distiller opened the door, let the officer in, slammed the door shut, turned the key, and kept the tax man confined for three days. The farmer gave his prisoner only water during this time. According to the region's inspector, the farmer then assured the excise man, "that his life should not be in any danger, but he must submit to the mild punishment of having his nose ground off at the grindstone." The atrocity was prevented by more humane neighbors who persuaded the farmer to settle for beating the excise man on the road back East.[23]

The collection district for western South Carolina suffered from the same violence and refusal to pay the tax. According to Tench Coxe, "obstructions to the execution of the law have . . . occurred, which have been carried so far . . . [and] menaces so violent and serious as to occasion the collector to refrain from the execution of his duty." Coxe and Hamilton were also informed of similar resistance in Georgia. They knew of the widespread violence and that no revenue was reaching Philadelphia from the trans-Appalachian West. President Washington knew most of the story, and Chief Justice John Jay and Attorney General Edmund Randolph knew some but probably not all. News of smuggling, defiance, and anti-excise violence outside of Pennsylvania was not reported in Philadelphia newspapers. Treasury officials chose to publicize selectively and, historian Mary K. Tachau has argued, selectively to withhold information about challenges to the law in most frontier regions. The isolation of the frontier from eastern mercantile centers made it possible to hide westerners' ability to nullify the law.[24]

The plan to single out western Pennsylvania as the unique seat of excise resistance did not emerge immediately. It was not the obvious response to widespread opposition to the tax. Initially, Hamilton considered armed repression of tax resisters in western North Carolina. Edward Carrington reported to Hamilton on anti-excise violence in that region during the summer of 1792. "What you remark," Hamilton wrote back, "concerning the non-execution of the excise law in N[orth] Carolina is very interesting. The probable effect of a continuance of the affair in the same posture is obvious. . . . If process should be violently resisted in the parts of N. Carolina bordering on your state [i.e., Virginia], how much could be hoped from the aid of the militia of your state?"[25]

President Washington's response to the same information was far less bellicose. This should surprise no one since it marked a well-known personality difference between the two men. Hamilton seemed often to "wish there was a war." Washington, on the other hand, felt more deeply the horrors of military engagement, was generally slow to anger, and more measured in his responses to trying circumstances. In this case, Washington shared Hamilton's displeasure at reports from western North Carolina; he too believed "the picture drawn [by Hamilton and Carrington] . . . a very unpleasant and disagreeable one." Unlike Hamilton, however, the President thought a letter to the governor of the state expressing dismay was the appropriate action at this time.[26]

Other information was also leading Hamilton to rethink his advocacy of military operations on the southwestern frontier. Attorney General Randolph had examined the "evidence" supplied to him by the Treasury department. He interpreted the information gathered by Coxe and Hamilton as offering "no evidence, nor any prospect of evidence, sufficient for the objects of prosecution" in North Carolina. Randolph found, in other words, insufficient documentation of illegal actions on the Carolina frontier to warrant trials or a military response.[27]

The Chief Justice offered similarly unsupportive advice. Nothing, in Jay's opinion, could be worse for the government than a military humiliation. Only if all else failed should an expedition be considered. Perhaps he had in mind the disastrous defeats of Harmar and St. Clair during the previous two years. Government officials certainly had cause to suspect the military prowess of the nation's soldiers on the trans-Appalachian frontier. Jay advised political prudence and tact. Firmness would do more to solve a crisis than inflammatory proclamations and military preparations. "No strong declarations should be made," Jay believed, "unless there be ability and disposition to follow them with strong measures. Admitting both these requisites, it is questionable whether such operations at this moment would not furnish the antis with materials for deceiving the uninformed part of the community, and in some measure render the operations of administration odious."[28]

Such advice may have contributed to Hamilton's rethinking of the options before him. In any event, by September 9, 1792, the Treasury Secretary no longer advocated military operations against the frontier counties of North Carolina. He now favored armed reprisals against the

western counties of Pennsylvania instead. The western Pennsylvanians
were not any more reluctant to pay the tax than settlers in other states.
"It is now more than fourteen months," Hamilton informed the President, "since the duty in question began to operate. In the four western
counties of Pennsylvania and in a great part of North Carolina it has
never been in any degree submitted to." He had also recently learned
that "a spirit of discontent and opposition had been revived in two of the
[western] counties" of South Carolina, and he might have added Kentucky and northwestern Virginia to the list. In terms of both violence
and refusal to pay the tax, nothing marked western Pennsylvania as
unique.[29]

Hamilton had other reasons, however, for singling out western Pennsylvania. He favored testing the mettle of national law enforcement on
the Pennsylvania frontier rather than in the Carolinas because "the government, from several obvious considerations, will be left in condition to
do it." He apparently calculated that suppression of excise resistance in
western Pennsylvania would be less costly and more predictably successful for tactical reasons than in Kentucky or the Carolinas. "Decision
successfully exerted in one place will, it is presumable, be efficacious
everywhere," Hamilton predicted. Crush resistance at the most vulnerable point and the more remote regions would fall into line.[30]

Other factors weighed heavily in Hamilton's new-found enthusiasm
for focusing on western Pennsylvania as the center of anti-excise activity.
Meetings, petitions, and violence against the excise acquired in his mind
"additional consequence from their being acted in the state which is the
immediate seat of the government." The geographic proximity of unrest
in western Pennsylvania presented, then, the most embarrassing challenge to government authority and the most easily suppressible example
of anti-excise disorder.[31]

When he spoke disparagingly of western Pennsylvanians, Hamilton
also found President Washington a more receptive audience than when
he expressed the same views about Carolinians. Washington, too, believed that resistance to the excise in western Pennsylvania was a special
case. "Such conduct in any of the citizens of the United States," Washington wrote, "under *any* circumstances that can well be conceived,
would be exceedingly reprehensible; but when it comes from a part of
the community for whose protection the money arising from the tax was
principally designed, it is truly unaccountable, and the spirit of it much
to be regretted." Washington here endorsed the explanation of the excise as necessary to provide funds for frontier defense. Settlers of the
western country believed that the Indian wars in their region ought to
provide them special dispensation from the tax. President Washington
thought just the opposite. Each position seemed irrefutably logical to its
adherents. Each side would act on its own unique set of premises; and
their positions would parallel those of 1765.[32]

Hamilton was convinced that there was a "persevering and violent opposition to the law" in western Pennsylvania. He urged the Attorney General, at the President's insistence, to seek indictments against "the persons who were assembled at Pittsburgh" for the August meeting. "My present clear conviction is," Hamilton informed the President, "that it is indispensable, if competent evidence can be obtained, to exert the full force of the law against the offenders, with every circumstance that can manifest the determination of government to enforce its execution." If, as Hamilton expected, decisions of federal courts would have no effect in the western country, the government must "employ those means, which in the last resort are put in the power of the executive." If forceful action was not taken, "the spirit of disobedience . . . [would] naturally extend and the authority of the government will be prostrate."[33]

Washington agreed that the Pittsburgh meeting constituted a profound threat to order. He endorsed Hamilton's efforts to procure evidence for indictments of those who led such challenges to lawful authority. If such behavior persisted, Washington instructed Hamilton, "I have no hesitation in declaring, if the evidence is clear and unequivocal, that I shall, however reluctantly I exercise them, exert all the legal powers with which the executive is invested, to check so daring and unwarrantable a spirit." Washington knew the people in the region from long personal experience, and he could tell Hamilton with authority that "forbearance, under a hope that the inhabitants of that survey would recover from the delirium and folly into which they were plunged, seems to have no other effect than to increase the disorder."[34]

Attorney General Randolph examined the evidence Hamilton provided him of a crisis in western Pennsylvania—testimony concerning the attack on Faulkner's house and a copy of the broadside signed and posted by delegates to the August meeting at Pittsburgh. The former case was clearly an indictable offense, and judiciary officials proceeded, ultimately successfully, to prosecute the perpetrators of damage to Faulkner's home. No crisis there. The law had been broken, and the courts operated effectively to convict the guilty. The Pittsburgh meeting was a different case, however. The Treasury Secretary and the President seemed to think such assemblies a more serious challenge to authority. They saw these public meetings as manifestations of a "contemptuous resistance" to law. They thought meetings like those in Pittsburgh during 1791 and 1792 actually *caused* the violent eruptions in Washington County. Hamilton believed that in light of these flagrant challenges to order, it was "absolutely necessary that a decided experiment should without delay be made of the energy of the laws, and of the government to put them in execution." Washington agreed that his administration could no "longer remain a passive spectator of the contempt with which . . . [the laws] are treated."[35]

Randolph disagreed with Hamilton's assessment of evidence about the

Pittsburgh meeting. He found no indictable offense in the behavior of delegates to the assembly. "To assemble to remonstrate," he wrote to Hamilton, "and to invite others to assemble and remonstrate to the legislature, are among the rights of citizens." Even the final clause of the assembly's minutes, which called for ostracism of those who cooperated with enforcement of the law, seemed to Randolph not an indictable action: "The last [paragraph] indicates a hostile temper, as it exiles from the comforts of private friendship and intercourse, and marks for contempt, the officers of excise. Still, however, when we avert to the strictness with which criminal law is interpreted . . . I must announce that the law will not reach the conferees." Randolph could not agree that a "crisis" existed in western Pennsylvania. Unlike Jay, Randolph endorsed Hamilton's plan for a proclamation. He argued, however, for a more conciliatory tone than the Treasury Secretary advocated. He considered Hamilton's proposed responses too inflamed, too martial, and not grounded in the law.[36]

Despite this advice, Hamilton proceeded along his determined path. He urged the President to issue a proclamation concerning the "irregular proceedings" of the Pittsburgh meetings, "warning all persons to desist from similar proceedings and manifesting an intention to put the laws in force against offenders." Hamilton still saw a proclamation as the necessary first step in a process he expected to go quite a bit farther. He did not yet "despair that . . . the ordinary course of legal coercion will be found adequate," but both the tone and content of his letters during 1792 indicate that he was far from despair at the prospect for armed enforcement of the law.[37]

President Washington never instructed Hamilton to draft a proclamation on the excise disorders. The Treasury Secretary composed the document and circulated copies among other cabinet officers on his own initiative. On September 9, Hamilton informed Washington of the necessity for issuing a proclamation, and enclosed a rough draft, along with Randolph's penciled changes. Hamilton also included his own opinion that Randolph's reservations were unfounded and "unnecessarily diminish the force of the instrument." Washington signed the document on September 15 and immediately forwarded it to Secretary of State Jefferson for his signature. The President also instructed Hamilton to act with care, since the proclamation would "undergo many strictures." He wished to down-play the threat of force. "The Constitution and laws must strictly govern," Washington observed, "but the employing of the regular troops avoided if it be possible to effect order without their aid; otherwise there would be a cry at once, 'The cat is let out; we now see for what purpose an army was raised'." Troops must be used, and the threat of force expressed, only "as the dernier resort," lest "standing armies," rather than the enforcement of law, become the dominant public issue.[38]

It was a delicate political problem with potentially wide-ranging ramifications. Hamilton, as usual, was less sensitive to political concerns; he had "long since learned to hold popular opinion of no value." The President was more cautious and more receptive to alternative views. They were both on the same path, however, sharing a similar fealty to order and a disdain for the breakers of law, especially in western Pennsylvania.[39]

In its final form the proclamation was circulated throughout the nation as a broadside and was also published in newspapers. It decried all actions "tending to obstruct the operation of the laws of the United States for raising a revenue upon [distilled] spirits . . . subversive of good order, contrary to the duty that every citizen owes his country and to the laws, and of a nature dangerous to the very being of government." It noted that such actions were "the more unwarrantable" because of the "moderation" shown by the government and its attempts to "obviate causes of objection." The proclamation informed all citizens that the chief executive was constitutionally bound to enforce the laws of the nation, and that every "legal and necessary step" would be pursued "to prevent such violent and unwarrantable proceedings," to bring to justice infractors of the laws, and to secure order. It exhorted citizens to "refrain and desist from all unlawful combinations and proceedings whatsoever having for [an] object or tending to obstruct the operations of the laws aforesaid." It further charged all judicial officials to fulfill the duties of their respective offices and proceed to enforce the excise laws. The national government had now committed itself officially both to an interpretation of events over the previous two years and to a plan for receiving protests against the excise in the future. Violent actions or threats against tax collectors were illegal and would not be tolerated. Likewise, all "unwarrantable proceedings" and "all unlawful combinations and proceedings whatsoever having for object or tending to obstruct the operations of laws" would be interpreted as subversive of "good order," "dangerous to the very being of government," and would be dealt with harshly.[40]

No one man, not even the forceful and brilliant Alexander Hamilton, could create a "rebellion" alone. To blame the Secretary of the Treasury for the entire affair, as some contemporaries and subsequent historians have done, would be just as foolish as crediting him with single-handedly bringing about the Constitution. The President, Congress, and the men who fought for the national government would have to agree that the time, the place, and the issue warranted such a response. The so-called rebels would have to cooperate as well—no resistance, no violence, no public outcry for subversion of law, no "rebellion." As 1792 drew to a close, however, there was at least one man, and a very powerful one, in the national government who seemed to relish the idea of war over the excise. By now there may also have been some men to the west who, for different reasons, shared the same dream. The others were not pawns in their game, but no one now worked as hard to defuse East-West conflict as these men might work for war.

Much later, in thoughtful retrospect, Albert Gallatin and William Findley regretted the tone of the resolutions adopted by the Pittsburgh assembly in 1792. Gallatin termed his endorsement of these resolutions "my only political sin." Findley also later believed the resolves "intemperate and impolitic." Findley thought them "censurable on the ground of policy," since they "disgusted those members of Congress" who might have been sympathetic to repeal.[41]

Nonetheless, at the time and years later both men and other participants insisted on the legality of the proceedings. Delegates believed they had acted within their rights and in conformance with hallowed traditions of Anglo-American political discourse. The "principles were the same, " Gallatin argued, "as [those of] a Philadelphia society established during the late war to obtain a change in the Pennsylvania Constitution." Findley compared the situation to that of Stamp Act and Tea Party protesters, and thought the actions in each of the three cases "morally right." He later recognized, however, that "when the change of a government, a revolt from it, or a temporary opposition to its laws . . . is believed to be morally right, it is yet a matter of the greatest delicacy to calculate with accuracy with respect to the prudence or policy of commencing the opposition calculated." Years later, it became clear that the Pittsburgh remonstrants had miscalculated "the probable consequences" of their actions in August 1792.[42]

Years later it also became clear to Findley and others that the national government erred both morally and politically when it issued the proclamation denouncing such meetings in September 1792. As a matter of policy, Findley observed, "if those who administer the government attempt to issue denunciations against the liberty of expressing opinions of their measures and objects, or to prescribe rules by which men must be regulated in expressing their opinions, the very attempt will increase the evil it is intended to correct." It was by no means certain in the fall of 1792, however, that the government's "denunciations against the liberty of expressing opinions" would result in the very threat to order it sought to quell. It was not inevitable that advocates of liberty would confront defenders of order with anything but pen and ink. Events, perceptions, and individuals would influence the course of East-West conflict over the excise during the next two years. In the meantime, though, frontier moderates had their jobs cut out for them with local radicals on the one hand and bellicose Federalists on the other. Moderates had only their wits to combat those on both sides who itched for pitched battle.[43]

Chapter Eight

LIBERTY, ORDER, AND THE EXCISE

Even as plans for more active enforcement of the excise were laid, Hamilton recognized the need for better information about activities in the West. He admitted that his sources were unreliable. If the government was to begin active prosecution of the law or march an army to suppress a nascent rebellion, he must have a trustworthy informant on the scene. Unfortunately, he made a bad choice. George Clymer, supervisor of collection for Pennsylvania, was prone to fear, exaggeration, and poor judgment. He shared all the regional prejudices of metropolitan easterners, but he had little of Washington's experience or Hamilton's analytical skill to assist him in understanding the situation he confronted upon arrival in Pittsburgh during the fall of 1792. Nonetheless, government actions during the next two years would rely heavily on Clymer's reports. He became one of the government's primary interpreters of frontier unrest.

Clymer's trip west in mid-September was itself a farce displaying his inflated fears about "barbaric" frontiersmen. He adopted a series of aliases and disguises designed to protect him from the outrages that he expected to suffer if the westerners ever discovered his true identity. He was probably highly offended, then, when he found that almost no one west of Philadelphia had ever heard of him—even though he had been a signer of the Declaration of Independence and had traveled that way before. He reportedly posed first as Henry Knox, the rotund Secretary of War, thus immediately exposing himself as an impostor since Knox's corpulence was legend. All who met him in this guise knew he was on a surreptitious mission.

Clymer next adopted the unimaginative pseudonym of Smith. In this identity he traded horses with his servant and posed as a menial. He abandoned this pose when he was assaulted by a hostler "who called him an ill-looking fellow, and said he did not know how to rub down a horse." A failure as both a general and a servant, Clymer next tried his luck passing as "an ordinary person." This apparently worked. No one recognized him, cared who he was, or even asked his name as he skulked west in his soddened hat. In this fashion he entered Pittsburgh, got a *room at the inexpensive Indian Queen, and stayed under his hat until reaching army headquarters. After he secured protection, Clymer checked into the Bear Inn, more fitting for a man of his true stature. When it became generally known that he was associated with the excise, however, he was asked to leave the hotel and lodge elsewhere.*

Clymer's presence failed to arouse the furor that he anticipated. Nonetheless, he refused to venture outside Pittsburgh because he expected the farmers to display "something beyond the passiveness of hatred" for any officer of the national government. Judge Alexander Addison assured Clymer that such fears were unwarranted. According to this local judge, the "passions of the people" were very narrowly directed toward those who tried to collect the excise tax. Their respect for other officials continued undiminished. No one cared enough about Clymer to bother abusing him. Clymer was not convinced. He stayed in town and solicited information second-hand from anyone who would speak to him. Perhaps it was not only fear, but metropolitan affinities and disdain for rural peoples and conditions, that kept Clymer holed up in the town.

At first, Clymer tried to get Judge Addison to do the work of ferreting out subversion in the countryside. Addison refused on constitutional grounds, since he was an officer of the state, not federal, government. Clymer next attempted to subvert the anti-excise movement from within by intimidating vulnerable characters into testifying against their cohorts. He almost succeeded with John Cannon, chairman of the August 1792 local assembly, who "was not a man of the strongest mind." But Clymer failed when Cannon "fell into bad hands."

It was not a successful journey. According to William Findley, Clymer stayed "but a few days at Pittsburgh . . . [and then] returned to Philadelphia with the rapidity of a post rider, accompanied by a military guard through the most peaceable part of the country." Back in Philadelphia, Clymer was embarrassed by accounts of his undercover travels that appeared in the newspapers. Political opponents of the government made him look silly. He responded in what was for him a typically rash and counter-productive fashion. He denied vehemently that he had ever adopted a disguise of any sort and then, as if to undercut his own assertions, argued that such a "device" was perfectly justifiable "to any one in his predicament." He had sought "to escape the rage of the people," who were in "a state of actual insurgency against the government of the union," men who had openly engaged in "a dangerous confederacy, composed of almost all the magistrates, other public officers, and clergy" of western Pennsylvania. Affecting a brave demeanor to refute the accusations of cowardice, Clymer applauded himself for having "adventured at all through a country so circumstanced." It was an act of bravery "more hazardous perhaps than to have taken an honorable chance in an Indian war."

What Clymer could not see was how his efforts, including his public

assault on the clergy and magistrates of the western country, contrib-
uted to an escalation of conflict between enemies of the excise and those
who would enforce the law. He did not understand that the national
government's indictment of public assemblies as subversive of good
order served to undercut the efforts of moderates in the western coun-
try. By describing men such as John Cannon and Edward Cook as
"demagogues," and personally threatening them with prosecution, offi-
cials discredited the moderate leadership in the region, enraged the
populace, and played into the hands of the more radically inclined.[1]

CLYMER'S FRONTIER TRAVAIL was just one variation on the theme of political conflict played out in the young republic. The years from 1791 through 1794 were a time of fierce debate over the nature of political society. Those who wrote in newspapers seemed even to disagree about the "fixed principles" upon which government was based, and the excise served as a catalyst for these harangues. The liberty-order battle provoked by fiscal concerns was one among a constellation of issues that touched deep emotions during the 1790s and seemed threatening to the very survival of the republican experiment.

In one sense, the sallies of partisans in Philip Freneau's opposition (Republican) *National Gazette* and John Fenno's (Federalist) *Gazette of the United States* were not truly debates. Writers began from such diverse principles that they seldom engaged in a dialogue. The defenders of order and the champions of liberty often failed to credit the integrity of their opponents. The friends of order, as some dubbed themselves, generally shared a Hobbesian-type fear of anarchy as the starting point for their consideration of contemporary politics. Their opponents, who portrayed themselves as friends of liberty, took a more Lockeian-type stance. They argued that protection of liberty, not the maintenance of order, was the principal task of government. Defense of liberty and preservation of order are not, of course, necessarily conflicting polarities. As the more moderate on each side admitted, liberty and order could be compatible, indeed interdependent, goals. But writers disagreed over the priority of each in the canon of political thought and over the immediate threat to liberty, order, and survival of the political status quo.

The friends of liberty described a world visualized before them by adherents to Britain's Country tradition, by the British opposition writers known so well to eighteenth-century Americans, by the colonial pamphleteers who denounced the Stamp Act and who wrote their way through a Revolution, and by opponents of the Constitution. It was a convention steeped in reverence for liberty, a fear of its frailty, and ever conscious of the threat posed by "aristocratic juntos," "corrupt ministers," "stockjobbers" and other "moneyed-men," and, of course, the tyranny for which all of these were harbingers. "Free government, in any country," some men still argued in the 1790s, "naturally verges by imperceptible advances to tyranny, unless corrected by the vigilance of the people. Nothing but the perpetual jealousy of the governed has ever been found effectual against the machinations of ambition."[2]

These same words might have been written at any time over the previous century by an Anglo-American follower of this tradition; the same ideas were certainly expressed often from the 1760s through the end of the century. The Constitution provided no guarantee that liberty would not succumb in the United States just as it had in the Nether-lands, Rome, Greece, and in every other nation where it was known to have flourished and died. Eternal vigilance was the price paid for the blessings of liberty. Causes of ill-health wafted in every breeze, and excises were well-recognized symptoms of plagues that had struck lib-erty down in earlier days.

Writers self-consciously drew upon the authority of Revolutionary principles, as they understood them, to describe political relations dur-ing the 1790s and to justify their opposition to the policies—in this case the excise—of those administering the national government. Some, for example, lauded the "spirited conduct of some good old Whigs of 1775" when a crowd assaulted the office of an excise collector in Germantown. By destroying the sign over his door, these patriots had expunged "a disgraceful badge of slavery . . . [and, it was hoped] convince[d] our rulers that a free people will not be amused by financial palliatives." Others remembered the Continental Congress's plea to Canada in 1775. In an address to the people of Quebec, Congress had decried excises as "the most odious of taxes." Many still shared such opinions and believed citizens must not so quickly forget the ideas that launched the Revolution.[3]

In light of this allegiance to Whig principles, it is not surprising that the ideological controversies over internal taxation provoked by the Stamp Act and the Constitution arose again during the excise dispute. It was in the Stamp Act crisis, some men remembered in the 1790s, "that the quick sightedness and spirit of Americans [first] showed them-selves." It was in 1765 some still believed, that colonists "made the world sensible that usurped power could neither cheat them by sophis-try, nor awe them by force, giving a noble lesson to their posterity ever to watch against governmental encroachments, and to stifle them in their birth." In sum, friends of liberty frequently argued during the 1790s that the Stamp Act resistance was a landmark in the defense of liberty because Americans then first displayed their rejection of the authority of remote central governments to levy internal taxes on a free people.[4]

The issue of representation was again, as it had been in 1765 and 1787, at the heart of debates over just taxation. Some still argued that a national legislature was unable to know local conditions and hence unfit to lay internal taxes on products of domestic production or trade. According to one writer, "every judicious politician must anticipate the remark that even the House of Representatives must necessarily be too limited in point of numbers, and in point of information will possess too little knowledge of the citizens, and too feeble a participation in the particular circumstances of the subjects of taxation" to levy internal taxes justly. At the time the excise law was passed, according to this same author, the interests of about one-half the people of the nation were not represented. Since some states elected representatives-at-large before results of the first national census were available, and since almost all Senators were from the East, the needs and views of frontier people were very poorly understood. "If we had no other proof," he argued, "this is sufficient to demonstrate that the federal government never was intended to embrace extensive internal powers; and that the powers of that kind which it possesses were only intended for emergencies, in which the preservation of the government itself was at risk."[5]

An anonymous writer who signed himself "Sidney" recalled how advocates of the Constitution had promised that these internal powers would be reserved for the most dire emergencies. Clearly, the pledge had been disingenuous since a national emergency was neither evident nor proclaimed in 1791. "When the vestiture of extensive internal powers in the federal legislature gave a general alarm to the people of the United States," this friend of liberty now recalled, "the best advocates for its adoption, and such as were most active in its formation, declared that those powers would not be exercised, except in the last resort, and that particularly the powers of levying internal excises could only be practicable when every other resource failed, and when pressing danger would, by producing conviction of the necessity of the measure, insure its success."[6]

The opposition tradition offered friends of liberty a handy explanation for such perfidy. Conspiracy theories about Court intrigues conformed to the most paranoid conventions of Anglo-American Country thought. "Sidney" explained that the excise was necessary "to enable the minister [i.e., Alexander Hamilton] to try his hand upon the administration of internal powers, and to buoy up ministerial influence by an extensive patronage of appointments to office. For it is well known that internal revenues require a much greater number of officers to superintend and enforce the collection than those revenues which are collected at the ports of trade." The diagnosis of this case was simple for "Sidney": an unrepresentative Congress had succumbed to the influence of aristocratic ministers, "mercenary merchants," and speculators. Had the House of Representatives not been such a "partial representation of the people," liberty-threatening internal taxes would never have been adopted. Here was a classic Country indictment of Court ministers and politicians, and some writers specifically denounced their opponents as Court apologists.[7]

Such a rapid and total embrace of internal taxes by officials so soon after Americans had "extricated themselves from the hard grasp of British taxation" was difficult for opposition writers to comprehend in any other terms, "The style and language" of this administration seemed "well suit[ed] to the court of a despot." An "aristocratic fondness and attachment to an excise law" appeared incongruously worn by men who were "the living monuments of their own liberty." The influence of speculators in land and paper, "malicious merchants," "aristocratic factions," and corrupt ministers were the reflexive answers perceived by opposition writers to the administration's questionable practices.[8]

It was a short step from diagnosis of "aristocratic" symptoms to a fundamentally class- and occupation-based explanation for adoption of the excise. Indeed, republican and class-based analyses were compatible and mutually reinforcing. The tax seemed to be an attack by wealthy eastern merchants, cosmopolitan "moneyed men," and other speculators against the economic interests, the style of life, and the morals of a less wealthy agricultural society. "Brutus," for example, could not find "a single act [of the national government] whose object was to promote the interest of the yeomanry of the United States." Another writer described the two parties vying for control of the national government. The one now in power, the one that endorsed funding, assumption, and excises, consisted of those, "who from particular interest, from natural temper, or from habits of life, are more partial to the opulent than to the other classes of society." This party had already "debauched themselves into a persuasion that mankind are incapable of governing themselves." From this observation, the artistocratic party concluded "that government can be carried on only by the pageantry of rank, the influence of money and emoluments, and the terror of military force."[9]

It seemed clear that "the fate of the excise law will determine whether the powers of the government of the United States are held by an aristocratic junto or by the people." Instead of responding to the flood of petitions against the excise that filled the halls of Congress, the members of that body "very improperly" handed them over "to an executive officer [i.e., Hamilton] who was the occasion of the injury, and was very interested in supporting it." Now, instead of repealing the law, a "sanctified friend of aristocracy" in the Congress advocated a national day of fasting, prayer, and humiliation "that the clergy of all denominations from one end of the continent to the other may intercede with the Lord of Hosts to dispose the minds of the people to obedience." The arrogance of such a proposal infuriated opposition writers. Who were these aristocratic politicians to presume such a condescending attitude? Where was a recognition of republican principles, of the equality among men, for which the Revolution was fought? It now seemed that at least some who "passed under the name of federalists" embraced the Constitution only "because they looked on it as a promising essay towards a system of anti-republican orders and artificial palances." These Federalists asserted their right to rule over the nation of farmers because they were "men of wealth and opulence, who could buy and sell the whole ragged race of whiskey drinkers twenty times over." The question of the excise, friends of liberty warned, "is no longer between federalism and anti-federalism, but between republicanism and anti-republicanism."[10]

The Court, class, and occupational theories about adoption of the excise also fit compatibly with regional explanations offered by self-styled friends of liberty. They saw the excise as a conspiracy of men in the more settled, urban, mercantile, cosmopolitan East against the economic interests of the Country—the rural, agricultural, especially the western hinterlands. It was a theory that conformed to their perceptions of inter-regional relations since 1775.[11]

Enemies of the excise were encircling a definition of the "liberty" they defended, although none actually pinned down the boundaries of its meaning. In their eyes the excise threatened personal or individual liberty, the economic liberties of farmers, and the liberty of citizens to affect changes on institutions and law. The end foreseen if the excise was not repealed, and evil influences on the government not suppressed, would include slavery of the individual to the state, domination of agriculture by mercantile interests, tyranny, and civil war. The prognosis of these Country doctors was typically alarmist. Their prescription was the tried and true cure-all from the Whig pharmacopeia—less order from above, more liberty from below; more respect for the yeoman, less deference to "non-productive" elites.

George Logan represented an extreme position on a spectrum of liberty's friends. He incorporated many of their greatest fears into a raging indictment of the excise, and "half-informed lawyers and mercenary merchants." Logan perceived "a dangerous aristocracy" controlling the government "which, if not crushed in the bud, will destroy our liberties forever." If citizens were not quick to smite the excise and its aristocratic supporters, an army of mercenaries could be expected to enforce the law. It had happened in Europe; it could happen here. "Ambitious and designing men" had misled honest yeomen into believing that "whilst you enjoy the freedom of electing your legislators there is no danger of your rights being violated. This is a dangerous and false doctrine," Logan warned. He offered in its place a higher standard of representation, one closer to that of some anti-Stamp Act pamphleteers and Antifederalists. It was a localist argument in every sense. Only the most local, most representative bodies should assess internal taxes. Adopt a bill of rights for the Constitution, reject indirect taxes levied by remote central governments, maintain strong local militias to protect against the encroachment of mercenary armies, and the nation and liberty might again be safe, according to Logan.[12]

Foes of the excise found the greatest threat to personal liberty in

section thirty-two of the act—a clause granting authority to search for
contraband goods and illegal distilling operations. They conjured visions
of rapacious tax-gatherers breaking down their doors, ransacking their
households, defiling their wives and daughters, and dragging men from
their beds and off into the night for possession of a dram of un-excised
whiskey. It was a Hogarthian scene of lecherous tax collectors destroying
all that Americans held dear that the friends of liberty drew from their
collective British pasts. Excises laid open "the peaceful dwellings of the
inhabitants of a country to the entrance, insult, and rudeness of a set of
unprincipled excise men." Internal taxes subjected citizens to "the dis-
turbance of the peace and happiness of their families by the entering,
searching, and ransacking their houses and closets by a set of rude and
insulting excisemen."[13]

Opposition writers saw violence as the greatest threat posed by the
excise law to their lives, property, and political liberties. Some, such as
an anonymous North Carolina poet, seemed to relish the violent response the law might provoke from liberty's allies:

> The countrys' a' in a greetin mood
> An some are like to rin red-wud blud:
> Some chaps whom freedom's spirit warms
> Are threatning hard to take up arms,
> And headstrong in rebellion rise
> 'Fore they'll submit to that excise:
> Their liberty they will maintain,
> They fought for't, and they'll fight again.

More often, friends of liberty feared this violence; they shuddered at the
results of attempted enforcement by the bane of all free men—a standing army. "Hold your tongues," advised one writer, "and either pay the
excise duty, or break up your stills, lest an army of militia, collected
from gin and rum distillers, should be sent out into the back country to
make you sing a different tune over your whiskey." The scenario was a
familiar one to students of liberty's history. From excise laws, to enforcement by militias, to standing armies enforcing all the laws could
easily be the short and brutal history of the decline and fall of American
liberty.[14]

The rhetoric seems high and the fears exaggerated to the modern
reader of these eighteenth-century letters. Indeed, it is difficult to judge
how much was hyperbole and how little was genuine paranoia. Did
Pennsylvania Senator William Maclay exaggerate his opposition to the
excise when he termed it "the most execrable system that ever was
framed against the liberty of a people?" Did he truly believe that Congress had opened "the box of Pandora" by adopting this law? Some
readers might doubt whether Maclay really thought that "war and
bloodshed are the most likely consequence of all this," but he had no

obvious cause other than habit of mind for hyping the rhetoric for his own diary. When the private writings of public men reflect the same displeasures and the same fears as their public expressions, we must at least suspect them of honest intent.[15]

In any event, the attitudes expressed—if not the tone of rhetoric used to express them—represented a widely shared vision of the political world, past and present. The public and private utterances of friends of liberty displayed a contrasting philosophy from that endorsed by self-styled friends of order, one consistent with long-standing traditions of Anglo-American political thought.[16]

On the other side, friends of order would strictly limit popular participation in politics in a way that was anathema to their opponents. They took pride in their own quiescent attitude toward public affairs. "I am one of those peaceable characters," one man bragged, "that seldom attend popular meetings." The proper time and the *only* proper time for citizens to express their political preferences was on election day. As one friend of order put it, the fountain of free government "must be preserved from contamination by the virtue and vigilance of the people in their elections—and in this way alone." The opposition had perverted the meaning of liberty in the opinion of some. True liberty "invests a people with the right of electing their own rulers, whose task is to enact laws for the general good—and it enjoins upon the community a strict and perpetual obedience of them." Unlike such writers as George Logan, for example, these men defined representation very narrowly—to vote is to be represented. Unlike those who claimed to be friends of liberty, these men would circumscribe liberty with duty and obedience. They shared no fear of ministerial encroachments; they argued against the eternal vigilance in public affairs so crucial to their opponents. Public gatherings and debates had no place in the republicanism of these friends of order. "Voluntary obedience and love of order" supplanted "liberty" in the hierarchy of values endorsed by some supporters of the excise law.[17]

The gravest threat came, in the minds of friends of order, not from above—from the wealthy and from political leaders—but from below—from the ignorant, the poor, narrow-minded localists, and in sum, from what they termed "the rabble." Seeing the threat in this way naturally led them to advocate less liberty for individuals and more obedience, deference, and order. The greatest political traumas seemed to them to result from popular anarchy. The danger was that ambitious men would mislead the lower orders into disruptive actions. Theirs was an attitude toward republican governance shaped most by the turmoils of the 1780s and far less by the "time-worn" theories of British opposition writers that seemed to them no longer applicable to the American case.

Friends of order believed that "the busy and restless sons of anarchy" were attempting by defiance of the excise law "to bring us back to those scenes of humiliation and distress from which the new Constitution has so wonderfully extricated us." The Antifederalists, those "old enemies of the honor and happiness of our country," seemed again at work. Opposition to the excise appeared to represent nothing more than "a feint, a covert to their main design, that of subverting the Constitution." Masks of loyalty, claims to be true federalists, could not hide the fact that "a uniform federalist, a republican federalist and an anti-federalist, will pass for the same in the twilight of truth."[18]

Like Fisher Ames, other friends of order "dread anarchy more than great guns." They lived in a Hobbesian world where man would devour man if government did not restrain him. Every ounce of their political strength seemed dedicated to combating those "dragons watching the tree of liberty," who seemed most to threaten the orchard of republican government. They sought even to redefine liberty in conformance with this dedication to peaceful governance. "Liberty is order," explained one writer in an attempt to link political values of the 1770s and the 1790s. "Liberty . . . is reason," proclaimed another in a similar endeavor. These and other friends of order aimed to subdue the passions unloosed by the Revolutionary experience, reintroduce a more hierarchical political order with themselves at the top, and secure the obedience of those below. "Wild ranting fury" and addresses to the "passions of the people" threatened to subvert this enterprise. "Reason," as one wrote, "should govern one man—it should govern all men—it is opposed by passion, which should never govern at all."[19]

Antifederalists, those narrow-minded ranters of political unrest, seemed to the friends of order to be joined in their subversive schemes by foreigners, the ignorant poor, and backwoodsmen who were isolated from the eastern centers of urban enlightenment. Friends of order indicted each of these groups for threatening the republican experiment. Some supporters of the excise manifested metropolitan prejudices against rural folks. One writer, who signed himself "Order," found it "really amusing to hear little obscure spots of people" complain about the laws. Cosmopolitan elites who shared this prejudice just dismissed out-of-hand the opinions of those who lived on the frontier. Another writer exhibited the same prejudice when he described backwoodsmen as "narrow-minded men whose views, like those of the pismire, are limited to the hillock where they lived." Because they were denied the illuminating environment of the East, frontier people acquired "sour restless minds" and their petitions should, therefore, be ignored by national leaders.[20]

Since citizens of the back-country were unable, in the eyes of some, to think for themselves, it appeared likely that their opinions originated from some place else. France seemed the likely candidate in the era of its Revolution, but England and Ireland were also commonly mentioned as probable suppliers of both the "grumblings" of anti-excise polemicists and the "rabble" who shared such un-American views. "Those whom vice, ignorance, idleness, and the rod of despotism have driven from the just rank of men, are a rabble," according to one friend of order. Europe was full of rabble, "and the overflowing mass of their multitudes have more or less tainted the healthy mass of our large towns." No one "who knew anything of this country" could possibly think or write the nonsense penned by these so-called friends of liberty. None who acted with such wanton disregard for the tranquility of the nation could honestly claim allegiance to the nation. Enemies of the excise law must be either deluded masses or willful revolutionaries intent upon overthrowing the government. Perhaps some of the incendiary letters to the *National Gazette* were "the production of a person who, after landing from a vessel from Ireland, followed his nose from hence to Harrisburg without turning to the right or left." The unenlightened prejudices expressed by some foes of the excise must have been "acquired in another country and under slavish laws; for these violent grumbletonians, many of them at least, were born abroad." Others no doubt intended to mislead this ignorant foreign rabble into revolution in a cynical attempt to gain power.[21]

Anti-excise sentiment seemed the result of an alliance between these grumbling foreigners from France, Ireland, or "a certain street in London," and America's lower classes. All these groups allied on the frontier where English, Scottish, and Irish immigrants were led by the likes of the French-born Albert Gallatin and William Findley, a native of Ireland. The friends of order expressed little respect for the poor and less for their opinions. "The conversations of the lower class rise from themselves," according to one writer, "and terminate where they rise." "It is by force alone," argued another, "that an ignorant herd can be governed." The United States must beware to educate its lower orders to duty and obedience lest America suffer the horrors of the Birmingham riots in England or the excesses of the French Revolution. The multitudes must be led, in the view of friends of order; the leaders of society should not cater to the passions of the poor. The "natural aristocracy" of the nation should teach the impoverished, the foreign, and the ignorant to eschew their enslavement to the worn-out ideas of the past and their prejudices against the names of taxes rather than the realities they represented. If they could not be taught in schools or the press, they must learn by force of arms that laws and not men governed America.[22]

As parents to infantilized masses, friends of order believed that educated elites shared a responsibility to raise "the people" from their childish attitudes. By example, education, and in the last resort coercion, they felt obliged to teach the lower orders appropriate patterns of behavior and thought. The nation's leaders knew best what was good for the country. The whining demands of frontier wards should be ignored lest authorities appear to sanction or approve such untoward behavior.

Stubborn recalcitrance must be nipped in the bud or else such behavior would continue interminably. The people—like children—must learn duty, discipline, and obedience.

Friends of order were dismayed, therefore, by the irresponsible example set by those political elites who opposed the excise. The Pennsylvania House of Representatives should have known better than to declare publicly its disapprobation of the excise law. The actions of these state leaders were analogous to a mother questioning the authority of a father in the children's presence. When a state legislature censured the national government, "the citizens may say, this Assembly has power over my life and property—it decides other laws wisely, and without being disobeyed. . . . Those who make bad laws, and attempt to subvert liberty, are certainly very bad men, and very unfit to hold the reins of authority any longer." Such irresponsible behavior could have several possible repercussions. It could lead the people to "fear and hate the [national] government," by appealing to "the fears and prejudices of the people." Alternatively, the censure could have no effect, and the authority of the state legislature might be disregarded by the people, "which by abating the dignity and respectability of the censuring body, is an injury to the cause of good government, and brings it into contempt." In either eventuality, however, it was likely to undermine the collective authority of the parent governments and lead to the necessity for violence to overawe the masses. Not the strap or belt, as in the family, or the whip used to discipline recalcitrant slaves, but the sword would be necessary to reassert the authority of the national government over its citizens.[23]

Elites also had a positive role to play in affecting the behavior of the citizenry, and the friends of order saw the excise law as providing an unprecedented occasion to alter the morals of the people. "With one voice," the most enlightened "patriots and philosophers of Europe" joined educated men of medicine, religion, and law in America to "call on government to check the immoderate use of spirituous liquors." What better way to bring the order and decorum of elites to the under classes of society, to alleviate "the pernicious effects of spirits on the lower ranks of the people," than to institute an excise on the production of domestically distilled alcoholic beverages? The tax would lower consumption, that was clear: "Those who say that an excise does not diminish the consumption of spirituous liquors may as well affirm that the less money there is to purchase, the greater the quantity that will be bought." Lowered consumption would reduce crime and other disorders, and bring discipline to the lives of the lower classes.[24]

The excise would inspire those "who have a mind to be sober and frugal" to abandon drink, save money by this abstention, and develop enterprising work-habits that would bring wealth to their families. Physicians, philosophers, clergymen, politicians, and political writers did their best to convince the laboring classes that sobriety, discipline, and order would bring prosperity. It was a futile effort to alter the culture of drink in American society, but it was an honest attempt by some well-intentioned reformers to bring about constructive change. Others, perhaps less honestly, tried to use the temperance movement to rationalize the political goals of the excise.[25]

The parent-child metaphor and the attitudes it represented were also adopted by those friends of order who seemed actually to ridicule the dedication of other citizens to the principle of liberty. One writer portrayed the friends of liberty as unruly students who deserved disciplining by a teacher. During the spring and summer of 1793 communities celebrated the arrival of France's minister Edmund Charles Genet. "Citizen" Genet was widely feted in Philadelphia and elsewhere by the political opponents of Anglophilic friends of order. At one of these parties a "cap of liberty" was handed from head to head in a symbolic representation of the attendants' unity in a cause and for a principle. This cap struck the correspondent to the *Gazette of the United States* as bearing "some similitude to the cap occasionally worn at country schools commonly called a dunce's or fool's cap. With this cap, it is usual to compliment blockheads, and idle boys, who, dissatisfied with the circumscribed liberty they enjoy, attempt to subvert the authority of the master, and to put him upon a level with themselves—a situation more consonant to the present enlightened system of equality, and the rights of man."[26]

This story illustrates many of the values discussed above. Those who celebrated liberty seemed childish, idle, ignorant, stupid, and naïve to friends of order. Friends of liberty failed to recognize the necessity for circumscribing a liberty that was threatening to undermine the prosperity of the nation. Those who would put the schoolmaster or the President "upon a level with themselves" overstepped the bounds of liberty endorsed by the administration's most conservative supporters. The friends of order did not believe in the political equality of all free men. By defining liberty as synonymous with order or reason they offered a dramatically constricted definition of the central principles of the Revolution. These men would substitute order and prosperity as the reigning principles of republicanism.

In this sense they were correct to accuse liberty's friends of being shackled to old ideas. The friends of liberty were devoted to the more radical principles of liberty proclaimed by the Declaration of Independence. They were obsessed by the same fears of governmental tyranny that British opposition writers had expressed for over a century. But to portray the friends of liberty as fundamentally backward-looking and to describe their political opponents as modernizers would be to caricature each and misrepresent the complex interweaving of old and new in the fears and dreams of those who would become Republicans and Federalists. It would be to adopt the Federalist vision of the world without a critical appraisal of their arguments.

The forces of order and centralization clearly saw themselves as waging war against "narrow local prejudices," "narrow-minded men," and "worn-out ideas." To them, the world seemed "strangely fettered by custom" and their opponents wrong to let "old prejudice outweigh demonstrative experience." And there was an undeniably "modern" dimension to the fiscal policies introduced by the Hamiltonian centralizers during President Washington's first term. Their attitudes toward banking, finance, and the relationship between the government and the nation's commercial interests did resemble the nation's future more than its past, although the practices were drawn from British precedents and hence were not entirely new. They would be the winners in a long struggle between national and state sovereignty; they could be seen as the forefathers of American industrial and corporate capitalism, but it would take a bloody civil war and an evolution in constitutional law to secure these victories.[27]

Their attitude toward restraint of individual liberty, however, was truly a relic of the past. Theirs was a "classical republicanism," fearful of declining virtue and dedicated to the constitutional balance of government among different social estates. To the friends of order, the personal freedom unloosed by the Revolutionary experience seemed little more than "the wild liberty of an individual." They longed for return to the patriarchal days when "the power of a good government . . . [was] naturally an object of love and admiration. Every man considering in the benevolent disposition of his rulers, consider[ed] their power as his own—and we consider[ed] our power with great complacency and regard." Now, many men seemed "so wicked and foolish as to fly in the face of authority"; they seemed to forget that "voluntary obedience, and a love of order, are among the most distinguished honors in the character of a soldier, as well as a citizen. It is but too notorious to be forgotten, that a contrary conduct, during our struggles for freedom, often produced the most unhappy consequences."[28]

The integrated patriarchal systems of the past, where everyone knew his place in a hierarchical community structure, had to some degree fallen apart during the Revolution. A polarized world seemed to result, a world where the actions and motives of leaders were questioned at every turn. It seemed necessary to restore the "good order" of the past if the nation was to survive. "Without this support of the lovers of order," one writer argued, "the government of this country would not have so much as the shadow of force." Only "law and order" could save the nation from slipping into licentiousness and then anarchy. The stakes were high and the friends of order would fight to defend the "fixed principles" of the Constitution from attack.[29]

Ever willing to experiment in fiscal matters, the friends of order steadfastly refused to budge from the formulas embodied in the Constitution. They saw assaults on the excise as threatening to annihilate those principles and the constitutional form of government that enshrined them. "If there are no fixed principles," one man wrote, "we must be perpetually afloat. This world may do for those that love to fish in troubled waters, but as to peace or permanency in existence, or government, or security to freedom, person, or property, they are all entirely out of the question." The majority had no right "to modify or annihilate their constitution whenever they think fit." The time of revolution, of questioning, of experimentation with forms of government was over. The choice was clear. Americans could return to the "anarchy and disgrace" of the 1780s or rest secure with "government and honor . . . to crown our labors."[30]

Fisher Ames took an extreme position among these thinkers. His dedication to "classical republicanism," his rabid intolerance for those who did not share his views, and his scorn for those who were less educated, less wealthy, and less eastern than he marked him as outside the mainstream of Federalist thought. Few other friends of order would ever, like Ames, actually write an assault on the principle of liberty— "The Dangers of American Liberty" (1805). Not all friends of order shared his belief that true liberty could exist only in a society of codified laws restraining the common man. His uniqueness was only in the inflated tone of his rhetoric, however, in the degree of his disdain for those who challenged the "friends of union and order" in Congress. Others shared his abhorrence of the "factious, levelling spirit" pervading politics and others also "dread anarchy more than great guns." Like Ames, his political colleagues saw the opposition to the excise as no more than "antis" bent upon resistance to every act of the government, determined to bring down the Constitution and their social betters. Ames was not alone in dismissing the integrity of his political opponents, or in relishing the opportunity to engage the enemies of government on a battlefield. It was a matter of honor with dishonorable men who cried out for "liberty" but meant "power" for themselves. Ames was prepared to duel them for the future of republican rule.[31]

Washington and Hamilton shared this view of the political world, although neither was so cynical and intolerant as Ames. In their eyes they tried to compromise, to be reasonable in dealing with the opposition faction and resisters to the excise law. Ames, of course, was more of an ideologue than either of these men and hence less willing to compromise on matters of order and fixed principle. Washington and Hamilton would do their best to amend the law in response to reasonable objections; they would even temper enforcement with patience and prior warning. In the end, however, theirs was an absolute dedication to the rule of law, to the maintenance of order, and to the circumscription of liberty. They, too, were friends of order.

Hamilton never shared the ideology of those who opposed the levying of internal taxes by remote central governments. In *Federalist* XXXVI he had addressed and dismissed arguments against granting such authority to the national legislature. He found no wisdom in Antifederalist fears. He could not agree that the House of Representatives would lack adequate knowledge of local conditions to lay equitable internal taxes because it was an insufficiently representative body. "Is the knowledge of local circumstances, as applied to taxation, a minute topographical acquaintance with all the mountains, rivers, streams, highways, and bypaths in each state," Hamilton asked rhetorically, "or is it a general acquaintance with its situation and resources, with the state of its agriculture, commerce, manufactures, with the nature of its products and consumptions, with the different degrees and kinds of its wealth, property, and industry?"[32]

Enlightened nations everywhere trusted individuals or committees to obtain necessary information on local conditions and to make judgments about fiscal policy. "Inquisitive and enlightened statesmen are everywhere deemed best qualified to make a judicious selection of the objects proper for revenue," Hamilton observed, "which is a clear indication, as far as the sense of mankind can have weight in the question, of the species of knowledge of local circumstances requisite to the purpose of taxation." Hamilton found no reason why such a system would not work in America; he saw no cause to deny the national government such a productive species of revenue on ideological grounds.[33]

By 1792 Hamilton had not changed his mind. He could still find "nothing in the nature of an *internal duty* on a *consumable* commodity more incompatible with liberty than in that of an external duty on a like commodity." According to the Secretary of the Treasury, "a doctrine which asserts that all duties of the former kind (usually denominated excises) are inconsistent with the genius of a free government is too violent, and too little reconcilable with the necessities of society to be true." In his opinion, such a philosophy would throw "an undue proportion of the public burden on the merchant and on the landholder."[34]

In every respect, Hamilton defined his views on taxation in opposition to the ideology shared by friends of liberty. They maintained a higher standard of representation, denied the authority of insufficiently representative bodies to levy "internal" taxes, and mistrusted the ability of "inquisitive and enlightened statesmen" to set policy for their less-informed inferiors. Opponents of the excise law *wanted* to put a heavier taxation burden on the merchant and the landowner. Since the government seemed to labor primarily for the interest of merchants and speculators, they should pay to finance it. The attractiveness of either ideology was largely dependent upon one's social and economic perspective. One would be far less likely to find an established international trader or large-scale eastern speculator in western lands who shared the political values of the friends of liberty. We cannot be surprised that the small distillers, laborers, tenants, and small farmers who populated the frontier lacked the same dedication to maintenance of the status quo displayed by the friends of order. It was ideology *and* interest that fused to create a truly volatile controversy. It is ideology *and* interest that help to explain the dynamics of conflict.

Dedication to Court or Country ideologies was not a blind allegiance to the century-old politics of Great Britain. The Court and Country positions displayed a semblance, but not an identity, to their earlier British counterparts. The American Country opposition shared its progenitor's preference for militias over standing armies, limited revenues, local administration, small government, extinction of the debt, and frequent elections. They went farther than their British predecessors in their desire to expand the meaning of representation and participation of the common man in the political sphere. They were less dedicated to "public order" than their British counterparts. Indeed, as argued here, degree of dedication to liberty or order was a defining characteristic of America's Country and Court factions during the 1790s. This was not true for the earlier British groups.[35]

The American factions also parted ways on the issue of internal taxes, a controversy which also had parallels in British politics, as in the case of Walpole's excise and Bute's cider tax. The Country opposition still expressed in the 1790s, as some Americans had in 1765 and 1787, a strong ideological opposition to remote central governments levying internal taxes. Court politicians thought such an ideological stance on representation and taxation entirely out of place under the republican government of the United States.

America's Court party would have liked to establish a permanent army and a permanent debt. Also like their British predecessors, they favored restriction of the democratic elements of government. One Congressman for every 40,000 rather than 30,000 constituents would better fit their principles. Maintenance of public order, tightening the reins of central government, seemed to them the essential tasks of administration. The greatest threat foreseen by the friends of order came from below, from ignorant masses, not from ministers of state or beneficiaries of government patronage.

Friends of order accused their opponents of being shackled to the shopworn ideas of the past, of being slaves to the prejudices of unenlightened European peasants. Federalists saw themselves as men of the future, able and willing to adapt old practices—i.e., excises—to new conditions. They saw themselves as progressive, Enlightenment figures who could learn from mistakes of their ancestors and modify their economic principles to fit changing times. In truth, of course, both friends of liberty and friends of order stitched their ideas from a complex array of timeworn fabrics—wisdom, fear, and prejudice—and more modern threads of each. The friends of liberty heralded the nineteenth-century's commitment to individual freedom; they trumpeted the triumph of the common man and longed for the unrestrained freedom to expand across the space of the continent as fast as their oxen could carry them. In this sense the friends of order were much more backward-looking, more fearful of trends unloosed by the Revolution. They waged a battle to restore the hierarchical order of patriarchal pasts. In the short run, however, and over specific issues, the victory of either was by no means secure.[36]

These were not absolute standards endorsed by all members of Federalist or Republican factions. They were points on spectrums of dedication to the principles of liberty and order within each sphere of thought. Men like George Logan and Fisher Ames represented extremes, but in the end, priority of liberty or order within a hierarchy of political principles represented a fundamental division between two radically different perceptions of the political world. As much as any domestic issue of Washington's presidency, the excise controversy fell into this ideological chasm. Like the Stamp Act, the whiskey excise produced a simultaneous challenge to ideology and interest and thus created a truly volatile situation. It served to divide East against West, city against country, settled versus wilderness societies, mercantile versus agricultural interests, in a way few other issues could. These divisions already existed; the excise debate revealed long-festering wounds from past and continuing controversies. They were disagreements of importance to people on either side—to their politics, their morals, their purses, and their ways of life.[37]

Chapter Nine

ALTERNATIVE PERSPECTIVES

On August 5, 1793, Philadelphia doctor Benjamin Rush visited the sick child of his friend Dr. Hodge. Rush found the boy running "a fever of the bilious kind." The physician's ministry—primarily bleeding the patient and prescribing a variety of purgatives—was for nought, and the youngster's illness "terminated (with a yellow skin) in death" two days later. On the 6th of August, Rush was called to the home of Thomas Bradford, whose wife also suffered with a bilious fever, but the symptoms "were so acute as to require two bleedings and several successive doses of physic." Eventually, Mrs. Bradford recovered, but for some time thereafter, "her eyes and face were of a yellow color."

On successive days Rush treated several more patients, who shared a range of symptoms—constipation, dull pain in the right side, loss of appetite, flatulency, perverted taste, a burning sensation in the stomach, headache, a dull, watery, yellow or red eye, dim and imperfect vision, hoarseness of voice, sore throat, alternating moods—from depression to giddiness—moist palms, and drenching night sweats. What most struck the physician upon entering the sick room was the patient's face. "The eyes were sad," Rush recorded in his notebook, "watery, and so inflamed in some cases as to resemble two balls of fire. Sometimes they had a most brilliant or ferocious appearance. A redness or yellowness in them was nearly universal. . . . The face was suffused with blood . . . and the whole countenance was downcast and clouded."

The son of Mrs. McNair seemed to respond when Rush "purged him plentifully" with salts and cream of tartar, and took ten ounces of blood from his arm. Four days later, though, the patient suffered a hemorrhage from the nose, and died soon after. Mrs. Palmer's two children were struck down with the fever, one on the 7th and the other on the 15th of the month, but both recovered. Mrs. Leaming also got better, but Peter Aston on the 18th and Peter Le Maigre on August 19th expired after several days of acute symptoms, and Rush began to suspect something more than the sporadic cases of fever that Philadelphia often experienced in summer months. He started visiting the dead as well as the dying, and noted the "deep yellow color within a few minutes—in some skin became purple, and in others black. . . . Some putrefied in a short time after their dissolution. . . . Many discharged large quantities

of black matter from the bowels, and others blood from the nose,
mouth, and bowels after death."

Now Rush was sure; it was the yellow fever, and an epidemic was
sweeping the city. Comparing notes with other doctors, the plague's
chronicler discovered that nine Philadelphians had succumbed on Au-
gust 1, twelve on the 7th, eleven on the 13th, twenty-four on the 29th,
and many more on the days in between. Ninety-six perished on Septem-
ber 24; 102 on October 9; and 119 on the single day of October 11. By
November 9, when the siege had all but ended, over 4000 were dead
from a population of about 55,000.

The result, not surprisingly, was panic in the streets. Ultimately,
virtually all who were not confined to the city by poverty, or their
ministrations to the sick and dying, fled the scene. At its height 6000
were ill with the fever at one time. The epidemic became "the most
appalling collective disaster that had ever overtaken an American city."
For over a century thereafter Philadelphians remembered the summer
and fall of 1793 for "the worst, the most frightening, the very classic of
plagues."[1]

OTHER FEVERS, of political rather than physiological sorts, also
infected Philadelphia during 1792 and 1793. Domestic and international
intrigues heated the exchanges between national politicians in an un-
healthy way. Not surprisingly, conflict over the excise was both a symp-
tom and a cause of this political malady. But the government's attention
to anti-excise unrest was distracted during much of 1793 while officials
faced what seemed to be even more serious threats to the health of the
body politic.

Although he denied the worth of any ideological arguments against
the excise, Alexander Hamilton was quite willing to consider reasonable
amendments to the law. Practical-minded man that he was, the Treasury
Secretary approached enforcement of the excise with an eagerness to be
flexible and to compromise in light of experience. Ultimately, he was
concerned that collections operate efficiently, fairly, and profitably. In
the short run, he believed it "preferable to weaken the efficacy" of
specific clauses of the excise act rather than "give just cause of complaint
of the rigorous execution of the law in a particular in which it is improvi-
dent in its provision."[2]

Uniformity of practices seemed the first step toward smooth operation. Instructions issued by the Treasury department to collectors were
extremely detailed. The first set of printed directions in 1791 ran to
eighteen pages and included a section-by-section interpretation of the
law. Identical hydrometers were issued to guarantee consistent mea-
surements. Uniform stamps for kegs, buildings, and stills soon followed.
Directions on enforcement included definitions of terms, the exact oaths
to be administered, and even the appropriate abbreviations of Christian

names on forms. Hamilton and Tench Coxe began execution of the law with striking efficiency and attention to detail.[3]

In the first year of enforcement Hamilton wanted to forestall as much criticism as possible. He hoped to avoid conflict between collectors and distillers who honestly misunderstood the law. In this way perhaps he could disarm some of the critics of administration policy by demonstrating that their worst fears about tax collectors were ill-founded. Flexibility should help minimize "inconveniences" to distillers and importers of alcoholic beverages. Hamilton believed that the gravest threats to the success of the law might come from the impolitic acts of overzealous collectors, and he took great pains to prevent confrontations. He even instructed tax men to forbear prosecuting distillers when their illegal actions "proceeded from ignorance of the law." He preferred "relaxation" of controversial provisions rather than creating resentment at rigorous execution. He advocated "due care" and argued for sympathy to the *intentions* of those who failed to conform at first.[4]

As early as December 1791, in his "Report on Manufactures," Hamilton recommended to Congress several modifications, including lowering the tax on domestically distilled alcoholic beverages to make them even more competitive with foreign products. Again, and in much greater detail, he reported on March 6, 1792, about problems of enforcement. Hamilton's statement was in response to an order of Congress. The House had given the Secretary all of the numerous anti-excise petitions it had received during 1791 and thrust upon him the burden for responding to these remonstrances.[5]

In the report, Hamilton first addressed himself to the ideological issues associated with internal taxes and protection of liberty. He did this by dismissing the fears of petitioners as unreasonable. Other objections, however, seemed more rational. Some petitioners, for example, believed that the 1791 tax law "by laying a smaller *additional* duty on foreign spirits than the duty on homemade spirits, has a tendency to discourage the manufacture of the latter." This was the kind of practical dollars-and-cents argument Hamilton appreciated, and he took it seriously. "This objection merits consideration," he reported to Congress, "and as far as it may appear to have foundation ought to be obviated." He was convinced by the argument of a New York distiller to recommend a one-cent-per-gallon reduction in the domestic excise and a two-cent-per-gallon increase on imported spirits.[6]

The Secretary also responded favorably to complaints that the inspection system threatened the "secrets or mysteries" of production. To protect distillers, Hamilton agreed that they should be forewarned of inspections and have the option of closing their operations to officers during any two hours of the day. Finally, among the "reasonable" requests for change was that of large New York distillers of domestic Geneva, who believed that the marking of casks prejudiced the public against their product. It seems that Americans preferred foreign Geneva and so merchants tried to hide the origins of native spirits. Treasury stamps gave away the liquor's domestic origins, and made it hard to sell. Hamilton reasoned that "if the want of a distinction between foreign and home made spirits were an occasion of fraud upon consumers, it would be a reason for continuing it, but as far as such a distinction gives operation to a mere prejudice, favorable to a foreign and injurious to a domestic manufacture, it furnishes a reason for abolishing it." So much for truth in advertising! The Treasury department would promote the efforts of distillers to prevent Americans from exercising yet another of their silly prejudices.[7]

Other objections to the law utterly failed to impress Hamilton. Small distillers complained that the operation of the law discriminated against them to the advantage of larger businesses. Hamilton reported that "it is objected that the duty by being laid in the first instance upon the distiller, instead of the consumer, makes a larger capital necessary to carry on the business." He dismissed the argument out-of-hand. The law extended credits for six to nine months on the quantities distilled. In other cases the duty was charged on the capacity of a still and collected only once every six months. According to Hamilton, then, "sufficient time is . . . allowed to raise the duty from the sale of the article, which supersedes the necessity of a greater capital." Smaller distillers also maintained that the law's requirement "to keep an account from day to day of the quantity of spirits distilled is . . . a hardship and impossible to be complied with." This complaint offended Hamilton's sense of good business practices. If they did not each day take "the trouble of setting down in the evening the work of the day in a book," they really ought to. He was willing to amend the forms to make them even easier to understand, but could find no merit in the complaints of such unbusinesslike businessmen.[8]

These were the objections of "a general nature" (those from numerous sources in geographically dispersed regions) that had reached Congress. Hamilton considered them all in his report and, in his eyes, showed great flexibility in answering "reasonable" complaints. He also responded, with much less sympathy, to remonstrances "of a local complexion," those arguing that the excise discriminated unfairly against the West. He addressed the petition from the Pittsburgh assembly of August 1791. Its signers had argued that "circumstance and the scarcity of cash combine to render the tax in question unequal, oppressive, and particularly distressing" to settlers hundreds of miles away from eastern markets. Hamilton did not deny that the tax might be less fair to some regions. "It may be safely affirmed," he argued in response, "to be impracticable to devise a tax which shall operate with exact equality upon every part of the community. Local and other circumstances will inevitably create disparities more or less great." Of all taxes that the

Secretary could conceive, however, none operated more equally than a tax on consumption, and no commodity was "an article of more equal consumption" throughout the United States than distilled spirits. If the complaining counties were greater consumers of whiskey than other regions, it was, according to Hamilton, in "their interest to become less so. It depends on themselves by diminishing the consumption to restore equality." Anyway, other taxes bore more heavily on other areas. It all evened out in the end, Hamilton asserted. If they were obliged by transportation costs to convert grain to whiskey for sale in the East, the duty would ultimately be paid by consumers, not by producing frontiersmen. According to Hamilton, the westerners "will still pay only upon their own consumption."[9]

Finally, the argument about scarcity of money in the West seemed to Hamilton a false issue. He had "no evidence to satisfy his mind that a real scarcity of money will be found on experiment a serious impediment to the payment of the tax anywhere." Nonetheless, if Congress had evidence of such dearth of specie, Hamilton was willing to accept payment in kind, provided distillers were required to deliver their product to offices of inspection in each county. He thought such a procedure unwarranted, but would, of course, honor the decision of Congress. Exceptions to paying the tax at all owing to extreme local circumstances were out of the question. Such exemptions were expressly forbidden by the Constitution, which required uniformity of taxes throughout the nation.[10]

There was a pattern to what Hamilton saw as reasonable complaints about the excise in March 1792; there were also common elements in the petitions he dismissed as "inaccurate and misconceived." Hamilton's flexibility was prejudiced toward large, innovative distillers; he was less sympathetic to the small, seasonal operators who ran less businesslike affairs. The result of a policy that encouraged mass production was not only class and occupationally prejudiced legislation, but regional discrimination as well. Each of the petitions favored in Hamilton's report came from eastern distillers; indeed, each was from New York. The petitions were from individuals whose opinions Hamilton respected because they were successful businessmen and who, like the New York City petitioner Hendrick Doyer, appeared to the Treasury Secretary "likely to be well informed on the subject." Hamilton also displayed a lack of understanding about rural conditions. His unsympathetic attitude toward agrarian culture discriminated most harshly against frontier regions where the contrasts with cosmopolitan life were greatest. He so admired efficiency, and he was so personally accomplished in keeping accounts, that he harbored no tolerance at all for those less endowed with these traits. Hamilton lived in a metropolitan world where such qualities were the very stuff of success. He personally rose from obscurity on the strength of his dedication to detail. If businessmen could not meet the standard of practice dictated by large eastern mercantile con-

cerns, Hamilton believed they must change or justly suffer the consequences of failure.[11]

As a man of enterprise, Hamilton simply could not picture a social
structure that brought little or no cash at all to men who owned property
or who labored for others. It was partly a crisis of imagination that struck
eastern elites when they read the petitions of frontiersmen. And it was
partly inter-cultural incomprehension that afflicted relations between
East and West. The culture of drink itself had regional, ethnic, and class
dimensions that, although hazily understood by eastern elites, elicited
no sympathy from them. They ridiculed those differences. They dismissed alien behavior as irrational. Theirs was the dominant way of life.
They were right in the way they lived. Less educated, less wealthy, less
"American" frontiersmen must learn to conform to dominant patterns of
life, labor, and leisure.[12]

One historian has recently gone so far as to argue that it was the
intention of Hamilton and others who supported the excise to eliminate
inefficient country distillers and to centralize the business for the "alleged moral and economic benefits associated with these changes." A
conspiracy of this sort is difficult to document, if indeed such intent ever
was widespread or shared by Hamilton. It is clear, however, that the
legislation was perceived by small distillers to be the result of such a
conspiracy. It also seems likely that in its effects, whether intended or
not, the law actually did threaten the economic survival of those who
would not or could not expand their production and innovate in their
methods. And it also appears that commercial operators seized the opportunity to enhance their competitive advantage over small distillers.
According to western Pennsylvania Congressman Willian Findley, large
distillers "thought they could avail themselves of the [excise] law to
advantage, by running down the occupiers of small stills in disadvanta-
geous situations."[13]

Distillers who ran year-round operations and who were able to devote
time and capital to their business could actually gain a competitive
advantage over smaller producers as a result of the excise law. Producers
had the option either of paying nine cents per gallon on the actual
whiskey they distilled or of paying a fixed rate on the capacity of their
stills. Hamilton acknowledged in his report that by taking the latter
option "and using great diligence, the duty may in fact be reduced to six
cents per gallon." Since the stills of farmers tended to be smaller, less
efficient, and idle for most of the year, it would not benefit them to pay
a fixed rate on the capacity of the still. Only those who operated their
stills on a continuous basis could profit by this option and hence only
these larger and more innovative operations would be able to realize the
three-cent-per-gallon advantage described by the Secretary of the
Treasury.[14]

There was, then, an acknowledged prejudice built into the law against the farmer who once a year distilled his surplus grain into whiskey in a battered and inefficient still. In effect, although perhaps not consciously in intent, this bounty to innovative producers worked as a severe handicap more in the West—where many distillers were small farmers of this description—than in the East—where most distilleries were larger commercial concerns. It is easy to see why westerners saw the law, in this regard, as yet another piece of class, occupational, and regionally biased legislation. It would probably not be accurate, however, to jump with the western farmers to the conclusion that Hamilton and his eastern friends engaged in a conscious conspiracy to drive them into economic despondency. If that were the Treasury Secretary's intent, he could have listened to those eastern petitioners who wanted to eliminate entirely the option to pay the tax on only the whiskey actually produced rather than on the capacity of stills. Hamilton specifically rejected that suggestion in his report. He advised against such a prejudicial amendment of the law because it would create "great inequality, arising from unequal supplies of the material at different times and at different places, from the different methods of distillation practiced by different distillers, and from the different degrees of activity in the business which arise from capitals more or less adequate."[15]

Few, if any, frontiersmen read Hamilton's report or ever heard about his defense of their interests in this regard. What they knew was that if they paid the tax, those in their community who operated large stills would undersell them by as much as six cents per gallon. Most did not even own their own still; of those who did, most lacked the capital to introduce innovative techniques to their distilling practices. They recognized that the excise disrupted traditional patterns of exchange and made demands for cash that seldom reached their hands in a fundamentally barter economy. They saw how the law benefited the Nevilles and the Craigs, for example, wealthy western Pennsylvania families who operated stills with capacities of 600 gallons apiece. They saw these large distillers gaining a virtual monopoly on whiskey sales to the army. It was this sort of advantage that owners of stills with capacities of seventy-five gallons, forty gallons, or even less would attempt to counterbalance by collective action. To some marginal farmers—those who did not even own stills of their own—the law seemed even more oppressive. They paid one-half their grain to a large operator to distill their rye. The tax would then "be paid out of the farmer's part, which reduces the balance to less than one-third of the original quantity. If this is not an oppressive tax," one petitioner observed, "I am at a loss to describe what is so."[16]

The perspective from Hamilton's Philadelphia office was, of course, quite different. He knew how flexible he had tried to be in enforcing the law. He knew how he had defended the interests of rural distillers against the arguments of eastern petitioners. And he knew that Congress accepted all his suggestions for amending the law during the spring of

1792. Now the excise operated even more reasonably and to an even greater competitive advantage for domestic over imported spirits.

In light of his miscomprehensions of conditions in the West, it is easier to understand the Treasury Secretary's chagrin at continued resistance to the tax during the summer of 1792. It seemed to him that the government had shown every leniency, had made every compromise possible within the best interests of the nation. Ideological incomprehension, inter-regional prejudices, and personality would combine with this lack of understanding to determine the bellicose plans for armed enforcement of the excise and the proclamation issued by President Washington during the fall.

As 1792 drew to a close, it appeared that Washington and Hamilton had succeeded in breaking the back of the extra-legal, but peaceful, protest movement against the tax. They had utterly failed, however, to exact excise taxes from frontiersmen even in the test-case region of western Pennsylvania. And they had not snuffed out alternative means of direct action and protest against the excise. John Neville remained unable even to establish offices outside Pittsburgh throughout 1793. He could get no guarantee of protection from magistrates in Washington County even if he did find a suitable location. During June he communicated his frustration to George Clymer. "At all events," Neville wrote, "I will venture to say that the law will not be carried into execution until government find it convenient to make examples of some offenders. Every exertion that has hitherto been made by two or three . . . officers has been defeated. The delinquents have passed unpunished, and in fact triumphed over the officer." Without force to back up his efforts, Neville thought it unlikely that his district would produce any excise revenue. "It cannot be expected," Neville complained, "that people who have distilled spirits . . . in direct contradiction to the law will suffer an individual in a remote, unsettled quarter to make seizure of it." On the contrary, only "slight and insult" would ever be the consequence of his labors on the frontier unless the national government took a more active role in enforcement.[17]

Over the course of 1793 the slights and insults mounted against Neville and his collectors. At a meeting of the Washington County militia in June, "General Neville the excise man" was burned in effigy. According to Neville, about one hundred people gathered to express "a great deal of illiberal stuff against me and the law. They exposed it [the effigy] during the day and in the evening consigned it to the flames, regretting that it was not me instead of the effigy."[18]

Benjamin Wells suffered worse. During the spring a mob broke into his Fayette County house. Fortunately for Wells, he was not at home. The band terrorized his wife and children with threats to the family unless the collector resigned his office. Mrs. Wells thought she recognized some of the perpetrators, but no sheriff or magistrate would cooperate in prosecutions. On November 22 at about 2:00 a.m., six armed men again broke into Wells's home. Their faces were blackened and handkerchiefs covered the mouths of four of the intruders. Two aimed cocked pistols at the excise man. They demanded that Wells surrender his commission and all official books and papers related to his office. He refused. The men more forcefully displayed the two pistols to Wells and "swore that if he did not produce his said commission and books they would instantly put him to death." This caused Wells to fear for his life. He went into the next room, returned with the documents, and put them on the table. Several of the men demanded that he actually place the account books and commission in their hands. Again, he refused. This time the intruders acquiesced, but not before they ordered Wells to publish his resignation in the *Pittsburgh Gazette* within two weeks, "otherwise they would pay him another visit and would not leave one log upon another at his house."[19]

It was not their refusal to pay the excise tax that marked as unique the intruders to Wells's house or the crowd that burned Neville in effigy. During 1793 no excise revenues were flowing east from Kentucky or the western counties of North Carolina and Virginia. Two years after Congress had adopted this internal tax, frontiersmen in every state south of New York (except New Jersey and Delaware) still successfully resisted the law. Two other factors did, however, distinquish western Pennsylvania from other tax-resisting regions on the frontier. The first was discussed in Chapter Seven. This was the decision of Washington and Hamilton to single out the western counties of Pennsylvania as a test case of national law enforcement. The second related not to the degree of overt resistance to the law, but the stubborn support for the excise among a small, but influential group of the region's populace. William Findley explained this distinction to Governor Mifflin. "It is well known," Findley reported, "that in some counties, as well of Virginia as of Pennsylvania, men have not, and cannot be induced by any consideration to accept of the excise offices. In those counties there have been no riots nor threatening resolutions; but this arises from the perfect unanimity which subsists in the dislike to the law."[20]

In other words, western Pennsylvanians opposed the excise no more rabidly than other frontiersmen. In other regions, however, those who accepted offices as collectors were quickly discouraged from their tasks and no others would assume their duties. By late 1792 there were no inspectors or collectors of the excise willing to step foot in the northwestern counties of Virginia. The same was true in Kentucky and on the North Carolina frontier. Where no one tried to collect the tax, the unrest quickly subsided after an initial uproar, a few tarring and featherings, several petitions, and other actions to intimidate would-be collectors and demonstrate disdain for the excise. Western Pennsylvania looked like a special case only because the Treasury department repeat-

edly pushed the issue there and, perhaps even more importantly, because of John Neville.[21]

Neville's experiences, his wealth, and his opinions were unlike those
of his fellow western countrymen. His life was not that of the average
settler. Neville was born to Virginia planter society in 1731; he passed
his youth on his father's estate at the headwaters of the Occoquan River.
He served in Braddock's expedition and acquired a patent to 1000 acres
of land on Chartier's Creek for his service in Dunmore's War (1774).
Neville was commandant of Fort Pitt for the first two years of the
Revolution and then served with Washington at Trenton, Germantown,
Princeton, Monmouth, and was a winter soldier at Valley Forge. He
ultimately achieved the rank of brigadier-general in the Continental
Army and equipped a company of soldiers at his own expense. After the
war he settled on the first large estate in the Pittsburgh region, his
"Bower Hill."

This mansion (by frontier standards) was one of the first clapboard
houses built in the area, contrasting starkly with the rough-hewn hovels it
overlooked from a palatial summit. It was constructed of materials trans-
ported from the East and from Great Britain. Most of its furnishings were
imported from Europe. The interior walls were painted and papered.
Two dozen paintings in gilt frames also adorned the walls. The floors of
every room, hall, and stairway were carpeted. Five feather beds with
bedsteads provided accommodation for family and visitors. Eighteen
Windsor chairs were distributed about the house. Neville worked at "a
desk neatly finished with [the] best mounting." He told the time from an
eight-day clock, with a fine mahogany case. Maps of the world, a collection of guns and swords, and a library of indeterminate size complete the
picture of Neville's environs. He valued the house and contents at over
$5000, a far cry from the worth of most frontier quarters.[22]

Neville's ideas reflected the same contrast between his cosmopolitan
experiences and wealth, and those of his fellow frontiersmen. He opposed every regional independence movement on the frontier from 1776
onward and took it upon himself to act as informant to eastern political
leaders on schemes that came into his view. He favored restraint in
settlement of the frontier, with strong central control of immigration and
land sales by eastern-based governments. He disapproved of his neighbor's cruel and counterproductive assaults on local Indians. In Pennsylvania politics he was an "anti-constitutionalist," opposing the democratic
state constitution of 1776. In national politics he supported ratification of
the Constitution and became a devout Federalist. In every case, Neville's position opposed that of most of his neighbors. His array of experiences in war and politics; his wide travels, exposure to cosmopolitan
life, fashions, and ideas; and his comparative wealth all gave him immense self-confidence when it came to dealing with his less-endowed
neighbors. He was brave, principled, and stubborn. He believed him-

self superior in judgment and capacity to those around him, and he was unyielding in his dedication to fulfilling his responsibilities as patriarch of Bower Hill and as regional inspector of the excise. Whether dealing with his slaves, his tenants, or other inferiors who came within his purview, Neville confidently insisted on pursuing his own lights.[23]

Without this one man—John Neville—as unrelenting symbol and active agent of all the contrasts and conflicts between cosmopolitan East and frontier West that the excise represented, the timing and the very nature of the confrontation in western Pennsylvania would have been different. A man of Neville's stubborn resolve was essential for the Treasury department to keep the excise issue alive in the western country for three years after passage of the tax. What made matters even worse within the context of western Pennsylvania politics was that Neville had originally opposed the excise. He was a member of the Pennsylvania assembly when that body adopted a resolution condemning the tax in 1791. Neville voted with the majority on that occasion. Shortly thereafter he accepted the office of excise inspector. According to William Findley, this quick turn-around by Neville caused his neighbors to believe that the inspector was giving "up his principles for a bribe, and bartering the confidence they had in him for money, and were the more irritated at his speaking contemptuously of their good opinion, which he had been formerly so solicitous to obtain." A long-standing prejudice against salaried officers of government—an inheritance of radical Whig principles—also operated in the region. And a rumor circulated about Neville that confirmed local fears about the corruption caused by such offices. "The people were the more irritated against him," according to Findley, "on being informed that when he was told that he would forfeit the good opinion of his neighbors . . . [Neville] answered [that] he did not regard their good will. He had got an independent salary of 600 a year."[24]

Whether it was true, the story had its effect. People who had once respected Neville now thought him corrupt. He became a catalyst for mounting opposition to the law, a symbol of its hydra-headed threat to the liberties and economy of the region. Neville and the collectors who served under him became the visible embodiments of the growing class distinctions felt by many who lived in the western country. Long-term social-structural changes had left an increasing number of residents landless and with no real hope for acquiring enough property in the region to become self-sufficient farmers. The excise controversy presented an occasion and symbolic personages against whom the frustrations of poverty could be directed. When some of the most wealthy residents of the region—the Nevilles, the Craigs, John and Benjamin Wells, Kirkpatrick, and others—defended the law, settlers made connections between wealth, politics, and their own economic plight. Assaults on property became an important dimension of excise protest.

The stage was set, then, for the drama of armed conflict anticipated by Neville, Clymer, and Hamilton. From the perspective of Philadelphia, and from Bower Hill, the national government had displayed patience. It had amended the tax in response to reasonable complaints. Its officers had tried repeatedly to explain and enforce the excise. And those who broke the law had been warned of the probable consequences by Washington's proclamation, by Hamilton's emissary George Clymer, and by local officials including John Neville and Benjamin Wells. To men who had sworn to uphold the Constitution, the situation now justified harsher measures. As they saw it, duty required them to take additional steps to enforce the laws.

The view from log huts on the banks of the Monongahela was different. Small farmers, sometime distillers, and the landless poor found the national government grossly unfair. It had adopted an internal tax hostile to their economic interests and to their way of life. The government had been unyielding in its attempts to exact the excise from them, seemingly ignoring their petitions and the harsh conditions under which they lived. The national government had failed to crush the Indian menace in their region and had neglected to secure open trade on the Mississippi, the only two demands on its offices made by frontier settlers. In return it expected money from people who had none under a regressive tax that favored the rich while it handicapped the only widely successful local industry. Life was becoming even harsher for impoverished frontiersmen, and government demands seemed a cruel joke to pile on top of the other frustrations of western life. They were desperate men grasping for someone to lash out against. As the massacre of the Moravian Indians had shown, any Indian would do when settlers needed to vent their anger at the cruelties of an elusive enemy. Tax collectors were similar sitting ducks for local people who had a wide range of scores to settle. Wells and Neville felt the wrath, as had others—Graham, Johnson, Roseberry, Wilson, and Connor—associated with the hated tax. They would also suffer the lash of local hostility toward invisible landlords, merchants, and politicians from the East who seemed to the settlers largely responsible for the bleakness of frontier life.

The government did not respond on cue, however, when the behavior denounced by the President's proclamation of 1792 continued the following year. One might have expected reprisals to the "slights and insults" suffered by Neville and his collectors during 1793, but no proclamations, no warnings, no army issued from Philadelphia. The excise remained uncollected on the frontier, and small farmers were no more willing than ever to surrender their liberties or the fruits of their labor to despised agents of the central government.

Other issues absorbed the attention of government officials during 1793. Insults to national authority in western Pennsylvania paled by comparison with threats posed by other enemies of public order. Beginning in 1793 and continuing for the next three years Europe was constantly at war. On January 21, Louis XVI was beheaded. Ten days later France declared war on Great Britain, Holland, and Spain. The Jacobins began a "Reign of Terror" in which more than 20,000 traitors, aristocrats, and alleged enemies of the French Revolution were executed. In June, Britain declared France under blockade, ordered the seizure of all neutral vessels carrying goods to France, and drastically broadened the traditional limits of blockades by including wheat and other foodstuffs on its list of contraband articles. Britain also subsidized a treaty between Portugal and Algiers in hopes of freeing Portugal to wage war on France. Each of these twists in European affairs posed profound consequences for the United States. The byproduct of Britain's machinations between Portugal and Algiers, for example, was the freeing of Algerine pirates to plague Atlantic shipping. Americans interpreted this secondary result as a primary aim of Britain. Interference in American trade also contributed to straining relations between the two nations and promoted sentiment in the United States for another war with the British.[25]

Coincidentally, Britain and Spain renewed their efforts to organize Indians on the frontier during 1793. Coming at such a time of crisis, however, the maneuvers of foreign nations on America's borders appeared to be the opening volley in yet another struggle for European hegemony over North America. When the American governor of the Northwest Territory heard that the Spanish were "arming themselves on the upper parts of the Mississippi," he and officials back in Philadelphia feared the worst. Superimposed on the European war, every move of Britain and Spain seemed purposefully aimed at drawing the United States into hostilities.[26]

In fact, American affairs were of little concern to the British Foreign Office at this time. Britain was basically oblivious to any repercussions its actions might have on its former colonies. British officials in Canada, however, were obsessed with fears about the intentions of the United States. They believed that the Americans would use the occasion of European war to attack the frontier forts and ultimately Quebec. Governor Simcoe of upper Canada believed that American General Anthony Wayne drilled troops on the frontier in preparation for an offensive campaign against Detroit. Simcoe organized his defenses to meet the invasion and formulated plans for a counter-assault. Friction between New York settlers and Canadian woodcutters seemed to Lord Dorchester, Governor-General of Canada, part of an orchestrated attempt by the United States to provoke war. He connected these incursions with Wayne's advance and perceived a coordinated policy of aggression by the United States against Canada.

Anticipating all-out war, Simcoe now plotted an offensive campaign to annex the American frontier. He advocated an alliance with Indian tribes and with Spain to separate settlements west of the Allegheny ridge from the Union. A strong showing against America's army in the West would undoubtedly lead to widespread defection of the frontiersmen. According to Simcoe, "two such glorious communications with the Ocean as the St. Lawrence and the Mississippi and the occupying of Pensacola would make the state of Kentucky look up to . . . [Great Britain] for union and alliance, as commerce cannot traverse the Appalachian Mountains to get to them; they must therefore experience great disadvantages if they continue an American state."[27]

British officials rejected Simcoe's advice, and Lord Dorchester disavowed any connection with such impolitic schemes. American officials knew only of the plots, however, and expected to see them hatch. Washington and Hamilton probably shared Simcoe's belief that about 80 percent of the frontiersmen were disloyal to the United States. From Philadelphia it looked as though Spain and Britain were plotting war and that these foreign powers might be supported by disloyal westerners. The threat of another international war for the continent seemed imminent to the President, and the outcome by no means assured.

Other threats also besieged President Washington. For the first time, he was personally attacked in the press. Never before had the hero of America's Revolution been so publicly assaulted as "infamously niggardly" in his private affairs, or as a "most horrid swearer and blasphemer" despite his apparent piety. This campaigner in so many wars was wounded to see himself described as ignorant, a man educated only in "gambling, reveling, horseracing, and horsewhipping." The celebration of his birthday, for years past an event of public rejoicing, was now being ridiculed as a "monarchical farce." The French Revolution seemed responsible. The atmosphere that promoted the assassination of Louis, the anarchy and terror sweeping France, was blowing west and American authorities were not immune to the effluvia carried by this wind. To Washington it all seemed a personal affront. The newspaper stories, the establishment of eleven "Democratic" societies, and disobedience to laws of the nation seemed to the President part of an international conspiracy against law and order. Privately, Washington suffered from these assaults "more than any person I ever yet met with," according to Thomas Jefferson. He longed for an opportunity to silence his enemies, those so-called friends of liberty who sought the downfall of America's constitutional republicanism.[28]

The arrival on American shores of French Ambassador Edmund Charles Genet seemed yet another dimension of an international conspiracy against order. Genet's schemes were viewed by the President within the context of international war and other treacherous spillovers from the French Revolution. Genet's efforts to raise an Armée du Mississippi, an Armée des Floridas, to commission privateers, and to recruit volunteers to aid his nation's cause seemed particularly threatening because of the already tense situation on the frontier. His efforts seemed to exploit stresses within American society. The irascible French emissary created a profound stir in American politics and occupied much of the energies of government officials from April through July.[29]

The gravest threat to the government in 1793 came not from political societies or newspaper attacks on the President; it did not come from the revolution in France or Genet's mission to the United States; and it was not the result of British blockades, Algerine pirates, Indians, or Canadian and Spanish plots to dismember the frontier. Although all of these problems combined to distract the administration from other domestic concerns, it was the yellow fever epidemic of the summer and fall that brought the operations of government to a virtual standstill. The plague was a personal, communal, and civic disaster. City government broke down in September, and the national government almost ceased to function. Hamilton came down with the fever and, enjoying one luxury of the rich in such dismal times, retired to a New York mansion to convalesce. Six Treasury clerks took the fever and left the city. Comptroller of the Treasury Oliver Wolcott tried in vain to preserve the routines of the department. With only one clerk, with few other officers of the government in the city, and with even fewer people willing to enter Philadelphia or receive messengers from its environs, there was little anyone could do to continue operations. Eventually even Wolcott left. President Washington also abandoned the town since his heroic presence could not alone run the nation or halt the panic of plague. He did his best, however, to transact business from his Mount Vernon plantation.[30]

As a result of the international challenges between February and August, and as a result of the epidemic that emptied Philadelphia of almost all who could afford to leave, the western country plummeted down the list of national concerns. Other assaults seemed more threatening, other insults more demeaning, and a plague more injurious to the continued existence of republican government in the United States. Western Pennsylvanians misunderstood the inaction of the federal government during 1793, just as they had misunderstood its earlier intentions. They miscalculated the resolve of Washington, Hamilton, and others in authority to enforce the law and to make an example of one small outpost of wilderness life. It was a crucial miscalculation, one that would lead to even greater suffering than inhabitants of the region already endured. It was a miscalculation born of the different perspectives of West and East.

Chapter Ten

FEDERALISM BESIEGED

John Neville actually succeeded in establishing an office of excise in-spection in June 1794. John Lynn agreed to sublease part of his house to the excise inspector. Neville's joy at this breakthrough was tempered by fear that the office would not last and, indeed, not long after the arrangement became known, Lynn was visited by a group of about twelve armed men with blackened faces. Lynn barricaded himself up-stairs and refused to come down to face the intruders. They promised Lynn that his person and house would be spared injury if he sur-rendered peacefully. When Lynn complied, the men seized him, threat-ened to hang him, and finally, after abusing him further, carted Lynn off to a remote section of the forest where they cut off his hair, stripped him naked, and tarred and feathered him. They made him swear never again to suffer an excise office to operate in his home and never to reveal their names to any person associated with the national government. When Lynn had submitted to all their demands, the crowd tied him to a tree and left him there, alone, over night. The next morning someone "found" Lynn still naked and lashed to the tree, and released him.

Battered and humiliated, Lynn kept his word, but was personally ruined, nonetheless. According to Neville, "he was an innkeeper and lived in a rented house. His custom has left him, his landlord ordered him off, and the people of the town are for immediately banishing him." It was a sure lesson to Lynn and any other men who might consider succoring the excise law within their premises. It was another defeat for Neville's efforts to enforce the law in Pennsylvania's four western counties.

Benjamin Wells was no more successful with the excise office he tem-porarily established in the Westmoreland County home of Philip Regan. The house and its occupant were besieged by armed assailants several times during June. The attackers were repulsed, but the office never functioned as an agency of excise collection. During the same month, incendiaries burned the barns of people who had volunteered as wit-nesses against perpetrators of anti-excise violence; the vandals were never identified.[1]

THE SPECTER of yellow fever faded for Philadelphians in early 1794. Only memories of the horror plagued residents as politicians arrived in January for the new session of Congress. The visage of war, however, had materialized to supplant the terror of disease in the minds of federal officials. War fever now swept all before it and threatened even greater mortality than the plague.

The moment seemed decisive for the American government and people. "In every direction in which this country is to be viewed," British consul Phineas Bond reported, "its situation must be deemed exceedingly critical—critical in respect to the powers of war—critical as to the continuance of peace—and immensely so as to its constitution and government." Politicians of all persuasions shared Bond's view of the crucial juncture the nation now had reached. "You see the situation of our country," Congressman Francis Preston informed his Virginia constituents, "without money, and on the one hand tormented by the savages of the West; in the East our commerce [is] laid prostrate, and our citizens carried into cruel captivity by the Algerines; and moreover we are daily injured and insulted by that proud and vindictive nation, Great Britain, with whom a war is almost inevitable." According to New Englander Fisher Ames, "if John Bull [i. e., Great Britain] is a blockhead, and puts himself on his pride to maintain what he has done, and should refuse reparation, it will, I think, be war."[2]

What Great Britain had done to provoke the ire of Americans was to invoke the "Rule of War of 1756" and implement new Orders in Council on November 6, 1793. British war ships were directed to seize every neutral vessel carrying supplies to and from the French West Indies. The orders were then kept secret until late December, when hundreds of American merchant vessels were plying the Caribbean trade. Then, in a spectacular raid, the British fleet captured over 250 ships and towed them into British ports. Over half were condemned as wartime prizes by British admiralty courts.

Almost simultaneous with reports of the attack on America's merchant fleet, news reached Philadelphia of hostile British maneuvers on the frontier. The establishment of Fort Miamis on the Maumee seemed yet another "serious aggression on the sovereignty, and an invasion of the territory of the United States." Philadelphians also now learned that Governor Dorchester of Canada had made an "inflammatory address" to a delegation of western tribes on February 10. Americans East and West already linked the renewed fervor of Indian assaults in the western country with British aggression. When the attacks began in the summer and fall of 1793, after a period of relative calm, Americans were inclined to blame Britain for supplying and encouraging the Indians. Now they had proof. The arming of Detroit for war and rumors of an Anglo-Spanish alliance on the frontier also flamed the fires of Anglophobia in the United States.[3]

The Spanish, too, seemed intent on a frontier war. Ambassador Jaudenes believed that "the present situation in which we find ourselves in this country is critical. It is necessary that we take decisive action quickly." This included attempts to negotiate a treaty between the Creeks and Cherokees in order to enlist the tribes against settlers on the southwest frontier. Carondolet, Spanish governor of Louisiana, also dispatched an emissary to Canada soliciting an Anglo-Spanish alliance against the United States. By late spring British Governor Simcoe in Detroit was asserting confidently the ability of Britain and Spain to annex Kentucky and the other "colonies" of the United States west of the Alleghenies. Such plans seemed credible to British and Spanish officials in North America; they appeared frighteningly possible to those in Philadelphia who heard rumors, if not details, of frontier intrigues.[4]

In response, Federalists advocated a 10,000-man army and authorizing President Washington to activate 80,000 militiamen. Some of the more bellicose members of Congress proposed a navy to defend American shipping on the high seas. Provisional war taxes were also recommended to finance these proposals.

At such a moment of national distress, amid the building tensions of preparation for war, administration officials had little patience with domestic unrest. In the face of international threats to the sovereignty of the nation, internal disorders appeared even more provocative than in earlier years. The fate of the republic again appeared to hang on every decision, just as during the period immediately following the Revolution. Each challenge to the established order seemed to portend cataclysm. Indeed, Washington's address of 1783 was being reprinted eleven years later; the spring and summer of 1794 was again a "moment to establish or ruin the national character forever."[5]

Hamilton felt personally besieged. British assaults on American shipping resulted in reduced trade, less income from the impost, and hence a deficit in the budgetary system he had so carefully designed. Hamilton also came under attack by his political enemies in early 1794. They now had evidence that he had violated the law, reallocating funds without an executive order. An embarrassing congressional investigation resulted, an inquiry conducted also in the press by political foes who reveled in the cloud that hung over Hamilton's public career. The shortfall in revenues could be remedied by new taxes that Hamilton proposed during the spring. Counter-assault on his political enemies was a more difficult problem; for now, forbearance was necessary.

Hamilton's response to the projected budget deficit—the Revenue Act of 1794—appeared before Congress as a series of tax bills during the spring. At the heart of these proposals were new excises on snuff, sugar, and carriages. A stamp tax, a tax on stock transfers, and an increase in tonnage duties were also warmly debated in the House. Again, just as with the excise of 1791, the Treasury Secretary was advocating internal taxes. This time, however, the proposed excises struck at the interests of urban manufacturers from the East. Many of those affected by these excises were as wealthy and as cosmopolitan as the Federalist politicians who voted for the taxes. Not surprisingly, then, their response to these economic threats was less violent and, ultimately, more successful than the efforts of poor, rural, frontier farmers and laborers to overturn the excise on distilled spirits. Urban easterners confined their opposition to economic issues and seldom attacked the taxes on ideological grounds. "If the system of excise is not early checked," a typical protest averred, "it will hamstring, in turn, every manufacture in America." This was not an attack on "internal" taxes, and the manufacturers seldom resorted to localist doctrines.[6]

This is not to say that some of the same political instincts were not at work in the opposition to the excises of 1791 and 1794. The Pennsylvania Democratic Society in Philadelphia believed all "excise systems to be oppressive [and] hostile to the liberties of the country." Manufacturers also mustered a distinctively localist argument in a petition to the Pennsylvania Assembly. As "the more immediate guardian of the rights and liberties of the citizens of Pennsylvania," the assembly could justly censure the national government's actions. The memorialists remembered how the state legislature had indicted the national government for adopting the earlier excise. They hoped the assembly would again reprimand Congress; but the state politicians ignored their protests.[7]

Nonetheless, the ideological postures of wealthy snuff and sugar manufacturers are unconvincing. The localist ideology affected by the manufacturers appeared less frequently, was expressed less heatedly, and, even then, was used only to bolster economic grievances that were the focus of their protests. Localist pleas, although perhaps genuine, were certainly secondary to economic concerns. Indeed, they appear as afterthoughts to compendious lists that attempted to gather every available arrow for the manufacturers' quiver of protests. Cultural, class, regional, and perhaps even ideological differences separated those in the East and West who opposed excise taxes. No riots rocked Philadelphia over the new excises; indeed there were few attempts to organize popular opposition to these taxes. Philadelphia manufacturers apparently disapproved of extra-legal protest; they harbored no sympathy for the direct actions of western Pennsylvanians. Their anger was confined within the sanctioned bounds of the electoral process. The excises became the central issue of several congressional elections in Philadelphia during the fall, and the manufacturers were largely successful in campaigns for anti-excise candidates.[8]

The new snuff and sugar taxes were approved by large majorities in both houses during the first nine days of June, and operations began shortly thereafter without significant incident. According to James Madison they were part of the administration's plan "to supplicate for peace, and, under the uncertainty of success, to prepare for war by taxes and troops." John Jay was dispatched to Britain as the supplicant for peace. Before he sailed, Great Britain had already repealed the Orders in Council of November 1793 and issued new orders permitting direct trade between the United States and the French West Indies.[9]

Plans to prepare for war met with staunch opposition when the act "to increase the Military Force of the United States" came before the House. There was no war declared; Congress had not been asked to declare one. Why, then, inquired those who feared for liberty, should the constitutional separation of powers be muddled by Congress abdicating its sole authority to raise armies? Madison thought it unwise to grant the President permission to arm over 10,000 men on his own initiative. He saw no "immediate prospect of a war as could induce the House to violate the Constitution." Madison believed it a wise principle "to make one branch of government raise an army, and another conduct it." He thought that Congress should resist the administration's repeated attempts to establish a standing army. Other Congressmen were even more suspicious of the administration's intent. John Smilie objected that "there must be some other purpose for these troops than any that had been acknowledged; for he could see none." William B. Giles also "was at a loss to discover against whom these ten thousand men were to be employed." Such suspicions contributed to the defeat by a vote of 50 to 32 of the administration's plan to ensure the defense of order.[10]

Madison and other "Republicans" favored economic reprisals against Britain rather than preparations for war. They believed that trade restrictions—embargoes—on the importation of British goods would reflect the nation's anger and have a better chance of success than armed encounters. Embargoes would be less costly in lives and dollars; they would obviate the need for greater taxation burdens on the people. The response to external threats thus became a "party" issue. The administration could not count on a unified national effort to meet its European foes; and the domestic conflict over the European war exacerbated the crisis atmosphere.

Pennsylvania's Governor Mifflin recognized the tension in Philadelphia's air. He perceived the paranoia provoked by external threats on the high seas, fears of European-inspired turmoil on the frontier, and the rage of party in Philadelphia. Mifflin tried to warn his fellow citizens of the probable consequences of domestic unrest in such a political climate. For people to challenge the national government at this moment, "to neglect the natural and safe resource of a free people for the purpose of protecting themselves and of repelling the injuries offered to their rights, is virtually to invite the use of those artificial expedients which have been fated, and must ever be dangerous to republican freedom and independence." Nonetheless, inhabitants of Pennsylvania's southwestern frontier continued to assert their displeasure with the policies of the Washington administration. They continued in 1794 to challenge the right, the authority, and the power of the central government to collect an internal tax in the hinterlands of rural America. Again, the protests took various forms, all of them threatening to defenders of public order.[11]

Extra-legal organizations, such as the democratic societies springing up around the country and the representative assemblies that met at Pittsburgh in 1791 and 1792, especially aroused the wrath of Federalist officials. To them it seemed that "self-created societies" were meant to challenge constitutional institutions. They appeared to pose a unique threat to order by overseeing, chastising, and even supplanting the normal functions of lawful authority. The Mingo Creek Society, founded in western Pennsylvania on February 28, 1794, qualified on all counts. It served as a proto-political organization for nominating candidates to public office. It operated as an extra-legal court of equity among members, intended to circumvent the more costly, complex, and time-consuming processes of established tribunals. And, it acted as a political machine, as an "engine of election" in the words of Hugh Henry Brackenridge, for county offices and state representatives. It was a novel sort of political society in America, although it had roots firmly anchored in the traditional associations of artisans and Revolutionary Sons of Liberty. It also prefigured nineteenth-century forms of party organization. In 1794, however, its popular base, its range of extra-legal functions, and its opposition to official policies, all marked it as an evil novelty, a threat to public order, an "engine" of unacceptable party politics.[12]

Some of the grievances that led militiamen in Washington County to establish the society are contained in its remonstrance to the President and Congress. At the top of their list was the unsettled matter of free navigation of the Mississippi. It seemed to the remonstrants that they were "entitled by nature and by stipulation to the undisturbed navigation of the river Mississippi and consider it a right inseparable from their prosperity that in colonizing this distant and dangerous district they always contemplated the free enjoyment of this right and considered it as an inseparable appendage to the country they sought out and fought for, and acquired." The national government had promised them the security of this right from Spain, according to the frontiersmen, and they had waited patiently, but in vain, for the fulfillment of this pledge. Similarly, the petitioners believed themselves entitled to protection against the Indians who invaded their homes. The settlers perceived, however, that the "government of America extends its arm of protection to all the branches of the union, but to your remonstrants." To the frontiersmen it seemed that the government was competent "to every end but that single one by which alone it can benefit us, the protection of our territorial rights. It is competent to exact obedience but not to make that return which can be the only trust and natural exchange for it."[13]

This brought the Washington County petitioners to their final point. Until they began to enjoy some benefits from their association with the United States, they thought it unjust that demands were made on them for contributions to support the federal system. "To be subject to all the burdens and enjoy none of the benefits arising from government," the frontiersmen avowed, "is what we will never submit to." In sum, they were unwilling to make sacrifices for a government that ignored their needs: "If the interest of . . . eastern America requires that we should be kept in poverty, it is unreasonable from such poverty to exact contributions. The first, if we cannot emerge from, we must learn to bear, but the latter we never can be taught to submit to."[14]

The petition was an eloquent testament to the western view of interregional relations in 1794. It was a summary of the handicaps the settlers believed they labored under as a result of their union with the East. It was a plea for redress, however, not a declaration of independence. Although framed in uncompromising language about the precariousness of their future in a united country, the petitioners sought the reciprocity of benefits that would balance the prices exacted for membership in the nation. It was the most recent in a series of petitions from the West seeking to achieve the promised benefits of independence.

From a Philadelphia perspective such an expression of discontent at a moment of national crisis seemed subversive in design, and potentially treasonous. It appeared to be yet another display of frontier disloyalty. Eastern officials read the petition within the context of long-term interregional stresses dating back to the founding of the nation. It was forwarded to the Justice department along with the bylaws of the Mingo Creek Society and other manuscripts furnished by a spy within the organization. The government was building a file and a case against its perceived enemies on the frontier.[15]

In retrospect it seems that at least some, and probably almost all, of those who formed the society harbored no subversive intentions. To local elites instrumental in drafting its rules, organizing its membership, and chairing its meetings, the association offered the best hope for restoring political quiescence to stormy western Pennsylvania. According to John McDonald, "the people had been all running wild and talked of taking [John] Neville prisoner and burning Pittsburgh; and this forming the society was thought of by moderate persons to turn the people off to remonstrating and petitioning, and giving them something to do that way to keep them quiet." The designs of men like McDonald were misinterpreted by the administration. Again, as with the Pittsburg assemblies of 1791 and 1792, the assumption was that a radical leadership must be misguiding the simple folk; that designing men were manipulating an ignorant rabble for their own political ends. The association would also be judged within the context of subsequent events. As violence spread, the Mingo Creek Society and a similar organization established in Allegheny County in April would appear to be "the cradle of . . . insurrection."[16]

No evidence links the societies to violent protest against the excise. It is possible, however, that they unwittingly contributed to an existing atmosphere of opposition, providing a forum for reinforcement of local concerns. People in the region already leaned toward independent action. By providing yet another example—in the societies' judicial functions—of the local people's ability to govern themselves better than easterners could govern them, the groups perhaps did contribute to the tensions between western Pennsylvanians and the central government. And they certainly did fuel the growing paranoia in Philadelphia about secession movements on the frontier.

To jump with the Federalists, though, to the conclusion that the people of western Pennsylvania were manipulated by elites is to misunderstand class relations and the sources of anti-excise protest in the region. Unrest bubbled up from below. Usually, professional men in the area responded to lower-class initiatives. In most cases—in the meetings of 1791 and 1792, the formation of the Mingo Creek and Allegheny societies, and in subsequent events—men of substance were unsuccessful in their attempts to direct or redirect lines of protest. More often, elites were manipulated by the rage of small farmers and laborers. Meetings and societies were not the causes, as friends of order insisted, but the consequences of unrest in the western country. Henry Marie Brackenridge's insight is helpful here: "The holding responsible the 'influential men' who attended the meetings goes on the idea that the masses take no part in them, but as they are acted upon by a few individuals; [this is] a very great mistake, but very natural in those who hold the people in a low estimate, and doubt their capacity for self-government. This was the great error, or rather 'political sin,' of the Federal party."[17]

Some western Pennsylvanians were resorting to traditional means of organizing protest against oppression, but the results do not challenge the veracity of McDonald's claims about the intentions of the societies' organizers. Violence continued during the spring of 1794 despite the best efforts of the societies. Nor did the proclamation of President Washington in late February seem to have any effect. Again, the President denounced the resistance to law in the West; again, he expressed the government's determination to enforce the law. Washington even offered a reward for the apprehension of the men who broke into excise-collector Benjamin Wells's house on November 22, 1793, and forced him to surrender his commission. Again, the warning went unheeded.[18]

During March, John Neville and excise collector Robert Johnson embarked on an expedition "to visit some of the most obstinate distillers" near the border between Washington and Fayette counties. They met no hostile crowds themselves, but Neville later learned that a mob of about sixty men had followed them around all day "swearing vengeance

against us" and checking to ensure that no distillers had complied with
the law. James Kiddoe [or Kildoe] had registered his still in response to
threats from the excise officers. When the crowd heard of this perfidy,
they destroyed the still and fired on the house of the unfortunate distiller. Kiddoe, in his first experience of good fortune that day, escaped
with his life. William Coughran [or Cochran] was also threatened, then
attacked, for entering his still. His still and grain mills were destroyed
and he was ordered to publish an account of what had happened to him,
and why, in the *Pittsburgh Gazette* as a warning to others.[19]

Several days thereafter, Neville himself suffered the wrath of local
vengeance. He, his wife, and their granddaughter were returning home
from Pittsburgh. As they rode up a steep incline, the saddle on Mrs.
Neville's horse loosened and slipped. Neville dismounted to adjust his
wife's gear. As he stood there, his back to the road, a man rode up and
asked if he was Neville the excise officer. Without turning around,
Neville answered yes. In an instant the man responded, "then I must
give you a whipping"; sprung from his horse; and grabbed Neville by
the throat and hair. The women were "screaming prodigiously," raising
the possibility that others would hear and come to assist the assailant.
After some scuffling, Neville managed to swing around and knock "the
villain prostrate." Neville grabbed the man by the throat, releasing him
after the fellow begged for his life, and lest others arrive to aid this
vanquished foe. It was a frightening experience for the Nevilles, whose
economic and social status generally isolated them from the rough
knocks of frontier life.[20]

Neville was also warned shortly after this encounter that a plan was
laid to seize him, force him to surrender his commission, and take him
prisoner. Thereafter, candles burned in the windows of Bower Hill
throughout the night and well-armed slaves guarded the house at all
times. Neville would not, however, compromise his duties as excise
inspector. He still hoped to make collections under the law in early July.
He still refused to accept payment of the excise tax in kind from those
distillers who were willing to comply, but who pleaded inability to pay
in cash. Neville was willing to accept payment in casks of whiskey, and
he believed the offers genuine; but he needed authorization for such
variance from the letter of the law and permission was not granted by
the Secretary of the Treasury.[21]

The willingness of some distillers to pay the tax in kind revealed that
opposition to the law was not absolute or unanimous in the western
country. These were generally the larger commercial distillers eager to
exploit their commercial advantage and gain lucrative contracts for supplying whiskey to General Wayne's army on the frontier. There were
also other circumstances under which the national government might
begin to collect the tax. Judge Addison believed that in the event of war
the people of the western country would not "shrink from its burdens,

and if the payment of the excise, odious and unequal as this revenue is, be necessary for its support, this payment, thus become the price of our independence, and the fruit of our duty, will, I trust, be made cheerfully and honestly." Localists had always acknowledged that in time of war extraordinary taxing methods that were ideologically repulsive under normal circumstances, might justly be collected.[22]

Even without the tragedy of war, Addison thought the government might succeed in collecting some excise taxes in the West. In his opinion, personnel changes would spur compliance. "If the collection of the excise were in proper hands," Addison advised, "it might now be made. But it seems to be intrusted to men without spirit or discretion, and in whose principles the people have no confidence." Some of the men Addison described as among the "most strenuously opposed to the excise law" in the region claimed their willingness to pay the tax "provided Benjamin Wells was removed from office, and some honest man appointed in his stead."[23]

These claims were never tested. The government refused Addison's and Governor Mifflin's pleas for flexibility and compromise. Hamilton's attitude toward enforcement had hardened since 1792; he was determined to make an example of those who had so long resisted the law. The reasonableness displayed by Washington in 1791 had evaporated. In its place stood a resolve to enforce the letter of the law. Hamilton would not accept offers to pay the tax in kind; he would not dismiss officers discredited by local experience. "The removal of either of the officers objected to," Hamilton assured the President in June, "after the persecution they have suffered and the perseverance they have displayed, would be a hazardous step—and a suspicion is warranted by the conduct of the parties that it may have been recommended with an insidious view."[24]

The violence continued in western Pennsylvania during the spring despite the efforts of Judge Addison to reconcile the hostile parties, despite John McDonald's attempts to channel protest into lawful paths, and despite President Washington's and Governor Mifflin's warnings about the probable consequences of continued resistance to the law. Mixed signals about western attitudes toward authority continued to arrive in Philadelphia. For those who were prone to see conspiracy under every western still, there was ample evidence to rekindle the wildest fears of anarchy.

Despite the claims of those who would defend the behavior of anti-excise rioters in western Pennsylvania, little progress was being made to reconcile local people to the tax. John Neville reported no new entries of stills for the fiscal year ending June 30. He could not send money or even secure reports from his collectors. Wells was repeatedly engaged in armed confrontation with his neighbors. John Lynn, who had lost his home and business for associating with Neville, was a refugee hiding in the house of excise collector Johnson until emotions toward him cooled. Johnson, out of disgust with the national government, was about to resign his office. According to Neville, "Mr. Johnson finding that government is not about to interfere in the abuses he suffered three years ago, dreading no doubt fresh instances of similar conduct, and thinking the compensation inadequate, is now about to decline the business." Neville's letter reporting these facts may not even have reached George Clymer before the end of June when Clymer, too, resigned.[25]

The times looked dismal for those who hoped to extract excise taxes from the western country. There are few grounds for agreeing with contemporaries and historians who have claimed that "the people [of western Pennsylvania] were becoming resigned to submission." Those signs still visible today suggest that, if anything, resistance was hardening, even as the determination of the government grew to enforce the letter of the law.[26]

Class divisions between large and small distillers continued to produce conflict in the western country. Men like William Coughran, who owned a large still, a saw mill, and grain mills, were willing to comply with the law. It was the small farmers, sometime tenants who owned little more than a dilapidated still, and artisans and laborers who owned nothing at all, who violently resisted the excise. Local elites were also divided in their attitudes toward the law. Some, like Addison, Cannon, McDonald, and others yet to appear on the stage, were sympathetic to local opposition to the excise, but not to the commission of violent acts. They sought to channel protest through peaceful petitions for redress drafted by representative assemblies, open meetings, or political societies. Many even argued for submission to the law during the petitioning process. Other elites, such as Neville, the merchant-collector Wells, and large distillers, actually favored the law, provoking violence by their uncompromising demands for compliance. As yet, no radical leadership had emerged from the ranks of the wealthy or professional classes. Small bands of the early "Regulator" type planned and executed attacks on complicit distillers and excise officers with little aid or sufferance from their social betters.

These divisions among residents of western Pennsylvania marked the region as different from other areas on the frontier. The ability of small numbers of the most economically powerful inhabitants to keep the excise alive distinguished the Pittsburgh area from Kentucky or frontier North Carolina, for example. Proximity to Philadelphia and the determination of the national government to make a test case of enforcement in western Pennsylvania contributed to the efforts of Neville and other individuals in the region to maintain a semblance of enforcement. The direct involvement of the national government in this one region would continue to provide a dynamic element in the confrontation over the excise. During June, federal officials took yet another step to assist

enforcement of the law. When Neville heard of the substantial amendments to the excise act passed by Congress, however, he still thought
the most crucial element was missing. In his opinion, "until government
find it convenient to adopt very different measures from what they have
hitherto done," there seemed little potential for collection in the West.
Neville thought he needed armed force to secure obedience to the law.[27]

President Washington was no more hopeful than Neville that a change
in the character of western countrymen was about to appear. Washington had had enough of the trials brought to him by his lands in Washington and Fayette counties. Despite the fact that they were "the cream
of the country in which they lie," Washington's lands had heaped upon
him "more plague that profit." His 32,323 acres on the Ohio and Great
Kanhawa rivers had also been "more pregnant of perplexities than profit" and, if he could get his price, Washington was eager to sell. In
mid-June he relieved John Cannon, the man George Clymer had tried
to intimidate in 1792, of responsibility for collecting rents on the western Pennsylvania tracts. "The continual disappointments I meet with in
the receipt of my rents under your collection in the counties of Fayette
and Washington," he informed Cannon, "lays me under the painful
necessity of placing this business in other hands." No one needed to
convince the President about the difficulties of exacting money—rent or
taxes—from the western country. Few knew better the problems of
establishing authority over the frontiersmen. Personally, Washington
was about to give up. As President, however, he would never abdicate
responsibility to bring the Constitution to every corner of the nation
and, perhaps, especially to western Pennsylvania.[28]

Nor had Congress resigned itself to regional noncompliance with the
excise law. On February 7, the House had established a committee to
study "if any, and what, further legislative provision may be necessary
for securing and collecting the duties on foreign and domestic distilled
spirits, stills, wines, and teas." The committee reported in May that
"there remains some opposition to the law in two western surveys of
South Carolina, in the survey of Kentucky, and the western survey of
Pennsylvania." Indeed, Treasury department reports showed that no
revenue was collected in the entire state of Kentucky and that collections on domestic spirits from Pennsylvania, North Carolina, South
Carolina, and Georgia were far below the costs of enforcement. The
supervisor of collections for Pennsylvania—George Clymer—could not
even furnish the committee with answers to its inquiries because some
of his collectors failed to file accounts.[29]

The result of the committee's report was the adoption of a long—
nineteen-paragraph—bill amending the 1791 and 1792 acts on domestic
and imported distilled spirits. Several provisions of this new law were of
particular relevance to inhabitants of the western country. Neville no
longer needed to establish offices in each of the four counties of his

survey. He could now commence operations from even one central office in Pittsburgh. Section ten of the act provided for the contingency Neville faced when residents of several counties combined to shut down excise offices. Nonexistence of an excise office in one's county of residence could no longer serve as an excuse for noncompliance. And under extraordinary circumstances, where no suitable dwelling could be leased for such purposes, the law authorized the President to purchase a building, provided the cost did not exceed $10,000.

Two of the most serious frontier complaints about operation of the excise were also remedied by the new law. Small distillers could now license a still for less than one year at a time. They could pay for as little as one month's use at a fraction of the former fee. This was a concession to small distillers who were transient producers of domestic whiskey. Finally, and most importantly from both an economic and ideological perspective, was the provision of the new law that authorized the trial of excise cases in state courts.

In the past, federal District Attorney William Rawle had refused to compromise on prosecution of delinquent distillers. He refused, on at least one occasion, to accept the entreaties of an attorney for the accused that transportation of witnesses to Philadelphia was a cruel exaction for defendants who lived on the frontier. "I wish you would reconsider," the lawyer wrote to Rawle from Fayette County, "the expense and trouble which the defendants must incur on this occasion; and if it is not positively incompatible with your ideas of duty and justice pray agree to have them what will arise from the attendance of, perhaps, twenty witnesses residing at a distance of more than 300 miles from Philadelphia." Rawle refused to accept the proposed expedient of admitting depositions from witnesses rather than requiring their physical presence at court. It was inflexible enforcement, perceived by western Pennsylvanians as profoundly unjust and strikingly similar to Great Britain's trampling three decades before on the rights of English colonists to trial in their vicinage. In this particular case the court met in February. Traveling would be difficult and dangerous over the mountains during the dead of winter. At least, however, the defendant and the witnesses he could finance would not be torn from their fields at a critical harvest time.[30]

No longer, after passage of the new enforcement act, would the specter of defending oneself hundreds of miles away from home, family, friends, and witnesses hang over the heads of frontier distillers. No more would the localist fear of alien courts and juries be associated with the excise law. Economic ruin because of travel expenses and time away from crops and animals should cease to exact cruel punishment on even the innocent. Now frontier distillers could avoid the nightmare of unjust verdicts by juries of strangers who neither understood nor sympathized with the culture, conditions, and people on the frontier. Or so it seemed when the law was adopted on June 5.

Even with the new changes in the excise act, inter-regional relations stood at an impasse at the end of June 1794. International war and strife-torn domestic politics set the stage, establishing one set of short-term contexts within which incidents during July would be read and interpreted. The personal beleaguerment of Washington and Hamilton would also affect profoundly their roles in unfolding events. Each felt besieged by political enemies; each had hardened his commitment to domestic order in the face of unprecedented assaults on authority at home and abroad. Eruptions on the frontier—Indian attacks, Spanish and British intrigues, and anti-excise violence—all seemed to national officials strands in a seamless web threatening to envelop the nation and doom the republican enterprise. And there was nothing from the long-term experience of national leaders in the East to diminish the most inflated interpretations of occurrences on the frontier.

British officials in North America believed that the United States was about to crumble. To Dorchester and Simcoe in Canada, and to Hammond in Philadelphia, it appeared that "from a distinction of interests between western and eastern America, it is manifest that the adherence of the former to the federal constitution, and the political connexion itself between the two divisions of the continent, depends on a very precarious sort of tenure." Kentucky seemed to the British about to secede; western Pennsylvania appeared ripe for British plucking. The Kentuckians might attack New Orleans at any time, in an effort to secure navigation of the Mississippi. The western Pennsylvanians were fed up with the lack of protection provided by the national government against the Indians, its inaction on the Mississippi question, and its attempts to exact a discriminatory excise despite its failure to deliver any cures for the region's ills. The American cauldron was boiling and British agents were doing their best to stir discontent at every opportunity. The time seemed critical to British observers in North America; to Spanish agents on the frontier; to settlers in Kentucky, western Pennsylvania, and elsewhere on the frontier who suffered economic depredations and Indian attacks; and to those men in Philadelphia who were charged with defending the nation, upholding the Constitution, and maintaining public order.[31]

PART THREE: CONSEQUENCE

The end of man is knowledge, but there is one thing he can't know. He can't know whether knowledge will save him or kill him. He will be killed all right, but he can't know whether he is killed because of the knowledge which he has got or because of the knowledge which he hasn't got and which if he had it, would save him.

Robert Penn Warren, *All the King's Men*.

Chapter Eleven

REBELLION

The debacles suffered by Generals Harmar (1790) and St. Clair (1791) did not end the federal government's efforts to crush the Indian menace in the Northwest. The defeats did, however, affect the confidence, deplete the resources, and slow the progress of America's army on the frontier. On May 25, 1792, General Anthony Wayne received orders to proceed against the nation's savage enemies. These instructions included President Washington's personal warning that "another defeat would be inexpressibly ruinous to the reputation of the government."

Since the army was decimated (almost literally) in the previous encounters, Wayne's legion had to be recruited virtually from scratch. Most of the experienced officers who were not slain in combat resigned shortly after St. Clair's defeat. Wayne had to find new ones competent for the job. In addition, he had to recruit and train 5120 non-commissioned officers and enlisted men in the rigors of warfare. These tasks could not be accomplished overnight. Hundreds of fresh recruits deserted during the march from Carlisle to Pittsburgh. Once in the field, according to Wayne, "such was the defect of the human heart that from excess of cowardice one-third of the sentries deserted from their stations."

Constant drill, daily marksmanship practice, and a system of rewards and punishments whipped Wayne's army into a credible force. Frontier civilians complained that as the army rehearsed its crafts, Indians plied their trades of plunder, torture, and murder across the countryside. But the soldiers continued to practice for months that stretched into years, and the general even invited some Indian chiefs to witness the martial displays. Months in the field produced the usual divisions within officer ranks, with some questioning whether Wayne's harsh hierarchical discipline was appropriate in the age of liberty, fraternity, equality, and the French Revolution. The government added delays on top of Wayne's cautious preparation, refusing combat authorization throughout 1793 due to its preoccupation with other affairs and out of a desire to exhaust all avenues of negotiated settlement. Influenza and smallpox depleted the effective forces by half toward the end of the year. Slow communications, irregular arrival of supplies, and harsh weather delivered the clinching blows to any plans for movement before the summer of 1794.

Indeed, the Indians moved first with an attack on Fort Recovery on June 30, 1794. Wayne's army repulsed them, thus besting the enemy on the very ground of St. Clair's defeat. By mid-July, with the arrival of mounted reinforcements from Kentucky, Wayne was ready to counterattack. Finally, on August 8 the main force secured a position about seventy miles in advance of Greenville, in the heart of Indian country. Were it not for the treachery of a lone deserter from Wayne's army, the Indians would have been totally surprised. As it was, his troops "gained possession of the grand emporium of the hostile Indians in the West without loss of blood."

Greater victory came on August 20, but with much bloodshed on both sides. At about eight o'clock that morning, the army advanced in the tight columns they had practiced for so many months. After traveling in this fashion for about five miles, the left flank came under heavy fire from an invisible enemy secreted in the woods and high grass. The ground was strewn for miles around with the dead trees that would later give the Battle of Fallen Timbers its name, and the Indians utilized the natural conditions to advantage. Wayne issued a complicated series of commands designed to roust the enemy from its cover, to flank them, and pin them between the American troops and the Maumee River. To the general's glee, "all those orders were obeyed with spirit and promptitude, but such was the impetuosity of the charge by the first line of infantry that the Indians . . . were drove from all their coverts in so short a time that although every possible exertion was used by the officers of the second line of the legion . . . to gain their proper positions . . . [only part of the reinforcements] could get up in season to participate in the action, the enemy being drove in the course of one hour more than two miles through the thick woods."

The victory was accomplished against a foe that outnumbered Wayne's troops by about two to one and that occupied a superior tactical position. About 2000 Indians had been routed by 900 novice combatants. The victors suffered 107 deaths; the vanquished lost about twice that many. News of the battle reached England in time to help John Jay secure a treaty that dictated removal of the British frontier forts. The definitive articles of peace with the Indians were exchanged the following year in the Treaty of Greenville, effectively eliminating the threat to white frontiersmen in western Pennsylvania and Ohio. Thus with one dramatic blow in August 1794 Wayne's army set in motion a series of events that within a year fulfilled two of the western country's conditions for loyalty to the Union.[1]

WAYNE'S TRIUMPH came too late to have an impact on the interregional tensions unloosed that summer in western Pennsylvania. The government had determined in June to prosecute the law more vigorously in the test-case region. According to Secretary Hamilton, "the increasing energy of the opposition" dictated sterner efforts to enforce the excise. Leniency over the past three years had failed to effect compliance with the tax. The law itself had been revised to appease the opposition, but to no avail. "The experiment," as Hamilton called it, "had been long enough tried to ascertain that, where resistance continued, the root of the evil lay deep and required measures of greater efficacy than had been pursued." There was no reason for the government to expect that western Pennsylvanians would ever comply, since violence against those who enforced and those who obeyed the law increased over time. Furthermore, easterners now complained of the injustice suffered by those who paid while others evaded the tax with impunity. Under these circumstances, Hamilton concluded, "there was no choice but to try the efficiency of the laws in prosecuting with vigor delinquents and offenders."[2]

With such a view in mind, District Attorney William Rawle secured processes from the federal court in Philadelphia ordering the appearance of over sixty western country distillers before the court during August. Although the writs appeared on the docket for May 31, it was not until June 22 that United States Marshal David Lenox traveled west to begin serving the processes, and it was not until mid-July that he completed his rounds in Cumberland, Bedford, and Fayette counties. On the evening of July 14 Lenox was entertained at the home of Hugh Henry Brackenridge in Pittsburgh. The marshal expressed relief to his host that he had suffered no violence during the course of his duties. Brackenridge was surprised that Lenox entertained such fears. He explained to his guest that the local people distinguished quite scrupulously between officers of the law and tax collectors, and that only the latter were the subjects of popular venom.[3]

Despite this advice about local prejudices, Lenox accepted John Neville's offer to serve as his guide through Allegheny County the next day. Perhaps the men assumed that respect for the marshal's office would shield them both from the wrath generally reserved for Neville and his collectors. In any event, Lenox's experiences in the company of Neville contrasted dramatically with the respect he received while traveling alone. The two men left Bower Hill early on the morning of July 15 and, according to the marshal, "in the course of a few hours I served process on four persons all of whom showed much contempt for the laws of the United States." At about noon they arrived at the home of William Miller. Lenox and Neville rode up to the farmer, and read the summons ordering him to set "aside all manner of business and excuses" and appear before the judge of the District Court in Philadelphia on August 12. Miller was enraged. "I felt myself mad with passion," he said afterwards. "I thought $250 would ruin me; and to have to go [to] the federal court at Philadelphia would keep me from going to Kentucky this fall after I had sold my plantation and was getting ready. I felt my blood boil at seeing General Neville along to pilot the sheriff to my very door."[4]

Miller refused to accept a copy of the summons and exchanged harsh words with the marshal. While Lenox was attempting to convince the farmer of the folly of his ways, Neville noticed that thirty or forty men were approaching them down the lane. Since the writ was already legally served, despite Miller's refusal to receive it, the two officials rode off to confront the crowd bearing down upon them. The group was armed—some with muskets, others with pitchforks—and angry. The men had been working in a field nearby when someone ran up and breathlessly announced that the "federal sheriff" and Neville the excise man were carrying people off to Philadelphia. It was harvest time, a hot day, and the laborers were intoxicated—an inauspicious moment to arouse this agricultural populace. They had dropped their work, grabbed their weapons, and marched off to prevent the outrage.

Accounts of the confrontation differ, although the crowd certainly milled around the lawmen. When the laborers discovered that the rumor they heard was not precisely accurate—people were being summoned to Philadelphia, not dragged off—they became somewhat confused and purposeless. They let the two horsemen pass, but when Neville and Lenox had gone about fifty yards a shot rang out. Afterwards, some people—including Alexander Hamilton—claimed that it was an attempt to injure the two men. Others reported that the shot was fired in frustration and into the air. Perhaps it was intended as a warning, more likely it was the unthinking gesture of an inebriated worker just letting off some steam. Lenox reined in his startled horse, turned around, and "upbraided them with their conduct." The laborers answered him "in a language peculiar to themselves,"—in other words, in dialects, accents, or patterns of speech alien to the Philadelphian. The two men then rode off—Lenox to Pittsburgh, Neville to Bower Hill. The incident was over, and Lenox had performed his duty in all but one case.[5]

By coincidence, the Mingo Creek militia was gathered that same day to fulfill President Washington's call for additional Indian fighters. When the militiamen heard the same rumor that had propelled farm hands from the fields to William Miller's aid, they too were enraged. To them it seemed that another central government had run amok, trampling on the ancient Saxon right of trial in the vicinage, sporting with the freedoms proclaimed by the Declaration of Independence and defended in the Revolution. They felt driven to defend this same liberty against those who abused it.[6]

The militia determined to capture the federal marshal and then decide, apparently on the basis of his testimony, what to do next. According to John Holcroft, there "was no mention of General Neville, only of the marshal at this time. The marshal [was] to be taken and brought

[back], then [it was] to be determined what [was] to be done in regard to his sending precepts on the different people." Two bands were selected to pursue the marshal; Holcroft led "37 guns" to Bower Hill, wrongly believing that Lenox had returned there with Neville.[7]

At about daybreak on July 16, Neville heard noises outside his garrisoned house. When he opened the door he realized that the place was surrounded and challenged the intruders to identify themselves. Holcroft later claimed that he thought the demand came from the marshal and shouted back that they were friends from Washington County come to guard him. Neville was not fooled; he ordered them to stand back, then fired, mortally wounding Oliver Miller. The militia shot back. Neville blew a signal horn and his slaves opened fire from their quarters at the rear of the crowd. Several more of the attackers fell wounded; none of the Neville household suffered injury during the twenty-five-minute exchange. The militia retreated to Couche's Fort, where another meeting swelled their numbers, and considered their next move throughout the night.[8]

The "murder" of Oliver Miller by John Neville, as the local people saw it, coupled with the attempt to summon thirty men from Fayette County to trial in Philadelphia, altered the nature of confrontation over the excise. Now, with the first mortal blow struck, self-imposed limits on extra-legal protest were reconsidered. A measure proposed and narrowly defeated on the evening of July 16 called for "a sum of money [to] be raised and given to some ordinary persons to lie in wait and privately take the life of General Neville." In a final piece of business, the company determined to march again on Bower Hill the next day. Sentiment was high for avenging Miller's death. Another new dimension of anti-excise violence now arose as well. In the past, few "men of substance," few "respectable characters," had engaged in such behavior. This was changing. As excise collector Johnson observed in his letter of resignation several days after the attack on Neville's house, he was willing to act as an agent of enforcement when the lawbreakers were only the "rabble." Now, "feeling the opposition changed from dignified rabble to a respectable party," he was withdrawing from the fray. The events of July 15–17 provoked this new development.[9]

Neville anticipated another assault on his house and applied to the judges, generals of militia, and sheriffs of Allegheny County for protection. They declined, claiming lack of authority. More bravely, Major James Kirkpatrick and ten soldiers from Fort Pitt agreed to assist in defense of Bower Hill. At about 5:00 p.m. on July 17 between 500 and 700 men paraded before Neville's mansion to the cadence of drums and with all the pomp and majesty that a frontier militia could muster. The mark of participation by community leaders was stamped on the organization and purposefulness of this parade compared with the more haphazard confrontations of the previous day and the past several years.

This was no rag-tag gathering to brutalize a tax collector, but a serious military encounter. Alexander Hamilton would later correctly portray it as something more than a spontaneous riot, although it seems something less than the treasonous "rebellion" against the United States that he and other easterners perceived.[10]

Major Kirkpatrick and his command smuggled Neville into a thicketed ravine before the rebel army surrounded the house. After about half an hour of posturing and drill by the militia, James McFarlane, who commanded the expedition, sent a written summons to the house demanding the surrender of Neville, his resignation, and his agreement to accept no further offices under the excise. Kirkpatrick informed his counterpart that Neville was not at home, but that he would submit to a search of the house by a deputation of six of their number and would permit them to take any official papers they desired from the premises. McFarlane responded that the soldiers must evacuate the mansion and ground their arms. Kirkpatrick refused, saying that it was obvious that the invaders intended to destroy property since they would not accept his offer. Negotiations were halted, the militia surrounded the house from about sixty to eighty yards' distance, and set fire to one of the slave cabins and a barn. The defending soldiers held their fire until they were able to evacuate Neville's family. The battle then began and lasted over an hour.

During the exchange McFarlane believed that he heard a call from the house. Thinking that the soldiers inside wished to parley, he ordered the militia to cease firing and he stepped out from behind a tree to begin negotiations. Shots rang out from the house and McFarlane fell. This popular militia officer and veteran of the Revolutionary war was dead. His comrades were stunned; they believed that Major Kirkpatrick himself had shot McFarlane after tricking him out into the open. The militia continued to set fire to the buildings that comprised Bower Hill. Barns, storage bins, and eventually the kitchen next to the main house were in flames—although several structures were spared at the request of Neville's slaves. According to Kirkpatrick, the heat inside the house was intense. When the kitchen began to burn, the soldiers recognized that all was lost, and they surrendered.

Accounts of casualties vary. It seems that two of the soldiers deserted in the course of the battle and that about four were seriously wounded. It is possible that one soldier later died of his wounds. At least one militiaman besides McFarlane, and perhaps two, also died on the field of battle, but there are no reliable estimates of injuries among the attackers. The leaders who took Kirkpatrick prisoner did not even know if they left wounded behind. Despite their anger and their belief that Kirkpatrick had slyly murdered their leader, the frontiersmen treated him tolerably well. "I had no great reason to complain of their behavior to me while a prisoner," he later reported. "Some indeed damned me and said I ought to be put to death for attempting with ten men to

defend the house against their numbers. Some [said] I should be put to
death for their commanding officer who fell, but the more moderate
among them protected me."[11]

Later that evening some of the rebels captured the federal marshal
and brought him to Couche's Fort. Lenox had cause to fear for his life as
drunken militiamen fired muskets in his direction and others attacked
him with knives. Fortunately for the marshal, senior officers defended
him, but not before he suffered superficial wounds to the throat and a
good deal of humiliation. Enraged rioters ordered Lenox to surrender
the remaining writs and promise not to make returns on those he had
already served. They instructed the marshal to lay his hand on the dead
militiaman's beard and swear an oath never to inform on those present,
never to return to their side of the mountains, and to have nothing to do
with the excise again. Witnesses later disagreed about whether Lenox
took the oath after his initial objections to the procedure. Somehow,
perhaps with the complicity of the "respectable characters" who had
earlier protected him from the mob, Lenox escaped the scene and the
next day floated down river on a barge to avoid the main roads out of
Pittsburgh.[12]

The Rebellion lacked a coherent purpose, but some rebels favored
seizing the opportunity provided by Lenox and Neville to realize long-
standing goals of regional independence from the state and/or central
governments. Others remembered their success in resisting and, they
believed, overturning the Pennsylvania excise tax some years before.
These less ambitious participants sought only to compel Neville's resignation, and nothing more. Judge Alexander Addison believed that initially most of the rioters fell within this latter group, and "presumed
their numbers sufficient to extort by fear alone, without actual force, a
ready compliance. Irritated by refusal, resistance, and repulse, and too
deeply engaged to retreat, in their frenzy they drew into their guilt all
within reach of their terror, and proceeded to the extremity of burning
the house." Theirs was an unthinking, uncalculated, emotional rebellion, doomed to collapse when tempers cooled, organized opposition
appeared, or contingencies demanded sophisticated planning.[13]

Several men died, others were seriously injured, and there was much
loss of blood at Bower Hill. The second encounter at Neville's was a
direct consequence of Miller's death the previous day. The "murder" of
McFarlane led to further violence that might otherwise have been
avoided. John Neville played a decisive role in this course of events.
Neville, alone, did not cause the Rebellion, but he certainly triggered
the riots. If this proud and stubborn patrician could have brought himself to resign his commission and surrender his official papers on July 16,
the mob probably would have dispersed. He saw the situation differently, though, and instead fired the first fatal shot.

Others, back in Philadelphia, might also have helped avoid this conflagration, and it was a string of ironic coincidences that led to Neville's door on July 16. The national government need not have issued the processes demanding the appearance of so many frontiersmen in a Philadelphia court. The enforcement act signed by President Washington on June 6, a law which everyone knew was imminent throughout the month of May, permitted the trial of tax evaders in local state courts. Although the government was technically within the law in acting under the previous legislation, some have wondered ever since why, unless a confrontation was desired, officials did not pursue the more conciliatory path. Why, when the other alternative was available, did the government choose to assault the well-known sensibilities of western Pennsylvanians and create a predictably explosive situation? Rather than securing compliance with the law, delivering writs to western owners of middling and small farms created a union of interest between these men and propertyless laborers who imagined themselves as having nothing to lose in an all-out challenge to the existing social and political order. It seems so certain a formula for disaster that the question about motives must always remain.[14]

District Attorney William Rawle actually sought the indictments. There is also direct evidence that Rawle, at least, sought something less than war in western Pennsylvania; that he never intended to prosecute over sixty frontiersmen in a Philadelphia court. According to Attorney General William Bradford, "the suits that were brought were merely for the purpose of compelling an entry of the stills. Whenever this was done and in Fayette County it was done in several instances—the rule has been to stay the prosecution—remit the forfeiture—and discharge the suit even without costs." In other words, the writs were a bluff, a threat to induce compliance with the law. According to this account, the only one that offers reliable interpretation of government intent, mass trials of frontier distillers would never have occurred. This interpretation is substantiated by the final irony of the whole affair. The summonses ordered defendants to appear before the district court in August, but the tribunal was not scheduled to meet during the heat of that month. The processes were thus technically invalid; and had westerners known the schedule of the eastern court, they could have—legally—challenged the writs.[15]

If the federal government had acted under the new law; if Marshal Lenox had arrived before harvest time or had not accepted John Neville's offer to guide him through Allegheny County; if the rumor that people were being dragged off to Philadelphia by the excise man had not circulated like wild-fire; if the Mingo Creek militia had not met on July 15; if western countrymen had known that the writs were technically invalid and that government attorneys had no intention of prosecuting over sixty distillers; or if Neville had surrendered his commission and restrained himself from firing the first shot, there might have been no

Whiskey Rebellion that summer. But then again, this string of tragic ironies and coincidences was only the trigger, not the cause, of the Rebellion. Inter-regional stresses were longer-term and more complex. The confrontation might not have erupted in July 1794 without this chain of unlikely circumstances, but as long as western Pennsylvanians remained rabidly divided over the excise law and the national government was determined to make a test-case of their opposition, any trigger would do.[16]

The death of McFarlane in the second attack on Neville's house was a critical moment in the whole affair. McFarlane was a local hero of the Revolution, a popular military leader, and now a martyr to the cause of liberty. He quickly became a symbol of the linkage between the Revolutionary and anti-excise struggles, an embodiment of what the Whiskey Rebellion seemed all about to those who supported the cause. The tombstone on McFarlane's grave asserted this canonization; and his funeral on July 18 provided the occasion for planning the next stage of rebellion, an assembly at the Mingo Creek meetinghouse on July 23.[17]

New actors now stepped onto the stage, "respectable" sorts whose names, as in the case of Hugh Henry Brackenridge and William Findley, had not previously been linked with unrest, and others—such as Albert Gallatin, Edward Cook, and David Bradford—who would take on different roles. This change in the class of participants was obvious to all who viewed the political landscape. "The people engaged in the present opposition to government," wrote an unsympathetic observer, "must not be considered as an inconsiderable mob; they are a respectable and powerful combination." The conclusion that elites now "led" the riots was the inaccurate, though rational, analysis of the government's friends; it was the logical perception of alienated witnesses who saw professional men addressing crowds of illiterates and assumed a hierarchical relationship between the two. In fact, these "leaders" were recruited against their will, although some quickly developed a passion for the role of demagogue. James Marshall and David Bradford, later two of the most incendiary favorites of the crowd, were bluntly told that "if you do not come forward now and support us, you shall be treated in the same or a worse manner with the excise officer." Brackenridge thought that Edward Cook also participated "at the solicitation and under the fear of the people."[18]

All of these men worried about their lives, their careers, and their property, and imagined themselves in a "delicate" relationship with their incensed country neighbors. They chose different methods and pursued different ends, but they were creatures rather than creators of the mob. At Mingo Creek, Bradford made a violent address, although Brackenridge "doubted whether he spoke according to his wish or harangued according to the humor of the people, and from a fear of them." Others tried a different tactic to save their hides; they aimed during this meeting to avoid taking a side. "There was but a moment between treason on the one hand, and popular odium on the other," Bracken- ridge later recalled. He sought to alter the sullen mood of the gathering by telling jokes, tried to dissuade his audience from marching on Pitts- burgh by recounting in a humorous way how the liberty-loving citizens of that village had closed down their local excise office and run Marshal Lenox out of town. Then Brackenridge ventured, as a lawyer, to give the assemblage some advice. "What had been done [at Neville's] might be morally right," he told them, "but it was legally wrong." They had, in his opinion, committed treason and it was now within the power of the President to call out militia against them. He encouraged a mass applica- tion for amnesty, and the appointment of those not yet involved as a committee to mediate negotiations with the government. He sought to convince the frontiersmen that they had no chance in a military contest with the better-armed and more populated East, but that an amnesty was likely if violence ended at this point. The crowd was not sympa- thetic to this analysis, and Brackenridge departed quickly, frightened by the mass grumbling that met his speech. [19]

Bradford was more successful by playing to the audience's hostile temper. He received cheers for his verbal assaults on the government, but had no coherent plan to offer the assembled. Debate continued, but to no decisive end. Finally, the meeting agreed to call another assembly several weeks later, and directed townships to send not more than five or fewer than two delegates to Parkinson's Ferry on August 14 "to take into consideration the situation of the western country." Moderates were content with this result. No war was declared, no program for secession proclaimed, no military campaign plotted against the town of Pittsburgh or the garrison stationed there; and no one proposed to march on Philadelphia to enforce demands. The delay of three weeks before another gathering bought time for tempers to cool and hope among some that a confrontation with national authorities could be avoided. [20]

Radicals, inspired by the crowd's enthusiasm, were not so content to rest. A letter recruited back-country Virginians for the cause. "We have fully deliberated," Bradford wrote, "and have determined with head, heart, hand, and voice that we will support the opposition to the excise law. The crisis is now come: submission or opposition." At about this same time, notices from the anonymous "Tom the Tinker" began to ap- pear. These warnings, typical of rural movements in Europe and Amer- ica, were designed to intimidate waverers and enlist the non-committed to the cause. The first letter was found by John Reed posted on a tree near his distillery. It instructed Reed, who had recently registered his stills in compliance with the excise law, that "I, Tom the Tinker, will not suffer any certain class or set of men to be excluded [from] the service of this my district, when notified to attend on any expedition carried on in order to obstruct the execution of the excise law, and obtain a repeal thereof." The broadside threatened punishment to those who "opposed the virtuous principles of republican liberty," and the tinkers were good on their word in destroying stills and other property of opponents during the summer of 1794.[21]

Other actions now accompanied these words. A small band with Bradford at its head schemed to discredit moderates within the western Pennsylvania movement. They determined to rob the mail carrier from Washington County to Pittsburgh, hoping to discover correspondence that might be used to enrage the populace against those who sought peace. But their timing was off, and the thieves missed the rider. Next they determined, with a similar intent, to intercept the Pittsburgh to Philadelphia post, and on July 26 they succeeded. This self-appointed "Canonsburgh Committee" found several letters from alienated town-dwellers that condemned the riots. These were used as justification for calling a military assembly on August 1.

Within the circular letter announcing this meeting at Braddock's Field was a thinly veiled call-to-arms against the town of Pittsburgh and the garrison stationed there. The time had now come, reasoned the seven men who signed the address, "that every citizen must express his sentiments not by his words, but by his actions." They instructed sympathetic rural people to arrive on the field by two in the afternoon, armed and with four days' provisions. "If any volunteers shall want arms and ammunition," the committee promised, ". . . they shall be supplied as well as possible. Here, sir, is an expedition proposed in which you will have an opportunity of displaying your military talents and of rendering service to your country."[22]

Expecting the worst, Pittsburgh citizens gathered in a town meeting on the evening of July 31 to determine how best to handle this threat from their bellicose country neighbors. They decided to banish the three men whose intercepted letters made them "particularly obnoxious" to the anti-excise rioters; to appoint a committee to inform those gathered at Braddock's Field of the town's actions and sympathy for the cause; to march out en masse to join the insurgents, thus displaying their united purpose with the country; and to elect delegates to the Parkinson's Ferry meeting called for August 14. These propositions reflected fear more than support for the rural rebellion; they were designed to placate radicals and thus save the town from being burned to the ground. The village committee displayed solicitude for the three exiled residents, doing its best to ensure the safety of persons and property. Even as the Pittsburgh committee and militia traveled to Braddock's Field, wives and children were hiding valuables before the anticipated assault.[23]

During the interval between issuing the summons to Braddock's Field and the appointed hour of arrival, those responsible for the plan lost their nerve. Alarmed at their own rashness, and concerned that the countryside would explode out of control, the Canonsburgh Committee issued orders countermanding the rendezvous. These went unheeded and resulted in vilification of "leaders" who appeared to waver. The door to Thomas Marshall's house was tarred and feathered after he publicly suggested that the gathering was probably a bad idea. He and Bradford felt obliged in the face of such threats to assert more adamantly their commitment to overturning the excise law. According to Brackenridge, "Bradford seeing the violence of the multitude, by which he was always governed, became more inflammatory than he had ever been [and] denied that he had consented to a countermand." Militia officers who disapproved of the proceedings had to continue nonetheless; "it was the people commanding the officer, not the officer the people." To Bracken-ridge, and to other moderates, the whole region seemed "one inflam-mable mass." Men who had witnessed the Stamp Act riots and the Revolution remembered the popular fervor accompanying these earlier events as "by no means so general and so vigorous amongst the common people as the spirit which now existed in this country." The revolution-ary potential of opposition to internal taxes, first revealed in American cities during 1765, was being realized on the frontier in 1794.[24]

The hierarchical relationship between classes assumed by eastern na-tionalists was actually reversed in a manner that horrified moderates and conservatives who followed the French Revolution's progress. "A revo-lution did not suit me, nor any man else who had anything to lose," recalled the frightened Brackenridge. "A secession of the [western] country from the government presented nothing that could be an object with me. For my part, I had seen and heard enough of revolutions to have any wish to bear a part in one. But to lie by was impossible; no man would be suffered to remain neutral." Going along, appearing sup-portive, "endeavoring to moderate the multitude and prevent outrages," seemed the best approach available to moderates, and the Braddock's Field meeting was a test of their ability to resist the demands of rural laborers for more aggressive commitment. Rebels debated simultane-ously whether Brackenridge would make a good governor of their new state, if they sought and achieved such an end, and whether to burn his house when they marched on Pittsburgh. His stance was ambivalent, and interpreted in different ways; some viewed him as a partisan, others as a traitor to liberty. It was indeed a delicate position that he and others like him—such as Findley and Gallatin—occupied, one complicated by the eastern government's vision of such men as responsible for the Rebellion.[25]

Most of the 7000 rebels who attended the August 1 assembly were propertyless and only about one-third owned stills. Contemporaries char-acterized the great mass of participants as "miserably poor." For the most part they had come to Neville's mansion and now to Braddock's

Field from townships where over half the residents owned no land; they lived in places beset by economic dislocation and resultant social tension. Not surprisingly, then, their grievances were generally economic in character; their victims were primarily members of wealthier commercial classes; and the property they envied was often the object of violence.[26]

Opposition to excise enforcement focused the frustrations of impoverished frontier life, but once unloosed, the anger of whiskey rebels transcended the persons and property most directly associated with the hated tax. On the day of the Braddock's Field meeting, as if to express symbolically this turn of events, a horseman rode through the streets of Pittsburgh brandishing a tomahawk and chanting his warning: "This is not all that I want: it is not the excise law only that must go down; your district and associate judges must go down; your high offices and salaries. A great deal more is to be done; I am but beginning yet." The defining characteristic of victims became, in the summer of 1794, commercial wealth, not complicity with the excise. Resident owners of large tracts of land, manufacturers, millers, and shopkeepers joined the ranks of the Rebellion's victims; nearly half of those assaulted after the burning of Neville's house had only indirect connections, or no visible link at all, to the central government's internal tax.[27]

Pittsburgh had become the symbol of this alien way of life. "Sodom," as the rebels renamed the town, was the local exemplar of urban culture; an embodiment of all that was wrong with cosmopolitan merchants, manners, and governments back East. The rebels claimed that they came to take Pittsburgh; some favored plundering it, while others thought it should just be leveled. "It was an expression," Brackenridge remembered, "that Sodom had been burnt by fire from heaven; but this second Sodom should be burned with fire from earth." Country women accompanied the rural horde primarily for the purpose of specialized household plundering during the anticipated fall of Pittsburgh. They reveled in their opportunity to humble comparatively wealthy village matrons and to strip the townhouses that seemed mansions to mistresses of rural hovels. Men dreamt aloud of the new hunting rifles and ammunition they would take from village stores. One rebel entertained the crowd by twirling his hat on the barrel of a rifle while shouting, "I have a bad hat now, but I expect to have a better one soon."[28]

Their dreams were never realized; the plotted destruction of Pittsburgh was never accomplished by this rural mob. Town residents credited the liberality of their hospitality and the shrewdness of their negotiators with preserving the village. Certainly the casks of whiskey distributed gratis to the crowd and the sly camaraderie practiced by town-dwellers were instrumental in turning the tide. The decision to expel the most offensive townsmen was critical, and convincing the inebriated rural poor that it was impossible to burn houses selectively without threatening the rest was a major triumph. At least as important, though, was fear.[29]

Fear of Fort Fayette's heavy artillery was decisive in altering the path and purpose of the mob. The primary goal of the Canonsburgh Committee was assault on the garrison and taking its arms and ammunition for their own defense. According to William Findley, "they considered the conduct of Congress in seizing the British post, arms, etc. while they remained colonies, petitioning the throne, acknowledging their dependence on it, and endeavoring to have their just grounds of complaint removed, to be a precedent perfectly applicable to their case." Again, when faced with the actual battle, these "leaders" lost their nerve. In the end, they asked permission of the fort's commander to march peacefully past it into Pittsburgh and there to cross the Monongahela on their way back home. Major Butler responded that "their peaceable intentions would be evinced by their passing the fort at proper distance," out of reach of its guns. The rebels abandoned even the pretense of confronting the army and skirted the fort by another road.[30]

Deprived of their primary goals, the so-called rebel army became purposeless and began to disperse. The town had escaped destruction; the garrison was probably never in any great danger from this poorly armed throng of rural laborers. Never again would the Rebellion reach such a fevered pitch; no more crowds of this size and temper assembled to combat their cosmopolitan foes. But that is hindsight. There was every reason to believe at the time that worse was yet to come. A six-striped flag, representing four Pennsylvania and two Virginia counties, was raised on August 1. Independence seemed the goal of these 7000 rebels in arms. Across the Monongahela, farm buildings of Major Kirkpatrick—alleged murderer of McFarlane and defender of Neville's home—were burned to the ground. Marauding bands garbed in the traditional outfit of Indian fighters—yellow hunting shirts with handkerchiefs tied around their heads—populated the countryside, raising liberty poles with inflammatory slogans; burning buildings; holding mock trials and banishing whomever they pleased; and brutalizing tax collectors and other enemies to the cause. Liberty-pole raisings became the occasion for fiery speeches, physical intimidation of critics, and the flying of the rebel flag. Slogans attached to the poles proclaimed liberty, equality, fraternity, and no excise. Men in blackened faces—imitating the fashion of Indian warriors set for battle—screamed "Death to traitors" and threatened enemies with guillotining. And worse, from the government's point of view, violence was spreading into Virginia, Maryland, Ohio, and central Pennsylvania.[31]

Still, there was no organized movement with clearly defined goals. No individuals with the talents of Sam Adams, John Wilkes, or Robespierre emerged to unite and direct this inchoate movement of disgruntled frontiersmen. Individuals spoke of independence, civil war, and union with Great Britain or Spain, but no mass enterprise of this sort ever existed, and no careful plans were laid for realizing these ends. By August 14, when about 250 delegates from western Pennsylvania and Virginia met at Parkinson's Ferry, moderates again appeared to hold a fragile ascendancy over advocates of violence. "The only rational scheme," Gallatin later recalled, "was to prevent the adoption of any criminal resolution, or to obtain a dissolution of the meeting without doing any act." This meeting more closely resembled those at Pittsburgh and Redstone Old Fort in 1791 and 1792 than the rowdy gatherings at Mingo Creek and Braddock's Field during the previous month. Many vented their spleens, but the four resolutions adopted by the assembly were conciliatory, rather than provocative. Delegates protested attempts to bring citizens to trial outside their neighborhood. They appointed a committee to petition Congress for repeal of the excise law and substitution of a "less odious tax"; and pledged that such a tax "will be cheerfully paid by the people of these counties." They committed themselves to "support of the municipal laws of the respective states," but declined to guarantee compliance with all federal laws. Finally, delegates agreed to appoint a committee to meet with any commissioners sent by the state or federal government to negotiate an end to the rural upheavals.[32]

These seemed steps in the right direction to moderates such as Brackenridge, Findley, and Gallatin. The resolutions were the best they could achieve in the face of demands for harsher statements of discontent. Among the gallery of witnesses to the meeting, the cry was still for war, but within the delegates' ranks no whispers of violent ambitions were heard. Moderates now had visible proof to support their contentions that the Rebellion was over, in western Pennsylvania at least, and that submission to lawful authority would soon be restored without the aid of outside force. "Time alone," Gallatin believed, "was sufficient to obtain a progressive restoration of order." The greatest potential for rekindling rebellion now apparently came from the East. Moderates, and some alienated conservatives, agreed that an eastern army was the spark most likely to reignite western embers of discontent. The Rebellion's status now seemed in the federal government's hands. Negotiations with commissioners sent west by state and national authorities thus appeared critical to delegates chosen at Parkinson's Ferry to perform this sensitive task.[33]

Chapter Twelve

RESPONSE

The French menace in Europe drove American and British governments closer together during the summer of 1794. After preparing for war against Great Britain earlier in the year, the Washington administration now feared the French Revolution on the one side and its own back-country citizenry on the other even more than it resented British assaults on neutral trading vessels. For reasons having more to do with France than the North American wilderness, Britain had also decided to abandon, temporarily at least, its efforts to annex Vermont, western Pennsylvania, and Kentucky. Wayne's victory at Fallen Timbers came at a critical time in negotiations between the two nations, and it convinced British officials that an American treaty was more urgent, and more likely, than an Indian alliance to help dismember the United States.

Canadian officials and Tory refugees had collaborated since 1783 with disaffected citizens in western Pennsylvania for secession of the region and reunion with Great Britain. Canadian Governor Simcoe still hoped that there might be an American war, and continued during 1794 to shuttle agents into and out of the western country. He tried to capitalize on the fortuitous uprising of whiskey rebels during the summer, but he received no support from his superiors back in London. Indeed, his correspondence was leaked to the American government, thus providing the Washington administration with details of negotiations between rebel sympathizers and British agents. Simcoe exaggerated his possibilities for success, inflated the numbers of frontiersmen sympathetic to reunion with Great Britain, and minimized the costs of British connivance in such schemes. Washington and Hamilton took Simcoe's analysis at face-value, however, and this information became a source of fear and provided a justification for armed suppression of the insurgency.

As early as March 1794, British Ambassador to the United States George Hammond had reported that frontiersmen were arming for war. An estimated 2000 Kentuckians were poised to attack the Spanish outpost at New Orleans, hoping to free the Mississippi for transportation of western crops to market. By June, Britain's ambassador was convinced that "the project of opening by force the navigation of the Mississippi is not merely a transient sentiment of individuals, but is the fixed universal determination of the great mass of the inhabitants of that part of the American territory." He conceived the federal government powerless to

prevent such enterprises and interpreted the series of presidential proc-
lamations forbidding such actions as futile. Hammond assessed the com-
mercial interests of western and eastern states as so utterly conflicting
that "the adherence of the former to the federal Constitution and the
political connection itself between the two divisions of the continent
depend on a very precarious sort of tenure."

When the Whiskey Rebellion erupted some months later, British ob-
servers were not in the least surprised. Although opposition to the excise
provided an "avowed pretext" for hostilities, Hammond was convinced
that the real cause was the same as in previous inter-regional conflicts,
"a rooted aversion" to central governance. Other British officials on the
scene agreed that the United States now faced its gravest crisis since the
Revolution; that events in western Pennsylvania during July and August
were the culmination of western unrest over the past twenty years. Some
predicted victory for the rebels in a frontier-wide independence move-
ment, while others anticipated that "a temporary suppression of this
revolt may happen." But all commentators believed that the Union
would not long survive in its present form.

The opinions of foreign observers were reinforced by persons claiming
to be agents of the rebels. On two separate occasions, men "of very
decent manners and appearance" contacted the British ambassador for
the purpose of negotiating an alliance between the western country and
his nation. The visitors told Hammond that "they were dissatisfied with
the [U. S.] government and were determined to separate from it." In
return for arms and perhaps other support, they were prepared to offer
the allegiance of their region to the British monarch. The minister
feared that word of this meeting would leak out and embarrass his
nation's ongoing negotiations with the United States. He delivered the
rebels a stern rebuff and apparently reported the unsolicited rendezvous
to Alexander Hamilton as well as to London The Washington adminis-
tration thus had good reason to share Hammond's interpretation of
events on the frontier.

The Spanish minister in Philadelphia received similar visits by Ken-
tuckians and western Pennsylvanians during 1794, and also assumed a
connection between the whiskey rebels and other frontier conspirators.
Since Ambassador Joseph de Jaudene's government was, for reasons
similar to the British, uninterested in dismembering the American fron-
tier at this time, he paid small sums to frontier agents in return for
future information and good will, encouraged them in their pursuits,
and promised Spanish interest in an alliance after they secured indepen-
dence from the United States. Federal officials learned of these discus-
sions as well, and thus knew that frontier incendiaries actively sought
the assistance of European powers for secession attempts. They feared
that fluctuations in European events might quickly lead to changes in
policy. Overnight, Spanish and British officials could become more ac-
tively concerned in schemes to subdivide the United States.[1]

WITH THE INTERNATIONAL ramifications of back-country unrest in mind, President Washington called a cabinet meeting for August 2. Settlers throughout the frontier had struck "at the root of all law and order" during July, and the administration now had to consider decisive steps for preserving the Union from dismemberment by internal and external foes. Armed Georgians were moving into Creek Territory for the purpose of establishing an independent state. Spies also reported that these same back-country rebels were "setting out upon some military expedition against the dominions of Spain with whom we are at peace."[2]

In a similarly threatening fashion, Kentuckians were again up in arms over navigation of the Mississippi. A series of remonstrances during May and June proclaimed their natural right to "the free and undisturbed navigation of the river"; demanded protection against Indians; and denounced the central government's ineffectual efforts in these regards. They also decried the recent appointment of John Jay, that "enemy of the western country," to negotiate with Great Britain for frontier demands that he was known personally to oppose. From Kentucky's perspective, sending Jay to Europe seemed testimony to the government's insincere devotion to frontier allegiance; it augured a return to the inter-regional tensions that afflicted the nation during the 1780s. Federal officials by now had heard the same rumors that frightened Spain's minister in Philadelphia; Kentucky conspirators appeared determined to open navigation of the river by force, secede from the Union, and ally themselves with Great Britain. Over 2000 Kentuckians might already be invading New Orleans, and were perhaps now united with back-country Georgians in a war that the national government was powerless to prevent.[3]

On top of all this, and rumors of worse, the Whiskey Rebellion posed an even greater threat than it would have in more tranquil times. The Rebellion also provided a tangible occasion for the government to test its prowess on the frontier. In the face of a series of challenges that frustrated the will of central authority, it seemed the one opportunity for successful assertion of federal dominance. Secretary Hamilton forthrightly acknowledged the linkage in his mind among events in Georgia, Kentucky, and Pennsylvania. In response to these challenges, he "insisted upon the propriety of an immediate resort to military force" in western Pennsylvania. The logic of Hamilton's diagnosis, and the methods he prescribed as a cure, were identical to those that he offered during the fall of 1792. This time, however, there was a genuine crisis in the western country, and he could develop the case in a more convincing legal fashion.[4]

Even so, there was no guarantee that other cabinet officials and President Washington would agree to Hamilton's plan. The Militia Act of 1792 required certification by a Supreme Court justice that the situation was beyond the control of civil authority before troops could be called to the central government's aid. And at the August 2 cabinet meeting, guests from Pennsylvania's state government uncooperatively asserted that "the judiciary power was equal to the task of quelling and punishing the riots." Hamilton's case had yet to be made, and the administrative process was slow to unfold. The task ahead, from Hamilton's point of view, was to convince the President of the need for a military response while adhering strictly to constitutional forms. Research, persuasion, and meticulous attention to detail were the orders of the day, and no one on either side was better prepared than the Secretary of the Treasury to meet such a challenge.[5]

Although he knew better, Hamilton emphasized the local nature of excise opposition, portraying the western Pennsylvanians as uniquely recalcitrant in that regard. He emphasized the role played by "formal public meetings of influential individuals" in the western country, and asserted a connection between the petitioning movement and the "general spirit of opposition" that produced violence in the region. Elites "fomented" unrest, Hamilton asserted, by sanctioning discontent in any guise. "These acts of violence," the Treasury Secretary averred, "were preceded by certain meetings of malcontent persons who entered into resolutions calculated at once to confirm, inflame, and systematize the spirit of opposition." Rebellion had built to a crescendo over the past four years despite his best efforts to modify the law. He pointed to resolutions of a Pittsburgh assembly in 1792 as evidence that incendiaries were uncompromising in their resistance to "all internal taxes on consumption." "The immediate question," Hamilton concluded, "is whether the government of the United States shall ever raise revenue by any internal tax." His inescapable conclusion was that only a nationalized militia of 12,000 men would suffice to enforce internal taxes in the face of ingrained ideological hostility toward central governance.[6]

The President was determined "to go every length that the Constitution and laws would permit, but no further" to end the Rebellion and enforce the excise. He shared Hamilton's conviction that "certain irregular meetings" chaired by frontier elites were responsible for the outrages in western Pennsylvania, and that ill-disposed "leaders" had escalated the rhetoric of insurrection "with every appearance of a disposition among the people to relax in their opposition and to acquiesce in the laws." Washington's greatest fears transcended the problem of collecting internal taxes; "anarchy and confusion" seemed to him the likely outcome if wilderness rebels continued to trample the laws with impunity. He found it distressing that the very people on whom the government spent the bulk of its resources were the ones disloyal to the Constitution; but given his personal experiences in the western country, the President was not surprised by the violence or irresponsible character of its citizens. He had no reason to expect a transformation in their "pre-

disposition . . . to be dissatisfied under any circumstances, and under
every exertion of government . . . to promote their welfare."[8]

Washington also thought he detected a cause of unrest in the democratic societies that had sprung up in the wake of Genet's visit one year
before. These political clubs, somewhat novel precursors of those associated with modern political parties, struck the President as designed
"primarily to sow the seeds of jealousy and distrust among the people of
the government." He portrayed members as "incendiaries of public
peace and order," who spread their "nefarious doctrines with a view to
poison and discontent the minds of the people." The notion of a permanent censoring or opposition party struck him as calculated to undermine law and order. The Whiskey Rebellion was the "first ripe fruit" of
the democratic societies, according to the President. It presented the
occasion for another confrontation between friends of order and those
who claimed to be friends of liberty, but who only masked "diabolical
attempts to destroy the best fabric of human government and happiness
that has ever been presented for the acceptance of mankind."[9]

Newspapers again became arenas for jousts on these same themes,
with combatants using the Rebellion to illustrate their favorite maxims
about liberty and order. Some correspondents dubbed themselves de-
scriptively; "Peregrine Peaceable," "Order," and "A Friend of Liberty"
were popular names. Others adopted satirical pseudonyms; "Anarchy,"
"One of the People," and "Hah! Hah! Hah!" were among the more
whimsical signatures designed to ridicule those with opposing views.
Proponents of conflicting ideologies had not altered their beliefs since
the liberty versus order debates of earlier years, but friends of liberty
were now on the defensive.[10]

Self-styled friends of order denounced the rebels' "total subversion of
government," and the reign of "anarchy, rapine, and devastation" portended by events on the frontier. Contempt of the laws had become the
high road to anarchy, just as friends of order had predicted all along, and
now the "Vendeites" of western Pennslyvania were trying to impose by
force of arms the principles of Thomas Paine's *Rights of Man*. The
"Jacobin" or "insurgent" clubs, as their detractors now termed the
democratic societies, were portrayed as agents of these hideous principles, and as advocates for renaming Washington County "La Vendee,"
while substituting "Lyons" for Pittsburgh after the region seceded from
the United States. Some friends of the national government were de-
lighted that the Rebellion had exposed the "vipers who would overturn
all order, government, and laws." They were certain that western Pennsylvania's "sinners in the midst of perfect light" would fail in their quest
to dethrone the Constitution, and that the Union would become
stronger by repulsing the challenge.[11]

With the French Revolution as their context and seminal cause for the
Rebellion, friends of order had only to explain how Jacobin ideals had

come to infect the "sans culottes of Pittsburgh." Immigration seemed the obvious answer, although Irish and Scots-Irish aliens were the ethnic groups most often blamed for the violence. Foreigners also predominated in the lists of "leaders" identified by easterners. The Swiss-born Albert Gallatin, Scots-Irishman William Findley, and the native Scot Hugh Henry Brackenridge were most frequently named as fomenters of unrest. Western Pennsylvania became known as "a center of terrorism under the guiding hand of Albert Gallatin" to many at the time, and the assertion has stuck for almost two hundred years.[12]

Class explanations for the riots fit compatibly with ethnic slurs. The impoverished, lazy, idle wretches who inhabited the frontier seemed bent on taking by force property belonging to frugal and industrious Americans. These illiterate "ciphers" had no right, in the eyes of advocates for order, telling the national government how to do its business. The ignorant poor, who had yet to learn the meaning of virtue, had confused licentiousness for liberty; and they were destined to inspire a reign of anarchy unless brought to their senses by more knowledgeable easterners. "Ambitious and designing men" in the region had taken advantage of these child-like waifs, and now the deluded were following the demented in a death-march for liberty.[13]

Friends of liberty responded with their own version of a class-analysis, and with ideological explanations that generally stopped short of justifying the Rebellion. They portrayed the federal government as representing an upper-class commercial interest and suggested that an army of eastern bankers would be appropriate for crushing the insurrection. "As violent means appear the desire of high toned government men," observed a correspondent to Philadelphia's *General Advertiser*, "it is to be hoped that those who derive the most benefit from our revenue laws will be the foremost to march against the western insurgents. Let stockholders, bank directors, speculators, and revenue officers arrange themselves immediately under the banners of the treasury, and try their prowess in arms as they have done in calculation."[14]

Drafting the eastern poor to fight the impoverished of the West seemed the ultimate hypocrisy to those who opposed the Federalist regime. Since the funding system was designed to accumulate great wealth in a few hands, create a "political moneyed engine," and suppress the state assemblies by "depriving them of the political importance resulting from the imposition and dispensation of taxes," cynical analysts of the political scene were neither shocked nor chagrined by riots among rural Americans. "If the state debts had not been assumed," friends of liberty concluded, "the general government [would have] had no call for internal taxes; the revenues arising from commerce being fully sufficient for every other demand." It was this adoration of British forms, this ambition to recreate the very conditions under which Americans had revolted from Great Britain, that now brought the United States to the brink of internal war. Friends of liberty were certain that they detected in this internal tax the cause of unrest, and advocated repeal as the high road to restoring peace.[15]

Even as the newspaper wars between advocates of liberty and order raged, and as western Pennsylvanians rampaged against symbols of commercial wealth and internal taxes, federal officials continued their quest to pacify the frontier. The administration decided, under President Washington's guidance and Secretary Hamilton's management, to pursue two paths at once, thus preparing for all contingencies. Political considerations dictated modification of the militant stance adopted by the government during the first two weeks of the Rebellion. In order to secure the cooperation of Pennsylvania's Governor Thomas Mifflin, the national government had first to exhaust all peaceful means of quelling unrest. In return for the governor's cooperation in mobilizing troops, President Washington reluctantly agreed on August 2 to suspend military operations for several weeks. The President's fear that the militia would not respond to his call for an army to put down the rebels, a divided cabinet, and lack of enthusiasm among state leaders for a military solution, led Washington to offer "reconciliation . . . with one hand" while brandishing "terror . . . in the other."[16]

After securing Supreme Court Justice James Wilson's official confirmation on August 4 that a state of rebellion existed in western Pennsylvania, Washington tested the waters of public opinion with a preliminary call for troops. On August 7, the President issued a proclamation that detailed his interpretation of events on the frontier since 1791. Washington again denounced "combinations to defeat the execution of the laws" and the influence of "certain irregular meetings" in the western country. The relationship between leaders and followers was clear to the President, and he blamed those elites associated with the meetings and petitions for fomenting unrest among the ignorant poor. Washington informed the nation of his preliminary efforts to raise troops, and ordered insurgents "to disperse and retire peaceably to their respective abodes" by September 1.[17]

The administration publicly committed itself to a peaceful solution of the problem during the three weeks following the proclamation, and for two weeks officials abided by that pledge. The President dispatched a peace commission composed of Attorney General William Bradford, Pennsylvania Supreme Court Justice Jasper Yeates, and Senator James Ross to the insurgent region on August 7, and granted them wide latitude to mediate an end to the Rebellion. The commissioners were empowered to grant an amnesty for all past criminal behavior in return for assurances that "the laws be no longer obstructed in their execution by any combinations, directly or indirectly, and that the offenders against whom process shall issue for a violation of or an opposition to the laws, shall not be protected from the free operation." They were instructed to adopt a conciliatory tone, but to commit the government neither to repeal of the excise nor a guarantee to prosecute future offenders in local courts.[18]

This effort to secure a peaceful end to the unrest reflected the administration's ambivalence toward negotiations with the rebels; as historian Richard H. Kohn recognized some years ago, it was "a shaky commitment, more a tactic than a policy, and indicative more of the President's uncertainty and fear than of a belief that force could be avoided." Certainly, the Treasury Secretary hoped that a contest of arms would settle the dispute in the government's favor, and President Washington shared Hamilton's belief that the use of force was inevitable, even before the commissioners left on their journey. The ministers of peace also put little stock in their potential for success. Bradford had already concluded that the riots were "a formed and regular plan for weakening and perhaps overthrowing the government," and the others were no more confident about their likely reception by the rebels. Ross and Bradford thought that a show of force by the government was necessary, whatever promises of fealty and remorse settlers might express. Even before he reached western Pennsylvania, Yeates was sure that there was too little time allotted for negotiations.[19]

The commissioners' ambivalence towards the mission was only exacerbated by their first-hand observations on the scene. A liberty-pole raising greeted the arrival of Yeates and Bradford in the rebellious counties. Local moderates at least prevailed on liberty's exuberant friends to raise the fifteen-striped flag of the United States on the pole rather than the preferred six-striper emblematic of the regional independence movement. Nonetheless, the ceremony seemed an ill-omen to those who hoped for a peaceful end to inter-regional tensions. Nor was Ross's report on the Parkinson's Ferry assembly entirely reassuring. He interpreted the meeting as split in three directions. One group of delegates was committed to a violent renunciation of all ties to the United States. Another faction was loyal to the Union, but determined to resist the excise. The third, or moderate party, consisted of propertied men who, "whatever might be their opinions of the excise, are disposed to the national will rather than hazard the convulsions of a civil contest." Fortunately, from the commissioners' point-of-view, the most violent group was also the least numerous, and the moderates had prevailed at the meeting. This preliminary analysis alone, however, was enough to reinforce the Treasury Secretary's conviction that the insurgency had to be forcibly suppressed.[20]

The first meeting between the commissioners and the committee of twelve appointed by the Parkinson's Ferry assembly was indecisive. The committee claimed authority only to listen and report back the government's proposals; the commissioners required a preliminary pledge in writing of the committee's submission to the laws and of their willingness to proselytize for law and order. The commissioners demanded a similar statement of fealty from the committee of sixty before September 1, and arrangements for polling the local populace on the question of submission by September 14. In return, the government offered a general amnesty for crimes committed during the riots, conditional on the restoration of order for one full year. The commissioners also committed the government to the "experiment" of trying federal cases in local state courts and to making "beneficial arrangements" for distillers who were delinquent in their excise payments.[21]

The federal negotiators were encouraged by the preliminary round of talks. The moderate party seemed to be gaining political strength, and in time would probably convert or overwhelm the other factions. But the commissioners also witnessed daily the comportment of "violent individuals" who refused to succumb to the logic of peace. Since they found it "impossible to predict with certainty the issue of this business," the commissioners were reluctant to recommend postponement of military arrangements beyond September 1. Bradford again privately advised Hamilton, in a letter of August 23, to recruit an armed force "to overawe the disaffected individuals," whatever the outcome of negotiations.[22]

By the third week in August, the administration was avowedly no more committed to peace than Bradford. Hamilton had expressed his opinion on August 8 that nothing short of a western-country plea for the despised tax man Robert Johnson to resume his duties should be accepted as evidence of submission. Two weeks later, in the first of his pseudonymous "Tully" letters to Philadelphia newspapers, the Treasury Secretary tried to undermine peace negotiations by branding the frontier riots as part of a concerted plot to overthrow the government. And he continued to fan the fires of political conflict over the next few weeks in essays attacking the "anarchists" who committed acts of "treason against society, against liberty, against everything that ought to be dear to a free, enlightened, and prudent people." Washington and Hamilton wished to preserve the public appearance of their dedication to negotiations, while privately abandoning the pacific policy that they had adopted out of political necessity earlier in the month. So even before they received the commissioners' preliminary evaluation, even before they read the report of the first meeting between the commissioners and the committee of twelve, and even before western delegates met on August 28 and 29 to consider the government's proposals, the President and his most trusted advisor planned for war.[23]

Hamilton directed Governor Henry Lee of Virginia, who would become the commander-in-chief of the expedition, to prepare his troops for the march. He also cautioned Lee to keep the maneuvers secret (although he did not suggest how to hide the draft of a 12,950-man army from public view), and he insisted that orders be post-dated to September 1. For "particular reasons" of a political nature, no one was to know that the decision to raise an army had been made before August 25. The peace negotiations were a sham, but a necessary political maneuver to forestall criticism of the administration's policy. It must *appear* that the President had made every effort to settle the dispute without resort to arms, even though he privately longed to teach the western Pennsylvanians a stern lesson.[24]

Washington and Hamilton had sufficient reasons to justify an abandonment of the peace negotiations to themselves; but they wished to avoid the political repercussions that would accompany a public renunciation of the process that they had endorsed only two weeks earlier. They knew of the visits by rebel agents to ministers of the Spanish and British governments. They had learned from sources in the western country that revolution was afoot, and that committees of correspondence were attempting to unite conspirators against the Union in western Pennsylvania with others in Virginia, Maryland, Kentucky, North Carolina, and Georgia. Hamilton's most trusted informant reported that the commissioners had little chance of "bringing the misguided multitude to a sense of their duty as citizen[s] of the United States."[25]

Under the circumstances, it seemed to the President and his advisor that waiting for the negotiations to run their course would only play into the hands of the rebels. Unless the government moved swiftly to organize an army, the opportunity would be lost for the season. Washington knew from personal experience that if the troops did not march soon, they might be stranded by the western country's harsh winter cold and vicious spring floods. The government would probably have to choose in a few weeks between risking a military debacle of major proportions and allowing the Rebellion to go unchecked for almost another full year. The President decided to err, if err he must, on the side of order; he committed the government to a stalwart defense of the Constitution without awaiting the unlikely news that the people he knew so well in western Pennsylvania had awakened to their responsibilities. Overreaction seemed preferable to inaction given the region's history and the President's knowledge of the rebels, the risks, and the stakes of the game.[26]

Neither the peace commissioners nor the western delegates who met at Redstone Old Fort (Brownsville) on August 28 and 29 were privy, of course, to the administration's decision. Actors in western Pennsylvania proceeded under the assumption that the negotiations were legitimate. As a consequence, if the committee of sixty accepted the government's conditions, and if the general populace overwhelmingly endorsed them, the President would suffer a major political embarrassment. But unanimity was always difficult to attain among the disaffected frontiersmen, and from its beginning the meeting promised to be a contentious affair. The first business at Redstone concerned the case of one Samuel Jackson, who was charged with calling the Parkinson's Ferry assembly a "scrub congress." Jackson's jest had all but condemned him to suffer the destruction of his house, mill, and barns. Moderates again triumphed, though, against the inflamed passions of the multitude, and "Scrub" Jackson escaped with a new nickname, the fine of one round of whiskey for all, and a good bit of teasing.[27]

The light mood engendered by the trial of Jackson did not survive the report on the commissioners' proposals. Some of the delegates were offended; they had expected to negotiate a conditional amnesty for the government, rather than a pardon for themselves. The initial hostility was so intense that moderates maneuvered to adjourn until the next day in the hope that tempers would cool overnight. And, indeed, Albert Gallatin's two-hour speech the following morning marked the turning of the tide in the moderates' favor. Gallatin eloquently explored the distinctions, as he saw them, between the western country's plight in 1794 and that of the united colonies in 1776. He sought to overturn the popular justification for regional secession by depriving the radicals of their claim as heirs to the Revolutionary tradition. "In our case," Gallatin observed, "no principle was violated; we had been represented and were still to be represented in the body which enacted the law." He warned against thoughtless sedition, reminding the assembled about the consequences of Shays's Rebellion. Before that agrarian insurrection, Massachusetts was a model democracy; since that event, according to Gallatin, the state had become the most aristocratic in the Union. "For certain it is," he instructed the audience, "that illegal opposition, when reduced, has a tendency to make the people abject and the government tyrannic."[28]

Gallatin and Brackenridge, who spoke next, appealed to the logic, the fears, and the patriotism of the crowd. The speakers agreed on the absurdity of expecting Spain and/or Great Britain to assist the region in a civil war with the East; they argued for the impracticality of secession at this particular time. With no seacoasts, and without free navigation of the Mississippi, an independent western country would be at the mercy of the nations surrounding it. The United States, Great Britain, and Spain would freely lay imposts on all of the region's trade; the new nation would be even more vulnerable to Indian attacks and wield less clout than the United States in peace negotiations with their savage foes. "There is no manner of question," Brackenridge predicted, "but the time will come when the western country will fall off from the eastern, as north will from south, and produce a confederacy of four; but surely it is our mutual interest to remain together as long as possible, to bear with inequalities or local and partial grievances while we enjoy general advantages and avoid general evils." Finally, there was abundant evidence that the westerners would lose a war with the United States. Like the Miami Indians who defeated the armies of Harmar and St. Clair only to be driven from their lands by troops under Anthony Wayne, the western country must also eventually fall to the superior force of eastern population and an eastern economy far better equipped to finance a war. In light of these circumstances, and "after what has happened," Brackenridge advised, "any terms, short of life, ought to be accepted" from the central government.[29] After the moderates had their say, David Bradford harangued for war. He ridiculed the moderates' concern for personal property and safety when liberty was at stake; he reasserted the linkage between the rebels' situation and that of Boston's Sons of Liberty in 1765 and 1776; and he confidently proclaimed that frontiersmen could disarm and defeat any number of eastern militiamen. Next there was a long debate, but many still feared to express their opinions in the face of an armed gallery hostile to any discussion of submission. Finally, the delegates agreed to a secret ballot, and voted by a margin of thirty-four to twenty-three for accepting the commissioners' proposals. Later, six of them claimed to have voted no by mistake, erroneously believing that the question was cast in negative terms. The delegates also selected a new committee of twelve charged to obtain "further modification" in the government's demands and a grant of more time to continue negotiations. They also agreed to arrange a public ballot on the question: "Will the people submit to the laws of the United States upon the terms proposed by the commissioners of the United States?"[30]

The deliberations of the Redstone meeting seemed indecisive to the commissioners, and, they believed, "only to involve us in new difficulties." The vote was too close to constitute an affirmation of peace. The refusal of delegates to proclaim their response to the offer in a public rather than a secret ballot represented an apparent rejection of the government's terms. And yet, the positive vote seemed progress toward reconciliation, and the commissioners wanted to encourage movement in that direction. They were convinced that "the authority of the laws will not be universally and perfectly restored without military coercion," but they sought to deceive westerners about the possibilities for avoiding the army.[31]

Since the commissioners had "no longer any hopes of a universal or general submission," they pushed for an immediate public declaration by loyal citizens in the region. They wanted at least to sort out the friends of government from the anarchists before troops arrived, thereby simplifying the job of judicial officials who would have to decide which frontiersmen to prosecute for treason. The commissioners considered their work ended, and two of them left for home on September 3. Only David Ross remained to supervise the balloting and to receive the army that was now almost certain to arrive in the near future.[32]

Moderates in western Pennsylvania had other ambitions for the September 11 ballot. In their ignorance about the government's plans, they still entertained hope for a peaceful resolution of the conflict. Members of the standing committee of Fayette County had not changed their minds about the excise, but they did recommend lawful efforts to gain its repeal. They, too, had opposed the excise when it was first proposed, and they shared their neighbors' ideological abhorrence of internal taxes. "An internal tax on consumption essentially differs from a tax on visible property," Gallatin and other members of the committee reasoned, "because, in the last case, nothing is more requisite than an account of what a man appears to be possessed of, whilst, in the other, it is necessary to know the quantity and quality of the article consumed; and in order to attain that knowledge a severe inquisition must take place . . . and, of course, extraordinary and dangerous powers must be given to the collectors."[33]

The federal excise on whiskey was especially loathesome, according to the Fayette County committee, because of the class and regional prejudices built into the tax. Small producers were often incapable of performing the complex record-keeping required by the law, and the region least able to afford it carried a disproportionate burden of taxation. Frontiersmen had a long history of willingly paying direct taxes on land, and an equally distinguished tradition of opposition to excises. They had long shared the sentiments of those who opposed Great Britain's Stamp Act on ideological grounds; and they endorsed the logic of the Continental Congress's letter to the people of Quebec in 1774. Nothing had changed, in their eyes, to warrant a renunciation of those principles. The government's recent extension of excises to other commodities, and its determination to try frontier offenders hundreds of miles from home, only confirmed the worst fears of liberty's friends.[34]

Despite their dedication to Revolutionary principles, Gallatin and the Fayette committee strongly recommended adherence to the law. They envisioned no alternative between submission and civil war; and they sought to convince their neighbors "how ruinous . . . to this country a [military] contest would be." Unlike their Revolutionary predecessors, the aggrieved were represented in the legislature that enacted the tax, and "every mode of redress which can exist in a republican form of government" was still open to them. Reason, patriotism, and fear all pointed toward submission as the appropriate response.[35]

A clear majority of the western Pennsylvanians who assembled on September 11 shared the Fayette committee's dedication to a moderate course. Many who had the requisite skills rewrote the oath to clarify their continued opposition to the excise, but their commitment to repeal by lawful means. They sought to communicate their loyalty to the principles under which the Revolution was fought, even while questioning the dedication to liberty of those who now ruled the land. In some townships there was no visible opposition to the loyalty oath, and in others there was only a smattering of dissent. Cross Creek Township, Allegheny County, for example, voted 170 to zero for submission; Derry Township cast 139 ballots for adherence to the law, and only three for resistance. In other districts, however, most citizens rejected the amnesty; and in several townships opposition was violent. In Franklin Township, Washington County, "a great majority being against the signing of any paper, and who had voted in the negative, came forward and demanded the paper in order to get the names of those who had voted for peace." Out of fear for the signers, the list was destroyed. "Turbulent bandits" disrupted the Unity Township, Westmoreland County proceedings, stole the list of signatories, and made off with the booty. Residents in several other districts felt so intimidated by their neighbors that they sneaked into more tranquil townships and took the oath there. The pattern of resistance and submission was not random, as some witnesses recognized at the time. We now know that violence persisted in those townships where the percentage of property owners was lowest, where the gap between rich and poor was greatest, and the tensions between agrarian poverty and mercantile wealth was most visible. In those jurisdictions where radicalized laborers set the tone of local life, violent resistance continued unabated throughout the month of September. Elite "leaders" who had only reluctantly come to the fore during July and August now abandoned the cause to a man, and retreated farther into the wilderness, or took the loyalty oath. Only the "ignorant and deluded" poor maintained their dedication to open rebellion.[36]

Elsewhere in the region, submission replaced resistance in the popular vocabulary. William Findley believed that if just one more week had been allowed for deliberations, reconciliation would have been almost complete. By the third week in September, even those witnesses unsympathetic to the rebels recognized that no armed force would meet the federal army when it arrived in western Pennsylvania. "The few friends of government" were soon "holding up their heads, and the leaders of the insurrection [were] begin[ning] to tremble." Somebody cut down the liberty pole in the town of Washington, and no one put it back up. Pittsburgh citizens declared at a town meeting that the Rebellion was over, and repealed the orders that had banished seven of their neighbors during August. Delegates to the final Parkinson's Ferry meeting on October 2 made similar and unanimous oaths of fealty to the government and dispatched two representatives—Findley and David Redick—to convince the President that all was well, and that the army's journey to the West could only prove counterproductive.[37]

Simultaneously with the western country's new-found loyalty to the national government came the President's announcement that the time for "overtures of forgiveness" had ended. Federal officials were not convinced that the frontiersmen's commitment to peace was sincere, and they knew that it was far from unanimous. Washington and Hamilton believed that the army was still necessary to complete the process of reconciliation; if troops were halted short of their destination, hostilities might quickly resume. If the westerners responded only to large doses of fear, perhaps a 12,950-man army would cure their ill-temper. The administration also had larger concerns than the the evolving situation in western Pennsylvania. The lesson they hoped to teach in the western counties of Pennsylvania was meant for a wider audience and was designed to solve a range of inter-regional and international problems. Indeed, it was those larger concerns, and events in other frontier regions, that provided the decisive impetus pushing the army over the mountains.[38]

Chapter Thirteen

A TALE OF TWO RIOTS
AND A WATERMELON ARMY

When nationalized troops sent to crush the Whiskey Rebellion reached Carlisle, Pennsylvania, in late September 1794, passions on both sides were high. Civilian-soldiers unused to the military life—either too young to have experienced the hardships of Revolutionary warfare or too old to suffer easily such trials again—were hungry, weary, and determined to use the new muskets and bayonets issued to them for this campaign. They were enraged by the derisive name "Watermelon Army" coined by detractors of their military prowess in the West. They had now reached the eastern edge of organized opposition and found liberty poles, symbolic of anti-excise protest, still standing. On the civilian side, there was resentment born of preexisting disaffection from the government and anger at this assault on the political liberties of those who protested federal policies. Local people resented this martial intrusion into their daily lives, the damage caused by marauding soldiers who broke down fences, trampled crops, and stole food, firewood, and shelter as it suited them. The scene was ripe for conflict despite the best efforts of senior officers to prevent violence, and two separate episodes resulted in civilian fatalities.

The first death caused by the army came on September 29. Dragoons galloped across the countryside that day in search of suspects associated with the raising of liberty poles in Carlisle. Among those rounded up in nearby Myerstown was a young man who was physically ill. The fellow declared his innocence and the debility that kept him from standing as directed by his captors. The sick boy next "attempted to go into the house without leave; the lighthorseman ordered him to stop, on the peril of being shot, and if he could not stand to sit or lay down, and in the mean time cocked his pistol. When the boy was in the posture of laying himself down, and the lighthorseman about to uncock his pistol, it went off and shot the boy mortally." The murder was an unfortunate accident. The youth who suffered an excruciating death from the wound to his groin, was not complicit in the anti-excise activities. He had obeyed the guard to the best of his ability. The soldier had no intention of killing him, but was perhaps a bit trigger-happy and unused to handling *the weapon. Nonetheless, an innocent person was dead in the sort of incident likely to damage the army's reputation and to arouse further disrespect for the government. Federal officials hoped to instill fear among dissidents, but not necessarily to kill them; friends of order had no wish to open themselves to charges of oppression or to create martyrs useful to the political opposition.*

The second fatality inflicted by the army occurred two days later, at a tavern in Myerstown. Several officers stopped to quench their thirsts, and a drunken civilian named Charles Boyd greeted them at the door with raised glass and a provocative toast—"Huzza for the whiskey boys!" The officers warned Boyd off with a threat to arrest him and then sought to avoid confrontation by retiring to another room. Boyd pursued them, "using vulgar and degrading expressions against the troops and the cause they were going upon." Captain Crain [Crane?], one of the victims of Boyd's diatribe, then ordered Private Zaccaria Burwell to take the belligerent man into custody. Boyd resisted the arrest, first beating back Burwell's pointed musket with a stick, then grabbing its protruding bayonet in an apparent effort to wrest the weapon from its owner. Again the private warned Boyd off, but the contest continued and in the scuffle Boyd got stabbed by the bayonet. Falling to the ground mortally wounded, the victim uttered his last words: "Success to the whiskey boys."

President Washington expressed "poignant regret" for the deaths and directed that the perpetrators be turned over to state magistrates. After taking testimony, a judge released both without charge. Washington also ordered officers to redouble efforts to avoid similar incidents. As Alexander Hamilton informed Governor Mifflin for the President, "it is a very precious and important idea that those who are called out in support and defense of the laws should not give occasion or even pretext to impute to them infractions of the laws."[1]

DURING AUGUST and September 1794, before the march of the Watermelon Army, violence associated with the Whiskey Rebellion shook at least twenty trans-Appalachian counties in four states and the Northwest Territory. In Pennsylvania alone, eight counties were affected—in addition to Allegheny, Fayette, Washington, and Westmoreland, where the Rebellion is generally recognized as occuring, Bedford, Cumberland, Franklin, and Northumberland experienced unrest. Allegany and Washington in Maryland; Ohio, Harrison, Monongalia, and Randolph in Virginia; Washington County, Ohio; and several Kentucky jurisdictions had citizens acting out protests against the national government.

Two of these "rebellions"—in Carlisle, Pennsylvania, and Hagerstown, Maryland—depict the range of anti-excise violence outside of western Pennsylvania that the Justice Department defined as illegal. Elsewhere, protests were either too remote from the centers of power for officials to make any credible show of law enforcement—as in Kentucky and western North Carolina—or they were so close as to diminish the possibility for successful resistance and thus undercut the intensity of protest movements—as in Northumberland and Franklin, Pennsylvania, and Augusta and Isle of Wight, Virginia. These two exemplary outbursts help to chart the geographical limits of central power and bear witness to the extension of that authority to heretofore isolated jurisdictions.[2]

Carlisle (Cumberland County) residents shared many of the grievances voiced by those further west, although they were not immediately threatened by Indians and had no obvious pecuniary interest in navigation of the Mississippi. On August 14 interested parties from the town's environs—most of them were not town-dwellers—met and drafted yet another petition to federal officials. They, too, decried the "oppressive, unjust, and unconstitutional" decision of the national government to assume state debts, and the "enormous load of taxes particularly the excise law" that resulted from the decision. They advocated land taxes in place of the excise, with higher rates for speculators who did not live on their property.[3]

These protesters were incensed by a land acquisition policy that they described as "unjust and impolitic; unjust because it is destructive of an essential principle in every republican government [namely] the equal division of landed property which ought to be encouraged . . . by law [as] far as is consistent with the encouragement due to industry; impolitic because it tends to alienate the affections of the common people from the federal government by being themselves deprived of becoming purchasers upon the same terms with the favorites of government." For these rural Americans, as for others, attempted enforcement of the excise served as both a cause for unrest and an occasion for voicing a range of related grievances against the standing order. Theirs, too, was a regionally, locally, and agriculturally based vision of the political scene, both a more traditional *and* a more radical blueprint for the nation's political future.[4]

As in western Pennsylvania, these Cumberland County protests shot off in several directions at once, with some people trying to channel dissent into meetings and petitions, and others of a more radical bent pursuing their own violent lights. There were individuals who advocated civil war and a separation of West from East. A fellow named Peterson, for example, proclaimed that "the people of the West had better separate themselves from the government of the United States than undergo such hardships as they were subjected to and they had better form a government for themselves, that they should have a government . . . [with] no President and no King." Robert Lusk (or Luske) was later prosecuted for sending an incendiary letter of support to the western Pennsylvania rebels. "As you have begun a good work," Lusk wrote, "we wish to have a hand in the fire." Others eschewed words for actions

against the excise. On August 27, about eight armed men with blackened faces visited the home of tax collector John Hurling, threatened
him with cocked pistols, demanded the papers associated with his office,
and departed with a cheer and a volley of gunfire. But few residents
engaged in such practices and, as in western Pennsylvania, no evidence
links organizers of the Cumberland County petitioning campaign to
these more violent episodes. There was no credible movement for disunion in Carlisle, although it is easy to see why nervous officials who
received reports of these incidents perceived that the back-country was
on the verge of a war for independence.[5]

Cumberland County riots associated with the Whiskey Rebellion were
placid affairs compared to those in other areas. Efforts to raise and defend
liberty poles in Carlisle during September 1794 showed the sorts of inter-
class cooperation and respect for property for which the Boston Tea Party,
among other incidents, is legendary. Intimidation, but little physical violence, occurred. One overly enthusiastic friend of liberty did forcibly
"borrow" a shovel from some workers, but no blows were exchanged.
More typical was the offer to pay an artisan for his expertise in splicing
two sections of the edifice together. He accepted the price and helped
carry the pole to its destination for no extra charge. Another man asked,
and was granted, the loan of an axe by a neighbor who declined to join the
proceedings. Artisans and professional men, laborers and farmers from
outlying districts united in this communal celebration and protest that
self-consciously harkened back to the days of the Revolution.[6]

The pole-raising itself, on September 11, was unremarkable among
Revolutionary-era displays for the symbols and ceremonies associated
with the event. Sections of timber were joined together into a shaft and
buried deeply enough to stabilize the structure. Then workers nailed a
sign to the pole proclaiming the slogan "Liberty and Equality." Jugs of
whiskey circulated liberally among the cheering throngs and guns were
fired to enhance the raucousness. One man balanced a bottle on his
head and stumbled around asking rhetorically, "Who will sell whiskey at
nine pence a quart without paying excise?" Effigies of prominent politicians were hanged and then committed to "blue blazes." Some physical
intimidation was associated with guarding the pole over the next two
days. Guards brandished pistols, and made threats against imagined
enemies who might try to fell the tree of liberty. They ordered passers-
by suspected of spying for the government to treat them to unexcised
whiskey. No one was actually injured, although several people were
chased down the street, grabbed, and had pistols or swords waved in
their faces. The crowd terrorized two men and detained them for about
half an hour, but that was the limit of force employed during the riots.
Neighbors also complained about the noise that continued through the
night.[7]

Under the circumstances, given the timing of such displays, federal officials perceived pole-raisings to be profound threats to order. Prose-cutors denounced this and similar protests in Chambersburg (Franklin County) and Northumberland (Northumberland County) as "having an obvious tendency to spread sedition and excite, encourage, and promote tumults and insurrections." Government attorneys missed or ignored the ironies of their resort to the same common law rules favored by British prosecutors during the two decades preceding the Revolution; they shared with their predecessors the conviction that "every good and wise government must provide for its own security and preservation." The obvious intentions of those who raised liberty poles made their actions seditious. Revolutionary traditions were not, in the eyes of the government, hallowed symbols sanctified by their association with that historic event. Times had changed, conditions dictated abandonment of anarchistic customs and strong measures to defend the status quo.[8]

In Maryland, Hagerstown's version of the Whiskey Rebellion was more locally divisive, aimed more clearly at overthrowing established institutions of authority, and was repressed more brutally by officials outside its environs than the Carlisle pole-raising. In all of these ways the Hagerstown riots resembled those in western Pennsylvania and con-formed with dominant traditions of American agrarian violence dating back to the seventeenth century.

State and federal officers knew of links between Pennsylvania insur-gents and western Marylanders during August 1794. Reports from the west revealed that rebel emissaries sought to purchase arms and inflame the tempers of the ignorant with wild stories about oppressive taxes. People isolated from eastern governments by distance and illiteracy heard that the excise now included grain—specifically wheat, rye and oats; that plans were afoot to extend the tax to all agricultural products, and that male children were to be excised at fifteen cents and females at ten. In response, according to government spies, the rabble was in arms and plotting to attack the federal arsenal at Frederick to secure arms for a frontier-wide independence movement. Friends of order now believed that western Committees of Correspondence modeled on their Revolu-tionary predecessors foretold the real object of the insurgents, "that the [protest against the] whiskey [excise] is only given out for the purpose of intoxicating the multitude, and that ANTIFEDERALISM will be their order of march."[9]

Events during the first two weeks of September only reinforced such fears, and by the middle of the month rumors reached Baltimore and Philadelphia that thousands of armed rebels were marching on the Fred-erick arsenal. These reports grossly exaggerated conditions, but were nonetheless relied upon as a basis for decisions. In fact, crowds includ-ing as many as 300 participants—about 50 from the town and 250 from its environs—had erected liberty poles in Hagerstown on two occasions. There was interpersonal violence associated with the tearing down of the first pole, and the threat of much more. Conflict was primarily between rural members of lower classes—laborers and owners of very little land—and more economically successful residents of the town. The pole-raisings were described as "invasions" and accounts noted that "very few persons of any character or property [were] involved in the business."[10]

Attempts to draft these men into militia units to help suppress the western Pennsylvania insurgency provided the occasion for the eruptions. Militiamen "beat their officers from the field" on September 1, raised a liberty pole, and hoisted a flag upon it emblazoned with the words "Liberty or Death." The next morning, after the crowd had dispersed, magistrates and "some of the better disposed part of the inhabitants" chopped the pole down. Enraged by this assault on their labors and principles, "the mob gave the alarm in the country adjacent [to the town] and were joined by a number of the country people, who assisted in putting up a second pole, and swore they would kill any person who should attempt to take it down. They also formed in ranks to the amount of three or four hundred, beat some who refused to join them, and threatened to march to Middletown and Funk's Town and put up liberty poles at those places." The Hagerstown rioters guarded the second pole for several nights, threatened town-dwellers, denounced the draft, the excise, and the federal government, and sought enlistments for a march on the Frederick arsenal. One unsympathetic witness believed that recruitment efforts by the rural rabble "would have collected 1000 men had not the Frederick people got notice of their intentions and armed themselves to the number of 500." For several days the mob reigned over Hagerstown, enjoying what one account described as a "complete ascendancy" that local officials were powerless to resist.[11]

Word that the residents of Frederick Town were prepared to meet them in the field sapped the martial ardor of the rioters and reduced their numbers to about ninety men, "who concluded it prudent to disperse and return home." Hagerstown officials were then able, even before reinforcements arrived, to muster the nerve and the manpower to destroy the "poles of anarchy" and send out a posse to arrest "leaders" of the unrest. They rounded up twenty rural folks and returned to the town where the liberty poles were ceremoniously committed to flames under the pillory, and the prisoners confined in jail.[12]

In the interim, Maryland Governor Thomas Simm Lee ordered 800 militiamen, an artillery company, and mounted troops to put down the insurgency. When the Baltimore Light Dragoons swept through Washington County during the third week in September, they gathered up twenty-two country types and delivered them to the Hagerstown jail, which already must have been bursting at the seams. Over the next few days they brought in over one hundred more, for a grand total of about 150 prisoners. The selection process for arrests must have been difficult (one suspects almost random) because "not one person could be seen by the troops that had the least appearance of hostility." "The inhabitants that I saw," commented another Baltimore officer, "were perfectly quiet and happy, tilling their land, and expressed a wish that all of their neighbors would do the same."[13]

Local magistrates, assisted by their out-of-town enforcers, then summarily tried and sentenced to death a schoolteacher whom they identified as the leader of the rebellion. If the inspiration of fear was their goal, these methods of repression were a success. One officer described the inhabitants as "terrified beyond anything he ever saw." The scene struck the soldiers as pathetic, with dirty, ignorant, poverty-stricken wretches begging for mercy in accents and languages that the dragoons found difficult to comprehend. This "alarming insurrection of lawless banditti" apparently seemed less threatening to the established order when examined close-at-hand than it had in rumors circulating throughout the East.[14]

Six of the accused, including the condemned schoolteacher, were then marched back East to stand trial for treason before the General Court of the Western Shore. Prosecutors charged each with waging war against the state, arming himself to that end, and attempting to convince others to join in an assault on law and order. All were acquitted by juries that were unconvinced by the state's eighteen witnesses. It was not possible to establish to the satisfaction of a fair-minded panel that any of these men had led the unrest. Like much rural upheaval in Europe and America, the Hagerstown riots were more spontaneous than led. To the disbelief of many friends of order, grievances and methods of seeking redress originated among the people who acted them out.[15]

As these episodes in Hagerstown and Carlisle illustrate, the variety of riots against the excise defy any single mode of analysis. The Carlisle crowds looked just like their most consensual Revolutionary counterparts, with parades, burning of effigies, and the construction of liberty poles. There was virtually no violence aimed at individuals, except those who threatened festivities or the symbols of protest, and membership reflected a homogeneity of class and occupational interests. Nonetheless, nationalists within and without the town perceived the activities a profound threat to order and responded forcefully to destroy the poles and prosecute fomenters for rebellion. The community was apparently no more divided over the excise than it and many others had been over the Revolution, but those who found such displays offensive were able in the 1790s to call upon a national military and judicial apparatus more effective than anything ever mustered by Great Britain. Some men again saw liberty poles as expressions of treason rather than symbols of ideological union, but this time they were able to enforce their views.

Conflict erupting in Hagerstown, on the other hand, bore closer resemblance to Great Britain's agrarian violence than to the Revolution's consensually based urban riots. Demonstrations split the region along both class and urban-versus-rural lines. Violence transformed the riots into a threatened march on a federal arsenal, and brought in response a swift and decisive counter-strike by Baltimore's elite corps of militia. Protestors lacked organization and leadership and had no sophisticated design or dedication to large-scale operations. They disbanded at the first sign of reprisals and begged for mercy or fled into the wilderness rather than combat better armed and trained soldiers.

The government successfully exploited these opportunities and used Carlisle and Hagerstown as staging areas for military operations against more remote opponents of central authority. These riots, and the eastern perception that more could erupt any day, were also the propellants that launched the federal army west. News of the Hagerstown uprising convinced Alexander Hamilton that "the disease . . . with which we have to contend appears more and more of a malignant nature." As Treasury Secretary, acting Secretary of War, and President Washington's most trusted adviser, Hamilton prescribed an immediate response lest this plague spread out of control.[16]

Raising and supplying an army of 12,950 men from New Jersey, eastern Pennsylvania, Maryland, and Virginia was a monumental task. Transporting troops through rain and mud across the Appalachian Mountains proved even more difficult, and the approaching seasonal changes augured worse if maneuvers were not quick and decisive. Disease, lack of discipline, insufficient rations, and squabbles over rank and command exacerbated harsh conditions and threatened disaster even before arrival at the scene of potential combat. The laws, the Constitution, and the Union seemed anything but secure as federal officials led the army to its wilderness destination. Rumors of a frontier-wide independence movement and negotiations between rebels and representatives of Great Britain and Spain heightened the tension, inflamed the passions, and inspired eastern nationalists with military fervor.[17]

Not all citizens shared this martial compulsion, and draft resistance was common. Class and regional variables defined the nature and degree of conflict, as exhibited in the Hagerstown riots. Opposition was not entirely confined to remote rural areas, however, or to those at the fringes of central control. "Small parties of the lower order" in Norfolk refused to enlist, and based their objections "upon a plea of serving against their countrymen, who were oppressed, and could no other way obtain redress but by resort to arms." Philadelphia and Baltimore experienced resistance of a similar nature. In all three cases the force of public opinion and power combined to overwhelm expressions of discontent. A Baltimorean, for example, publicly damned Congress and aroused his small following with cheers of "God save King George." A pro-government mob of middle and upper-class sorts, with the sufferance of public officials, tarred and feathered the dissenter; then they paraded him around the countryside and released him at the county line. "Whatever inconveniences may in general result from such acts," reasoned a witness not accustomed to justifying mob violence, "the present has had the most salutary effects and almost wholly silenced the clamors of the malcontents of that quarter of the county."[18]

Wealthy urbanites were often eager to enlist *if* arrangements suited them. Hundreds volunteered conditionally, agreeing to serve if they received a rank comporting with their self-perceived worth and if they did not fall under the command of men (whom they often named) that they considered social inferiors. Struggles over rank and command produced bitter quarrels and undermined the government's ability to organize troops. Marching the army as four separate divisions—one from each state—helped to alleviate inter-state rivalries of this sort and left intra-state competition to the discretion of the governors. Negotiations over uniforms—color, design, and accoutrements—occupied the energies of wealthy young men. Where egos and sartorial tastes went unsatisfied, refusal to serve or, in the case of draftees, purchase of substitutes were the choice alternatives for men of substance. Honor and ambition often supplanted patriotism as the highest priorities of both the resplendent dragoons riding west and those who petulantly stayed behind.[19]

Among the lower classes, especially in Maryland and Virginia and more often outside the cities, draft evasion by hiding was the most common response to calls for troops. Volunteers represented a very small percentage of enlisted men—as low as zero and seldom above 25 percent among rural brigades. The commanding officer of the Cecil County, Maryland, militia found "such a general unwillingness amongst the people to engage in this service, I very much fear that we shall find great difficulty to complete the number required. I have not heard of a volunteer in the County." He was unable to organize even a token contingent before the first week in November, too late to join the march west.[20]

Virginia suffered from the same "spreading backwardness" among its citizens; "obscure individuals," "refractory and mutinous persons," and other "delinquents" hampered efforts to raise an army. Officers in outlying areas were "sorry and ashamed to inform" the governor that "there is so many in favor of them [i.e., the whiskey rebels] that those drafted cannot be made to go." The state even experienced its own versions of the draft riots that erupted in Hagerstown. On September 11, militia officers in Surry County assembled their units first to seek volunteers and then, if necessary, to draft men to fulfill quotas for the national army. For the whole county there were only eight volunteers. A captain had just finished haranguing his company for its lack of patriotism and was about to begin procedures for a draft, when one Benjamin Bilbro stepped from the ranks. Bilbro confronted the captain and stated that if the officer was done he had something to say to the men. He then turned around to face the group and shouted that all who were for liberty should follow him. All but about ten left the field.

Eventually, the ranks of Bilbro's army swelled to almost 200 and rumor spread that they intended to attack the arsenal at Cabin Point. In the face of a well-armed defense and threats of execution for treason, the movement collapsed, with some men escaping to the wilderness and others volunteering for service to avoid prosecution. A similar episode disrupted the draft in Dinwiddie County and lesser numbers confronted their officers in Isle of Wight County as well.[21]

Drafting an army was only the first of many problems faced by officers of the state and federal governments. The rate of desertion was high, discipline proved difficult to maintain, and illness reduced the numbers and sapped the strength of effective troops even before the march began. Rough terrain, poor weather, and late arrival of supplies worsened conditions on every count.

In effect, the government marched two armies west to suppress the whiskey rebels. The militia corps was composed largely of draftees and substitutes who enlisted for the bounties they received. Almost to the man in some brigades these were the flotsam of early American society; poor, propertyless, often foreign-born, these soldiers were often in it for the pittance they received in pay or because they had no viable alternative. The other army consisted of gentleman volunteers who joined for a variety of personal, patriotic, and/or political reasons. Militiamen were poorly clad and had no service uniforms; the gentlemen dressed in a rainbow of colors and designs unique to each brigade. According to William Findley, the very word "militia" became an epithet attached by officers and volunteers only to the lower-class regiments. "To have a militia distinguished into gentlemen privates and plebeian privates is wholly anti-republican," Findley later reflected. "In the late expedition, the name militia was understood to have the same idea fixed to it as *plebeian* or *lower order of citizens*. An army arranged in this manner never can have confidence within itself, nor embrace the confidence of their fellow citizens."[22]

Partly as a consequence of tense inter-class relations within the army, discipline was a constant problem. Officers spent much of their time combing the countryside for deserters, and typical morning fare for the troops included the whipping of a penitent "example" to the rest. Officers had constantly to weigh the beneficial effects of public corporal punishments against the potentially disruptive influence of such displays. When soldiers were sympathetic to the victims, mutiny rather than deference could be the result. Late in the campaign, for example, officers reconsidered the sentences of three soldiers in response to threats from the enlisted ranks. On some days, soldiers simply refused orders to strike their tents. In the wake of one such protest among

Pennsylvania and New Jersey brigades on October 26, officers were forced to distribute an extra ration of whiskey and give everyone the day off. Drunkenness was widespread among officers—including the governors of Pennsylvania and Maryland—and enlisted men, and the random firing of guns during the night persisted despite numerous orders to desist. On November 7, New Jersey troops decided by general acclamation to drain four days' ration of whiskey at once, and discipline suffered accordingly. Gambling was rampant, to the chagrin of senior officers who felt powerless to stop it. Periodic rumors—such as those predicting late payment of troops and that the army was really intended to march on Detroit to fight Indians and British regulars—undermined discipline and slowed the army's pace until they could be refuted to the satisfaction of reluctant soldiers.[23]

Illness afflicted the contingents from all four states. Dysentery, with its accompanying diarrhea and fever, was the most frequently debilitating disease. Dr. Robert Wellford, who attended the Virginia troops, noted as early as September 28 that "the numbers of . . . [indisposed soldiers] in the cavalry are greater than could have been suspected." Throughout the month of October, Wellford treated about thirty-five new cases per day, and the bad weather that began in the middle of that month swelled the ranks of the unwell. By the third week in October over half the men in the Pennsylvania corps were incapacitated, making it "doubly hard on the remainder."[24]

When President Washington arrived at the Carlisle staging area on October 4 the army greeted him with all the pomp and ceremony that its depleted ranks could muster, and officers apparently succeeded in keeping the men relatively sober during his stay. The Commander-in-Chief reviewed the troops, "bowing in the most respectful manner to the officers," and at least one Pennsylvania soldier was overwhelmed by the glorious scene. "Amidst all this reflected blaze of armory," he wrote, "THE MAN OF THE PEOPLE, with a mien intrepid as that of Hector, yet graceful as that of Paris, moved slowly onward with his attending officers, nor once turned his eagle eye from the dazzling efulgence of the steel clad band. . . . The scene was augustly picturesque and inspiring." It was an event calculated to inspire not just the army but the nation. The audience was intended to encompass friends and foes from the East and West, and the President played to an international gallery as well. Long accounts of Washington's presence among the troops appeared in newspapers throughout the nation; and they were dutifully forwarded by European ministers to their home governments. The President wished to communicate to the world that the power and the majesty of this young nation were not to be trifled with, and he was a master of symbolic imagery.[25]

William Findley and David Redick, the representatives of the Parkinson's Ferry meeting, arrived in Bedford on October 9. They hoped to

convince the President that order was being restored in the western
country and to dissuade him from sending the troops over the mountains. They failed to change Washington's mind. He told the westerners
that he "considered the support of the laws an object of the first magnitude," and that nothing short of "unequivocal proofs of absolute submission" would deter the march of the army. He assured Findley and
Redick that every possible measure would be taken to guarantee that
the troops offered no insult or damage to innocent inhabitants of the
western country. Washington told his guests that "the army, unless
opposed, did not mean to act as executioners, or [to] bring offenders to a
military tribunal; but merely to aid the civil magistrates." "I believe
they are scared," was the President's pleased assessment of his conversation with the two men.[26]

The western delegates began their journey back home with the bad
news on October 11. On the same day, Washington left for Fort Cumberland, Maryland, to review the southern wing of the army. Again the
President added his majesty to the proceedings and received the adula-
tion of his troops in return. On October 20, convinced that all was going
tolerably well and that the army would meet little or no resistance when
it reached its destination, Washington put General "Light Horse Harry"
Lee in charge and headed back for Philadelphia. He also left Hamilton
as unofficial civilian head of the entire expedition, and he expressed his
hope that the Secretary of the Treasury would "be enabled to send B
[David Bradford] and H [Herman Husband] . . . to Philadelphia for
their winter quarters." The order was swiftly obeyed, and Husband and
three others were locked in the city jail at about the same time that the
President arrived home. Bradford had already retreated further into the
wilderness, from which the army was powerless to extricate him.[27]

After Washington departed, the army began its arduous journey
across the mountains. The march was not, however, equally difficult for
all involved. Enlisted men suffered a disproportionate burden of the
labor, the shortness of rations and supplies, and even the harsh weather
compared with those in higher ranks. The problems with provisions
were monstrous ones, and as late as October 7 Secretary Hamilton was
distressed to find "that the troops are everywhere ahead of their supplies. Not a shoe, blanket, or ounce of ammunition . . . is yet arrived."
Some men were so poorly clad that they had to be left behind. Even
when clothing and blankets did reach them, rather late in the campaign,
much of it was unfit for use. Shoes disintegrated in the rain and mud,
and soldiers found the going easier in bare feet despite the snow and
rocky terrain. Shortage of food led to plundering, thus complicating
relations with civilians along the army's path. President Washington,
during the time that he had accompanied the troops, was upset that in
some places they "did not leave a plate, a spoon, a glass, or a knife"
behind as they swept across the countryside in search of provisions.[28]

Officers selectively inflicted severe punishments on those caught stealing—one hundred lashes to a Virginia soldier who took a bee hive and beat the owner—but enlisted men continued to tear down fences for firewood, steal chickens and, where they could find them, cattle and sheep for food. Finally, confronting the inevitable, Hamilton authorized impressment of civilian property to feed troops in a more orderly fashion. The quartermaster corps initiated these procedures with full knowledge that they threatened the lives of civilians who needed crops, poultry, and cattle for the harsh winter ahead. As one authorized thief confessed in his diary, "it is a disagreeable act . . . but we were in a starving condition, our provisions out and none within eight miles; therefore necessity, which has no law, impelled us to it."[29]

Officers generally avoided the worst of these trials by boarding at inns or private homes. Ration allowances were considerably higher for officers, who could also afford to supplement their diet where civilians were willing to sell their fare. Those in higher ranks seldom slept in tents or open air and thus missed the leaky roofs and sodden ground that undermined the health of enlisted men. The journals of officers often read like tourist guides to taverns and scenery along the route, while enlisted men's diaries recounted weeks of hunger and cold. Officers' complaints were generally confined to the quality of accommodations rather than lack of food and warm beds. On occasion, however, where civilians were united in their disdain for the army, officers were gouged for services or were denied them entirely. In the wake of the army's two civilian murders at Carlisle, for example, officers were unable to obtain a chicken at any price to make soup for a sick comrade.[30]

From the earliest stages of the campaign, the army encountered disaffected civilians hostile to its purpose. In eastern-most climes evidence of opposition was scattered and largely confined to the lower classes, what one officer termed "the most ignorant and uninformed part of society." As troops approached the mountains, more frequent displays demonstrated widely shared opposition to central control. Civilians were intimidated, but not entirely cowed by this show of the federal government's might. Liberty poles marked the paths of dissent and convinced the troops that proclamations of fealty were not entirely sincere. Officers were convinced that in every town "we daily pass and repass the most violent abettors of the insurgents," but it was difficult to detect which were the ones who constructed the "whiskey poles" that sprouted up each night along the army's route. The poles could be destroyed, but the sentiments behind them were difficult to subdue.[31]

When it became obvious to everyone in late October that no rebel army would take the field, gentleman soldiers sought other outlets for their hostile tempers. Mounted contingents made no distinction between persons taken as witnesses and those captured for interrogation and possible prosecution. All were treated badly in a misplaced enthusiasm for restoring order. The most substantial roundup of suspects in western Pennsylvania occurred on November 13. Mounted troops struck in the dead of night, in some cases literally dragging men from bed and without permitting prisoners to dress themselves for the journey ahead. About 150 half-naked frontiersmen, some of them with bare feet, were then "driven before a troop of horse at a trot through muddy roads seven miles from Pittsburgh." At the army's quarters some of the prisoners were impounded in a muddy pen with no roof to shield them from the sleet that fell through the night. They had also to endure the taunts of guards who joked about hanging or shooting the lot, and suffer the ungentle prods of bayonets when they inched too close to the fires that warmed their captors. Others spent days in a wet stable, where they were treated to the small quantities of uncooked dough and raw meat their captors tossed on the ground. General "Blackbeard" White insulted and abused his forty captives personally before ordering them tied by twos back-to-back and thrown into the unfinished basement of a tavern. The suspects languished in that state for two days without food or fire; then White drove his herd of prisoners twelve miles through the mud and rain. When one of them collapsed in convulsions, the general ordered him lashed to the tail of a horse and dragged the rest of the way. Fortunately, some of the cavalry were revulsed by their commander's inhumanity and shared their mounts with those unable to walk any farther. Innocent and guilty, friends and foes of the government that now imprisoned them, endured the physical abuse and humiliation that accompanied it. Many had their health damaged or ruined, and at least one man died from exposure to the cold.[32]

Once the suspects (and witnesses) were apprehended, Alexander Hamilton and judges accompanying the army began the arduous task of interrogation. They hoped to identify leaders of the tumult and transport them back East for prosecution. Officials had no wish to indict mere followers who were too ignorant or deluded to comprehend the severity of treasonous actions. They wanted "examples" whose trial and execution for treason would deter other disaffected citizens from plotting rebellion or secession. Unfortunately, the likes of David Bradford and perhaps as many as 2000 "rebels" had fled deeper into the wilderness before the army arrived. Thousands more had availed themselves of the amnesty generously offered by the President. That left moderates such as Brackenridge, who had not signed the pledge, and undistinguished participants who did not conform to the prevailing vision of a leadership class. Attention focused on Brackenridge as the most prominent and vulnerable "rebel" on the scene. Senior officers prevented an assassination attempt aimed at Brackenridge by militiamen only with confident assurances that the rascal would be strung up soon enough by lawful authority. Hamilton's hostile tone, and Henry Lee's cold reception of his old friend, convinced Brackenridge that he was to be a scapegoat for the

whole affair. Only after two days of interrogation and interviews with
members of the Neville connection did Hamilton realize that the moderates' role in the Rebellion had been grossly misrepresented. "Had we
listened to some people," Hamilton concluded, "I do not know what we
might have done."[33]

As things stood, the government was left with about twenty obscure
characters in custody to shoulder blame for the Rebellion. Sheriff John
Hamilton and the Reverend John Corbley were the most prominent
among them, but neither had been major actors in events of the previous six months. More typical of "rebels" eventually prosecuted were
farmers who had lost economic ground over the past ten years and
laborers who owned no land at all. Two of those who later went on trial
for their lives were described by neighbors as "simple," perhaps psychologically impaired, and certainly incapable of organizing and leading a
secession movement against the United States. John Mitchell's farm had
dwindled from one hundred to thirty-five acres, and he could not afford
a still; Philip Vigol (Wigle) owned nothing at all. These two became the
only "examples" convicted of treason, but were later pardoned by President Washington. The army had utterly failed to discover and capture
"leaders" of the unrest, and contemporaries theorized that Judge Peters
authorized the detention of so many unlikely villains from political
rather than strictly legal motives. He knew that most could not be
convicted, and in fact few were ever brought to trial, but the times
demanded scapegoats, and the army, the government, and the eastern
citizenry required symbols of their victory over enemies of the state.[34]

The main body of the army began its trek home on November 19; the
suspects and their guards followed six days later. General White ordered
the escort to travel with swords drawn at all times and to chop off the
head of any insurgent who attempted escape. The journey was again an
arduous one, and accounts abound of hardships, unruly troops, and
abuses suffered by the captives. By the time the legion reached Philadelphia on Christmas day, prisoners "wore the appearance of wretched-
ness," and even Presley Neville (son of the excise man) "could not help
being sorry for them, although so well acquainted with their conduct."
To enhance the captives' humiliation, and perhaps to ensure that crowds
could discern miscreants from militia, officers stuck badges of white
paper in the hats of the "rebels." The triumphant army then paraded its
prizes down Broad Street to the cheers of a huge crowd and the celebratory discharge of artillery. Ships displayed their colors in the harbor,
and the bells of Christ Church rang peals of gratitude and welcome. A
band played as the procession passed the President's house, and the
great man emerged to bask in the glory of the moment. Newspapers
reported the next day that "the father of his country expressed more in
his countenance than can be described."[35]

The "rebels" were then delivered to jail, where some of them lan-

guished for four and others for up to six months. Ultimately, all but two
were acquitted. Juries freed defendants for a variety of reasons including
mistaken identity, lack of the requisite two witnesses to a treasonous act,
and imprecisions of testimony. The judges were liberal in their definitions of treason and provided juries a narrow latitude within which to
determine the facts in each case. Not surprisingly, given the political
significance of the trials, judges' instructions to juries were heavy-
handed by the standards of the day. Justices apparently succumbed to
self-perceived pressure for convictions and out of fear that all the rebels
would go free. Lawyers witnessing the trial of Vigol and Mitchell, the
two "simple" souls convicted of treason, reported that the verdicts were
inescapable given the judge's behavior. Supreme Court Justice Paterson
informed Vigol's jury that "with respect to the evidence, the current
runs one way; it harmonizes in all its parts." Likewise, the jury was told,
"with respect to [Vigol's] intention . . . there is not, unhappily, the
slightest possibility of doubt." Dutifully, the jury agreed; and the judiciary was spared the embarrassment of total failure. The government
had its examples, and the President an occasion for a magnanimous
gesture in pardoning the convicted felons.[36]

Left behind in Pittsburgh when the main army departed were 1500
volunteers under General Daniel Morgan, whose job was the maintenance of order over the winter months. Instead, the soldiers disrupted
the region's tranquility. According to Brackenridge, "they were noisy in
taverns [and] late in their patrols through the streets; the cow of a man
that had but one was stabbed, the horse of another run through the
body." Officers attacked a wagoner for no apparent reason, slicing his
skull in two or three places and cutting off a finger during the brawl that
ensued when friends came to his aid. Soldiers frequently looted houses
and destroyed property, and resistance entailed the risk of worse damage to persons and possessions. On one occasion officers demanded food
from a man who declined the request; he suffered physical abuse and
the destruction of his home in return. Civil suits eventually recovered
some losses, but most of the plunderers went unidentified and unpunished by a populace that feared worse acts of reprisal.[37]

Such was the "order" restored by the federal government's "glorious,
successful, and bloodless expedition." The triumph for central control
was, of course, neither glorious nor bloodless; and victors' hyperbole
masked the hardships endured by victims on all sides of the affray. The
confrontation settled nothing, as violence is wont to do, but it was a
transforming episode in a larger pattern of events. President Washington had his own understanding of the Rebellion's significance; he believed "this event having happened at the time it did, was fortunate."
The troops had "terrified the insurgents," and the government had
taught its enemies within and without the nation about the spirit and
power that bolstered the Union.[38]

But the nation was still not safe from internal disorder, and Washington thought he knew the cause of unrest. "My mind is perfectly convinced," he wrote, "that if these self-created [democratic] societies cannot be discountenanced . . . they will destroy the government of this country." The President believed that these societies had sowed the seeds of distrust in the minds of citizens, attempted to bring about a violent revolution, and fomented the western disturbances. Grievances articulated by the westerners seemed only a front for the real designs of anarchists and rebels. "Their malevolence was not pointed merely to a particular law," he told Congress, "but . . . a spirit inimical to all order . . . actuated many of the offenders." Fortunately for the country, these "enemies of order" had showed their hand too soon, and the "army of the Constitution" had ably defended the laws. The eyes of all well disposed people should now be opened to the evil designs of those who opposed his administration. This misfired Rebellion should convince all true friends of order, as it had the President, that diligence was the order of the day.[39]

Not everyone was convinced, and the House refused after much debate to endorse the President's attack on "self-created societies." Washington himself, his opponents observed, belonged to the Order of the Cincinnati, a self-created society by any reasonable definition of the term. Friends of liberty offered instead an explanation of the Rebellion just as cynical as Washington's, placing the entire blame on the government. "We have been accused of wearing the mask of conspirators," Benjamin Franklin Bache reported in the Philadelphia *Aurora*. "As well we might say . . . that the pretended friends of law and order had secretly fomented the insurrection that they might borrow another argument against republicanism and be furnished with a stronger evidence in favor of a standing army." To James Madison it seemed that Washington's attack on the democratic societies was "the greatest error of his political life." To Thomas Jefferson, the President's denunciation of the societies appeared to be "one of the extraordinary acts of boldness of which we have seen so many from the faction of monocrats. It is wonderful [i.e., full of wonder] indeed," Jefferson continued, "that the President should have permitted himself to be the organ of such an attack on the freedom of discussion, the freedom of writing, printing, and publishing."[40]

The Rebellion and the government's response thus exacerbated rather than cured the political conflict that rent America in the 1790s. It contributed as much as any single event to widening the breach between self-styled friends of liberty and friends of order, and to the birth of the Republican and Federalist parties in the years following 1794. And this was only one effect of the Rebellion on the transforming political scene. It was only one of the consequences of this last violent battle over the meaning of the Revolution.

CONCLUSION

At nine o'clock on Wednesday morning, August 19, 1795, Secretary of State Edmund Randolph was on his way to the President's house. Randolph was stopped on the street by Washington's steward who delivered the message that the scheduled meeting had been postponed until later in the day. When Randolph returned at the appointed hour, he found Washington, Timothy Pickering, and Oliver Wolcott waiting for him. The President was curt with his old friend and asked him to read and interpret a letter that he drew from his pocket. Randolph unfolded the large paper and began to read French Minister Joseph Fauchet's dispatch number ten to his home government, dated October 31, 1794.

The letter purported to analyze the underlying causes of the Whiskey Rebellion, and to explain the "repressive means" employed by the American government to crush the insurgency. At points the dispatch asserted, and in others it seemed to imply, that Randolph was the source for the information that it contained. It portrayed Washington as the puppet of Anglophilic ministers (most notably Alexander Hamilton) who despised the citizenry and who had monarchical ambitions for the President. The letter intimated that the government consciously provoked violence in the western country, magnified the danger to the republic, and used the occasion as an excuse for assaulting the administration's political enemies. The dispatch also referred to two other letters—numbers three and six—that were not included with the document that Randolph was reading for the first time.

When the Secretary of State had finished his perusal and initial analysis of the letter's content, President Washington invited the other men present to ask questions. At this point, Randolph perceived that more was amiss than he had detected from a quick reading of the dispatch. He was deeply offended by Washington's manner, and by the President's handling of this initial inquiry with others present in the room. "I came to this conclusion," Randolph later recalled; "if the President had not been worked up to prejudge the case, he would not have acted in a manner so precipitate in itself, and so injurious and humiliating to me." Under the circumstances, Randolph saw no recourse for himself but immediate resignation from the cabinet and the publication of a vindication of his conduct.

Randolph did not interpret the letter as implicating him in improper communications with a foreign minister; and he was incensed by the charge that he had solicited a bribe. Randolph read Fauchet's correspondence as overstating the confidential relationship between the two men, but not as claiming that the Secretary of State had compromised either himself or his government. Randolph's political foes, among whom he now counted the President, understood it differently, though, and discovered evidence within Fauchet's obscure prose that Randolph sought aid for the rebels and attempted to enrich himself in the process.

Fauchet and Randolph certainly had different recollections of their conversation on August 5, 1794, at the height of the administration's concern over the Rebellion. They agreed, however, that Randolph had sought to diminish rather than increase the chances for civil war. Fauchet remembered that Randolph sought money to pay informants knowledgeable about Great Britain's role in the affair. Randolph recalled vaguely only a suggestion that Fauchet pursue their mutual suspicions about the British, and share the information with the United States. Randolph was convinced that Fauchet embellished the story to impress his superiors about his influence among American ministers of state; he was certain that political enemies within the administration—and also outside it, now that Alexander Hamilton was retired from office—purposefully misconstrued the dispatches to bring about his political ruin.

In retrospect, it seems that Randolph was probably indiscreet in his conversations with the French minister, but no more so than Hamilton had been in his long relationship with British Ambassador George Hammond. Randolph, however, got caught by his political enemies. The proposition that Randolph solicited a bribe appears absurd. There is no evidence within the dispatches to support the charge, and Fauchet did not even imply that Randolph sought to profit financially from their relationship. Nonetheless, the political atmosphere was such that anything seemed possible. And Washington's fears for the nation, and distrust of his political foes, had reached new heights in the aftermath of the Whiskey Rebellion. Randolph believed, and probably rightly, that the President became enraged by rumors that Randolph was actively campaigning for Thomas Jefferson's succession to the presidency. Washington's suspicion of his Secretary of State's personal loyalty, a mistrust confirmed by Fauchet's dispatches, was enough to require Randolph's resignation from the administration. Randolph had not shared Washington's and Hamilton's enthusiasm for armed repression of the Rebellion, and now the President thought he understood why.[1]

IN THE AFTERMATH of the Whiskey Rebellion over 2000 of the most disaffected frontiersmen migrated farther into the continent's interior, thereby ensuring for themselves at least a temporary escape from the ever-lengthening arm and increasingly strong grip of central governance. The wilderness moved ahead of them. Shortly after the Rebellion, western Pennsylvania no longer defined an edge of settlement. Treaties with Great Britain (1794) and Spain (1795) secured evacuation of the Northwest by foreign troops and navigation of the Mississippi River, thereby enhancing the region's economic potential. The battle at Fallen Timbers (1794) and the Treaty of Greenville (1795) diminished the Indian threat, thus permitting population of the Ohio country at a quickened pace. Many of the conditions that precipitated conflict in the western country during the thirty years prior to 1795 were thus changing shortly thereafter. Much of the harshness of frontier life traveled further west and south, where the pangs of hunger, the squalor of poverty, and the horror of Indian-white encounters became the stories of nineteenth-century frontiers. The Whiskey Rebellion came at a critical moment in the transformation of one border region and the creation of others.

The army sent west to crush the Rebellion made its own unintended contributions to the local economy. The government spent huge sums in western Pennsylvania to supply the soldiers with food and whiskey. This brought the largest injection of specie that the region had ever experienced. Cash-poor farmers now had money to spend, and they spent it on land. Soldiers visiting the western country for the first time espied plots that were much to their liking, and many of them purchased ground and moved their families west in the years following 1794.

Eastern speculators who owned vast wilderness tracts were also direct beneficiaries of these transformations in the fortunes of the Old Northwest. George Washington, for one, had actively renewed his quest to sell frontier real estate only one month before the Rebellion, and the coincidence was certainly a propitious one for his finances. As he observed later in the year, "this event having happened at the time it did was fortunate," but in more ways than he implied. When the "army of the Constitution" crushed the "enemies of order," it also helped raise the value of Washington's property by about 50 percent. For the foreseeable future, the acreage would "continue to increase in price . . . especially in the western counties of this state [Pennsylvania], since the restoration of tranquility and the influx of money there have taken place." A fortuitous resurvey of one extensive plot revealed that the President owned hundreds of acres more than he had previously declared or paid taxes on. So the prospects were sunny for parcels that Washington (now that he was selling rather than acquiring) honestly described as "the cream of the country in which they lie, being the first choice of it." There was no rush since it was now a seller's market, but he would renew leases for only one year at a time lest they interfere with sales. With the Whiskey Rebellion behind him, the Indians overwhelmed by Anthony Wayne's army, and order brought to the frontier, the President could begin to realize his dreams for the region and for himself.[2]

Historian Charles Beard was thus correct to assert connections between pecuniary self-interest and political action in post-Revolutionary
America, but he needed the perspective of Frederick Jackson Turner to
make the charges stick. It is difficult, if not impossible, to understand
the politics of the 1780s and 1790s without reference to the frontier, and
to the personalty *and* property concerns of nationalist leaders. Self-
interest alone, consciously pursued, did not dictate policy, but neither
did disembodied ideology, virtue, or selfless demigods.[3]

Localists and nationalists were inspired by both economic and ideological concerns that at times superseded their commitments to the
United States. Either group, in any region, was capable of endorsing
secession under the right circumstances, as witnessed by the frontier
independence movements discussed here, the Hartford Convention,
and the Civil War. Over time, nationalist sentiments certainly grew, but
localism retained a dedicated following that was willing to renounce
allegiance to the nation long after the Whiskey Rebellion.[4]

The Rebellion's meaning, of course, transcended as well as incorporated the economic interests of regions and individuals. The language
of discourse on the excise controversy reveals some of the continuities
in American politics through and beyond the Revolutionary era, and
teaches the error of sharply dividing our history into periods defined
by ratification of the Constitution. When eighteenth-century Americans
discussed politics, they generally spoke in a shared political language.
They theorized in terms of scales and spectrums, incorporating meta-
phors from the marketplace and Newtonian physics, and thus revealed
their British heritage, their Enlightenment sensibilities, their distinctive brands of Whig ideology, and their capitalist experiences and values. They conceived of governance as something of a balancing act
between the few and the many, the rich and the poor, the powerful
and the weak. They imagined a delicate scale with liberty on one side
and order on the other. Too much weight on either side, they believed, could bring disarray to the political world—anarchy if the
masses ran amok, tyranny if the rulers became corrupted by power.
They envisioned the various levels of government—town, county, colony or state, and empire or nation—as points on spectrums of representation and authority.[5]

This is not to say that Americans always agreed about the political
issues before them, as the excise controversy plainly reveals, or that an
ideological consensus always helped them resolve peaceably the crises
they faced. On the contrary, America's internal Revolution widened and
deepened gulfs between classes, ideologies, and regions at the same
time that it honed the language of political discourse. Nor were wounds
healed by the Constitution. Indeed, problems were aggravated by the
struggles between localists and nationalists that the new political order
sustained, and by the 1790s republican language was one of the weapons

used in an increasingly bitter political war. By the 1790s it was by no means certain to Americans that they could coexist within their republican form of government; it was clearer that many wished they would not. The Whiskey Rebellion did not assure the allegiance of rural America, as Fries's Rebellion demonstrated only four years later, but it did demonstrate the federal government's commitment to a perpetual Union and its ability to enforce that commitment hundreds of miles distant from the centers of its power.

Even as the Washington administration's response to the Rebellion established precedents for executive branch law enforcement, it also demonstrated the limits of federal authority. After the crushing of opposition in western Pennsylvania, the excise law was still difficult to administer west of the Appalachian divide, where the costs of collection were never recouped. Frontiersmen remained willing to pay land taxes, poll taxes, and tariffs on imported products; and state and federal authorities encountered little systematic resistance to such levies. But trans-Appalachian Americans continued to resist internal taxes on grounds of ideology and self-interest.[6]

Federalists had made their point about the power of the new government, but still could not collect internal taxes on the frontier; and they had helped to create a constituency for the Jeffersonian-Republican challenge to their reign. The Rebellion was a critical episode in the ongoing battle between the center and the periphery, cosmopolitans and localists, East and West, between those who favored strong central control and those who demanded local autonomy. It was a signal victory for the self-styled "friends of order," who would rule the nation for another six years. It was not a decisive triumph, though, and the "friends of liberty" celebrated Jefferson's succession to the presidency as a "revolution" in both senses of the word—as a dramatic change and as a return to the principles of 1776, as they understood them.

During the first term of Republican governance, the whiskey excise and all other federal internal taxes were struck down. The dominant ideological faith from 1800 through 1860 interpreted constitutional authority to levy taxes on domestic productions and trade as reserved only for grave national emergencies. By the time that Alexis de Tocqueville visited the United States in the 1830s, it had become a folk belief that any attempt to enforce a national excise on liquor, except during time of war, would be met with another insurrection by liberty-loving Americans. Before the Civil War, the federal government never challenged this axiom established by the Whiskey Rebellion.[7]

This victory for localist ideology was not of course a consensual or permanent triumph. The lines that defined the Federalist-Jeffersonian breach became blurred in the nineteenth century and remain so today. But the heirs to these fundamentally irreconcilable visions of the political world continued to do combat in election campaigns, with Democrats carrying the torch of localism in the mid-nineteenth century, while Republicans, at times, claim its legacy in the late twentieth century.

The Whiskey Rebellion also provides important lessons about the decades that preceded the event. The Rebellion occurred almost twenty years after Americans had gone to war to secure self-determination, a larger measure of representation in government, and protection against unjust taxes on items they produced or consumed. The Rebellion came over ten years after Americans won that war and more than five years after they drafted and adopted a Constitution to implement the hard-won gains of independence. And yet, they were still fighting about taxes, still burning politicians in effigy, still tarring and feathering tax collectors, planting liberty poles, circulating petitions of protest, and again forming political action societies to defend the cause of liberty against its enemies in government. Something had clearly gone wrong, or so at least some Americans believed.

The story of the Whiskey Rebellion is also, then, one of disenchantment, not with the seeds, but with the fruits of revolution. Indeed, it was the very principles of the Revolution, as they understood them, that the whiskey rebels so lustily espoused. It was the Revolution's principles, the rebels argued, that they defended against another central government gone awry. And they are not the only ones in our history who have been disillusioned for the same reasons.

Thus, in some ways, the most striking revelation of this exploration into the contemporary meanings of the Whiskey Rebellion is the degree of continuity from the Stamp Act crisis through and beyond the anti-excise disorders of the 1790s. It is remarkable how little changed in the nature of conflict and the parameters of political discourse during three decades of Revolutionary upheaval. There is little of substance to distinguish the rhetoric, perspectives, ideology, or methods of Tories and British bureaucrats in the earlier period from those of the friends of order thirty years later. There is an ideological identity between many of the suspicions, fears, diagnoses, and prescriptions for the cure of political ill-health in the writings of Thomas Hutchinson, James Otis, George Grenville, and Lord North in the years preceding the Revolution, and those of George Washington, Alexander Hamilton, Fisher Ames, and other Federalists after the war. The attitudes of the friends of order certainly had more in common with the enemies of America's Revolution than they did with the ideals of Stephen Hopkins, Thomas Paine, the Antifederalists, and the Republicans either before or after the War for Independence and the French Revolution.

Some readers may also be surprised that heroes of the American Revolution espoused during the 1790s the very ideas that, we are told as children, they had once risked their lives and fortunes to oppose. Hence change, as well as continuity, and also some unpatriotic questioning of our national myths, seem crucial to the story of the Whiskey Rebellion.

These revelations are not easily reconciled with popular understandings of the Revolution; nor are they readily absorbed by existing syntheses of late eighteenth-century ideology and politics. The Whiskey Rebellion and the relevant contexts surrounding it raise questions about consensus interpretations of the period as well as more radical understandings of the Revolutionary ferment. Conflict *and* continuity coupled with the central role of ideas, but not a universally shared ideology, are fundamental to the argument presented here. Contrasting and sometimes conflicting ideologies, styles, experiences, and interests were essential dimensions of the Revolution and the politics that followed it.

Neo-Progressive historians will not be surprised to read that neither Thomas Hutchinson nor George Washington was a radical Whig, ever; and that these two men were not alone, nor unopposed, in either the Patriot or Tory camp. Nonetheless, and here neo-Progressives might be expected to disagree, an understanding of radical Whiggery remains essential to comprehension of the Revolutionary contest and the political combat that followed it. Although conflict over economic and other interests was at the heart of the Revolutionary experience, so were principles; and it is possible to generalize about those ideologies and interests beyond the local, state, and sometimes even regional levels. The identification of class or other economic conflict does not warrant abandoning the study of the history of ideas, rather it dictates a closer attention to the rationales people used (and use) to explain their actions to themselves and others. There is no necessary conflict between the two dominant schools of Revolutionary historiography, as some scholars have long recognized; neither school has "won" the interpretive battle over the Revolution, although from time to time myopic observers of the battlefront have made such claims for one or the other combatant.

None of us will abandon our cherished beliefs about the nature and consequences of the American Revolution in the face of the interpretation of the Whiskey Rebellion presented here, nor should we. Nor would it be appropriate to jump cynically from recognition of some cracks in neo-Whig and neo-Progressive perspectives to an abandonment of the insights of brilliant students in both schools. Some of us, however, may come to reexamine and rethink our personal syntheses of the late eighteenth century, and may even come to question the ruling paradigms within which we now work. There may be potential in the liberty-order construct for organizing more than just the taxation debates of the 1790s. Only further research will reveal the concept's utility for defining the breaches that provoked conflict over the basic principles of political culture during the eighteenth century. A liberty-order paradigm does, however, offer the potential for defining those struggles in terms meaningful both to the eighteenth century and to our own time.[8]

AFTERWORD

THE SPELLING and punctuation of eighteenth-century sources have been modernized and standardized in the text, and abbreviations expanded to conform with modern usages. Historiographical controversies have been relegated to the notes, lest they interfere with the story I have to tell. Readers with further interest in my disagreements with fellow historians, as well as my debts to them, might read my historiographical essay on the Rebellion and my article on internal taxes, which develop these points in more detail. "The Friends of Liberty, the Friends of Order, and the Whiskey Rebellion: A Historiographic Essay," in Steven R. Boyd, ed., *The Whiskey Rebellion: Past and Present Perspectives* (Westport, Conn., 1985), 9–30, was the dissertation prospectus from which this book grew; "The Tax Man Cometh: Ideological Opposition to Internal Taxes, 1760–1790," *WMQ*, XLI (1984): 566–591, became part of Chapter One. I thank the *Quarterly* for permission to reprint portions of that article here.

At Oxford University Press, Sheldon Meyer's early and continued confidence in this project has been most gratifying, and Leona Capeless and her editorial staff have helped much to improve the manuscript. Denise Thompson prepared the index. I greatly appreciate my association with each of these people and their contributions to the final product.

Over the past ten years, I have been greatly influenced by people who sparked my desire to belong to their community of scholars, and who helped me learn how to try. Alison Olson first inspired me by her imagination and enthusiasm as a teacher when I was an undergraduate at the University of Maryland. These lessons were reinforced by Miles Bradbury, Marvin Breslow, Ron Hoffman, John McCusker, and Al Moss. From McCusker I also learned how much work it is to do it right, and by his patient instruction and example I learned how to begin to work hard. Other friends who were students with me at Maryland were equally instructive and supportive in the study of history and the experiencing of life. Craig Donegan, Liz and Ken Fones-Wolf, and Jeff Looney are all valued friends and much admired colleagues.

While I was a graduate student at Princeton, Lawrence Stone gave me some hard lessons in how to think, Stan Katz taught me how to read more effectively, John Murrin showed me how much I do not know, and

Doug Greenberg invested much ink and energy in teaching me how to write better. To the extent that I write at all clearly, think at all coherently, read anywhere nearly as perceptively as I ought, or exhibit the least humility about how much I have yet to learn, I owe it to this group of teachers. By example, Nancy Weiss also taught me much about the humane dimensions of teaching. Fellow students at Princeton were also invaluable intellectual and personal resources. Val Martinez and Lou Masur were (and are) particularly helpful in those regards. As director of the dissertation from which this book grew (actually, in length it has shrunk), Murrin gave me the absolute liberty to follow my own lights and to make my own mistakes, thus contributing all the more to the lessons I learned from the experience. I also thank Greenberg, Katz, Murrin, and Jack Main for serving as a committee of readers for the dissertation.

Since I left graduate school, several people have assisted me in revising the dissertation into a book. Steve Innes, Chris Lee, and Dan Rodgers gave the original manuscript thorough readings and constructive criticisms. Innes and Jack Rakove were commentators on an overview of the project; and Innes has over the past six years relentlessly batted these ideas back at me, from which the book and (I hope) our friendship have benefited greatly. Lou Masur read the dissertation at least twice, offered insightful analyses each time, and suffered the projected hostility that I served up on the racquetball court in return, with no visible damage to our friendship.

My colleagues and students at Rutgers continue to provide more support and encouragement than I have a right to expect. Their tolerance, advice, and friendship have made my first years of teaching a joy in all respects. Paul Clemens and John Gillis read the dissertation carefully and offered good advice, some of which I even took. Rudy Bell, Philip Greven, and Dick McCormick provided equally insightful suggestions after reading a revised version of the manuscript. The book is a better one for their help.

Without financial support I could never have begun my graduate studies at Princeton, and without the grants that I have received over the past few years I would not have finished the book. My four years at Princeton were financed by the University's scholarship fund, the Davis Center for Historical Studies, the Danforth Foundation, and the Whiting Foundation. Since then, the American Bar Foundation and the American Association for State and Local History have provided generous research grants, as has the Research Council at Rutgers. A Constitutional Fellowship from the National Endowment for the Humanities and a Henry Rutgers Research Fellowship bought the time for me to complete the writing and revisions.

Librarians and archivists have, with rare exceptions, enhanced the process of research. Beth Carroll of the American Philosophical Society and Brian Driscoll of the Canadian Archives in Ottawa generously provided copies of manuscripts in their collections. Jodi Bilinkoff, who was in Spain doing her own research, secured copies of manuscripts from the Archivo Historico Nacional in Madrid, and translated them for me. Archivists at the following places also assisted me when I visited their institutions: Connecticut Historical Society, New-York Historical Society, New York Public Library, New Jersey Historical Society, New Jersey State Library and Archives, Alexander Library (Rutgers), Firestone Library (Princeton), Pennsylvania Historical Society, Pennsylvania State Archives, Maryland State Archives, Maryland Historical Society, Enoch Pratt Library, Library of Congress, National Archives, Virginia State Library and Archives, Virginia Historical Society, North Carolina State Library, William R. Perkins Library (Duke), and the Tennessee State Library.

Finally, and most of all, I thank Dennee. She read the dissertation more times than anyone, and even typed the final copy. She has read every chapter of the book at least five times, and suggested numerous improvements. Through it all—the long commutes from Maryland during my first year in New Jersey; my compulsive behavior while studying for general exams; the uncountable hours she has spent alone while I was in a library, away on a research trip, lecturing or worrying about lecturing, and at my desk or in front of the computer—Dennee has been there for me. In partial return for a debt that can never be repaid, this book is for her.

ABBREVIATIONS USED IN THE NOTES

AHR	*American Historical Review*
AN	Archivo Historico Nacional, Madrid, Spain
APS	American Philosophical Society
AQ	*American Quarterly*
CA	Canadian Archives, Ottawa
CHS	Connecticut Historical Society, Hartford
EHR	*English Historical Review*
HSP	Historical Society of Pennsylvania, Philadelphia
JIH	*Journal of Interdisciplinary History*
JAH	*Journal of American History*
JSH	*Journal of Social History*
LC	Library of Congress, Washington, D. C.
LCP	Library Company of Philadelphia
Md HR	Hall of Records, Annapolis, Maryland
MVHR	*Mississippi Valley Historical Review*
NA	National Archives, Washington, D. C.
NEQ	*New England Quarterly*
NJHS	New Jersey Historical Society, Newark
PA	*Pennsylvania Archives*
PAH	*Pennsylvania History*
P&P	*Past and Present*
WMQ	*William and Mary Quarterly* 3d series
WPHM	*Western Pennsylvania Historical Magazine*

NOTES

INTRODUCTION

1. John R. Howe, Jr., "Republican Thought and the Political Violence of the 1790's," *AQ*, XIX (1967): 147–165.
2. Gordon S. Wood, "Rhetoric and Reality in the American Revolution," *WMQ*, XXIII (1966): 3–32. Van Beck Hall made a related point when he advocated using the early national period "to analyze the connections between social change and political decision making before the upheaval of industrialization." Hall, "A Fond Farewell to Henry Adams: Ideas on Relating Political History to Social Change During the Early National Period," in James Kirby Martin, ed., *The Human Dimensions of Nation-Making: Essays on Colonial and Revolutionary America* (Madison, Wis., 1976), 323.
3. For a more detailed analysis of the Whiskey Rebellion's historiography see, Thomas P. Slaughter, "The Friends of Liberty, the Friends of Order, and the Whiskey Rebellion: A Historiographic Essay," in Steven R. Boyd, ed., *The Whiskey Rebellion: Past and Present Perspectives* (Westport, Conn., 1985), 9–30.
4. Leland D. Baldwin, *Whiskey Rebels: The Story of a Frontier Uprising* (Pittsburgh, 1939).
5. John Marshall, *The Life of George Washington* (Fredericksburg, Va., 1926), V, 170–190. The reference to "duck soup" was a dismissive comparison to the Marx Brothers movie of the same name. It was made by a commentator on an overview of this project that I presented at a historical conference. The vision of the Rebellion as "almost charmingly benign" was Richard Hofstadter's in Hofstadter and Michael Wallace, eds., *American Violence: A Documentary History* (New York, 1970), 10, and referred also to the Boston Tea Party and Shays's Rebellion. Dorothy E. Fennell, "From Rebelliousness to Insurrection: A Social History of the Whiskey Rebellion, 1765–1802," Ph.D. diss., University of Pittsburgh, 1981, is an excellent local study of the social dimensions of excise tax resistance in western Pennsylvania. Robert Eugene Harper, "The Class Structure of Western Pennsylvania, 1783–1796," Ph.D. diss., University of Pittsburgh, 1969; Andrew Robert Lee Cayton, " 'The Best of All Possible Worlds': From Independence to Interdependence in the Settlement of the Ohio Country, 1780–1825," Ph.D. diss., Brown University, 1981; and James Patrick McClure, "The Ends of the American Earth: Pittsburgh and the Upper Ohio Valley to 1795," Ph.D. diss., University of Michigan, 1983, likewise provide essential insights to the local social and political structures of the Old Northwest. Without them, my interregional interpretation of the Rebellion would not have been possible. The same applies to Mary K. Bonsteel Tachau, "The Whiskey Rebellion in Kentucky," *Journal of the Early Republic*, II (1982): 239–259, the only published account of excise tax resistance outside of western Pennsylvania.
6. See, for example, Lawrence Stone, "The Revival of Narrative: Reflections on a New Old History," *P&P*, no. 85 (1979): 3–24; E. J. Hobsbawm, "The Revival of Narrative: Some Comments," *P&P*, no. 86 (1980): 3–8; and, for a very different perspective, Hayden White, "The Question of Narrative in Contemporary Historical Theory," *History and Theory*, XXIII (1984): 1–33.

Chapter One: THE TAX MAN COMETH

1. Dorsey Pentecost, Washington County, to the president and members of the Su-
    preme Executive Council of Pennsylvania, April 16, 1786, *PA* ser. 1, X (Philadelphia,
    1854), 757–758; Findley, *History*, 33.
2. *Journals of the House of Commons*, I, 392–454; [William] *Cobbett's Parliamentary
    History of England* (London, 1806), I, 1121–1149; Steven Dowell, *A History of
    Taxation and Taxes in England*, 6 vols. (London, 1884), I, 188.
3. Edward Hughes, *Studies in Administration and Finance, 1558–1825* (Manchester,
    1934), 118–152; William Kennedy, *English Taxation, 1640–1799* (London, 1913), 51–
    75; Peter Mathias, *The Brewing Industry in England, 1700–1830* (London, 1959),
    343–355.
4. Hughes, *Studies in Administration*, 118–152; Kennedy, *English Taxation*, 51–75;
    Mathias, *The Brewing Industry in England*, 343–355; John Brewer, "War and Bu-
    reaucracy: From the Land Tax to the Excise; English Revenue Collection from 1660
    to 1790," unpublished paper presented to the Davis Center Seminar, Princeton
    University, February 18, 1983; P. G. M. Dickson, *The Financial Revolution in Eng-
    land: A Study of the Development of Public Credit, 1688–1756* (London, 1967);
    Stephen Baxter, *The Development of the Treasury, 1660–1702* (London, 1975); C. D.
    Chandaman, *The English Public Revenue, 1660–1688* (London, 1975).
5. Hughes, *Studies in Administration*, 118–152; Kennedy, *English Taxation*, 51–75;
    Mathias, *The Brewing Industry in England*, 343–355; Brewer, "War and Bureau-
    cracy"; Dickson, *Financial Revolution*; Baxter, *Development of the Treasury*; Chan-
    daman, *English Public Revenue*.
6. Sir John Glanville, *Excise Anatomized* (London, 1659); *A Letter from a Gentle-
    man . . .* (London, 1691), 14; [William Prynne?] *A Declaration and Protestation
    Against the Illegal, Detestable, Oft-condemned, New Tax and Extortion of Excise in
    General . . .* (London, 1776), III, 369, 370.
7. Dowell, *History of Taxation*, I and II; Hughes, *Studies in Administration*, 118–152;
    Kennedy, *English Taxation*, 51–75; Mathias, *Brewing Industry*, 343–355.
8. Ibid.; Dowell, *History of Taxation*, I and II; Hughes, *Studies in Administration*, 118–
    152; Kennedy, *English Taxation*, 51–75.
9. Kennedy, *English Taxation*, 61; Thomas Hobbes, *Leviathan* (London, 1651), 251; Sir
    William Petty, *Treatise of Taxes and Contributions* (London, 1662), 71–75, 91; Tho-
    mas Sheridan, *A Discourse on the Rise and Power of Parliaments* (London, 1677),
    172–174; *Considerations Touching the Excise . . .* (London, 1644?); Sir Josiah Child,
    A New Discourse of Trade (London, 1698); Edward Raymond Turner, "Early Opinion
    About English Excise," *AHR*, XXI (1916): 314–318.
10. Edward Raymond Turner, "The Excise Scheme of 1733," *EHR*, XLII (1927): 34–57;
    Paul Langford, *The Excise Crisis: Society and Politics in the Age of Walpole* (London,
    1975); B. Williams, "The Duke of Newcastle and the General Election of 1734,"
    EHR, XII (1897): 448–488.
11. Ibid.; Turner, "Excise Scheme of 1733"; Paul Langford, *Excise Crisis; A Collection of
    Parliamentary Debates in England*, X (London, 1741), 148, 149, 187.
12. *Collection of Parliamentary Debates*, X, 152, 157, 163, 164, 168, 195, 197; XI, 15–16,
    18, 26, 30–31, 39–41, 43–48, 77, 89, 91.
13. *The Country Journal: Or, the Craftsman*, Oct. 28, Nov. 11, Nov. 25, and Dec. 16,
    1732, Feb. 10, 1733; *St. James Evening Post*, March 24–27, 1733; *Northampton
    Mercury*, Jan. 15, 1733; *Fog's Weekly Journal*, Feb. 17, 1733. Reports on violence in
    Kent, Sussex, Yorkshire, Norfolk, Great Yarmouth, and Wales were printed in the
    Norwich Mercury during September and December 1743; *St. James Evening Post*,
    May 7–9, 1743; *General Evening Post*, May 4–7, 1734, June 11–13, 1734; *London
    Evening Post*, May 7–9, 1734.

14. Caroline Robbins, *The Eighteenth-Century Commonwealthman: Studies in the Trans-mission, Development and Circumstance of English Liberal Thought from the Restoration of Charles II until the War with the Thirteen Colonies* (Cambridge, Mass., 1959); Bernard Bailyn, *The Ideological Origins of the American Revolution* (Cambridge, Mass., 1967); J. G. A. Pocock, *The Machiavellian Moment: Florentine Political Thought and the Atlantic Republican Tradition* (Princeton, 1975).

15. *Parliamentary History*, XV, 1307–1314; *The North Briton*, XLIII, March 26, 1763; Mathias, *Brewing Industry*; Kennedy, *English Taxation*; Hughes, *Studies in Administration*; Dowell, *History of Taxation*, II.

16. Paul S. Boyer, "Borrowed Rhetoric: the Massachusetts Excise Controversy of 1754," *WMQ*, XXI (1964): 328–351; [Samuel Cooper] *The Crisis* (Boston, 1754); *The Eclipse* (Boston, 1754); *A Letter From a Gentleman to his Friend, Upon the Excise-Bill Now Under Consideration* (Boston, June 7, 1754); [John Lovell] *Freedom, The First of Blessings* (Boston, 1754); *A Plea for the Poor and Distressed, Against the Bill, For Granting an Excise Upon Wines, and Spirits distilled, sold by Retail, or consumed within this Province, &c* (Boston, 1754); *The Relapse* (Boston, 1754); *The Review* (Boston, 1754); *Some Observations on the Bill Entitled, "An Act for Granting to His Majesty an Excise Upon Wines, and Spirits Distilled, sold by Retail or Consumed Within this Province, and upon Limes, Lemons, and Oranges"* (Boston, 1754); *The Voice of the People* (Boston, 1754); *The Monster of Monsters* (Boston, 1754); *The Cub new lick'd; or, A new Story of An Old Monster* (Boston, 1755); A. P., "To the Freemen of Pennsylvania," [1750?], Stauffer Collection, HSP; Charles M. Andrews, *The Colonial Background of the American Revolution* (New Haven, 1924, 1931), 54.

17. For an analysis of American opposition to internal taxes with a more historiographical focus, see Thomas P. Slaughter, "The Tax Man Cometh: Ideological Opposition to Internal Taxes, 1760–1790," *WMQ*, XLI (1984): 566–591.

18. In England, the terms "excise," "inland" tax, and "interior" tax were apparently still synonymous during the eighteenth century. (See, *Craftsman*, Nov. 25, 1732, 1.) In America, excises were viewed as a subset of the more inclusive term "internal" tax. Stamp taxes, for example, were internal taxes, but they were not called excises. British politicians made operational distinctions between inland or internal taxes and customs duties, so the words were not new. It was the ideological distinction articulated by some Americans that the British were not used to hearing.

19. William Beckford, Feb. 6, 1765, in R. C. Simmons and P. D. G. Thomas, eds., *Proceedings and Debates of the British Parliaments Respecting North America, 1754–1783* (New York, 1983), II, 10–13, 82, 86, 87, 91, 135–143, 285, 294, 298.

20. Ibid., 86, 87, 129, 132, 140, 145. North's observations came in his speech of Dec. 8, 1768, Cavendish Diaries, Egerton MSS, 215, fol. 302, British Library; P. D. G. Thomas, ed., "The Parliamentary Diaries of Nathaniel Ryder, 1764–1767," *Camden Miscellany*, no. 23, Camden 4th ser., VII (1969): 233–238, 253–276, 291–300; John L. Bullion, *A Great and Necessary Measure: George Grenville and the Genesis of the Stamp Act, 1763–1765* (Columbia, Mo., 1983); Thomas, *British Politics and the Stamp Act Crisis: The First Phase of the American Revolution, 1763–1767* (London, 1975), esp. ch. 12; Thomas P. Slaughter, "The Empire Strikes Back: George Grenville and the Stamp Tax," *Reviews in American History*, XII (1984): 204–210.

21. Hutchinson, quoted in Edmund S. Morgan, "Thomas Hutchinson and the Stamp Act," *NEQ*, XXI (1948): 476.

22. *Proceedings*, II, 113–121, 134–135, 166, 194, 199–218, 228–233.

23. Edmund S. Morgan and Helen M. Morgan, *The Stamp Act Crisis: Prologue to Revolution* (Chapel Hill, N. C., 1953; rev. ed., New York, 1963); Pauline Maier, *From Resistance to Revolution: Colonial Radicals and the Development of American Opposition to Britain, 1765–1776* (New York, 1972); *Boston Evening-Post*, Sept. 2, 1765.

24. *The examination of Doctor Benjamin Franklin, before an August Assembly, relating to the Repeal of the Stamp Act &c.* (Philadelphia, 1766), in Leonard W. Labaree *et al.*, eds., *The Papers of Benjamin Franklin* (New Haven, 1959–), XIII, 139. In a letter of March 13, 1768, to his son William, Franklin again affirmed Parliament's authority to lay duties on imported goods, but not "internal taxes" [ibid., XV, 76].

25. Malcolm Freiberg, ed., *Journals of the House of Representatives of Massachusetts* (Boston, 1971), XLI, 76.

26. Franklin to Jackson, May 1, 1764, *Franklin Papers*, XI, 186.

27. Thomas Fitch *et al.*, *Reasons Why the British Colonies in America Should Not Be Charged with Internal Taxes . . .* (New Haven, 1764), 4–5, in Bernard Bailyn, ed., *Pamphlets of the American Revolution* (Cambridge, Mass., 1965), 386–387; [Stephen Hopkins], *The Rights of Colonies Examined* (Providence, 1765), in Bailyn, ed., *Pamphlets,* 513.

28. Richard Bland, *The Colonel Dismounted . . .* (Williamsburg, Va., 1764), 22, in Bailyn, ed., *Pamphlets,* 320; Fitch *et al.*, *Reasons Why,* in Bailyn, ed., *Pamphlets,* 378–407.

29. Franklin to Jackson, May 1, 1764, *Franklin Papers*, XI, 186.

30. James Otis, *The Rights of the British Colonies Asserted and Proved* (Boston, 1764), 38, 42, in Bailyn, ed., *Pamphlets,* 447, 450–451, and *A Vindication of the British Colonies . . .* (Boston, 1765), 5, ibid., 555; *Proceedings,* II, 119, 201, 207, 209, 210.

31. *Boston Evening-Post,* Feb. 4, 1765, March 18, 1765, May 13, 1765, Aug. 13 and 26, 1765; *Connecticut Gazette,* Sept. 9, 1765, reprinted in the *Boston Gazette,* Sept. 9, 1765; [Hopkins] *Rights of the Colonies Examined,* in Bailyn, ed., *Pamphlets,* 508, 512, 513, 515–517.

32. [Hopkins] *Rights of the Colonies Examined,* in Bailyn, ed., *Pamphlets,* 516. "Localist," as used here, describes those Americans whose loyalties and perspectives were more local than national on a spectrum that described the late eighteenth-century political scene. The term is generally synonymous with "Country" and later "Jeffersonian-Republican," at least on the issue of taxation. It distinguishes the ideology of this group from those variously termed "nationalist," "cosmopolitan," "Court," and "Federalist." For a different, and more precise definition of "localist" and "cosmopolitan" see Jackson Turner Main, *Political Parties before the Constitution* (Chapel Hill, N. C., 1973), 32–33. On American varieties of "Court" and "Country" see, for example, Joyce Appleby, "Commercial Farming and the 'Agrarian Myth' in the Early Republic," *JAH,* LXVIII (1982): 833–849, and "What Is Still American in the Political Philosophy of Thomas Jefferson?" *WMQ,* XXXIX (1982): 287–309; John M. Murrin, "The Great Inversion, or Court versus Country: A Comparison of the Revolution Settlements in England (1688–1721) and America (1776–1816)," in J. G. A. Pocock, ed., *Three British Revolutions: 1641, 1688, 1776* (Princeton, N. J., 1980), 368–453; Robert E. Shalhope, "Republicanism and Early American Historiography," *WMQ,* XXXIX (1982): 334–356; James H. Hutson, "Country, Court, and Constitution: Antifederalism and the Historians," ibid., XXXVIII (1981): 337–368.

33. Standing armies, corrupt collectors of external taxes, and such repressive measures as the Boston Port Act were also perceived as threats to American liberty. See, for example, Oliver M. Dickerson, *The Navigation Acts and the American Revolution* (Philadelphia, 1951), ch. 9. Some Americans also opposed external taxes for ideological reasons. John Dickinson, for one, equated all taxation with representation. (*The Farmer's and Monitor's Letters, to the Inhabitants of the British Colonies* (Williamsburg, Va., 1769).) Among historians, even Edmund Morgan, whose major interpretive points concern the colonists' dedication to principle and the consistency of their principles over time, must acknowledge that colonial resistance to British taxes after 1766 was never again so dedicated or interregionally united. (*The Birth of the Republic, 1763–89* (Chicago, 1956), 49–51.)

34. Charles Francis Adams, ed., *The Works of John Adams*, 10 vols. (Boston, 1850–1856), II, 374.

35. Jack N. Rakove, *The Beginnings of National Politics: An Interpretive History of the Continental Congress* (New York, 1979), 157–158, 170, 303, 306–309, 315, 362, 380, 399; E. James Ferguson, "The Nationalists of 1781–1783 and the Economic Interpretation of the Constitution," *JAH*, LVI (1969): 241–261.

36. The fact that the controversy over the internal-external distinction never arose in the Continental Congress or the Constitutional Convention may indicate the unrepresentative character of those bodies. The isolation of each from the pressures of public opinion is well known. See, for example, Charles Warren, *The Making of the Constitution* (Cambridge, Mass., 1948), 627; U. S., *Constitution*, Art. I, sec. 8, par. I; Art. I, sec. 10, par. 2.

37. "Centinel," *Independent Gazette*, Oct. 5, 1787, in Cecelia M. Kenyon, ed., *The Antifederalists* (Indianapolis, Ind., 1966), 9.

38. "Letter from the Federal Farmer," no. 3, Oct. 10, 1787, in Kenyon, ed., *Antifederalists*, 223; Jonathan Elliot, ed., *The Debates in the Several State Conventions on the Adoption of the Federal Constitution, as Recommended by the General Convention at Philadelphia in 1787*, 2d ed. (Washington, D. C., 1861), IV, 93, 245. Similar amendments were offered in several other state conventions, including New York, Virginia, and Pennsylvania. See, for example, ibid., II, 331. These proposals were quite close to Lord North's of 1775. On opposition to internal taxes see also Merrill Jensen, ed., *The Documentary History of the Ratification of the Constitution*, Vol. II: *Ratification of the Constitution by the States: Pennsylvania* (Madison, Wis., 1976), 162, 307, 445, 447; Herbert J. Storing, ed., *The Complete Anti-Federalist*, 7 vols. (Chicago, 1981), III, 41.

39. "Letter from the Federal Farmer," no. 3, Oct. 10, 1787, in Kenyon, ed., *Antifederalists*, 223.

40. Ibid., 223–224.

41. "John De Witt," "To the Free Citizens of the Commonwealth of Massachusetts," letter no. 2, *American Herald* (Boston), Oct.–Dec. 1787, in Kenyon, ed., *Antifederalists*, 100; "Agrippa," no. 9, *Massachusetts Gazette*, Dec. 28, 1787, ibid., 137; Elliot, ed., *Debates*, IV, 87, 88; II, 344.

42. Elliot, ed., *Debates*, III, 411–412.

43. Ibid., II, 335; IV, 80, 88; II, 74, 531. On the linkage between representation and internal taxation see "Philadelphiensis," no. 10, *Independent Gazette*, Feb. 21, 1788, in Kenyon, ed., *Antifederalists*, 79; "Letter from the Federal Farmer," no. 3, Oct. 10, 1787, in Kenyon, ed., *Antifederalists*, 225, 217.

44. "The Address and Reasons of Dissent of the Minority of the Convention of the State of Pennsylvania to Their Constituents," *Pennsylvania Packet, and Daily Advertiser* (Philadelphia), Dec. 18, 1787, in Kenyon, ed., *Antifederalists*, 55–56, 57, 58; Patrick Henry, Debates in the Virginia Convention, in Storing, ed., *Complete Anti-Federalist*, V, 244. For further documentation of the Antifederalist position see the footnotes to Slaughter, "The Tax Man Cometh."

Chapter Two: THE QUEST FOR FRONTIER AUTONOMY

1. *Pennsylvania Gazette*, July 5, 1763; [Benjamin Franklin] *A Narrative of the Late Massacres in Lancaster County of a Number of Indians, Friends of this Province* (Philadelphia, 1764), John R. Dunbar, ed., *The Paxton Papers* (The Hague, 1957), 58–59. This sketch of the Paxton riots is based on Brook Hindle, "The March of the Paxton Boys," *WMQ*, III (1946): 461–486; James Kirby Martin, "The Return of the Paxton Boys and the Historical State of the Pennsylvania Frontier," *PAH*, XXXVIII (1971): 117–133; and Dunbar, ed., *The Paxton Papers*, especially Franklin's *Narrative*, 57–75; and *A Declaration and Remonstrance of the distressed and bleeding Frontier Inhabitants of the Province of Pennsylvania* (Philadelphia, 1764).

2. "Translator's Note," Marquis de Chastellux, *Travels in North America, in the Years 1780, 1781, and 1782* (Dublin, 1787), I, 218–219. See also, Charles Thomson to Hanna Thomson, July 25, 1783, Eugene R. Sheridan and John M. Murrin, eds., *Congress at Princeton: Being the Letters of Charles Thomson June–October 1783* (Princeton, N. J., 1985), 28–31; Charles Thomson to Hannah Thomson, Oct. 14, 1783, ibid., 66–67.

3. Timothy Pickering to Rufus King, June 4, 1785, in Charles R. King, ed., *The Life and Correspondence of Rufus King* (New York, 1894), I, 106–107; Tobias Lear to Benjamin Lincoln, Feb. 26, 1787, Benjamin Lincoln Papers, Boston Historical Society, microfilm, reel 8.

4. George Mason to George Mason, Jr., Jan. 8, 1783, Robert A. Rutland, ed., *The Papers of George Mason* (Chapel Hill, N. C., 1970), II, 761. For predictions of war see, "Nassau," *Pennsylvania Evening Herald,* Jan. 8, Feb. 10, 15, and 26, 1785; "Boston," *Providence Gazette,* Jan. 24 and 29, May 7 and 24, and June 4, 1785; *New York Journal,* Feb. 3, 1785; [Richmond] *Virginia Gazette,* March 12, 1785; *Newport Mercury,* May 4 and June 14, 1785; [Trenton] *New Jersey Gazette,* Feb. 12 and 21, 1785; *New Brunswick Political Intelligencer,* Feb. 22 and March 1, 1785.

5. Thomas P. Slaughter, "Mobs and Crowds, Riots and Brawls: The History of Early American Political Violence," unpublished essay.

6. William L. Saunders, ed., *The Colonial Records of North Carolina* (Raleigh, 1886–1890), X, 256–262; William Stewart Lester, *The Transylvania Colony* (Spencer, Ind., 1935), 121, 123, 125, 230; George Henry Alden, *New Governments West of the Alleghanies Before 1780,* Bulletin of the University of Wisconsin Historical Series, II, no. 1 (Madison, Wis., 1897); Peter Force, ed., *American Archives* (Washington, D.C., 1837–1853), ser. 4, VI, 543; *North Carolina Colonial Records,* X, 373–376; Edmund Cody Burnett, ed., *The Letters of the Members of the Continental Congress,* 8 vols. (Washington, D.C., 1921–1936), I, 123; *Journal of the Virginia House of Delegates,* Oct. 30 and Nov. 4, 1778.

7. Worthington C. Ford, ed., *Journals of the Continental Congress, 1774–1789* (Washington, D.C., 1904–1907), IV, 342; "The Memorial of the Inhabitants of the Country West of the Alleghany Mountains," Yeates Papers, HSP.

8. "To the Hon. the Provincial Council of North-Carolina," [1776?], J. G. M. Ramsey, *The Annals of Tennessee to the End of the Eighteenth Century, Comprising its Settlement* (Charleston, N.C., 1853; rpt. ed., Kingsport, Tenn., 1967), 134–138; A. W. Putnam, *History of Middle Tennessee* (1859; rpt. ed., Knoxville, 1971). See also, Frederick Jackson Turner, "Western State-Making in the Revolutionary Era," *AHR,* I (1895–1896): 267–268; Louise Phelps Kellog, ed., "Petition for a Western State, 1780," *MVHR,* I (1913–1914): 268; Theodore Roosevelt, *The Winning of the West,* II (New York, 1889), appendix E, 398–399; David Ramsay, *The History of South Carolina, from its First Settlement in 1670, to the Year 1808,* 2 vols. (Charleston, S. C., 1809); Thomas Paine, *Public Good,* in Philip S. Foner, ed., *The Complete Writings of Thomas Paine,* II (New York, 1945), 326, 330.

9. Ford, ed., *Journals of the Continental Congress,* IV, 205, 342, 357–358.

10. "The Declaration and Petition of the Inhabitants of the New Hampshire Grants, to Congress, announcing the District to be a free and Independent State," William Slade, ed., *Vermont State Papers* (Middlebury, Vt., 1823), 72; Thomas Young, "To the Inhabitants of *Vermont,* a Free and Independent State, Bounding on the River Connecticut and Lake Champlain," April 11, 1777, ibid., 76. Some of the same issues arose elsewhere in New England during this period. See, for example, Jere R. Daniell, *Experiment in Republicanism: New Hampshire Politics and the American Revolution, 1741–1794* (Cambridge, Mass., 1970); James Truslow Adams, *New England in the Republic, 1776–1850* (Boston, 1926), 109–165.

11. "Constitution of the State of Vermont, as Established by Convention, July 2, 1777," in Slade, ed., *Vermont State Papers,* 243. John N. Shaeffer, "A Comparison of the First Constitutions of Vermont and Pennsylvania," *Vermont History,* LXIII (1973): 33–43, demonstrates that although the Vermont convention "relied heavily" on the Pennsylvania constitution as its model, it made twenty-seven substantive changes in the earlier document. The quotation is from Peter S. Onuf, "State-Making in Revolutionary America: Independent Vermont as a Case Study," *JAH,* LXVII (1980–1981): 802. On the same subject see Willi Paul Adams, *The First American Constitutions: Republican Ideology and the Making of the State Constitutions* (Chapel Hill, 1980), 93–98.

12. Ford, ed., *Journals of the Continental Congress,* Sept. 27, 1799, XV, 1118; Samuel Flagg Bemis, *Pinckney's Treaty: A Study of America's Advantage From Europe's Distress, 1783–1800* (Baltimore, Md., 1926), 32–33; Richard B. Morris, ed., *John Jay: The Making of a Revolutionary* (New York, 1975), 649–835; Henry P. Johnston, ed., *The Correspondence and Public Papers of John Jay,* 4 vols. (New York, 1890–1893); William Jay, *The Life of John Jay: With Selections from his Correspondence and Miscellaneous Papers,* 2 vols. (New York, 1833), I, 100.

13. Peter S. Onuf, *The Origins of the Federal Republic: Jurisdictional Controversies in the United States, 1775–1787* (Philadelphia, 1983), ch. 2.

14. Public Archives of Canada, Ottawa, MG 21, Add. Mss 21880 (B 220), 173. I thank Mr. Brian Driscoll, British Archives Manuscripts, for his assistance in securing copies of this and related documents. The evidence supplied by Haldimand was two intercepted letters from Thomas Jefferson. Jefferson to George Rogers Clark, March 1780; Jefferson to John Todd, March 19, 1780, Public Archives of Canada, Ottawa, MG 21, Add. Mss 21880 (B 220), 174–180. These letters are printed in Julian Boyd, ed., *The Papers of Thomas Jefferson* (Princeton, N. J., 1950–), III, 316–321.

15. Thomas Scott to President Reed, Oct. 19, 1781, *PA* ser. 1 (Harrisburg, 1854), IX, 439; "Resolution of the [Pennsylvania] General Assembly, 1782," Nov. 19, 1782, ibid., 666; John Dickinson, "Instructions to Rev. James Finley, 1783," Feb. 6, 1783, ibid., X, 163, 164. Onuf, *Origins of the Federal Republic,* asserts that the commitment of western Pennsylvanians to the idea of independent statehood was "ephemeral" (61, 71), and he sees no evolution or development in relations between East and West over the course of the 1780s (39 and *passim*). He also implies that East-West conflict virtually ended with adoption of the Constitution (69 and *passim*); and he criticizes Gordon Wood and Charles Beard for perpetuating the "myth" of "social forces supposedly struggling for supremacy" during the 1780s (xiv). Onuf also seems to dismiss the relevance of Revolutionary ideology for understanding post-Revolutionary politics (xiv). At other points in the book, he seems to contradict each of these statements (e. g., xv, xvi, xvii). Onuf thus offers a contrasting interpretation of some of the same events discussed here in chapters two and three, but from the perspective of eastern nationalists and without attention to frontier conditions, ideology, or economic self-interest.

16. Samuel Cole Williams, *History of the Lost State of Franklin* (New York, 1933; rpt. ed., Philadelphia, 1974), 30.

17. Williams, *Lost State of Franklin,* 39–40, 46–48, 52–53, 67–71, 83–84; Ford, ed., *Journals of the Continental Congress,* IV, 525. Yet another frontier movement for independent statehood is revealed by an "Advertisement" of March 12, 1785, by one John Emerson notifying "the inhabitants of the west side of the Ohio River that there is to be an election for the choosing of members of the convention for the framing a constitution for the governing of the inhabitants, the election to be held on the 10th day of April next ensuing," William Henry Smith, ed., *The St. Clair Papers* (Cincinnati, 1882), II, 5. On Ohio, see also, Andrew Robert Lee Cayton, " 'The Best of all Possible Worlds': From Independence to Interdependence in the Settlement of the Ohio Country, 1780–1825," Ph. D. diss., Brown University, 1981.

18. Smith, ed., *St. Clair Papers*, II, 20–21; *North Carolina State Records*, XVI, 919, 733; Walter Faw Cannon, "Four Interpretations of the History of the State of Franklin," East Tennessee Historical Society, *Publications*, no. 22 (1950): 3–18; Williams, *History of the Lost State of Franklin*, 21.

19. [Daniel Davis] "The Proceedings of Two Conventions Held at Portland to Consider the Expediency of a Separate Government in the District of Maine," *Collections of the Massachusetts Historical Society* first ser., IV (1795): 25–40; Jeremiah Perley, *The Debates, Resolutions, and Other Proceedings of the Convention of Delegates Assembled at Portland on the 11th, and Continued Until the 29th Day of October, 1819, for the Purpose of forming a Constitution for the State of Maine* (Portland, 1820), 291.

20. Van Beck Hall, *Politics Without Parties: Massachusetts, 1780–1791* (Pittsburgh, 1972), 170, 179, 182; Robert L. Taylor, *Western Massachusetts in the Revolution* (Providence, 1954), 5.

21. Ibid., 73, 91, 160–161, 108, 109; David P. Szatmary, *Shays' Rebellion: The Making of an Agrarian Insurrection* (Amherst, Mass., 1980), 37–42.

22. David Sewell to George Thatcher, Oct. 16, 1786, "The Thatcher Papers," *Historical Magazine* 2d ser., VI (1869): 257–258; Szatmary, *Shays' Rebellion*, 46–48; *Worcester Magazine*, II (1786–1787): 336–338; Main, *Political Parties Before the Constitution*, 115 n.

23. Taylor, *Western Massachusetts*, 120–121; Hall, *Politics Without Parties*, 184–185.

24. Gerard to Vergennes, Oct. 20, 1778, in French Foreign Office, *Affaires Etrangeres, Etats Unis*, V, no. 33; Gerard to Vergennes, Feb. 18, 1779, ibid., VII, no. 100; Paul C. Phillips, "American Opinions Regarding the West, 1778–1783," *Proceedings of the Mississippi Valley Historical Association for the Year 1913–1914*, VII (Cedar Rapids, Iowa, 1914), 293; Michael Allen, "The Federalists and the West, 1783–1803," *WPHM*, VI (1978): 315–332; Payson J. Treat, *The National Land System, 1785–1830* (New York, 1910).

25. Edward Rutledge to John Jay, Nov. 12, 1786, in Henry P. Johnston, ed., *Correspondence and Public Papers of John Jay* III, 217; Richard Henry Lee to George Washington, July 15, 1787, James Curtis Ballagh, ed., *The Letters of Richard Henry Lee* (New York, 1914), II, 426. Michael Allen, "The Mississippi River Debate, 1785–1787," *Tennessee Historical Quarterly*, XXXVI (1977): 447–467, wrongly, I believe, paints a picture of united "southern" and "western" interests opposed by "northeastern nationalists" who wanted the Mississippi to remain closed to American trade. Similarly, Joseph L. Davis, *Sectionalism in American Politics, 1774–1787* (Madison, Wis., 1977), portrays the South as united against the North on the Mississippi question. His note 25 on page 14 offers one speech in the South Carolina legislature to document the argument.

     This is not to say that northern versus southern regionalism did not exist. For some issues, however, it is a less useful explanatory device than the East-West division, and the presumption of pervasive northern-southern conflict is often more a reflection of anachronistic knowledge of the Civil War than of research in the eighteenth-century sources.

26. Gardoqui to Conde de Galvez, Aug. 23, 1785, translated and reproduced in Bemis, *Pinckney's Treaty*, 83.

27. James Monroe to Patrick Henry, Aug. 12, 1786, in Burnett, ed., *Letters*, VIII, 422; Bemis, *Pinckney's Treaty*, 95.

28. Rufus King to Elbridge Gerry, Aug. 13, 1786, Burnett, ed., *Letters*, VIII, 425; Charles Thomson, Minutes of Proceedings, Aug. 18, 1786, ibid., 440; William Samuel Johnson, speech, Aug. 21, 1786, ibid., 447–449.

29. Monroe to Patrick Henry, Aug. 12, 1786, ibid., 424–425; Monroe to James Madison, Aug. 14, 1786, ibid., 427. See also Monroe to Madison, Sept. 3, 1786, in Robert A. Rutland and William M. E. Rachal, eds., *The Papers of James Madison*, (Chicago,

1962–   ), IX, 112–114; Timothy Bloodworth to Richard Caswell, Aug. 24, 1786, in Burnett, ed., *Letters*, VIII, 451.

30. Madison to Jefferson, Aug. 12, 1786, *Papers of Madison*, IX, 96; Jefferson to Madison, Jan. 30, 1787, ibid., 248; *Correspondence of Jay*, I, 329; Jay to Jefferson, April 24, 1787, ibid., III, 245.

31. J. Leitch Wright, Jr., *Britain and the American Frontier, 1783–1815* (Athens, Ga., 1975), 20–25, 31; Samuel Flagg Bemis, *Jay's Treaty: A Study in Commerce and Diplomacy* (New York, 1923), 5–7.

32. Haldimand to North, Oct. 24, 1783, Public Archives of Canada, Ottawa, Q. 22: 85.

33. Sydney to Haldimand, April 8, 1784, Public Archives of Canada, Ottawa, Q. 23: 55; Extract from the Minutes of the Council of State, Quebec, March 24 and 28, 1785, Public Archives of Canada, Ottawa, Q. 24: 450.

34. Hugh Williamson to Governor Martin, Nov. 18, 1782, *Letters of the Members of the Continental Congress*, VI, 545; *New Hampshire State Papers*, X, 381–383; *Falmouth Gazette*, Dec. 31, 1785; Onuf, *Origins of the Federal Republic*, 36.

35. *Falmouth Gazette*, Feb. 2, 1786; March 30, 1786. Onuf, *Origins of the Federal Republic*, 36, 150, who quotes all the sources in this note and the one above, gives more attention and detail than provided here to the nationalist perspective on East-West conflict up to the ratification of the Constitution.

Chapter Three: SECTIONAL STRIFE

1. "Account of the sufferings of Massy Herbeson [*sic*] and her family, who were taken prisoners by a party of Indians. Given on oath, before John Wilkins, esq., one of the justices of the peace for the commonwealth of Pennsylvania," Archibald Loudon, *A Selection of the Most Interesting Narratives of Outrages Committed by the Indians in Their Wars With the White People*, 2 vols. (Carlisle, Pa., 1808; rpt., in one vol., New York, 1971), 69–78.

2. Szatmary, *Shays' Rebellion*, 108.

3. Ibid., 71.

4. Seth Ames, ed., *The Works of Fisher Ames* (Boston, 1854), II, 97; *Massachusetts Centinal*, April 2, 1785; Nathan Dane to Samuel Phillips, Jan. 29, 1786, Nathan Dane Papers, LC; Dorchester to Sydney, Feb. 28, 1787, 50: B-39, 135, Colonial Office 42, Public Archives of Canada, Ottawa; *Hampshire Gazette*, June 6, 1787; Szatmary, *Shays' Rebellion*, 73, 75, 97, 108, 109. On Shays' Rebellion see also Marian L. Starkey, *A Little Rebellion* (New York, 1955); Andrew Cunningham McLaughlin, *The Confederation and the Constitution* (New York, 1905), ch. 10; and James Truslow Adams, *New England in the Republic, 1776–1850* (Boston, 1926).

5. Ronald F. Banks, *Maine Becomes a State: The Movement to Separate Maine from Massachusetts, 1785–1820* (Middletown, Maine, 1970), 10–12; William Willis, *The History of Portland from its First Settlement*, 2 vols. (Portland, Maine, 1865); Peleg Aldrich, "Massachusetts and Maine: Their Union and Separation," *Proceedings of the American Antiquarian Society* (1877): 43–64; Edward Stanwood, "The Separation of Maine from Massachusetts," *Massachusetts Historical Society Proceedings* 3d ser., I (1908): 125–165; Louis Hatch, *Maine, A History* (New York, 1919); *Cumberland Gazette*, Aug. 31, 1786. On Maine's continuing attempt to secure statehood into the nineteenth century, see Alan Taylor, " 'Stopping the Progres of Rogues and Deceivers': A White Indian Recruiting Notice of 1808," *WMQ*, XLII (1985): 90–103.

6. Banks, *Maine Becomes a State*, 22; Davis, "Proceedings," in Perley, *Debates*, 277–300.

7. Ethan Allen to Dorchester, July 16, 1788, Public Archives of Canada, Ottawa, Q. 36: 488. For another perspective on the Vermont independence movement see Onuf, *Origins of the Federal Republic*, chapters 5 and 6.

8. Memorial of Levi Allen to Lord Sydney, May 4, 1789, Frederick Jackson Turner, ed., "Relations between the Vermont Separatists and Great Britain, 1789–1791," *AHR*,

XXI (1915–1916): 553–554. See also, Memorial of Levi Allen, Nov. 22, 1786, Public Archives of Canada, Ottawa, Q. 28: 7; Proclamation of Dorchester, April 18, 1787, in *Records of Governor and Council*, III, 402; Ordinance of Governor and Council of Canada, April 30, 1787, ibid., III, 403; Dorchester to Sydney, June 18, 1787, Public Archives of Canada, Ottawa, Q. 28: 4; Sydney to Dorchester, Sept. 14, 1787, ibid., Q. 28: 28; Major Skene to his father, Dec. 16, 1787, ibid., Q. 36: 481.

9. In the summer of 1789 Spain seized several British ships that were on their way to establish a trading post at Nootka Sound on the western coast of modern-day Canada. During the spring and summer of 1790 both nations made preparations for war. The crisis was settled by October 28, 1790, when Spain and Britain signed a convention. Stephen Cottrell, Office of Committee of Privy Council for Trade, Whitehall, April 17, 1790, in Frederick Jackson Turner, ed., "English Policy Toward America in 1790–1791," *AHR*, VIII (1902–1903): 82.

10. Ibid., 84, 85.

11. Unrest in New Hampshire grew out of the same sort of economic and political turmoil exhibited in the rest of rural New England. See Daniell, *Experiment in Republicanism*, 184–201 and *passim*; Lynn W. Turner, *William Plumer of New Hampshire, 1759–1850* (Chapel Hill, N. C., 1962).

12. John Haywood, *The Civil and Political History of Tennessee* (Nashville, 1891), 160; Colonel Anthony Bledsoe to Governor Caswell, March 26, 1787, North Carolina State Library, Raleigh.

13. White to Miro, April 18, 1788[?], Archibald Henderson, "The Spanish Conspiracy in Tennessee," *Tennessee Historical Magazine*, III (1917): 232.

14. Sevier to Gardoqui, Sept. 12, 1788. Williams, *History of the Lost State of Franklin*, 241, argues that this letter does not constitute evidence of Sevier's disloyalty to the United States. Henderson, "Spanish Conspiracy," 233, disagrees, and so do I.

15. Robertson to Alexander McGillivray, Aug. 3, 1788, in Henderson, "Spanish Conspiracy," 239.

16. Robertson to Miro, Sept. 2, 1789, in Henderson, "Spanish Conspiracy," 242.

17. Malcolm J. Rohrbaugh, *The Trans-Appalachian Frontier: Peoples, Societies, and Institutions, 1775–1850* (New York, 1978), 66–87; Archer Butler Hulbert, ed., *The Records of the Original Proceedings of the Ohio Company*, 2 vols. (Marietta, Ohio, 1917); Jack Ericson Eblen, *The First and Second United States Empires* (Pittsburgh, 1968); William Henry Smith, ed., *The St. Clair Papers*, 2 vols. (Cincinnati, 1882); Clarence E. Carter and John Porter Bloom, eds., *Territorial Papers of the United States*, 27 vols. (Washington, D. C., 1934–   ), II. Cayton, " 'The Best of All Possible Worlds,' " discusses the internal divisions within the Northwest Territory and relations between the federal government and the region during the years before 1800 in a fashion that parallels, for the most part, the account of other frontier areas detailed here. Other frontier movements for independent statehood occurred in northeastern Pennsylvania and upstate New York during this same period. Both movements had their origins in the same sorts of grievances described here, evolved in a similar fashion over time, and found adherents unsuccessfully appealing to state governments in the language of America's Revolutionary pamphleteers. See Julian P. Boyd, "Attempts to Form New States in New York and Pennsylvania, 1786–1796," *The Quarterly Journal of the New York State Historical Association*, XII (July 1931): 257–270.

18. "The Memorial of Delegates and Revolutionary Officers to the Virginia Assembly, in 1786," Thomas Marshall Green, *The Spanish Conspiracy: A Review of Early Spanish Movements in the Southwest* (Cincinnati, 1891), Appendix C, 389–391. For another perspective on Virginia's relations with Kentucky see Onuf, *Origins of the Federal Republic*, ch. 4.

19. Green, *Spanish Conspiracy*, 61; Harry Innes to Edmund Randolph, July 21, 1787, ibid., 85.

20. "Circular Letter Directed to the different Courts in the Western Country," Danville, Kentucky, March 29, 1787, ibid., 110.

21. William R. Shepherd, "Wilkinson and the Beginnings of the Spanish Conspiracy," *AHR*, IX (1903–1904): 497, 498–499, 501.

22. Decision of the Council of State on Wilkinson's First Memorial, Nov. 20, 1788, William R. Shepherd, ed., "Papers Bearing on James Wilkinson's Relations with Spain, 1787–1789," *AHR*, IX (1903–1904): 749–750.

23. James Wilkinson to Estavan Miro, Sept. 17, 1789, ibid., 751–752.

24. Ibid., 754–755, 765–766.

25. See, for example, *Lexington Gazette*, Sept. 13 and 22, 1788; Green, *Spanish Conspiracy*, 186–187; Charles Gayarre, *History of Louisiana* (New Orleans, 1885; rpt. ed., New York, 1972), III, 277, 278, 280.

26. Gayarre, *History of Louisiana*, 285.

27. Ibid., 239, 250–253, 296; Lee to Madison, Oct. 25, 1786, *Papers of James Madison*, IX, 145; Onuf, *Origins of the Federal Republic*, 150, 178, quotes the fears of these and other nationalists in 1786. For western Pennsylvania perspectives on inter-regional affairs see the *Pittsburgh Gazette*, Aug. 26, 1786, 1; Sept. 2, 1786, 2; Nov. 4, 1786, 4; Dec. 2, 1786, 3, 4; May 5, 1787, 1; Nov. 10, 1787, 2; Madison to Edmund Randolph, April 15, 1787, *Papers of Madison*, IX, 379.

28. *Gentlemen's Magazine*, LV (August 1785): 656.

29. *London Chronicle*, Aug. 6, 1785.

30. F. O. America H, in Turner, ed., "English Policy Toward America in 1790–1791," *AHR*, VII (1901 1902): 717 718, 719. Turner misread "R. D." for "P. A." All dispatches sent by "P. Allaire" and "P. A." came from Peter Allaire who was an American and had been judged a spy by Benjamin Franklin as early as 1780 See Claude-Anne Lopez, "The Man Who Frightened Franklin," *PMHB*, CVI (1982): 515–526.

31. P. A. to Pitt[?], Nov. 4, 1790, Turner, ed., "English Policy Toward America," 724.

Chapter Four: LICE, LABOR, AND LANDSCAPE

1. From *A Narrative of the Sufferings of Massy Harbison* (Pittsburgh, 1828), 13–16. On Indian-white relations during this period, see also Rev. John Heckewelder, *An Account of the History, Manners, and Customs of the Indian Nations, Who Once Inhabited Pennsylvania and the Neighboring States* (Philadelphia, 1819); Anthony F. C. Wallace, *The Death and Rebirth of the Seneca* (New York, 1970).

2. James B. Finley, *Autobiography* (Cincinnati, 1853); John A. Pope, *A Tour Through the Southern and Western United States of North America* (Richmond, 1792; rpt., New York, 1888); Henry Marie Brackenridge, *Recollections of Persons and Places in the West* (Philadelphia, 1834); "Extract of Letters from an Officer in one of those Regiments to his friend in London" (London, 1755), reprinted in Archer Butler Hulbert, ed., *Braddock's Road*, IV of *Historic Highways of America* (Cleveland, 1903); "Colonel Eyre's Journal of His Trip from New York to Pittsburgh, 1762," *WPHM*, XXVII (1944): 37–50; Russell J. Ferguson, *Early Western Pennsylvania Politics* (Pittsburgh, 1938), 2–4, 18–19, 32, 36–37, 64–65.

3. Hugh Henry Brackenridge, *Gazette Publications* (Carlisle, Pa., 1806), "On the Situation of the Town of Pittsburgh, and the State of Society at That Place," *Pittsburgh Gazette*, July 26, 1786; McClure, " 'Ends of the American Earth,' " 118; Joseph Doddridge, *Notes on the Settlement and Indian Wars of the Western Parts of Virginia and Pennsylvania from 1763 to 1783* (Wellsburg, Va., 1824; Pittsburg, 1912); George Dallas Albert, ed., *History of the County of Westmoreland, Pennsylvania* (Philadelphia, 1882); "Copy of a Letter from a Gentleman at New Orleans," *The Maryland Advertiser and Baltimore Journal*, Nov. 30, 1790, 2–3.

4. Certainly Frederick Jackson Turner and his most loyal adherents have been prone to such stark geographical determinism. See, for example, Turner, *The Rise of the New*

West, 1819–1829 (New York, 1906); Ray Allen Billington, *America's Frontier Heritage* (New York, 1966); R. Carlyle Buley, *The Old Northwest Pioneer Period, 1815–1840,* 2 vols. (Indianapolis, 1950); Frederick Merk, *History of the Western Movement* (New York, 1978). This is by no means a wholesale indictment of the authors or books named above. On the contrary, each book is a classic in its own right and each author made major contributions to our understandings of historical processes and interregional development in the United States. My ruminations on the relationship between geographical paradox and ideological and political processes were influenced by Benjamin R. Barber, *The Death of Communal Liberty: A History of Freedom in a Swiss Mountain Canton* (Princeton, N. J., 1974).

5. See, for example, "Extracts of Letters from an Officer." Propagandists, such as G. A. Imlay, *A Topographical Description of the Western Territory of North America* (London, 1792), painted a far more pleasant portrait of westerners and their environs, for obvious reasons, than travelers who simply recounted experiences in their private journals or wrote accounts for relatives and friends. The personal reports seem a more reliable reflection of eastern attitudes about the frontier than the propaganda tracts. The quantifiable evidence on local economy offered below also provides independent validation for many of the personal observations in the literary sources.

6. Mary Dewees, "Journey from Philadelphia to Kentucky, 1787–1788," *PMHB*, XXVIII (1904): 184–185. On the same point, see also Colonel John May, "Journal of Colonel John May of Boston, Relative to a Journey to the Ohio Country, 1789," *PMHB*, XLV (1921): 101–179; Arthur Lee, Pittsburgh, 1783, in Richard Henry Lee, *The Life of Arthur Lee* (Boston, 1829), II, 385; John Wilkins, Pittsburgh, 1783, in *Centennial Volume of the First Presbyterian Church of Pittsburgh, Pa.* (Pittsburgh, 1884), 17; William Winans, "Recollections of Boyhood Years in Southwestern Pennsylvania, 1788–1804," *WPHM*, XXII (1939): 25; Virginia Beck, "The Evolution of Government in Allegheny County, 1788–1808," *WPHM*, XXIV (1941): 209–228; John W. Harpster, ed., *Pen Pictures of Early Western Pennsylvania* (Pittsburgh, 1938); Thomas Chapman, "Journal of a Journey Through the United States, 1795–6," *The Historical Magazine and Notes and Queries* 2d ser., V (1869): 357–368; Lewis Condict, "Journal of a Trip to Kentucky in 1795," New Jersey Historical Society, *Proceedings* new series, IV (1919): 108–127.

7. Wilkins, in *Centennial Volume,* 17; Winans, "Recollections," 25–26. For a similarly harsh evaluation of the people and life in the western country see Pope, *Tour.* David McClure, *Diary* (New York, 1899), 53, 105–106.

8. Dewees, "Journal," 185.

9. McClure, " 'Ends of the American Earth,' " 85, 114, 116; Elliott J. Gorn, " 'Gouge and Bite, Pull Hair and Scratch': The Social Significance of Fighting in the Southern Backcountry," *AHR*, XC (1985): 18–43.

10. Harper, "Class Structure," 36, 42, 45. Nor does the number of acres owned by frontier farmers reveal their actual standard of living. When we look at the figures for cleared land the problems appear even worse. On the average only about 10 percent of holdings were in cleared and arable land. Twenty acres was the median size of working farms during the 1780s. Historians have estimated that about 40 acres were necessary during this period for a viable family farm, and 75 acres for profitable commercial farming. See, Charles S. Grant, *Democracy in the Connecticut Frontier Town of Kent* (New York, 1961), 32–35; James T. Lemon, "Household Consumption in Eighteenth Century America and its Relationship to Production and Trade: The Situation Among Farmers in Southeastern Pennsylvania," *Agricultural History*, XLI (1967): 68–69.

11. Harper, "Class Structure," 79; McClure, " 'Ends of the American Earth'," 505. By comparison with either seventeenth-century New England or the eighteenth-century East, the concentration of wealth in western Pennsylvania was *not* more strati-

fied. The typical seventeenth-century New England town also found about 35 percent of wealth concentrated in the hands of the wealthiest decile of population. The poorest 30 percent of the population in eastern cities during the eighteenth century had about nothing as well. On eighteenth-century cities see Gary B. Nash, *The Urban Crucible: Social Change, Political Consciousness, and the Origins of the American Revolution* (Cambridge, Mass., 1979). On seventeenth-century Boston see James A. Henretta, "Economic Development and Social Structure in Colonial Boston," *WMQ*, XXII (1965): 75–92. According to Jackson Turner Main, *The Social Structure of Revolutionary America* (Princeton, 1965), "the wealthiest 10 percent owned about half of the inventoried property in Massachusetts, 40 percent in New Hampshire, and 45 percent in New Jersey, the last figure being the average for the North" (42).

12. Harper, "Class Structure," 81, 131; Main, *Social Structure*, 16, 17. James T. Lemon, *The Best Poor Man's Country: A Geographical Study of Early Southeastern Pennsylvania* (New York, 1972), 69, estimates that in Chester and Lancaster counties in 1782 over 30 percent of the population was landless. In Bedford County, according to 1783 tax records, nonresident speculators owned more than 50 percent of the land in some townships, while a high proportion of residents owned none. Maine, *Social Structure*, 16, 17. Harper's conclusion about the significance of absentee landlordism in western Pennsylvania has recently been challenged by Lee Soltow and Kenneth W. Keller, "Tenancy and Asset-Holding in Late Eighteenth-Century Washington County, Pennsylvania," *WPHM*, LXV (1982): 1–15. Soltow and Keller studied a 1791 tax list for Cecil Township, Washington County. From this record they have concluded that "landownership and tenancy seems to have been largely a relationship between local people in Washington County" (13). They also argue that "landless persons [in Cecil Township] were not as rich as the landowners, but they were not poverty-stricken dependents either" (14). Their second point seems questionable since they acknowledge that "quite possibly poor men were not included in the tax lists" (14). Their evidence and conclusions about the insignificance of absenteeism in Cecil Township, if correct, seems to constitute an exception to the overall portrait of landlord-tenant relations in western Pennsylvania as described by Harper, Main, McClure, and Cayton, rather than a challenge to Harper's thesis as Soltow and Keller believe. There is just too much contemporary literary evidence corroborating Harper's, Main's, McClure's, and Cayton's findings, in addition to their statistical evidence, to dismiss them on the basis of one tax list for one year in one township of the region.

13. Harper, "Class Structure," 29, 34; Cayton, " 'Best of all Possible Worlds'," 5, 6. Robert D. Mitchell, *Commercialism and Frontier: Perspectives on the Early Shenandoah Valley* (Charlottesville, Va., 1977), 69, 121, notes the same phenomenon in adjacent Augusta County, Virginia, where 36 percent of the taxable residents owned no land in 1762. He estimates that 30 percent of frontiersmen owned no land during the late eighteenth century and that the wealthiest 10 percent owned 40 percent of the property. See also, Robert D. Mitchell, "The Presbyterian Church as an Indicator of Westward Expansion in Eighteenth-Century America," *The Professional Geographer*, XVIII (1966): 293–299.

14. Solon J. Buck and Elizabeth Hawthorne Buck, *The Planting of Civilization in Western Pennsylvania* (Pittsburgh, 1939), 144; T. W. J. Wylie, ed., "Franklin County One Hundred Years Ago: A Settler's Experience Told in a Letter Written by Alexander Thomson in 1773," *PMHB*, VIII (1894): 323; John May, Journal, May 22, 1788.

15. Buck and Buck, *Planting of Civilization*, 150; McClure, " 'Ends of American Earth'," 451.

16. Buck and Buck, *Planting of Civilization*, 152–153; W. E. Mockler, "Surnames of Trans-Allegheny Virginia, 1750–1788," *Names*, IV (1956): 1–17, 96–118.

17. Harper, "Class Structure," 74–75.
18. Ibid., 77; Solon J. Buck, "Frontier Economy in Southwestern Pennsylvania," *WPHM*, XIX (1936): 117.
19. Harper, "Class Structure," 243, 250, 277.
20. Charles H. Ambler, *George Washington and the West* (Chapel Hill, N.C., 1936), 134; Imlay, *Topographical Description*, 33, 34–35.
21. Ibid., 88, 110–111, 127, 140.
22. May, "Journal," 116.
23. Ibid.
24. Ibid., 117.
25. Ibid., 122.
26. The poorest 10 percent of western Pennsylvanians owned a higher *percentage* of the region's riches than a comparable group of Bostonians during the same era. The wealthiest 10 percent of the western country's settlers monopolized no greater percentage of the community's resources than elites in southeastern Pennsylvania's Chester County. See notes 12 and 13, and Allan Kulikoff, "The Progress of Inequality in Revolutionary Boston," *WMQ*, XXVIII (1971): 375–412; James T. Lemon and Gary Nash, "The Distribution of Wealth in Eighteenth-Century America: A Century of Change in Chester County, Pennsylvania, 1693–1802," *JSH*, II (1968): 1–24.
27. Cayton, " 'The Best of All Possible Worlds'," 181 and *passim*, describes an economic structure in the Northwest Territory that parallels the one depicted here. McClure, " 'The Ends of the American Earth,' " Harper, "Class Structure," and Fennell, "From Rebelliousness to Insurrection," also provide evidence and interpretations consistent with the one offered here for western Pennsylvania.
28. "The Population of Pittsburgh and Contiguous Territory, Including the Names of Heads of Families as Shown by the United States Census of 1790," *WPHM*, II (1919): 164; Harper, "Class Structure," 150, 180, 191.
29. Buck and Buck, *Planting of Civilization*, 267–269.
30. Buck, "Frontier Economy," 120.
31. On patterns of consumption and the culture of drinking during this period see W. J. Rorabaugh, *The Alcoholic Republic: An American Tradition* (New York, 1979), especially chapters one and two. According to William L. Downard, *Dictionary of the History of the American Brewing and Distilling Industry* (Westport, Conn., 1980), xxi, a packhorse could carry only four bushels of raw grain, but twenty-four bushels converted into whiskey.
32. "Petition of Inhabitants of Westmoreland County—Excise on Liquors—1790," *PA* ser. 1, XI, 670–673. On the repeal of the excise tax see, "Address of Governor Thomas Mifflin to the Gentlemen of the Senate and House of Representatives of the State of Pennsylvania, Philadelphia, December 28, 1790," *Journal of the Senate of the Commonwealth of Pennsylvania* (Philadelphia, 1790), 41–48; Edward Bartholomew to the Governor and Executive Council, Dec. 2, 1790, McCallister Collection, Library Company of Philadelphia, yi 2 7313 .F .39; Lemuel Molovinsky, "Tax Collection Problems in Revolutionary Pennsylvania," *PAH*, XLVII (1980): 253–259. See also, Albert Gallatin, Draft of Report of the Harrisburg Conference of September 3, 1788, in Henry Adams, ed., *The Writings of Albert Gallatin*, 3 vols. (Philadelphia, 1879), I, 1–4. Frontiersmen's perceptions that they were under-represented in colony/state legislatures and in Congress were sometimes inaccurate or exaggerated, but the story is a complex one. See, for example, the maps equating population and representation in Lester J. Cappon et al., eds., *Atlas of Early American History* (Princeton, 1976), 25, 62. It was certainly true that frontier representatives were consistently outvoted during the eighteenth century, and that independent statehood helped to redress the balance.

33. "Petition of Inhabitants of Westmoreland."
34. Ibid.; W. J. Hayward, "Early Western Pennsylvania Agriculture," *WPHM*, VI (1923): 179, 185.
35. "Petition of Inhabitants of Westmoreland."

Chapter Five: GEORGE WASHINGTON AND THE WESTERN COUNTRY

1. George Henry Loskiel, *History of the Mission of the United Brethren Among the Indians in North America* (London, 1794); John Heckewelder, *Narrative of the Mission of the United Brethren Among the Delaware and Mohegan Indians, from Its Commencement, in the Year 1740, to the Close of the Year 1808* (Philadelphia, 1820; rpt., New York, 1971); *PA* ser. 1, IX (Philadelphia, 1854).

2. The first President's relationship to the frontier is documented in a series of monographs that constitute a small portion of the prodigious Washington hagiography. Even the most celebratory and condemnatory of the comprehensive modern biographies neglect, however, to establish the pattern of Washington's lifelong western business dealings or the relationship between his public actions and private interests. See, Archer B. Hulbert, *Washington and the West* (New York, 1905); Cora Bacon-Foster, *Early Chapters in the Development of the Patomac [sic] Route to the West* (Washington, D.C., 1912), Roy Bird Cook, *Washington's Western Lands* (Strasburg, Va., 1930); William R. Jillson, *The Land Adventures of George Washington* (Louisville, Kentucky, 1934); Charles H. Ambler, *George Washington and the West* (Chapel Hill, N. C., 1936); Hugh Cleland, *George Washington in the Ohio Valley* (Pittsburgh, 1955); Rick W. Sturdevant, "Quest for Eden: George Washington's Frontier Land Interests," Ph.D. diss., University of California, Santa Barbara, 1982. Sturdevant estimates that over 3000 authors have written about Washington since 1800 (2). James Thomas Flexner, *George Washington*, 4 vols. (Boston, 1965–1972), I, 5; Bernard Knollenberg, *George Washington. The Virginia Period, 1732–1775* (Durham, N.C., 1964), 135. The major interpretive biographies of Washington include those of Flexner and Knollenberg, as well as John Marshall, *The Life of George Washington*, 5 vols. (Philadelphia, 1805–1807); Jared Sparks, *The Life of George Washington*, 2 vols. (London, 1839); Washington Irving, *Life of George Washington*, 5 vols. (New York, 1855–1859); Douglas Southall Freeman, *George Washington: A Biography*, 7 vols. (New York, 1948–1957); Marcus Cunliffe, *George Washington. Man and Monument* (Boston, 1958); Gary Wills, *Cincinnatus: George Washington & the Enlightenment; Images of Power in Early America* (New York, 1984); John R. Alden, *George Washington: A Biography* (Baton Rouge, 1984).

3. Donald Jackson and Dorothy Twohig, eds., *The Diaries of George Washington*, 7 vols. (Charlottesville, Va., 1976), I, 9–10, 15, and 18. Hereafter referred to as G.W., *Diaries*.

4. John C. Fitzpatrick, ed., *The Writings of George Washington*, 39 vols. (Washington, D.C., 1931–1944), I, 17. Hereafter referred to as *Writings of G.W.*

5. G.W., *Diaries*, I, 127–128, 130, 132, 147, 154–155, 158. See Flexner, I, ch. 6, for a more detailed account of this journey.

6. G.W., *Diaries*, I, 132.

7. On the Seven Years War and Washington's role in it see the books listed in note 2 above and Francis Parkman, *Montcalm and Wolfe: The Decline and Fall of the French Empire in North America* (Boston, 1884); Lawrence Henry Gipson, *The British Empire Before the American Revolution* (Caldwell, Idaho, 1936–1970), VI, VII, and VIII; and Guy Fregault, *Canada: The War of the Conquest* (New York, 1969).

8. *Writings of G.W.*, I, 107, 34–35, 70, 105, 113–114, 112–113.

9. Ibid., I, 44.

10. Ibid., III, 66–70; I, 149–150, 159; II, 22, 276. My interpretation of Washington's

motives departs sharply here from Flexner's, where he quoted Washington's claim that "love of country" and the "affections of fellow citizens" were the motive forces behind his behavior. Flexner ignored the quotation that I offer, although he generally attempted to portray Washington in the best possible light without suppressing evidence. He did this by gross understatement when faced with a bold lie by Washington (e.g., I, 208–209, where he explained that Washington "neglected to state" the truth when offering misinformation about the superiority of Virginia over Pennsylvania routes to the West), by eschewing analysis where such would redound to Washington's discredit (e.g., I, 292, where he presented evidence of Washington's rapaciousness without comment), and by portraying the most blatant examples of Washington's shady dealings as exceptions to his usual behavior (e.g., I, 256, where he recounted Washington's attempt in 1761 to enlist the aid of a sheriff to corrupt an election in his behalf, cited Washington's attempt to disguise inferior quality flour for sale in Barbados, and then observed that sometimes Washington's "feet slipped"). My account is interpretively compatible with Knollenberg's, although I establish a broader context, incorporate more supporting evidence, and carry the story twenty years beyond his 1775 end date. See especially, Knollenberg, ch. 14 and Appendix to ch. 14. The second volume of Knollenberg's biography of Washington covers the years of the Revolution and thus does not pick up the theme of frontier land speculations. Knollenberg, *Washington and the Revolution: A Reappraisal* (New York, 1940).

11. Knollenberg wrote about Washington's land-grabbing before the Revolution at some length, so I will merely sketch the outlines of the relevant part of the story and supply context and details not included in existing accounts. *Writings of G.W.*, III, 1–4, 120–124; William Crawford, Springgarden, to G.W., Nov. 12, 1773, LC, G.W. Papers, reel 33.

12. *Writings of G.W.*, III, 2. See Knollenberg, ch. 14 and Appendix to ch. 14. Even Flexner (I, 302–304) recognized that in these maneuvers Washington acted the part of the "oversharp businessman," that he confused "moral and legal issues." Flexner offered a Watergate-style apologia, though, for the first President's actions. Washington did nothing, Flexner maintained, that "was not common practice with speculators in wilderness areas." That may be true, although we have no synthetic study of land speculation in eighteenth-century America to verify the impression. Still, the point is not that Washington was the only "oversharp businessman" of his day, but that his frontier land dealings and other business enterprises generally conformed to this pattern; that he lied, broke the law, and betrayed public trusts in pursuit of private gain; that this pattern of deceit and morally questionable behavior contradicts the portrayals of Washington usually drawn by his biographers (including Flexner, but excluding Knollenberg); and that self-interest was a conscious or unconscious motive for Washington's public activities.

13. Cook, *Washington's Western Lands;* Sturdevant, "Quest for Eden," 15.

14. *Writings of G.W.*, II, 467–471, 471–473.

15. Ibid., II, 468, 471–473.

16. Ibid., II, 467–470, 521–522. Washington once admitted that he was willing to break "the letter of the law" when it came to land speculation. *Writings of G.W.*, III, 498–499.

17. Ibid., III, 104–105.

18. Ibid., III, 154, 267, 209–211.

19. Ibid., III, 211.

20. Richard Thompson, Philadelphia, to G.W., Sept. 30, 1773, LC, G.W. Papers, reel 32; *Writings of G.W.*, XXIX, 317–318, 328–331.

21. Knollenberg, ch. 14 and Appendix to ch. 14. It should be noted that Washington refused the offer of additional frontier lands as partial compensation for his services in the Revolution. One might view this apparently selfless act as an exception to the

pattern of rapaciousness identified in this chapter or, as Flexner did (I, 303–304), as an attempt to escape "temptations" like the ones to which Washington succumbed after the Seven Years War, to the damage of his reputation. Such an interpretation is consistent with Gary Wills's contention that Washington was also obsessed by his public image (*Cincinnatus*, Part II, and *passim*). Accumulation of additional land did not fit into Washington's investment scheme by 1783. As Sturdevant ("Quest for Eden," 392) rightly points out, the retiring commander-in-chief hoped to reproduce the social structure of tidewater Virginia on the frontier. Thus he needed to gain control and supervision of large tracts. Too much land would be unwieldy, poor land unfit, and small tracts ill-suited to the enterprise. By 1784, Washington was seeking "to secure what I have." Congress's offer was thus unattractive to him, whatever his other motives for declining the gift. *Writings of G.W.*, XXVII, 437–438; C.W., *Diaries*, IV, 25; Gilbert Simpson, Jr., to G.W., Oct. 5, 1772, LC, G.W. Papers, reel 32; *Writings of G.W.*, XXVII, 329–330; Ambler, *George Washington and the West*, 153–154, 156–157, and *passim*.

22. G.W., *Diaries*, IV, 26.

23. Ibid., IV, 29 and 39, n. 3. Flexner (II, 58–61) recounted the story from Washington's perspective, emphasizing his legal claim versus the Scots' contention that their occupancy and improvement counted for more than his illegally secured patents. Flexner acknowledged that Washington was angry and that he perhaps "used profane language and was fined on the spot by one of the squatters, who happened to be a justice of the peace" (II, 59). Flexner no doubt saw this exchange as an exception to his belief that the mature Washington largely succeeded "in curbing the aggressive side of his nature when it was not to the advantage of his nation and his neighbors" (I, 254). I see it as consistent with Washington's passionate disdain for frontiersmen, part of a lifelong pattern of behavior that served as a counterpoint to his usual austerity. Washington knew from personal experience that there was a shortage of cash in the region. His 1784 auction of "Washington's Bottom" found only a bidder who could pay in wheat, and he rented the land for ten years at an annual rate of 500 bushels. G.W., *Diaries*, 23. Washington also knew first-hand of the Indian troubles plaguing the frontier. He was unable to visit his Kanawha lands in 1784 because of Indian unrest. Thomas Freeman to G. W., June 9, 1785, LC, G. W. Papers.

24. G.W., *Diaries*, IV, 32; Thomas Smith to G.W., Feb. 9, 1785, Nov. 17 and 26, 1785, and Nov. 7, 1786, LC, G.W. Papers, reel 98; G.W., *Diaries*, IV, 36–38, notes 4 and 10.

25. Ibid., V, 74 n. Some of the squatters became tenants; others moved elsewhere in the neighborhood. Washington sold the parcel in 1796 for $12,000.

26. Flexner, I, 302; *Writings of G.W.*, XXVIII, 112.

27. G.W., *Diaries*, IV, 58.

28. Ibid., IV, 66.

29. *Writings of G.W.*, XXVII, 373–377; Bacon-Foster, *Early Chapters*, 33–89; *Writings of G.W.*, XXVIII, 204–205; XXX, 123. Charles A. Beard, *An Economic Interpretation of the Constitution of the United States* (New York, 1923), was right to emphasize the self-interested motives of some supporters of constitutional reform during the 1780s, but wrong to elevate personalty over property as the dominant interest.

30. G.W., *Diaries*, IV, 66.

31. Ibid., IV, 68; *Writings of G.W.*, I, 100–101; XXVIII, 4, 64, 77–81, 202–205, 227–230, 230–232, 264–267, 291, 460–461; XXIX, 249–250; XXX, 123; Henry Lee to G.W., July 3, 1786, G.W. to Richard Henry Lee, Oct. 31, 1786, LC, G.W. Papers, reel 96.

32. *Writings of G.W.*, XXVIII, 227–230, 231, 460; G.W. to Henry Lee, July 26, 1786, LC, G.W. Papers, reel 96.

33. Ambler, *George Washington and the West*, 173; Cook, *Washington's Western Lands*, ch. 8 and *passim*; *Writings of G.W.*, XXIX, 381–385.

34. At one point, and in apparent contradiction to his other appraisals, Washington also described his hope that the frontier might serve as an active moral agent to preserve America from moral degeneracy. *Writings of G.W.*, XXX, 307; XXVIII, 202–203. Flexner, IV, 46, 157, 163; *G.W. Papers*, XXXII, 406, 427, 438–439. Washington also saw "such an intimate connection in political and pecuniary consideration between the federal district and the inland navigation of the Potomac that no exertions, in my opinion, should be dispensed with to accomplish the latter" (*Writings of G.W.*, XXXII, 18–19). As President of the United States and the Potomac Company he pursued the interests of both constituencies simultaneously. His selection of Harper's Ferry as the location of a national arsenal also aided the prospects of the Potomac Company, as he well knew. Merritt Roe Smith, "George Washington and the Establishment of the Harper's Ferry Armory," *Virginia Magazine of History and Biography*, LXXXI (1973): 416–417; Sturdevant, "Quest for Eden," 154. The Potomac Company did not, however, succeed in providing profits to its investors during Washington's lifetime.

25. See below, especially, Chapters Seven, Eleven, and Twelve.

Chapter Six: INDIANS AND THE EXCISE

1. "Copy of a letter from Mr. John Corbley, (a Baptist minister), to his friend from Philadelphia, dated Muddy Creek, (Penn.), Sept. 1, 1792," in *Narrative of Massy Harbison*, 94–95; Loudon, *Selection*, 60–62.

2. *Narrative of Massy Harbison*, 11. See, for example, the [Philadelphia] *Gazette of the United States*, April 9, 13, 23, and 30; May 7 and 28; June 18 and 25; and July 2, 9, 16, and 30, 1791 for reports of Indian-related matters on the Pennsylvania frontier. See also *The* [Annapolis] *Maryland Gazette*, June 9, 1791, 2 and *passim;* "A Proclamation," March 29, 1791, in "Executive Minutes of Governor Thomas Mifflin," *PA* 9th ser., I, 57. A small band of settlers also murdered four peaceful Indians in western Pennsylvania on March 9, 1791, and then crossed the border into Virginia, ibid., 89.

3. John C. Miller, *The Federalist Era, 1789–1801* (New York, 1960, 1963), 183. See, for example, *PA* 9th ser., I, 226, 233, 235, 311, 312, and *passim.*

4. Dorchester to Grenville, March 8, 1790 (no. 18, secret), printed in Douglas Brymner, ed., "Letters from Lord Dorchester and Minutes of Council, 1790," *Report on Canadian Archives, 1890* (Ottawa, 1891), 242; Deposition of Captain Asheton, Court of Inquiry on General Harmar, Fort Washington, September 24, 1791, *American State Papers, Military Affairs*, 7 vols. (Washington, D.C., 1832–1861), I, 28; Deposition of Major Ferguson, ibid., 20, 21; Deposition of Lieutenant Denny, ibid., 24.

5. Deposition of Lieutenant Denny, ibid., 24–25. Harmar lost 183 men, including 79 regulars during this campaign. See Dale Van Every, *Ark of Empire: The American Frontier, 1784–1803* (New York, 1963), 225. Thomas Jefferson, for one, hoped that the national government learned a lesson from Harmar's defeat. Apparently, it did not. "The federal council," Jefferson wrote, "has yet to learn by experience, what experience has long ago taught us in Virginia, that rank and file fighting will not do against Indians." Ford, ed., *Works of Jefferson*, VI, 210. Phineas Bond, British consul in Philadelphia, feared rightly that Harmar's defeat would bring a rededication of American military efforts in the region of British frontier forts. See Bond to the Duke of Leeds, Feb. 1, 1791, in J. Franklin Jameson, ed., "Letters of Phineas Bond . . . 1791–1794," *Annual Report of the American Historical Association for the Year 1897* (Washington, D. C., 1898), 473–474.

6. Samuel Johnson, *A Dictionary of the English Language*, 2 vols. (London, 1755), I, c. f., "excise," defined it as "a hateful tax levied upon commodities, and adjudged not by the common judges of property, but wretches hired by those to whom excise is paid." Langford, *The Excise Crisis;* Boyer, "Borrowed Rhetoric"; William Blackstone, *Commentary on the Laws of England*, 4 vols. (London, 1765–1769; rpt. facsimile ed.,

Chicago, 1979), I, 308; Dall W. Forsythe, *Taxation and Political Change in the Young Nation, 1781–1833* (New York, 1977), 43. See Robert A. Becker, *Revolution, Reform, and the Politics of American Taxation, 1763–1783* (Baton Rouge, 1980), for a description of late colonial revenue-raising measures. During the period from 1763 to 1775 approximately 75 to 90 percent of Pennsylvania revenues came from property taxes (Becker, 237).

7. Gales, *Debates*, II, 1692–1693, 1698–1700.

8. Fisher Ames to Richards Minot, June 23, 1790, *Works of Fisher Ames* (Boston, 1809), 81–83. According to Howard A. Ohline, these were not the only political trade-offs made in behalf of Hamilton's fiscal program. The Congress also "chose to extend federal power over the debts of the states instead of over domestic slavery." Ohline, "Slavery, Economics, and Congressional Politics, 1790," *Journal of Southern History*, XLVI (1980): 358.

9. Ames to Minot, June 23, 1790, *Works*, 81–83. The negative vote on taxing measures had other positive effects, according to Tench Coxe. It aroused the public creditors and fired their "jealousy" of those who opposed the tax. Coxe to A. H., July 10, 1790, *Papers of A. H.*, VI, 490–491.

10. A. H., "First Report on the Further Provisions Necessary for Establishing Public Credit" [Philadelphia, Dec. 13, 1790], ibid., VII, 225–226.

11. Ibid., 228.

12. Ibid., 230.

13. Ibid., 231, 232.

14. Ibid., 233.

15. Clinton Rossiter, ed., *The Federalist Papers* (New York, 1961), 93. In Federalist XXXVI, Hamilton also argued in favor of assigning the national government authority to lay "internal taxes." Tun Yuan Hu, *The Liquor Tax in the United States, 1791–1949* (New York, 1950), 11, mistakenly argued that A. H. "declared himself opposed to federal excise" in Federalist XII. On historians and Hamilton's motives see Slaughter, "The Friends of Liberty, the Friends of Order, and the Whiskey Rebellion." According to Freeman W. Meyer, "A Note on the Origins of the 'Hamiltonian System'," *WMQ*, XXI (1969): 579–588, this program can accurately be called Hamilton's since "the president . . . seemed to act as a mere onlooker in fiscal policy" (581).

16. *PA* 2d ser., IV, 19. The editor mistakenly dated this resolution June rather than Jan. 22, 1791. A contemporary printed copy of this document is in the McCallister Collection, Library Company of Philadelphia, and also in the *Gazette of the United States*, Feb. 5, 1791. The vote in favor of the resolution was 40 to 16. North Carolina's senators received similar instructions. See Benjamin Hawkins to A. H., Feb. 16, 1791, *Papers of A. H.*, VIII, 45; William L. Saunders, Walter Clark, and Stephen B. Weeks, eds., *Colonial and State Records of North Carolina* (Raleigh, 1886–1914), XXI, 962, 1029, 1044, 1049. The North Carolina instructions were reported in the *Gazette of the United States*, Jan. 5, 1791. The full text of the resolutions was printed in ibid., Jan. 19, 1791. For the New England perspective on the excise see, for example, Joseph Staunton (U. S. Senator from Rhode Island) to William Arnold, Feb. 22, 1791, Gratz Collection, case 1, box 29, HSP. For an example of a North Carolinian who voted in favor of the excise, and his explanations for doing so, see Fleming Nevin, "The Liquor Question in Colonial and Revolutionary War Periods," *WPHM*, XIII (1930): 196–197.

17. *Journal of the . . . House of Representatives of the Commonwealth of Pennsylvania*, Feb. 1, 1791, 145–147. The explanation of the majority arose in response to a statement of a minority in the House who contested the right of state legislators to interfere in the business of the national government, ibid., 142–145, 147–149.

18. Edgar S. Maclay, ed., *Journal of William Maclay* (New York, 1890), 376–377, 387–388.

19. John Sevier, Circular Letter, Jan. 10, 1791, in Noble E. Cunningham, ed., *Circular Letters of Congressmen to Their Constituents, 1789–1829* (Chapel Hill, N. C., 1978), I, 3.

20. Gales, *Debates*, II, 1890.

21. Ibid., 1891, 1892.

22. Ibid., 1901, 1905, 1906, 1907, 1925–1927; Thomas Rodney to A. H., Feb. 10, 1791, *Papers of A. H.*, VIII, 23. William D. Barber, " 'Among the Most Techy Articles of Civil Police': Federal Taxation and the Adoption of the Whiskey Excise," *WMQ*, XXV (1968): 58–84, noted that "southern congressmen claimed that their section would prefer a land tax to an excise, but little evidence supports the contention" (68, fn. 34). James Madison also expressed opposition to an excise in principle, but was resigned to its passage, thought opposition futile, and voted for the tax bill (J. M. to Edmund Pendleton, Feb. 13, 1791; J. M. to James Madison [Sr.], Feb. 13, 1791, in *Letters and Other Writings of James Madison* (Philadelphia, 1865), I, 527, 528, 529.

23. *Gazette of the United States*, Feb. 12, 1791. See also, "The Humble Address of Ten Thousand Federal Maids," ibid., Jan. 26, 1791. As tax theory, of course, this was all nonsense. Demand for alcoholic beverages is quite inelastic. Taxes have little or no effect on consumption, which is one reason that liquor is a reliable source of government revenue. As social and medical theory, however, the arguments of these and other contributions reflected the most enlightened knowledge of the day.

24. "The Memorial of the College of Physicians of the City of Philadelphia," Dec. 27, 1790, *Gazette of the United States*, Jan. 1, 1791. See also, ibid., June 8, 1791, for a warning about the particularly dangerous effects of over-eating and excessive consumption of alcoholic beverages during the summer months. On related issues, and on the culture of drink in the early republic see Rorabaugh, *The Alcoholic Republic*, 49 and *passim*. See also, Nevin, "The Liquor Question in Colonial and Revolutionary War Periods," 195–201.

25. Gales, *Debates*, II, 1890. The argument for health benefits was presented as part of the original bill in the spring 1790 session, ibid., 1692–1693.

26. Ames to Thomas Dwight, Jan. 6 and Jan. 24, 1791, *Works*, 92, 93; *Gazette of the United States*, Feb. 2, 1791, Jan. 8, 1791. These sentiments were shared by correspondents to the same newspaper on Jan. 22, Feb. 2, Feb. 5, and Feb. 19, 1791.

27. "Civis," *Dunlop's Daily Advertiser*, reprinted in the *Gazette of the United States*, Feb. 5, 1791; Ames to Thomas Dwight, Jan. 24, 1791, *Works*, 93–94; Gales, *Debates*, II, 1923–1924.

28. Ibid.

29. Reprinted in *Gazette of the United States*, Feb. 19, 1791; ibid., Jan. 15, 1791; Gales, *Debates*, II, 1897.

30. Gales, *Debates*, II, 1895, 1899, 1900.

31. Ibid., 1896, 1897, 1899; *Gazette of the United States*, Jan 22, Jan. 26, 1791.

32. *Gazette of the United States*, Jan. 22, Feb. 2, 1791.

33. Ibid., Jan. 29, 1791.

34. Ibid., Jan. 22, Feb. 9, 1791.

35. Marshall Smelser, "The Jacobin Phrenzy: Federalism and the Menace of Liberty, Equality, and Fraternity," *The Review of Politics*, XIII (1951): 457–482; Marshall Smelser, "The Federalist Period as an Age of Passion," *AQ*, X (1958): 391–419.

36. Politically, the most interesting group is the 37 Congressmen who voted "no" to the tax bill on either June 21, 1790 *or* Jan. 21, 1791. All but three of these opposed the bill in 1790, but then voted for it in 1791. Their opposition was clearly political, not ideological, and probably tied to the issue of moving the capital to the banks of the Potomac. Alexander White of Virginia, for example, strongly resisted the excise *until* the bargain was struck to move the capital. Thirteen different Congressmen voted against the excise both on June 21, 1790 *and* on Jan. 21, 1791. These included eight of ten representatives from frontier districts and four of six members who had histo-

ries of Antifederalism. Two Antifederalists from Massachusetts favored the excise. Alexander White of Virginia was from Frederick County, a frontier district. Four Congressmen *clearly* opposed only the excise provision of the bill. They voted "yes" to striking the excise provision from the bill on June 18, 1790, and when that action failed, voted "no" to the entire bill both on June 21, 1790 and Jan. 21, 1791. These four men might be viewed as the most ideologically consistent group within Congress who did not oppose all taxes, or at least import taxes. See the geographic distribution of the votes on maps in Slaughter, "Liberty, Order, and the Excise," Appendix II. See also, Barber, " 'Most Techy Articles of Civil Police,' " 78, n.57, and Gales, *Debates*, II, 1842–1852, 1857–1861, 1870, 1883–1884.

37. Deposition of Mr. Fitzsimons, "Causes of the Failure of the Expedition Against the Indians, in 1791, Under the Command of Major General St. Clair," communicated to the House of Representatives, May 8, 1792, *American State Papers, Military Affairs*, I, 36–37.

38. Quoted in Van Every, *Ark of Empire*, 233. See also, G. W. to David Humphreys, March 16, 1791, in Fitzpatrick, ed., *Writings of G. W.*, XXXI, 243.

39. Quoted in Van Every, *Ark of Empire*, 236. Braddock lost 714 of 1200 men, Grant lost 300 of 800 at Fort Duquesne, Bouquet's losses ran to 115 of 480 at Bushy Run, Herkimer lost 400 of 700 at Oriskany, and Butler suffered 302 deaths of 450 men in his defeat at Wyoming (236, fn. 4).

40. "Causes of the Failure of the Expedition Against the Indians," ibid., 39.

41. Executive Minutes of Governor Thomas Mifflin, *PA* 9th ser., I, 305, 309, 311, 312. See also, *Gazette of the United States*, Dec. 18, 1791.

42. Grenville to Hammond, Sept. 2, 1791, in Bernard Mayo, ed., *Instructions to the British Ministers to the United States, 1791–1812*, in *Annual Report of the American Historical Association for the Year 1936* (Washington, D. C., 1941), III, 16. See also, Bemis, *Jay's Treaty*, 94; Levi Allen to Henry Dundas, Aug. 9, 1791, Canadian Archives, Q. 54: 698, printed in *AHR*, XXI (1916): 555–558; Allen to Dundas, Nov. 27, 1791, in ibid., 559–560. See also, Douglas Brymner, ed., *Reports on Canadian Archives, 1889–1890* (Ottawa, 1890–1891), Note C: Vermont Negotiations, 53–58; and Frederick Jackson Turner, ed., "Documents: English Policy Toward America in 1790–1791," *AHR*, VIII (1902–1903): 78–86.

43. On Feb. 18, 1791, Congress voted to admit Vermont to the Union. President Washington signed the act admitting Kentucky on Feb. 4, 1791. Kentucky formally became a state in June 1792.

44. The dispatch of a British minister to the United States in 1791 led Spain to request a similar exchange, since the Spanish now feared an imminent rapprochement between the two English-speaking nations. But eighteen months elapsed before William Short actually arrived in Madrid. See Bemis, *Pinckney's Treaty*, 105. Nor were Spanish agents particularly active or successful in fomenting unrest on the southwestern frontier. They were pleased at the discontent aroused by the unsettled Mississippi issue and pleased at the rapid growth of settlement on the frontier, despite Kentucky's admittance to the Union, which they considered as by no means permanent. They were disturbed that the American defeats by the northwestern Indians might lead to the deployment of a 5000-man United States army on the frontier. And they were fearful of rumored schemes by American citizens to attack New Orleans. In brief, the Spaniards seemed merely to bide their time, still hopeful that discontent on the frontier might some day redound to their favor, but taking no serious active movements to foment this unrest at the present time. See Josef de Jaudenes and Josef Ignacio de Viar, Philadelphia, to Conde de Floridablanca, Madrid, July 17, 1791, Archivo Historico Nacional, Madrid, Estado, leg. 3896, t. 3, no. 297, no. 9. I thank Jodi Bilinkoff both for securing a copy of this and related documents for me in Madrid and for her invaluable assistance in translating the letters.

Chapter Seven: ASSEMBLY AND PROCLAMATION

1. James Brison to Gov. Thomas Mifflin, Nov. 9, 1792, *PA* ser. 2, IV, 44–45; John Neville to George Clymer, Nov. 7, 1791, Oliver Wolcott, Jr. Papers, XIX, CHS.

2. William Findley, *History of the Insurrection in the Four Western Counties of Pennsylvania in the Year MDCCXCIV* (Philadelphia, 1796), 41.

   William Findley (1741–1821) was a Scots-Irish immigrant who arrived in America in 1763. He had little formal schooling and initially worked as a weaver. He was an early supporter of the Revolutionary movement and served in a series of elective offices after he moved to a farm in Westmoreland County, Pennsylvania, in 1769. He was a member of the state Council of Censors from 1783 to 1790, served as an assemblyman, a state supreme executive councilman, and a delegate to the state constitutional convention of 1789–90, where he vainly fought for retaining the more democratic constitution of 1776. In national politics he was an Antifederalist and served as a Congressman continuously from 1791 to 1817.

3. Ibid., 41. This vision of American Revolutionaries as "paranoid," or at least prone to believe in conspiracies, derives from the interpretations of Bailyn, *Ideological Origins,* and Gordon S. Wood, "Conspiracy and the Paranoid Style: Causality and Deceit in the Eighteenth Century," *WMQ,* XXXIX (1982): 401–441.

4. Findley, *History of the Insurrection,* 42.

5. On the Redstone meeting of July 27, 1791, see Henry Marie Brackenridge, *History of the Western Insurrection in Western Pennsylvania, Commonly Called the Whiskey Insurrection, 1794* (Pittsburgh, 1859), 22–23; Hugh Henry Brackenridge, *Incidents of the Insurrection in the Western Parts of Pennsylvania, in the Year 1794* (Philadelphia, 1851), I, 228–236; *Maryland Journal,* Aug. 23, 1791; Oct. 7, 1791.

   Hugh Henry Brackenridge (1748–1816) arrived in America from Scotland with his parents at the age of five. As a youth, Brackenridge was a prodigious scholar; he became a schoolmaster at the age of fifteen, and entered the College of New Jersey (Princeton) in 1768. Writer, lawyer, politician, and jurist, Brackenridge is perhaps best remembered as the author of *Modern Chivalry,* an epic satirical novel set in late eighteenth-century America, that is modeled on Cervantes's *Don Quixote*. The huge book was published serially over the years from 1792 through 1815, and the themes and biting wit of the later parts were greatly influenced by Brackenridge's political misfortunes in the 1790s. William Findley, against whom he competed unsuccessfully for public offices on several occasions, is portrayed unflatteringly in the novel as Traddle the weaver. Brackenridge favored adoption of the national Constitution, became a Republican in national and state politics, and was appointed to the Pennsylvania Supreme Court in 1799. He moved from Pittsburgh to Carlisle in 1801.

6. Craig, *The History of Pittsburgh,* 236.

7. Minutes of the Meeting at Pittsburgh, Sept. 7, 1791, *Pittsburgh Gazette,* printed in *PA* 2d ser., IV, 20–22.

8. Ibid.

9. Ibid.

10. Two of the three western Pennsylvania counties (Westmoreland and Fayette) voted against ratification of the Constitution, and the third (Washington) recorded a tie vote. See Lester J. Cappon et al., eds., *Atlas of Early American History: The Revolutionary Era, 1760–1790* (Princeton, 1976), 63; Findley, *History,* 42.

    Dorothy Fennell's attempt to trace whiskey rebels through tax records verifies the impression of contemporaries on the scene, and supports the interpretation offered above. According to Fennell, "there was not a poor man at the meeting" in Brownsville [Redstone-Old Fort] on July 27, 1791. At least eighteen of the twenty-five men present were either justices of the peace or militia officers, or both. The Pittsburgh assembly of Sept. 7, 1791, was composed of the same class of men. Eight of eleven delegates were lawyers, and six of the eleven held a public office of some kind ("From Rebelliousness to Revolution," 47, 48).

11. Findley, *History*, 68; *PA* 2d ser., IV, 86; John Neville to George Clymer, Sept. 15, 1791, Wolcott Papers, XIX, CHS.

12. Neville to Clymer, Sept. 8 and Dec. 22, 1791, Wolcott Papers, XIX, CHS.

13. At least one other related incident occurred in western Pennsylvania in late 1791. A man named Roseberry suffered a tarring and feathering for voicing opposition to excise resistance. See Neville to Clymer, Dec. 11, 1791, Wolcott Papers, XIX, CHS. John Neville, "An Address to the Citizens of Westmoreland, Washington, Fayette and Allegheny Counties on the Revenue Law," *Gazette of the United States*, Jan. 7, 1792, 4; Jan. 11, 1792, 1; Jan. 14, 1792, 4.

14. Neville to Clymer, Aug. 23, 1792, Wolcott Papers, XIX, CHS, printed in *Papers of A. H.*, XII, 306.

15. Ibid. On Aug. 25 Faulkner took out an advertisement in the *Gazette*. "Notice is hereby given," read his ad, "as an inspection office has been kept by Gen. Neville at my house in Washington, I hereby inform the public that it shall be kept there no longer. Those who are uneasy and making threats may give themselves no further trouble." *Papers of A. H.*, XII, 306. The notice was reprinted in the [Philadelphia] *National Gazette*, Sept. 5, 1792.

16. Neville to Clymer, Aug. 23, 1792, *Papers of A. H.*, XII, 306. The above account is based upon the depositions of William Goudy, Allegheny County, Sept. 29, 1792; Reasin Beall, Pittsburgh, Sept. 29, 1792; Peter Myers, Allegheny County, Sept. 29, 1792; John Parmore, Allegheny County, Sept. 29, 1792; and Richard McKinsey, Allegheny County, Sept. 29, 1792, LC, Manuscript Division, Pennsylvania, Whiskey Rebellion Collection, MSS 16, 804.

17. Reprinted in the *National Gazette*, Aug. 4, 1792, and in *Papers of A. H.*, XII, 307. The regional convention of Aug. 21–22, 1792 had basically the same socio-economic composition as the 1791 assemblies (see note 10 above). Dorothy Fennell has located only four delegates to the 1792 convention who also participated in the violent remonstrances against the excise during 1791, and all of them tried to prevent further violence after the meetings. So the assemblies apparently served not only to bring together "respectable" opponents of the excise, who sought to diminish violence, but also to recruit other elites to the moderate cause ("From Rebelliousness to Insurrection," 49–50, 53, 54).

18. Minutes of the Aug. 21–22, 1792 meeting of the delegates from the western counties of Pennsylvania held at Pittsburgh, *Papers of A. H.*, XII, 308–309; *Gazette of the United States*, Sept. 1, 1792, 3; Sept. 5, 1792, 3. Four delegates to the assembly were members of the Pennsylvania Assembly—Albert Gallatin and John Smilie of Fayette County, and David Bradford and John Cannon of Washington County. Gallatin had been the secretary of the Redstone meeting in July 1791. Four delegates to the Aug. 1792 meeting—Edward Cook, David Phillips, James Marshall, and David Bradford—had represented their counties at the Pittsburgh meeting of Sept. 1791.

19. Ibid.

20. Ibid.

21. Thomas Marshall to Tench Coxe, Sept. 7, 1792, Whiskey Rebellion Papers, Record Group 58, Records of the Internal Revenue Service, NA. Neville to Clymer, Aug. 23, 1792, Wolcott Papers, CHS, XIX, confirms Marshall's suspicions. See also, Edward Carrington to Thomas Marshall, Dec. 31, 1793, Whiskey Rebellion Papers, NA.

22. The Augusta associators were later forced to sign a recantation to avoid prosecution, which confirms my impression that only resisters more remote from the centers of power could pull off such a direct challenge to law.

23. Coxe to A. H., Oct. 12, 1792, *Papers of A. H.*, XII, 599–600; Daniel Huger to A. H., [June 22–25, 1792], ibid., XI, 541–543.

24. Coxe to A. H., Oct. 12, 1792, ibid., XII, 600–601; Daniel Stevens to A. H., May 22 and May 26, 1792, ibid., XI, 417, letters not found; A. H. to G. W., Sept. 9, 1792, ibid., XII, 344–346; John Berrien to A. H., June 1, 1791, ibid., VIII, 404. *Gazette of the United States,* May 16, 1792, 3. Obstruction of excise collection was largely a frontier phenomenon, but it was not uniquely so. In Pennsylvania, for example, crowds did violence to excise collectors in Germantown, Chester, Cumberland, and York, all of which were east of the Appalachian chain. In some cases, direct action took the form of not-so-subtle warnings. Residents of Germantown, for example, removed an "office of inspection" sign from over a collector's door and replaced it with "the four quarters of a carrion" (*National Gazette,* May 31, 1792). When this failed to intimidate the collector, several persons "in disguise violently assaulted, beat, and abused . . . [him] with guns, clubs, etc" (D, Records of the Court of Quarter Sessions, Chester County, Pennsylvania, quoted in *Papers of A. H.,* XII, 594). Distillers in Northampton County simply refused to cooperate with collectors. People in Cumberland County forced a tax man to surrender his records. Inhabitants of the same county organized an association or collective pledge refusing to pay the tax (Edmund Randolph to G. W., Sept. 10, 1792, G. W. Papers, LC, Manuscript Division; Tench Coxe to A. H., Oct. 12, 1792, *Papers of A. H.,* XII, 594–596). On opposition in eastern and central Pennsylvania, see also William Rawle Family Papers, I, HSP. On the initial period of collections and reactions to resistance, see, for example, the *Carlisle Gazette,* Jan. 26, 1791; Feb. 16, 1791; March 23, 1791; July 27, 1791; Aug. 31, 1791; Sept. 7, 1791; Sept. 21, 1791. Frontier resistance was unique, then, only in the frequency of violence, the success of resistance to the law, the support for resistance by an apparent majority of the region's populace, and, most importantly, its persistence over time. Eastern resistance was crushed relatively quickly and the excise became a profitable tax east of the Appalachians within two years of its adoption. See also, Mary K. Bonsteel Tachau, *Federal Courts in the Early Republic: Kentucky, 1789–1816* (Princeton, 1978), 66–67; Mary K. Bonsteel Tachau, "The Whiskey Rebellion in Kentucky," *Journal of the Early Republic,* II (1982): 239–259.

25. A. H. to Edward Carrington, July 25, 1792, *Papers of A. H.,* XII, 84.

26. The quotation is from A. H. to Edward Stevens, Nov. 11, 1769, ibid., I, 4. The interpretation of Hamilton's personality and its contrast with Washington's is based on Jacob E. Cooke, *Alexander Hamilton* (New York, 1982), 5, 27–28, and *passim;* Gerald Stourzh, *Alexander Hamilton and the Idea of Republican Government* (Stanford, Calif., 1970). See also, G. W. to A. H., Aug. 31, 1792, *Papers of A. H.,* XII, 304–305; G. W. to A. H., Aug 5, 1792, ibid., XII, 166–167.

27. Edmund Randolph to A. H., Sept. 8, 1792, *Papers of A. H.,* XII, 336–340.

28. John Jay to A. H., Sept. 8, 1792, ibid., XII, 334–335. See also A. H. to John Jay, Sept. 3, 1792, ibid., 316–317.

29. A. H. to G. W., Sept. 9, 1792, ibid., 344–346.

30. Ibid., 344–346.

31. Ibid., 345.

32. G. W. to A. H., Sept. 7, 1792, Fitzpatrick, ed., *Writings of G. W.,* XXXII, 143–145.

33. A. H. to G. W., Sept. 1, 1792, *Papers of A. H.,* XII, 311–312.

34. G. W. to A. H., Sept. 7, 1792, ibid., XII, 331–333.

35. Ibid; A. H. to Tench Coxe, Sept. 1, 1792, ibid., XII, 305–310.

36. Edmund Randolph to A. H., Sept. 8, 1792, *Papers of A. H.,* XII, 336–340.

37. A. H. to G. W., Sept. 22, 1792, ibid., 412–415.

38. Edmund Randolph to A. H., Sept. 8, 1792, ibid., 336–340. The drafts of the proclamation have not been found.

39. A. H. to G. W., Nov. 11, 1794, ibid., XVII, 366–367.

40. "Proclamation," Sept. 15, 1792, ibid., 150–151; Thomas Jefferson to G. W., Sept. 18, 1792, Paul Leicester Ford, ed., *The Works of Thomas Jefferson,* 12 vols. (New York,

1904–1905), VII, 153–154; G. W. to the Governors of Pennsylvania, North Carolina, and South Carolina, Sept. 29, 1792, Fitzpatrick, ed., *Writings of G. W.*, XXXII, 169; G. W. to A. H., Sept. 17, 1792, ibid., 153–154.

41. *The Speech of Albert Gallatin . . . .* (Philadelphia, 1795), 7; Findley, *History*, 45 and 47.

42. *Speech of Albert Gallatin*, 6.

43. Findley, *History of the Insurrection*, 54.

Chapter Eight: LIBERTY, ORDER, AND THE EXCISE

1. This account of Clymer's journey is based on the report that appeared in the *Pittsburgh Gazette, Claypoole's Mail*, and was reprinted in the [Philadelphia] *National Gazette*, Nov. 28, 1792, 4; Findley, *History*, 70, 78; Alexander Addison to George Clymer, Sept. 29, 1792 and Clymer to Addison, Oct. 1, 1792, Wolcott Papers, XIX, CHS; Clymer to A. H., Oct. 4, 1792, *Papers of A. H.*, XII, 517–522; Clymer to A. H., Sept. 28, 1792, ibid., 495–497; A. H. to Tench Coxe, Sept. 1, 1792, ibid., 305–310; Coxe to Clymer, Sept. 6, 1792, Letters of the Commissioner of the Revenue, 1792–1793, Record Group 58, NA; Clymer to [?], Dec. 13, 1792, Gratz Collection, case 1, box 4, HSP; "A Western Clergyman," *National Gazette*, Jan. 16, 1793. McClure, "The Ends of the American Earth," 597, notes that Clymer had visited Pittsburgh in 1778 and pronounced it an excellent place "to do penance in."

Clymer was born in Philadelphia in 1739 to a Quaker family. He was a signer of the Declaration of Independence, a member of the Constitutional Convention, a Federalist in national politics, and an anti-constitutionalist in state politics. He was a member of Congress, federal supervisor of revenue for Pennsylvania, and a negotiator of the Creek Indian Treaty in Georgia in 1796. Clymer was a merchant, a landspeculator, and the first president of the Philadelphia Bank. He had the second highest residential tax assessment in the city of Philadelphia in 1774 (Dr. William Shippen was first) and the third highest income from real property. Clymer engaged in profiteering during the Revolution. He opposed the Bill of Rights for the national Constitution. He favored a bill that would allow Europeans to speculate in American lands, but opposed the establishment of local land offices that would have enabled Americans to make small purchases. He saw the latter as detrimental to the interests of land companies in which he had invested heavily. He owned land in western Pennsylvania, which he sold in 1795, after the government crushed the Whiskey Rebellion and land prices in the region rose dramatically (see Chapter Thirteen and the Conclusion). He also speculated in Kentucky lands. His son served in the federal army sent west to subdue the rebels in 1794 and died of lockjaw while in western Pennsylvania. There was some question about Clymer's accounting practices while he was supervisor of revenue, and the Treasury department tried for over twenty-five years to collect $3500 from him, and then from his estate. The case came to trial in 1819, seven years after Clymer's death, and his name was exonerated. Jerry Grundfest, *George Clymer: Philadelphia Revolutionary, 1739–1813* (New York, 1982).

2. *National Gazette*, Jan. 16, 1792, 3. On the Court-Country paradigm in early American politics see John M. Murrin, "The Great Inversion: or Court versus Country: A Comparison of the Revolution Settlements in England (1688–1721) and America (1776–1816)," in J. G. A. Pocock, ed., *Three British Revolutions: 1641, 1688, 1776* (Princeton, 1980), 368–453.

What I describe here as a debate between friends of liberty and order, Joyce Appleby depicts as a dispute over alternative visions of liberty—with the former a "Lockeian liberal" and the latter a "classical republican" definition (Appleby, *Capitalism and a New Social Order: The Republican Vision of the 1790s* (New York, 1984), 15–23). The problem with using Appleby's categories for the excise debate of the 1790s is that the language of Federalists (her classical republicans) was framed as an attack on "liberty," not as a defense of traditional usage of the term. Nor does her characterization of Republicans as "shedding the past" (79, 81, and *passim*) seem valid for essays published in "Republican" newspapers, endorsed by "Republican" politicians, or authored by pseudonymous "Republicans." These friends of liberty resorted far more often and far more reverentially to the lessons of history than their opponents. See also, James Roger Sharp, "The Whiskey Rebellion and the Question of Representation," in Boyd, ed., *Whiskey Rebellion,* 119–133.

3. *National Gazette,* June 18, 1792, 2; April 26, 1792, 2.

4. Ibid., Jan. 23, 1792, 3. See, for example, ibid., April 12, 1792, 3. This writer thought a law such as the Stamp Act "deservedly odious" whether adopted by a foreign government or "by a Congress of our own creating."

5. Ibid., May 24, 1792, 1.

6. Ibid., May 21, 1792, 4.

7. Ibid., May 24, 1792, 1, 2; July 4, 1792, 1.

8. Ibid., Jan. 12, 1793, 3, from the *Harrisburg Advertiser.*

9. *National Gazette,* Feb. 9, 1792, reprinted in Daniel Marder, ed., Hugh Henry Brackenridge, *Incidents of the Insurrection* (New Haven, 1972), 47–51; *National Gazette,* Feb. 2, 1793, 1, reprinted from the *Fayetteville* [North Carolina] *Gazette,* Jan. 15, 1793. The particular threat to the morals of the yeomanry was said to arise in part from the necessity of taking oaths—which would lead people to lie—concerning their distilling practices. On the excise's threat to morals see the *National Gazette,* April 23, 1792, 2–3; May 10, 1792, 1, 2. Appleby is wrong to assert a direct link between the execution of Louis XVI in 1793 and the origins of class-conscious conflict in the rhetoric of American politics, since, as these citations show, that debate predated 1793 (*Capitalism and a New Social Order,* 54, 55, 58, 74, and *passim*).

10. *National Gazette,* Sept. 26, 1792, 2; May 7, 1792, 2; Dec. 1, 1792, 3; May 14, 1792, 2. For another class-based analysis, see ibid., July 4, 1792, 2. "Gunpowder," *Gazette of the United States,* March 14, 1792, reprinted from the *American Daily Advertiser.*

11. H. H. Brackenridge, "Thoughts on the Excise Law, so far as it respects the Western Country," *National Gazette,* Feb. 9, 1792, reprinted in Marder, ed., Brackenridge, *Incidents,* 47–51.

12. Ibid.

13. *National Gazette,* Feb. 2, 1793, 1, reprinted from the *Fayetteville Gazette,* Jan. 15, 1793.

14. [George Logan], *Five Letters Addressed to the yeomanry of the United States . . . By A Farmer* (Philadelphia, 1792), letters 1, 3, 5.

15. "On the Excise Law," *National Gazette,* Feb. 2, 1793, 1, reprinted from the *Fayetteville Gazette,* Jan. 15, 1793. See also, *Gazette of the United States,* Oct. 27, 1792, 1–2, on the threat of searches to personal liberty.

16. "A Petition and Remonstrance to the President and Congress of the United States (Written by a North Carolina Planter)" (1791), in William K. Boyd, ed., *Some Eighteenth Century Tracts Concerning North Carolina* (Raleigh, 1927), 492; "Mum.," to the *National Gazette,* May 14, 1792, 2. *National Gazette,* Jan. 12, 1793, 3, reprinted from the *Harrisburg Advertiser.*

17. Edgar S. Maclay, ed., *Journal of William Maclay* (New York, 1890), 386, 387, 390. Of course, Maclay may have intended that his journal see the light of publication. This could affect the posture he took toward "private" writings.

18. For two contrasting examples of the liberty-order controversy as acted out on the floor of Congress, see *Gazette of the United States,* March 14, 1792, 3; March 15, 1794, 3.

19. Ibid., March 15, 1794, 3; Feb. 1, 1792, 3; July 13, 1793, 1, reprinted from the [Stockbridge, Mass.] *Western Star.* Murrin, "The Great Inversion," made essentially the same point, although specifically within a post-1794 context, when he wrote that

in the Federalists' "hierarchy of political values, liberty and equality had become subordinate to public order and energetic government" (411).

20. *Gazette of the United States*, Jan.. 7, 1794, 3; Nov. 10, 1792, 3; Dec. 5, 1792, 3.

21. Fisher Ames to Christopher Gore, Jan. 28, 1794, in Seth Ames, ed., *Works of Fisher Ames* (Boston, 1809), 140; *Gazette of the United States*, June 5, 1793, 4; Ames to George Minot, March 8, 1792, *Works*, 114; *Gazette of the United States*, Jan. 23, 1793, 3; May 11, 1793, 3; Aug. 29, 1792, 3.

22. *Gazette of the United States*, March 7, 1794, 2; Jan. 16, 1793, 3.

23. "A Farmer," ibid., Feb. 11, 1794, 2; Jan. 16, 1793; Sept. 5, 1792, 1, reprinted from the *Connecticut Courant*. On the foreign influence, see also the *Gazette of the United States*, Feb. 4, 1792, 3; March 7, 1792, 3.

24. *Gazette of the United States*, Feb. 4, 1792, 3; Oct. 29, 1791; Oct. 26, 1791. On the same issue, see also Dec. 10, 1791. During 1791 the newspapers printed full accounts of the riots in Birmingham, England. Some American elites feared the spread of lower-class violence from Europe. On the Birmingham riots see R. B. Rose, "The Priestly Riots of 1791," *Past and Present*, no. 18 (1960): 68–85.

25. *Gazette of the United States*, April 20, 1791. On "responsibility" see also March 25, 1794, 2. On "obedience" and "example" see also Dec. 31, 1791.

26. Ibid., Aug. 25, 1792, 3; April 4, 1792, 1; Sept. 22, 1792, 3; *The Carlisle* [Pennsylvania] *Gazette*, April 20, 1791, 3, reprinted from the *Connecticut Courant*. For a similar story with a related moral see the much longer "Portrait" in the *Gazette of the United States*, May 16, 1792, 1–2.

27. *Gazette of the United States*, Aug. 20, 1791, reprinted from the *Freeman's Journal*. On the culture of drink and the attempts to instill temperate habits during this period see Rorabaugh, *The Alcoholic Republic*.

28. *Gazette of the United States*, June 8, 1793, 3. On Genet's arrival and its broader meaning for American politics see Harry Ammon, *The Genet Mission* (New York, 1973).

29. "An Enquirer," *Gazette of the United States*, April 23, 1791; "Cato," ibid., Sept. 5, 1792, 1; Sept. 26, 1792, 3; May 27, 1794, 3.

30. On "classical republicanism" in late eighteenth-century America, see J. G. A. Pocock, *The Machiavellian Moment: Florentine Political Thought and the Atlantic Republican Tradition* (Princeton, 1975); Wood, *Creation of the American Republic*; Robert E. Shalhope, "Republicanism and Early American Historiography," *WMQ*, XXXIX (1982): 334–356; John W. Malsberger, "The Political Thought of Fisher Ames," *Journal of the Early Republic*, II (1982): 1–20. *Gazette of the United States*, Nov. 10, 1791, 1; April 20, 1791; Dec. 31, 1791; Aug. 28, 1793, 3; July 1, 1794, 2.

31. *Gazette of the United States*, Feb. 8, 1792, 3; Oct. 3, 1792, 3. The transformation of authority relationships during the second half of the eighteenth century is the subject of Rhys Isaac, *The Transformation of Virginia, 1740–1790* (Chapel Hill, 1982); and Jay Fliegelman, *Prodigals and Pilgrims: The American Revolution Against Patriarchal Authority, 1750–1800* (New York, 1982). See also Thomas P. Slaughter, "Family Politics in Revolutionary America," *AQ*, XXXVI (1984): 598–606.

32. *Gazette of the United States*, May 21, 1791; May 25, 1791. My citations are almost exclusively to Philadelphia newspapers because they epitomize the national debate and had the widest national circulation. Many of the letters quoted here, and hundreds of others like them, appeared in newspapers throughout the states. The extended essays, such as "Sidney" and "Brutus," were reprinted around the country, some of them appearing first in the Philadelphia papers, some of them originating in other states. For other examples of letters from "friends of liberty," see the [Hagerstown, Md.] *Washington Spy*, March 2, 1792, 3; April 4, 1792, 1; Aug. 13, 1794, 4; the *Pittsburgh Gazette*, Feb. 9, 1793, 1; Feb. 23, 1793, 1–3; Aug. 3, 1793, 3; April 19, 1794, 1; Aug. 26, 1794, 3; and the *Maryland Journal and Baltimore Advertiser*,

Jan. 21, 1791, 2; June 23, 1794, 3. For other examples of letters by "friends of order," see, the *Maryland Journal*, Feb. 1, 1791, 3; Aug. 17, 1791, 2; Nov. 23, 1791, 4; Aug. 6, 1794, 1–2; Aug. 13, 1794, 1–2; Aug. 20, 1794, 3. Letters on both sides were also frequently printed in New England and New York newspapers.

33. On Ames's political thought see Malsberger, "The Political Thought of Fisher Ames." My description of Ames and the quotations are taken from his correspondence between 1792 and 1794 printed in *Works*, 114–160.

34. Clinton Rossiter, ed., *The Federalist Papers* (New York, 1961), 218.

35. Ibid., 219.

36. "Report on the Difficulties in the Execution of the Act Laying Duties on Distilled Spirits" (Philadelphia, March 5, 1792, communicated to the Speaker of the House of Representatives, March 6, 1792), *Papers of A. H.*, XI, 79.

37. Murrin, "Great Inversion," 380, 381, 382; J. H. Plumb, *The Growth of Political Stability in England, 1675–1725* (London, 1967), ch. 6; and J. P. Kenyon, *Revolution Principles: The Politics of Party, 1689–1729* (Cambridge, 1977).

38. Recently, Joyce Appleby has criticized historians J. G. A. Pocock, James Henretta, Lance Banning, Drew McCoy, and John Murrin, among others, for portraying the Jeffersonians as losers in a heroic battle against modernity. On the contrary, she has argued, the Jeffersonian vision of America was both democratic and capitalistic, agrarian and commercial. In sum, she counters a tendency in the writings of these historians with an alternative caricature of Federalists and Republicans. Each of those named above has provided valuable insights to the political culture of the early Republic, although Appleby has offered an antidote to the overstated and in some instances misstated cases of those she assails. But we would be closer to the truth, if we recognized the amalgam of forward- and backward-looking elements in the thought and practice of Federalists and Republicans. See Appleby, "Commercial Farming and the 'Agrarian Myth' in the Early Republic," *JAH*, LXVIII (1982): 833–849; Appleby, "What Is Still American in the Political Philosophy of Thomas Jefferson?" *WMQ*, XXXIX (1982): 287–309; Appleby, *Capitalism and a New Social Order*; Murrin, "The Great Inversion"; Lance Banning, *The Jeffersonian Persuasion: Evolution of a Party Ideology* (Ithaca, 1978); Pocock, "Virtue and Commerce in the Eighteenth Century," *JIH*, III (1972): 119–134; Pocock, *The Machiavellian Moment*; Henretta, "Families and Farms: Mentalité in Pre-Industrial America," *WMQ*, XXXV (1978): 3–32; and Drew McCoy, *The Elusive Republic: Political Economy in Jeffersonian America* (Chapel Hill, 1980).

Appleby's vision of Republicans as economic modernizers, and Federalists as conservatives, fits neither the internal taxation debate discussed in Chapter One, nor the liberty-order debate described here. Her notion that the "promise of prosperity encouraged them [i.e., the Jeffersonians] to vault over the cumulative wisdom of the ages and imagine a future far different from the dreary past known to man" (*Capitalism and a New Social Order*, 49) does not fit the localist-Antifederalist-Republican side of taxation debates. McCoy's analysis of Republican political economy is more useful for this purpose.

In one other important sense, however, both the friends of liberty and friends of order were traditionalists in that they all assumed that *real* economic growth required a paternalistic society. Federalists thought that they could modernize the economy and the government only by building upon a traditional social hierarchy. Jeffersonian-Republicans could envision supplanting the traditional social hierarchy only by expanding—not by developing—the traditional economy. Republicans would attack the symptoms and symbols of a European-type hierarchical social structure in America—i.e., primogeniture and entail—but never the cause—slavery. Federalists were traditional for their fear of an expanding economy, but the Jeffersonians were no more "modern" for their endorsement of economic expansion. Both modern communism and capitalism assume that social equality can be protected only by some combination of economic growth and statism. Jeffersonian-Republicans were distinctively anti-statist; neither Republicans nor Federalists advocated true economic growth. Neither Federalists nor Republicans were proto-modern, then, in the sense of anticipating all of the major components of dominant economic thought today.

39. Murrin, "Great Inversion," 390, described the Stamp Act in this same way.

Chapter Nine: ALTERNATIVE PERSPECTIVES

1. Benjamin Rush, *An Account of the Bilious remitting Yellow Fever, as it Appeared in the City of Philadelphia in the Year 1793* (Philadelphia, 1794), 8–12, 36–37, 113–114; J H Powell, *Bring Out Your Dead: The Great Plague of Yellow Fever in Philadelphia in 1793* (Philadelphia, 1949; rpt., 1970), v; Wolcott Papers, XIX–XX, CHS.

2. A. H., "Treasury Department Circular to the Supervisors of the Revenue," Sept. 30, 1791, *Papers of A. H.*, IX, 249.

3. "Explanations and Instructions Concerning the Act . . . Passed in the third Session of Congress, On the 2d of March 1791" [Philadelphia, 1791], *Papers of A. H.*, VIII, 365–382.

4. A. H., "Treasury Department Circular to the Supervisors of the Revenue," June 27, 1791, *Papers of A. H.*, VIII, 510; A. H. to Jeremiah Olney, Sept. 24, 1791, ibid., IX, 236; A. H., "Treasury Department Circular to the Supervisors of the Revenue," Sept. 30, 1791, ibid., IX, 248–249; A. H., "Treasury Department Circular to the District Judges," ibid., IX, 402; William Ellery [Newport, R.I.] to A. H., Oct. 18, 1791, ibid., IX, 403.

5. "Report on the Subject of Manufactures, Dec. 5, 1791," *Papers of A. H.*, X, 1–340; "Report on the Difficulties in the Execution of the Act Laying Duties on Distilled Spirits" [Philadelphia, March 5, 1792, communicated on March 6, 1792], ibid., XI, 77–106. The orders that resulted in this report were issued by the House of Representatives on Nov. 1 and 2, 1791, *Journal of the House*, I, 446, and are reprinted in *Papers of A. H.*, XI, 78.

6. "Report on the Difficulties," *Papers of A. H.*, XI, 84, 86–90. On Hamilton's arguments against the ideological fears of petitioners see Chapter Eight above.

7. "Report on the Difficulties," *Papers of A. H.*, XI, 90–91, 92–93.

8. Ibid., 90–91, 93–94.

9. Ibid., 96–100. Congress did not amend the law to allow payment of the excise tax in kind until 1794. See below Chapter Ten.

10. Ibid.

11. Ibid., 90.

12. See above, Chapter Eight.

13. Dorothy Fennell, "By Calculation Oppressed: The Whiskey Excise and the Decline of Country Distillers," unpublished essay, which is a revised version of chapter seven of her dissertation, "From Rebelliousness to Revolution," 227–258; William Findley to [Pennsylvania] Governor Thomas Mifflin, Nov. 21, 1792, *PA* ser. 2, IV, 42. Fennell's chapter seven is a major contribution to our understanding of the distilling industry in western Pennsylvania and one to which the following discussion is heavily indebted.

14. A. H., "Report on the Difficulties," *Papers of A. H.*, XI, 98.

15. Ibid., 82. My interpretation of Hamilton's intent departs here from Fennell's.

16. The quote and some of the information in this paragraph are from Fennell, "By Calculation Oppressed." Her source for the quotation is *Annals of Congress*, III, 586. For a broader theoretical consideration of the sort of dispute discussed here, see Henretta, "Families and Farms"; T. H. Breen, "The Culture of Agriculture: The Symbolic World of the Tidewater Planter, 1760–1790," in David Hall, John M.

Murrin, and Thad W. Tate, eds., *Saints and Revolutionaries: Essays on Early American History* (New York, 1984), 247-284.

17. Neville to Clymer, June 7 and June 23, 1793, Wolcott Papers, XIX, CHS.

18. Ibid.

19. Neville to Clymer, May 24, 1793, and deposition of Benjamin Wells before Judge Richard Peters, Philadelphia, Jan. 29, 1794, Wolcott Papers, XIX, CHS.

20. Findley to Mifflin, Nov. 21, 1792, *PA* ser. 2, IV, 50.

21. Ibid.

22. From the list of property destroyed by insurgents at Bower Hill included with a "letter from the Secretary of the Treasury accompanying his report on the petition of Benjamin Wells and the Counter Petition of Sundry inhabitants of Fayett County 2nd April 1800, and referred to the Committee of claims," included as Appendix G of Margaret Moore Felton, "General John Neville," M.A. thesis, University of Pittsburgh, 1932.

23. John Neville to the President of the Virginia Council of Safety, June 13, 1776, *VMHB*, XVI (1908): 53-55; Neville to Patrick Henry, April 1, 1777, *PA* 1st ser., V, 286-288; Felton, "General John Neville"; *Dictionary of American Biography*, XIII (New York, 1934), 437-438.

24. Jacob E. Cooke, "The Whiskey Rebellion: A Re-Evaluation," *PAH*, XXX (1963): 316-346, also saw Neville as a pivotal figure in the events discussed here. According to Cooke, "if one man was responsible for the whiskey insurrection it was General John Neville" (336). Findley, *History*, 79-80.

25. On the events of 1793 and their impact on domestic politics see Dorothy Twohig, ed., *The Journal of the Proceedings of the President, 1793-1797* (Charlottesville, Va., 1981), Jan. 11, 1793; Feb. 9-10 and 27, 1793; March 12 and 23, 1793; May 16, 1793; Nov. 6, 1793; Dec. 3, 1793; *National Gazette*, July 6, 1793, 3; Aug. 10, 1793, 2; Aug. 10, 1793, 2; Aug. 24, 1793, 1, 3; Sept. 7, 1793, 3; Oct. 2, 1793, 1; *Gazette of the United States*, April 6, 1793, 3; John Spencer Bassett, *The Federalist System, 1789-1801* (New York, 1906; rpt. ed., 1969); John C. Miller, *The Federalist Era, 1789-1801* (New York, 1960); and Forrest McDonald, *The Presidency of George Washington* (Lawrence, Kansas, 1974).

26. Arthur St. Clair to A. H., Aug. 9, 1793, *Papers of A. H.*, XV, 211.

27. Quoted by Bemis, *Jay's Treaty*, 170-171, 171-172.

28. *New York Journal*, Dec. 7, 1793; *National Gazette*, March 2, 1793; McDonald, *Presidency of George Washington*, 133.

29. Harry Ammon, *The Genet Mission* (New York, 1973).

30. From Vice President John Adams's perspective some years after the event, the yellow fever epidemic seemed also a blessing in disguise. Twenty years later, Adams remembered 1793 as one of the most dangerous years in the republic's history—along with 1786 (Shays's Rebellion), 1794 (The Whiskey Rebellion), and 1798 (Fries's Rebellion), and he tried to explain his perspective on the disorder of the times. "You certainly never felt," Adams recalled for Thomas Jefferson, "the terrorism excited by Genet . . . when ten thousand people in the streets of Philadelphia, day after day, threatened to drag Washington out of his house and effect a revolution in the government, or compel it to declare war in favor of the French Revolution and against England. The coolest and the firmest minds . . . have given their opinions to me that nothing but the yellow fever . . . could have saved the United States from a total revolution of government." Adams, Washington, Hamilton, and others may have overreacted, but that is hindsight unaffected by the insecurity of the times through which they lived. There were good reasons in 1793 for the friends of order to fear that their world was tumbling down around them (Adams to Jefferson, June 30, 1813, in Lester J. Cappon, ed., *The Adams-Jefferson Letters*, 2 vols. (Chapel Hill, N. C., 1959), II, 346-347).

Chapter Ten: FEDERALISM BESIEGED

1. Neville to Clymer, June 13, 1794, Wolcott Papers, XIX, CHS; Findley, *History of the Insurrection*, 58, 60, 62; H. M. Brackenridge, *History of the Western Insurrection*, 28, 29; *Gazette of the United States*, Feb. 26, 1794, 2.

2. P. Bond to Lord Grenville, March 10, 1794, in J. Franklin Jameson, ed., "Letters of Phineas Bond, British Consul at Philadelphia, to the Foreign Office of Great Britain, 1790–1794," *Annual Report of the American Historical Association for the Year 1897* (Washington, D. C., 1898): 543; Francis Preston to his Virginia constituents, March 24, 1794, in Cunningham, ed., *Circular Letters*, I, 22. Similar sentiments were expressed in a circular letter from Congressman Thomas P. Carnes to his Georgia constituents, May 2, 1794, ibid., 26. Ames to Christopher Gore, Jan. 28, 1794, *Works*, 134.

3. Bemis, *Jay's Treaty*, 175; *Gazette of the United States*, June 30, 1794, 2; Bemis, *Jay's Treaty*, 170–176; Opening Address of Governor Thomas Mifflin to the Pennsylvania Assembly, 1793, PA ser. 4, IV, 258; Mifflin to Assembly, Sept. 4, 1793, ibid., 266; Wright, *Britain and the American Frontier*, 94; Governor Howell [New Jersey], to Senator John Rutherford, March 12, 1794, NJHS, G7, NJ Mss, IV, 67.

4. Jaudenes to Alcudia, March 13, 1794, AN, Estado 218, translation by Jodi Bilinkoff; Simcoe to Dundas, June 21, 1794, CA, Q, 280 281, 178; Simcoe to Dundas, Aug. 4, 1794, Canada, Public Archives, *Report* (1889), note C, 57–58; CA, Q, 69–71, 38, 41. Attempts to reconcile the Creeks and Cherokees were unsuccessful.

5. *Gazette of the United States*, June 28, 1794, 3.

6. Opponents of the 1794 excises succeeded in getting the taxes reduced in 1795 and suspended in operation on May 21, 1796, and again on March 4, 1797. On April 4, 1800, the tax on tobacco products was repealed. On April 6, 1802, the tax on sugar was repealed. Samuel Smith, *Annals of Congress* (Jan. 16, 1795), IV, 1115–1117. James Thompson Callender, *History of the United States for 1796* (Philadelphia, 1797), 8. I have not located a single reference to the excises of 1794 as "internal" taxes. This absence may demonstrate regional ideological differences if the earlier objections in the newspapers were written by westerners.

7. Democratic Society of Pennsylvania, Resolve, July 31, 1794, HSP; *Gazette of the United States*, Sept. 8, 1794.

8. The only crowd action that I have discovered was reported by Samuel Hodgdon to A. H., May 9, 1794, *Papers of A. H.*, XVI, 397. In this incident several men—Jacob Morgan, a businessman; Thomas Leiper, a tobacconist; Edward Pole, an ironmaker; and Edward Pennington, a sugar refiner—explained to the crowd the issues at stake in the proposed excises. One man then read a petition to the President and Congress that, in sum, objected to the proposed excises as "unjust, impolitic, oppressive, dangerous, and unnecessary" (*Gazette of the United States*, May 10, 1794; extract printed in *Papers of A. H.*, XVI, 398–399). The crowd was asked to ratify the petition, which they did vociferously. See also Roland M. Baumann, "Philadelphia's Manufacturers and the Excise Taxes of 1794: The Forging of the Jeffersonian Coalition," *PMHB*, CVI (1982): 3–39.

9. Madison to Jefferson, May 25, 1794, *Letters of Madison*, II, 17. The proposed stamp tax, the tax on stock transfers, and the increase in tonnage duties were defeated in Congress.

10. *Annals of Congress*, IV, May 30, 1794, 738, 735.

11. Mifflin to the Judges of the [Pennsylvania] Supreme Court, March 21, 1794, PA ser. 2, IV, 58.

12. According to section 8 of its bylaws, "the society shall have power with the concurrence of the districts and county to nominate and recommend such persons as in their opinion will be capable to represent us in the government of this state and the United

States. To hear and determine all matters [at] variance and disputes between party and party. To encourage able teachers for the instructions [of] youth. To examine into the conduct of their teachers. To introduce the Bible and religious books into their schools. To encourage the industrious, and promote the man of merit. . . ." According to Section 10, "all matters in variance and disputes within the districts shall be laid before the society, and no district or citizen within the districts shall sue or cause to be sued before a single justice of the peace or any court of justice a citizen or citizens of the districts, county, counties before they first apply to the secretary for redress, unless the business will not admit of delay" (Constitution for the district of Hamiltons (Feb. 18, 1794?), William Rawle Family Papers, I, 18, HSP). See also, "To the President and Congress of the United States of America: The Remonstrance of the society of Hamilton's district of Washington County in Pennsylvania," [1794] ibid.; A. J. Dallas to William Rawle, Jan. 18, 1794, ibid.; records of meetings of Hamilton district society, Feb. 11, Feb. 19, and Feb. 28, 1794, ibid.

13. The Remonstrance of the society of Hamilton's district of Washington County in Pennsylvania [Feb.–March? 1794], ibid., I, 12.

14. Ibid.

15. Volume I of the Rawle Family Papers contains District Attorney William Rawle's file of information on potentially treasonous activities in western Pennsylvania. The spy within the Mingo Creek Society cannot be identified from the papers, but his information was apparently forwarded to the government through excise collector Benjamin Wells. It has previously been thought that no records of the Mingo Creek Society survived. It is probable that the Society's own records were destroyed in the fall of 1794 lest they incriminate its members at a time when the national government was prosecuting western Pennsylvanians for treason. The copies in the Rawle papers may be all that remain. The documents in the Rawle papers were prepared for the President by Tench Coxe. After the President read them they were forwarded to Rawle. See also Rawle Family Papers, I, 15–17, and references in note 12.

16. Deposition of John McDonald [n.d.], in H. H. Brackenridge, *Incidents of the Insurrection*, III, 77. Notice of the Allegheny County society appeared in the *Pittsburgh Gazette* on April 26, 1794. The notice reported that "the articles of this society are to the same effect with that of Mingo Creek, and equally calculated to abstract the public mind from the established order of the laws." Brackenridge, *Incidents of the Insurrection*, III, 25, labeled the Mingo Creek Society "the cradle of the insurrection."

17. H. M. Brackenridge, *History of the Western Insurrection*, 25.

18. *Gazette of the United States*, Feb. 26, 1794, 2. The proclamation appeared again on page 1 of the issues of Feb. 27 and 28.

19. Neville to Clymer[?], March 21, 1794, Wolcott Papers, XIX, CHS.

20. Ibid.

21. Ibid.

22. Addison to Mifflin, March 31, 1794, *PA* ser. 2, IV, 60. See above Chapter One. In practice, internal taxes were repealed during Jefferson's first term and not reenacted until the War of 1812. After the war emergency passed, in keeping with Republican principles, the excises were repealed and none were again adopted until the Civil War.

23. Addison to Mifflin, March 31, 1794, *PA* ser. 2, IV, 60; Addison to Mifflin, May 12, 1794, ibid., 63.

24. A. H. to G. W., June 4, 1794, *Papers of A. H.*, XVI, 461. See also, Clymer to Tench Coxe, April 21, 1794, Wolcott Papers, XIX, CHS.

25. Findley, *History of the Insurrection*, 63; Baldwin, *Whiskey Rebels*, 91. Evidence does not substantiate the claims of these authors that resistance to the tax was declining in western Pennsylvania during 1793 and 1794. There were always some

men, generally larger distillers, who were willing or eager to see the law enforced. There were no doubt some, but very few, small distillers who considered registering their stills during 1793 and 1794. Hamilton misunderstood this to be a movement toward general compliance. See A. H. to G. W. [Aug. 5, 1794], *Papers of A. H.*, XVII, 45, 47. Neville seldom thought himself on the road to successful enforcement of the law. See, for example, Neville to Clymer, June 7, 1793, Wolcott Papers, XIX, CHS. Neville to Clymer, June 29, 1794, Wolcott Papers, XIX, CHS; *Gazette of the United States*, July 3, 1794, 2. According to the newspaper, Clymer was replaced by General Henry Miller of York, Pennsylvania.

During the winter of 1793–94 some of the larger distillers responded to the economic pressure imposed by the Quartermaster General. If they wanted to sell whiskey to the army, by far the largest potential customer on the frontier, they would have to register their stills and pay the tax. In response to this movement, tax resisters warned that they would burn out all who complied. True to their word, local firebrands destroyed the stills and mills of Kiddoe, Robert Shawhan, and William Richmond. These were apparently among the first attacks on those who complied with, rather than those who enforced, the excise law. In June resisters attacked the mills of William Coughran [or Cochran]. For more detail see Fennell, "From Rebelliousness to Insurrection," 65, 108, 109; Baldwin, *Whiskey Rebels*, 99–103. The very small number who attempted to comply and the swiftness with which they were put out of business by local resisters does not seem to justify the interpretation that this was a major breakthrough in enforcement. Nonetheless, it was a change, not of the minds but in the actions of large distillers, a breach in the apparent phalanx of resistance in western Pennsylvania.

26. Findley, *History of the Insurrection*, 36.

27. Neville to Clymer, June 20, 1794, Wolcott Papers, XIX, CHS.

28. G. W. to James Ross, June 16, 1794, *Papers of G. W.*, XXXIII, 403–405; G. W. to Presley Neville, June 16, 1794, ibid., 405–409; G. W. to John Cannon, June 16, 1794, ibid., 409; G. W. to Israel Shreve, July 28, 1794, ibid., 447–449; G. W. to James Ross, Aug. 1, 1794, ibid., 451–452; G. W. to James Ross, Aug. 6, 1794, ibid., 456–457. Again, Washington assumed that the responsibility for lost revenues lay with those at the top—in this case Cannon, who collected his rents—rather than with the underclass acting on its own initiative.

29. *Annals of Congress*, IV (Feb. 7, 1794), 437; *American State Papers, Finance*, I, 279–281. The case of excise collector Zacharius Biggs was also known to executive branch officials by this time. Biggs, collector in the Winchester, Virginia, area, had intercepted some illegal whiskey on the road, obtained evidence and witnesses, and proceeded toward prosecution of the delinquents. Biggs was then sued for trespass in his seizure of the whiskey. He lost the case, was fined by the local court, and resigned his office. The case was perceived by government officials as a decisive defeat for their efforts to collect the excise on the northwestern frontier of Virginia. See the report of Zacharius Biggs, Collector of Revenue, March 1, 1794; Edward Smith, Winchester, to Edward Carrington, Supervisor of the District of Virginia, April 21, 1794; Carrington to Tench Coxe, April 30, 1794; Biggs to Edward Smith, May 25, 1794; and Smith to Carrington, June 6, 1794, Rawle Family Papers, I, 2, 23, 24, HSP.

30. "An Act making further provision for securing and collecting the duties on foreign and domestic distilled spirits, stills, wines, and teas," June 5, 1794, *Annals of Congress*, IV, 1457–1461; A. J. Dallas to William Rawle, Jan. 18, 1794, Rawle Family Papers, I, 13, HSP.

31. Wright, *Britain and the American Frontier*, 86, 89, 92; Hammond to Grenville, March 7, 1794, Great Britain, State Papers Foreign, F. O. 5, IV, f113, no. 4; and Hammond to Grenville, June 27, 1794, F. O. 5, V., f131, no. 27. The quote is from

Hammond's letter of June 27. General Anthony Wayne reported in June that rebellion in Kentucky was likely and that sympathy for Britain was rampant on the frontier. According to Wayne, "I have but too much cause to apprehend a pervading spirit of opposition to the measures of the general government in the state of Kentucky." On May 24, state leaders gave what Wayne termed incendiary speeches and then one concluded by declaring that he "should not be displeased to see the British in possession of the northwest banks of the Ohio as our neighbors." Wayne to Henry Knox, June 11, 1794, Wayne Mss, XXXV, 116, HSP. See also *Gazette of the United States*, Feb. 15, 1794, 3; Feb. 24, 1794, 3; June 25, 1794, 3; June 27, 1794, 3; Twohig, ed., *Journal of the Proceedings of the President*, Feb. 11, 1794; Feb. 24, 1794; April 7, 1794; July 14, 1794.

Chapter Eleven: REBELLION

1. Wayne to H. Knox, Aug. 10, 1792, Richard C. Knopf, ed., *Anthony Wayne: A Name in Arms; The Wayne-Knox-Pickering Correspondence* (Pittsburgh, 1960), 63–66; Wayne to Knox, March 30, 1793, ibid., 208–213; Glen Tucker, *Mad Anthony Wayne and the New Nation* (Harrisburg, 1973); H. N. Moore, *Life and Services of Gen. Anthony Wayne* (Philadelphia, 1845), 170 and *passim*.
2. A. H. to G. W., Aug. 5, 1794, *PA* ser. 2, IV, 99.
3. Brackenridge, *Incidents*, I, 5–6; Findley, *History*, 78; H. M. Brackenridge, *History of the Insurrection*, 77.
4. Lenox to A. H., Sept. 8, 1794, Wolcott Papers, XIX, CHS; Brackenridge, *Incidents*, I, 5, 121; III, 26; Findley, *History*, 77–79.
5. Lenox to A. H., Sept. 8, 1794, Wolcott Papers, XIX, CHS; Findley, *History*, 74; H. M. Brackenridge, *History of the Western Insurrection*, 30. Findley and both Brackenridges believed that the incident never would have occurred if Lenox had not been joined by Neville, who was the true object of the crowd's hostility. Hamilton argued that Lenox and Neville escaped injury only by luck; that the shot was intended to injure or kill. See A. H. to G. W., Aug. 5, 1794, *Papers of A. H.*, XVII, 53.
6. H. M. Brackenridge, *History of the Western Insurrection*, 30.
7. Brackenridge, *Incidents*, III, 133–134.
8. Testimony of John Holcroft, ibid., III, 133–134, 136. Oliver Miller may have been the father of William Miller.
9. Testimony of James Therr, in ibid., III, 133; Robert Johnson to [?], July 20, 1794, *PA* ser. 2, IV, 71.
10. Brackenridge, *Incidents*, I, 8–9; III, 134–135; A. H. to G. W., Aug. 5, 1794, *Papers of A. H.*, XVII, 56; Abraham Kirkpatrick to G. W., July 25, 1794 and July 28, 1794, Wolcott Papers, XIX, CHS; Deposition of Francis Mentges, Aug. 1, 1794, *Papers of A. H.*, XVII, 2–5; Neville to Tench Coxe, July 18, 1794, ibid., n. 2, 3–4.
11. In addition to the sources cited in note 10, see Isaac Craig to Henry Knox, July 18, 1794, Wolcott Papers, XIX, CHS, which reported that two militiamen died and several were wounded, while one of Kirkpatrick's men died and four were wounded defending Neville's house on July 17. Of all the first-hand reports on events of that day, only Craig's mentioned the dead soldier from Kirkpatrick's command. Not even the major, in his detailed report to the President, announced the death of one of his men. Hamilton, in his emotional account of the outrage, never asserted the death of a soldier. He reported three soldiers wounded, one militiaman (McFarlane) killed, and several wounded.
12. Testimony of James McCallister, in Brackenridge, *Incidents*, III, 134–135; Lenox to A. H., Sept. 8, 1794, Wolcott Papers, XIX, CHS.
13. Deposition of Daniel Pugh, Nov. 19, 1794, Rawle Family Papers, I, 67, HSP; Addison to H. Lee, Nov. 23, 1794, Papers of Isaac Craig, Carnegie Library, Pittsburgh; John Wilkins to Clement Biddle, Aug. 1, 1794, *PA* ser. 2, IV, 81–82.

14. At the time, the administration's opponents theorized that Alexander Hamilton ordered the processes served under the old law. William Findley, among others, believed that "the head of the revenue department conducted the execution of the law in a manner that was calculated to promote the event that happened" (Findley, *History*, 312–313). No direct evidence has surfaced to support the accusation, but Hamilton's statements and other actions during his tenure as Secretary of the Treasury—as discussed in Part II above—were certainly consistent with such intentions. Findley's charge must remain plausible, indeed likely, but unproved.

15. W. Bradford to Elias Boudinot, Aug. 1, 1794, Wallace Papers, II, HSP.

16. Cooke, "The Whiskey Rebellion," shared my estimation of Neville's central role in the affair. "If one man was responsible for the whiskey insurrection," Cooke wrote, "it was John Neville" (336). For my disagreements with Cooke and other interpreters of these events see Slaughter, "The Friends of Liberty, the Friends of Order, and the Whiskey Rebellion." For more detail on events discussed in this chapter see Brackenridge, *Incidents;* Findley, *History;* H. M. Brackenridge, *History of the Western Insurrection.* Baldwin, *Whiskey Rebels,* also gave a more detailed account, but it was based primarily on Brackenridge, *Incidents,* as supplemented by Findley, *History.*

17. Brackenridge, *Incidents*, I, 32–36.

18. Ibid., 37; *Pittsburgh Gazette*, July 26, 1794.

Bradford had apparently been involved for years in frontier independence movements. The "papers" reportedly found in his house that listed members or "leaders" of such a movement and detailed their activities have not been found. See "Extract of a letter from a Gentleman in Mc Pherson's battalion, Camp near Washington, Nov. 14, 1794," *Gazette of the United States*, Nov. 21, 1794, 3.

Bradford was born about the year 1760, in Maryland, and immigrated to western Pennsylvania in about the year 1782. Shortly thereafter, he was admitted to the Washington County bar, and one year later he was appointed deputy attorney general for the county. He served in that office until he left the region in 1794. Bradford was an extremely successful lawyer and lived in the finest house in the town of Washington. Many of his fellow lawyers in the region considered him mentally unstable, however, and lacking in judgment. After his flight from the region in October 1794, Bradford resettled in Bayou Sara, Louisiana Territory, where he lived the rest of his life. Boyd Crumrine, *The Courts of Justice Bench and Bar of Washington County, Pennsylvania* (Washington, Pa., 1902), 263, n.2; Crumrine, *Washington County*, 483.

19. *PA* ser. 2, IV, 71–72; Brackenridge, *Incidents*, I, 38. John Holcroft was widely reputed to be the author of the "Tom the Tinker" letters, although the assertion has never been proved. It is, of course, possible that there was no single person, but rather several associated with the name. There certainly were multiple "tinkers" who "fixed" the stills of men who tried to comply with the excise law.

20. Bradford's letter, reprinted in Brackenridge, *Incidents*, I, 38; Bradford to John McCally, Kinny Robinson, Thomas Cottrell, John Black, etc., Aug. 6, 1794, Executive Papers, Gov. Henry Lee, box 86, VSL; *PA* ser., 2, IV, 78–79.

21. Ibid., 79–81; Brackenridge, *Incidents*, I, 47–50.

22. Ibid., 42–44, 85–86; Richard H. Kohn, ed., "Judge Alexander Addison on the Origin of the Whiskey Rebellion," Boyd, ed., *Whiskey Rebellion*, 49–60.

23. Brackenridge, *Incidents*, I, 42–50; Isaac Craig to H. Knox, Aug. 3, 1794, Richard C. Knopf, ed., "Personal Notes on the 'Whiskey Rebels,' " *Historical and Philosophical Society of Ohio Bulletin*, XII (1954): 314–315; John Wilkins to General William Irvine, Aug. 19, 1794, *PA* ser. 2, IV, 168–174; William Bradford to Edmund Randolph, Aug. 10, 1794, WR, LC. John Wilkins's report to Irvine on the Pittsburgh meeting and the sentiments of the town's residents supports Brackenridge's account.

24. Fennell, "From Rebelliousness to Insurrection," 76–85, 92, 97–98, 114, 123, 126–127, 135, 139, 144, 155, 160, 169–171; Brackenridge, *Incidents*, I, 86.

25. Ibid., 43–44, 69.
26. Fennell, "From Rebelliousness to Insurrection," 73–92.
27. Brackenridge, *Incidents*, I, 50–66. Both Brackenridge, *Incidents*, I, 66, and Fennell, "From Rebelliousness to Insurrection," estimate the size of the Braddock's Field crowd at 7000. William Findley, *History*, believed it somewhat less, and Isaac Craig guessed 4500 in Craig to Knox, Aug. 3, 1794, in Knopf, ed., "Personal Notes," 314–315. Other estimates reported in eastern newspapers ranged between 9000 and 12,000.
28. Findley, *History*, 102; Craig to Knox, Aug. 3, 1794, Knopf, ed., "Personal Notes," 314–315.
29. Brackenridge, *Incidents*, I, ch. 8.
30. Fennell, "From Rebelliousness to Insurrection," 113; John Webster to Neville, Aug. 2, 1794.
31. Brackenridge, *Incidents*, I, ch. 8; Fennell, "From Rebelliousness to Insurrection," 66, 99, 103, 117, 120, 121. Altogether, rebels banished seven men from western Pennsylvania during July and August (Fennell, 126).
32. *The Speech of Albert Gallatin . . .* (Philadelphia, 1795), 16; *PA* ser. 2, IV, 159–161. Brackenridge, *Incidents*, counted 260 delegates; Fennell, "From Rebelliousness to Insurection," has located only 240. Findley, *History*, reported "upwards of 200 delegates" (113).

Albert Gallatin (1761–1849) was born to an aristocratic family in Geneva, Switzerland, and was educated in that city in the era's Enlightenment ideals. He immigrated to America without consulting his family, in 1780. In 1784 he traveled to western Pennsylvania and set up a store in Fayette County. His first public office was as a delegate to the Harrisburg convention of 1788, which met to consider ways and means of revising the new United States Constitution. Gallatin had supported adoption of the Constitution, and later became a Republican in national politics. He was a member of the state constitutional convention of 1789–90, and was elected to the state legislature in 1790, where he served through 1793. The Assembly elected him a United States Senator in 1793, but he was denied a seat in that body on the dubious grounds that he had not been a resident of the U. S. for nine years. Beginning in 1795 Gallatin served three terms in the U. S. Congress, where he distinguished himself as a Republican partisan and an expert on fiscal affairs. He served as Secretary of the Treasury from 1801 to 1814. For ten years beginning in 1813 (even while he remained technically in his cabinet post) Gallatin served abroad almost continuously on diplomatic missions. From 1816 to 1823 he was Ambassador to France. Gallatin's last foreign mission was to England in 1826–27. He came out of retirement in 1831 to accept the presidency of John Jacob Astor's National Bank. Raymond Walters, Jr., *Albert Gallatin: Jeffersonian Financier and Diplomat* (New York, 1957).
33. *Speech of Gallatin*, 18; John Wilkens to Clement Biddle, Aug. 1, 1794, *PA* ser. 2, IV, 81–82; D. Bradford to Timothy Pickering, Oct. 4, 1794, Timothy Pickering Papers, reel 41; Kenneth A. White, ed., " 'Such Disorders Can Only be Cured by Copious Bleedings': The Correspondence of Isaac Craig During the Whiskey Rebellion," *WPHM*, LXVII (1984): 213–242. David Bradford's account of the Parkinson's Ferry meeting portrays Brackenridge as the fiery radical. See Bradford to Isaac Craig, Oct. 5, 1794, White, ed., "Correspondence of Craig," 235–236. The accounts of Findley, Gallatin, and the others cited above corroborate Brackenridge's version. See *Speech of Gallatin*, 27.

Chapter Twelve: RESPONSE

1. Wright, *Britain and the American Frontier*, 96–99; Great Britain, State Papers Foreign, F. O. V, f113, no. 4; V, f131, no. 27; V, f191d, no. 28; V, f266–268, no. 30; V, f279, no. 31; V, f202, no. 31; V, f324–326, no. 32; Bernard Mayo, ed., *Instructions to*

the British Ministers to the United States, 1791–1812, III (Washington, D. C., 1941), 24–27, 36–37, 60–61, 66–75; Jameson, ed., "Letters of Phineas Bond," 542–545, 554–559; *Gazette of the United States,* June 30, 1794, 2; Jaudenes to Alcudia, March 13, 1794, AN, Estado 217; Jaudenes to Alcudia, March 13, 1794, AN, Estado 218; Jaudenes to Alcudia, Oct. 31, 1794, AN, Estado 250; Jaudenes to Alcudia, July 25, 1795, AN, Estado 297; Bemis, *Jay's Treaty,* 246–247, 250–251; Bemis, *Pinckney's Treaty,* 239–248.

2. Edmund Randolph to William Bradford, A. H., and Henry Knox, July 11, 1794, *Papers of A. H.,* XVI, 588–590; *Gazette of the United States,* June 23, 1794; Anthony Wayne to Knox, June 11, 1794, Knopf, ed., *Wayne–Knox–Pickering–McHenry Correspondence,* 342–343; *American State Papers: Indian Affairs,* I, 482, 486, 501; *Papers of A. H.,* XVI, notes 1 and 2, 588–590.

3. Conference Concerning the Insurrection in Western Pennsylvania, Aug. 2, 1794, *Papers of A. H.,* XVII, 9–14.

4. Ibid.

5. Ibid. On Aug. 4, Associate Justice of the Supreme Court James Wilson fulfilled the legal requirement by declaring that the execution of law in western Pennsylvania was "obstructed by combinations too powerful to be suppressed by the ordinary course of judicial proceedings," thus freeing the administration for a military response. Judge Wilson to G. W., Aug. 4, 1794, *PA* ser. 2, IV, 82–83.

6. A. H. to G. W., Aug. 2, 1794, *Papers of A. H.,* XVII, 15–19; A. H. to G. W., Aug. 5, 1794, ibid., 24–58; note 88, ibid., 58; Minutes of the Meeting at Pittsburgh, Aug. 22, 1792, *PA* ser. 2, IV, 29–31.

7. *Papers of A. H.,* XVII, 10; Proclamation of President Washington, Aug. 7, 1794, *PA* ser. 2, IV, 124–125.

8. G. W. to Burgess Ball, Aug. 10, 1794, *Writings of G. W.,* XXXIII, 462–463; G. W. to Charles Mynn Thruston, ibid., 464 466; G. W. to Henry Lee, Aug 26, 1794, ibid, 474–476; G. W. to Burgess Ball, Sept. 25, 1794, ibid., 505–507.

9. Ibid. See Philip S. Foner, ed., *The Democratic-Republican Societies, 1790–1800* (Westport, Conn., 1976); Eugene Perry Link, *Democratic-Republican Societies, 1790–1800* (New York, 1942); Hazard to Belknap, Sept. 11, 1794, *Collections of the Massachusetts Historical Society,* 5th ser., III (1877): 350; G. W. to Henry Lee, Aug. 26, 1794, *Writings of G. W.,* XXXIII, 474–479; G. W. to Gen. Daniel Morgan, Oct. 8, 1794, ibid., 522–524.

10. *Gazette of the United States,* Aug. 2, 1794, 2, 3; Aug. 25, 1794, 2; Aug. 26, 1794, 2; Aug. 28, 1794, 2; Sept. 10, 1794, 2; Sept. 15, 1794, 3; Sept. 30, 1794, 3; Dec. 27, 1794, 2; Dec. 29, 1794, 2.

11. *Gazette of the United States,* Aug. 30, 1794, 2; Sept. 13, 1794, 3; Sept. 15, 1794, 3; Sept. 24, 1794, 3; Sept. 26, 1794, 3; Dec. 11, 1794, 3; Dec. 18, 1794, 2; *Maryland Journal,* Aug. 27, 1794, 2; Sept. 17, 1794, 2; *Worcester Intelligencer,* Nov. 11, 1794, 3; Nov. 25, 1794, 3; *Courier of New Hampshire,* Aug. 28, 1794, 2.

12. *Gazette of the United States,* Aug. 2, 1794, 3; Aug. 28, 1794, 2; Sept. 15, 1794, 3; Robert Hendrickson, *Hamilton,* 2 vols. (New York, 1976), II, 290. As discussed in Chapters One and Four above, there was certainly an ethnic dimension to the Whiskey Rebellion, and ethnicity has been offered as a causal explanation for the insurrection by several historians (see Slaughter, "Friends of Liberty, Friends of Order, and the Whiskey Rebellion"). Irish and Scots-Irish immigrants were the initial transmitters of distilling technology on the frontier, and they also brought with them national traditions of opposition to excises and other internal taxes. As Jacob E. Cooke pointed out some years ago, however, when he criticized ethnic interpretations of the Rebellion, there are certain interpretive dangers in overemphasizing the ethnic factors of revolt (Cooke, "The Whiskey Insurrection," 320–321). Other regions shared the same basic ethnic makeup of western Pennsylvania

but did not rebel. There were numerous exceptions to the ethnic rule within the western country as well. Germans, for example, were about evenly divided over anti-excise resistance; nor were Welsh and English immigrants unanimous in their political loyalties. It is difficult to sort out poverty from ethnicity, especially since recent immigrants occupied in disproportionate numbers the bottom rungs of the economic ladder. The explanation offered here emphasizes the ideological, political, inter-regional, international, economic, and class dimensions over ethnic ones because the revolt most certainly transcended ethnic and other cultural tensions, and because ethnic explanations tend to beg the wider questions that put native Americans on both sides of the controversy. This is not to say that ethnicity and culture are not relevant to the story.

13.   *Worchester Intelligencer*, Oct. 7, 1794; *Gazette of the United States*, Aug. 4, 1794; Aug. 20, 1794; Sept. 10, 1794, 2; Nov. 20, 1794, 2; Dec. 17, 1794, 3; *Courier of New Hampshire*, Nov. 15, 1794, 3; "Tully" no. 4, *American Daily Advertiser*, Sept. 2, 1794; *Carlisle Gazette*, Aug. 13, 1794, 1–3; Aug. 20, 1794, 3; [Hagerstown] *Washington Spy*, Sept. 24 and Oct. 7, 1794.

14.   [John Taylor,] *An Enquiry into the Principles and Tendency of Certain Public Measures* (Philadelphia, 1794); A Citizen [William Findley?], *A Review of the Revenue System Adopted by the First Congress Under the Federal Constitution* (Philadelphia, 1794); *Gazette of the United States*, Sept. 4, 1794, 1; Sept. 10, 1794, 2; Dec. 15, 1794, 3; Dec. 22, 1794, 3; Address of the German Republican Society; "Franklin," *Independent Gazetteer*, Aug. 30, 1794; *Washington Spy*, Sept. 3 and Sept. 10, 1794. Letters from friends of liberty frequently appeared in the *General Advertiser*, Boston *Independent Chronicle*, and *New York Patriotic Register*.

15.   *A Review of the Revenue System*, 1–3, 15, 17–20, 28; Taylor, *Enquiry*, 1–3, 5, 6, 47.

16.   PA ser. 2, IV, 82–136; Harry Marlin Tinkcom, *The Republicans and Federalists in Pennsylvania, 1790–1801: A Study in National Stimulus and Local Response* (Harrisburg, 1950), 113–131; *American State Papers: Miscellaneous*, 2 vols. (Washington, D. C., 1834), I, 85, 97–103; Randolph to G. W., Aug. 5, 1794, Washington Papers, LC; Richard H. Kohn, "The Washington Administration's Decision to Crush the Whiskey Rebellion," *JAH*, LIX (1972): 568–575.

17.   Judge Wilson to G. W., Aug. 4, 1794, PA ser. 2, IV, 82–83; Proclamation of President Washington, Aug. 7, 1794, ibid., 123–127.

18.   Instructions to the United States Commissioners, Aug. 7, 1794, WR, LC (also printed with wrong date (Aug. 8) in PA ser. 2, IV, 137–139); Randolph to Commissioners, Aug. 7, 1794, Simon Gratz Collection, case 2, box 14, HSP.

19.   Kohn, "Washington Administration's Decision," 576; Bradford to Elias Boudinot, Aug. 1, 1794, Wallace Papers, II, HSP. For a more detailed account of the administration's internal decision-making process, see Kohn, "Washington Administration's Decision," which stands as the best analysis of this aspect of the Rebellion from the government's point of view.

20.   Commissioners to the Secretary of State [Edmund Randolph], Aug. 17, 1794, Pennsylvania: Whiskey Rebellion Papers, I, LC (hereafter referred to as WR, LC); A. H. to Henry Lee, Aug. 25, 1794, *Papers of A. H.*, XVII, 143–145; Brackenridge, *Incidents*, I, 102; II, 5. Pennsylvania Governor Thomas Mifflin also appointed his own peace commissioners, Chief Justice of the State Supreme Court Thomas McKean, and General William Irvine, who cooperated with the national commissioners on the scene. See, Irvine Papers, XII, HSP; Executive Minutes of Governor Thomas Mifflin, PA 9th ser., I.

21.   Commissioners to Randolph, Aug. 21, 1794; Aug. 23, 1794, WR, LC; Proceedings of the First Conference, Aug. 20, 1794, PA ser. 2, IV, 182–185; Commissioners to the Committee of Conference, Aug. 21, 1794, ibid., 187–189; Committee of Conference to the U. S. Commissioners, Aug. 22, 1794, ibid., 190–191; Propositions Submitted

by the U. S. Commissioners, Aug. 22, 1794, ibid., 191–193; Yeates to Mrs. Yeates, Aug. 20 and Aug. 22, 1794, Yeates Papers Correspondence, folder 7, HSP; Irvine to Mifflin, [Aug.?] 1794, Irvine Papers, XII, HSP. Although it was known as the committee of twelve, fourteen delegates actually met with the commissioners. The extra two were from Ohio County, Virginia.

22. Commissioners to Randolph, Aug. 23, 1794, WR, LC; Report of the Pennsylvania Commissioners to Governor Mifflin, Aug. 22, 1794, *PA* ser. 2, IV, 194–198; William Bradford to A. H., Aug. 23, 1794, *Papers of A. H.*, XVII, 129–130.

23. A. H. to William Bradford, Aug. 8, 1794, *Papers of A. H.*, XVII, 76–77; "Tully" no. 1, *American Daily Advertiser*, Aug. 23, 1794, reprinted in *Papers of A. H.*, XVII, 132–135; "Tully" no. 2, *American Daily Advertiser*, Aug. 26, 1794, in *Papers of A. H.*, XVII, 148–150; "Tully" no. 3, *American Daily Advertiser*, Aug. 28, 1794, *Papers of A. H.*, XVII, 159–160; A. H. to Henry Lee, Aug. 21, 1794, *Papers of A. H.*, XVII, 121–122; A. H. to Thomas Simm Lee, Aug. 21, 1794, ibid., 122; A. H. to Isaac Craig, Aug. 25, 1794, ibid., 140; A. H. to Samuel Hodgdon, Aug. 25, 1794, ibid., 142; A. H. to Henry Lee, Aug. 25, 1794, ibid., 142–143; A. H. to Henry Lee, Aug. 25, 1794, ibid., 143–145; A. H. to Isaac Craig, Aug. 13, 1794, in White, ed., "Correspondence of Isaac Craig," 223; Craig to Henry Knox, Aug. 15, 1794, ibid., 223–224; Craig to Knox, Aug. 17, 1794, ibid., 224–225; Craig to Knox, Aug. 22, 1794, ibid., 225; A. H. to Craig, Aug. 25, 1794, ibid., 225–226, G. W. to Knox, Aug. 8, 1794, *Writings of G. W.*, XXXIII, 461; G. W. to Burgess Ball, Aug. 10, 1794, ibid., 463; Richard C. Knopf, ed., "Personal Notes on the 'Whiskey Rebels,' " *Historical and Philosophical Society of Ohio Bulletin*, XII (1954): 308–323. Pennsylvania Governor Thomas Mifflin, who attended the August 2 meeting with the President, was convinced that Washington had already determined on that date to raise an army. See Randolph to Mifflin, Aug. 30, 1794, *Papers of A. H.*, XVII, 163–167, and their correspondence throughout the month of August; A. H. to G. W., Sept. 2, 1794, *Papers of A. H.*, XVII, 180–190.

24. A. H. to Henry Lee, Aug. 21, 1794, *Papers of A. H.*, XVII, 121–122; A. H. to Henry Lee, Aug. 25, 1794, ibid., 142–143; A. H. to Henry Lee, Aug. 25, 1794, ibid., 143–145. The information did leak out, and each man blamed the other. See the Executive Letterbook, Aug.–Sept. 1794, VSL.

25. Craig to Knox, Aug. 17, 1794, White, ed., "Correspondence of Craig," 224. Ultimately, even Hamilton realized that Craig's reports misrepresented conditions in western Pennsylvania. But it was not until Hamilton arrived in the region during November 1794 and began personal inquiries that he learned how poorly Craig had served him in this regard. See Chapter Thirteen below.

26. *Papers of A. H.*, XVII, 1–169; A. H. to Thomas Simm Lee, Aug. 29, 1794, ibid., 162; *Writings of G. W.*, XXXIII, 451–490.

27. Brackenridge, *Incidents*, I, 108–109, Findley, *History*, 121–122; *Writings of Gallatin*, 19–20.

28. Brackenridge, *Incidents*, I, 112–115.

29. Ibid. For Bradford's account of these events, which contradicts all other surviving sources, see D. Bradford to T. Pickering, Oct. 4, 1794, Pickering Papers, reel 41.

30. Resolutions at Redstone Old Fort [Aug. 28–29, 1794], *PA* ser. 2, IV, 211–212; Brackenridge, *Incidents*, 116–121; Commissioners to Randolph, Aug. 30, 1794, WR, LC; Findley, *History*, 119–127; "The Speech of Albert Gallatin," 18.

31. Commissioners to Randolph, Aug. 30, 1794, WR, LC.

32. Commissioners to Randolph, Sept. 2, 1794, WR, LC; Kohn, "Washington Administration's Decision," 580–581.

33. Fayette County Standing Committee, Sept. 10, 1794, WR, LC.

34. Ibid.

35. Ibid.

36. John Redick to the Commissioners, Sept. 11, 1794, WR, LC; John McCarter[?] to James Ross, Sept. 16, 1794, ibid.; George Smith and James Montgomery to Ross, Sept. 15, 1794, ibid.; John Wilkins to Ross, Sept. 12, 1794, ibid.; Statement of Ross, Sept. 13, 1794, ibid.; reports of township votes, Sept. 11, 1794, ibid.; Resolves of Ohio County, Virginia, Sept. 8–9, 1794; *PA* ser. 2, IV, 269–271; Report of the U. S. Commissioners, Sept. 24, 1794, ibid.; Resolutions of the Pittsburgh Meeting, Sept. 27, 1794, ibid.; Isaac Craig to John Neville, Sept. 12, 1794, in White, ed., "Correspondence of Craig," 229–230; Craig to Neville, Sept. 19, 1794, ibid., 232; Craig to Knox, Oct. 10, 1794, ibid., 237; Craig to Samuel Hodgdon, Oct. 17, 1794, ibid., 237; Craig to Neville, Oct. 20, 1794, ibid., 238; Craig to Hodgdon, Nov. 21, 1794, ibid., 240; *PA* ser. 2, IV, 233–545; *Speech of Gallatin*, 21, 25; Findley, *History*, 131, 133, 135, 138–139; Jasper Yeates to Mrs. Yeates, Sept. 25, 1794, Yeates Papers, HSP.

37. Ibid. By early October, it was apparently even safe to make fun of the rebels. See the satirical campaign speech of "John Fling, Esq." in the *Pittsburgh Gazette*, Oct. 11, 1794.

38. Second Proclamation of President Washington, Sept. 25, 1794, *PA* ser. 2, IV, 361–363.

Chapter Thirteen: A TALE OF TWO RIOTS AND A WATERMELON ARMY

1. A. H. to Jared Ingersoll, Oct. 10, 1794, *Papers of A. H.*, XVII, 315–316; A. H. to Thomas Mifflin, Oct. 10, 1794, ibid., XVII, 317–318; *Gazette of the United States*, Oct. 4, 1794; *Dunlap and Claypoole's American Daily Advertiser*, Oct. 17, 1794; Diary of Captain Jonas Smith, Sept. 29, 1794, NJHS; Alexander James Dallas, "Letters on the Western Insurrection," George Mifflin Dallas Collection, box 18, folder 18, 5, HSP; Rawle Family Papers, I, 40–42, HSP; Journal of Major Gould, Society Collection, HSP.

    The derisive term "Watermelon Army" was apparently first used in a satirical essay entitled "An Indian Treaty" which was reprinted in newspapers throughout the East during September 1794. In this spoof of the inter-regional controversy over the excise, a character named "Captain Whiskey" warned the army to stay home. "Brothers," he proclaimed, "you must not think to frighten us with fine arranged lists of infantry, cavalry, and artillery composed of your watermelon armies from the Jersey shores; they would cut a much better figure in warring with the crabs and oysters about the Capes of Delaware." For obvious reasons, New Jerseyans were the ones most offended by the piece. It was probably not a coincidence that the New Jersey corps had a higher percentage of volunteers and suffered less draft resistance than the other states involved in the suppression of the Rebellion. New Jersey's troops were also the least disciplined and most violent and were responsible for both the civilian deaths in Carlisle. Plundering was also a greater problem among the militia of that state than with the others. See "An Indian Treaty," *PA* ser. 2, IV, 545–549; and "Jersey Blue's intended answer to Capt. Whiskey's intended speech to the Commissioners at Pittsburgh, if their Session continues till Sept. 1st, 1794," ibid., 549.

2. The major sources for information about other anti-excise violence outside of western Pennsylvania include the Rawle Family Papers, I, HSP; National Archives Microfilm Publications, M986, Criminal Case Files of the U. S. Circuit Court for the Eastern District of Pennsylvania, 1791–1840, reel 1, case files, 1791–1799; National Archives Microfilm Publications, microcopy no. 414, reel 1, Letters Sent by the Commissioners of the Revenue and the Revenue Office, 1792–1807; *Gazette of the United States;* [Hagerstown, Md.] *Washington Spy;* Maryland State Papers, 1 (ser. A), Md HR; Council Letterbook, Md HR; *Maryland Journal and Baltimore Advertiser;* Executive Papers and Executive Letterbook, VSL.

3. Petition, Carlisle, Pa., Aug. 14 [dated Aug. 29], 1794, Rawle Family Papers. I, 31, 132, HSP.

4. Ibid.

5. "Notes of Cumberland County Testimony" [n. d.], Rawle Family Papers, I, 119, 125, HSP; NA, M986, reel 1, U. S. v. Robert Luske; "Statement of John Huling, Oct. 8, 1794, Rawle Family Papers, I, 34, 48, 116, HSP.

6. Gordon S. Wood, "A Note on Mobs in the American Revolution," WMQ, XXIII (1966): 635–642; Pauline Maier, "Popular Uprisings and Civil Authority in Eighteenth-Century America," WMQ, XXVII (1970): 3–35; Slaughter, "Mobs and Crowds, Riots and Brawls"; Declaration of William Eaken, Sept. 29, 1794, Rawle Family Papers, I, 38, HSP; Declaration of Anthony Fearer, Sept. 29, 1794, ibid., I, 39; Examination of Francis Gibson, Sept. 29, 1794, ibid., I, 35.

7. Deposition of George Rowan, Sept. 27, 1794, Rawle Family Papers, I, 33, HSP; Deposition of James Dill, Jr., Sept. 28, 1794, ibid., I, 34; Examination of Francis Gibson, Sept. 29, 1794, ibid., I, 35; Warrant, Sept. 29, 1794, ibid., I, 37; Notes on testimony in Cumberland County [n. d.], ibid., I, 120; Deposition of James Bacon, Sept. 29, 1794, ibid., I, 36.

8. U. S. v. James Quigley and others, Rawle Family Papers, I, 124. The Chambersburg (Franklin County) and Northumberland (Northumberland County) riots were both more violent than the Carlisle episode and found communities more evenly split over the issue. In both cases the division appears, for the most part, to have occurred along class lines and found elites unsuccessfully (at first) attempting to convince non-deferential common folks of the error of their ways. In each case the poles were cut down by opposing groups and some violence surrounded attempts to rebuild the symbols. See NA M986, U. S. v. Frederick Reamer, U. S. v. Thomas Wilson, U. S. v. Thomas Caldwell, U. S. v. Andrew Billmeyer, U. S. v. William Bonham; Rawle Family Papers, I, 51–57, 74–101, 110, 123, 126–127, 135.

9. "Citizen, to the Enemies of Anarchy," Washington Spy, Aug. 27, 1794, 1; Gazette of the United States, Aug. 23, 1794, 3; Council Letter Book, 1793–1796, 42–43, Md HR 1883.

10. Gazette of the United States, Sept. 9, 1794, 3; Oct. 4, 1794, 2; Edward Carrington to James Wood, Sept. 24, 1794, Executive Papers, Box 87, VSL; Courier of New Hampshire, Oct. 4, 1794, 1.

11. Ibid.

12. Gazette of the United States, Oct. 4, 1794, 2.

13. Lee to Brigadier General Mountjoy Bayley, Sept. 13, 1794, Council Letterbook, 1793–1796, Md HR, 60–61.

14. Maryland Journal, Sept. 26, 1794, 2; Sept. 22, 1794, 3; Sept. 17, 1794, 2; Sept. 19, 1794, 3.

15. Papers of A. H., XVII, 231–233; Maryland Journal, Sept. 26 and Oct. 6, 1794; Council Letter Book, 1793, 1796, Md HR; Samuel Chase to [Gov. T. S. Lee?], Oct. 6, 1794, Scharf Collection, box 58, items 11A and 11B, Md HR; Thomas Scharf, History of Western Maryland, 2 vols. (Philadelphia, 1882); General Court of the Western Shore, Judgments, Oct. term 1794, J G 25, Md HR; General Court of the Western Shore, Docket, Oct. 1794 term, 260 Md HR; Adjutant General's Papers, box 57, Washington County, 1793–1808, Md HR; Will H. Lowdermilk, History of Cumberland (Washington, D. C., 1878); Harry I. Stegmaier et al., Allegany County: A History (Parsons, West Virginia, 1976); T. J. C. Williams, History of Frederick County Maryland, 2 vols. (Frederick, 1910); Thomas J. C. Williams, History of Washington County Maryland, 2 vols. (n. p., 1906). Norman K. Risjord, Chesapeake Politics, 1781–1800 (New York, 1978), ch. 16, is wrong on two counts about Maryland's role in the Whiskey Rebellion: (1) violence did spread beyond the generally recognized pockets of resistance; (2) Maryland had a much more difficult time filling draft quotas than Risjord believed.

16. A. H. to Thomas S. Lee, Sept. 17, 1794, *Papers of A. H.*, XVII, 242–243; A. H. to Rufus King, Sept. 17, 1794, ibid., 241–242. The decision to raise an army was made perhaps as early as Aug. 2, and certainly no later than Aug. 25. The decision to send the army at least as far as the staging areas in central Maryland and Pennsylvania came no later than Sept. 9. The final decision to march the army all the way to western Pennsylvania is the one referred to here, and came during the week after Sept. 9 and largely in direct response to events outside western Pennsylvania. See Kohn, "Washington Administration's Decision," 581.

17. Tench Coxe to Henry Lee, Aug. 29, 1794, Executive Papers, box 87, VSL; A. H. to Thomas Mifflin, Sept. 16, 1794, *Papers of A. H.*, XVII, 238–239. "Records of Officers and Men of New Jersey in the Pennsylvania Insurrection of 1794," *Records of the Officers and Men of New Jersey in Wars, 1791–1815* (Baltimore, 1970), records 2184 men actually serving in the army from that state. Approximately 5200 Pennsylvanians, 2350 Marylanders, and 3300 Virginians also served in the Watermelon Army. See, A. J. Dallas to William Irvine, Aug. 7, 1794, Papers of Brigadier General William Irvine, XII, HSP. The New Jersey and Pennsylvania troops rendezvoused at Carlisle, but maintained their separate identities as "wings" of the army; Virginia and Maryland regiments joined together at Cumberland, Maryland.

18. Willis Wilson to H. Lee, Sept. 15, 1794, Executive Department, Governor's Office, Militia Commission papers, box 11, VSL; *Gazette of the United States*, Sept. 13, 1794, 3; Sept. 30, 1794, 3; Jacob Rush, Warrant, Oct. 2, 1794, Rawle Family Papers, I, 43, HSP; General Matthews to James Wood, Oct. 12, 1794, Executive Papers, box 88, VSL; H. Lee to Brigadier General Bradley, Sept. 17, 1794, ibid.; H. Lee to Major Taylor, Aug. 22, 1794, Executive Letterbook, VSL; Circular to the Brigadier Generals, Oct. 4, 1794, Executive Letterbook, Oct. 4, 1794, VSL; Thomas S. Lee to Major Robert Morgan, Oct. 21, 1794, Council Letterbook, Md HR.

19. Charles Warfield to Thomas S. Lee, Aug. 29, 1794, Md. State Papers, box 76, item 33; C. [?] H. Williams to Lee, Sept. 2, 1794, ibid., item 34; ibid., items 36, 38, 46, 57; [?] Whittings to Archibald Blair, Nov. 18, 1794, Executive Papers, box 88, VSL; William Dillwyn to John Pemberton, Oct. 27, 1794, Gratz Collection, case 14, box 1, HSP; statement of "Old Blues of Mcpherson's Corps," Sept. 15, 1794, McCallister Collection, LCP; William Leddel Papers, Ms 33, NJHS; Reuben George to H. Lee, Sept. 12, 1794, Executive Papers, box 87, VSL; Thomas Nelson to H. Lee, Aug. 9, 1794, ibid.; James Wood to Brigadier General Jones, Aug. 28, 1794, Executive Letterbook, VSL; James Wood to Col. John Willson, Aug. 29, 1794, Executive Letterbook, VSL; H. Lee to Lieut. William Smith, Sept. 17, 1794, Executive Letterbook, VSL; [?] Whittings to Archibald Blair, Nov. 18, 1794, Executive Papers, box 88, VSL; Richard Willis, William Pile, John Cooke to James Woods, Sept. 18, 1794, Executive Department, Governor's Office, Militia Commission Papers, box 11, VSL; W. Martinsburg to H. Lee, Oct. 4, 1794, Militia Commission Papers, VSL.

20. [Edward] Oldham to Thomas S. Lee, Sept. 4, 1794, 1 Md. State Papers 1 (ser. A) 4 Md HR 6636, box 76, item 5; Lee to Oldham, Nov. 3, 1794, Council Letterbook, 90, Md HR; Lee to Mountjoy Bayly, Nov. 3, 1794, Council Letterbook, 91, Md HR; Lee to John Carlile, Sept. 4, 1794, Council Letterbook, 49–50; William Van Lear, Williamsport, to Lee, Sept. 1, 1794, Md. State Papers, box 76, item 8; John Briscoe, St. Mary's County, to Lee, Sept. 9, 1794, Md. State Papers, box 76, item 14, reported "only one volunteer from one regiment"; John Carlile, Harford Town, to Lee, Aug. 30, 1794, Md. State Papers, box 76, item 16, reported that "except the Light Dragoons who came forward voluntarily" the rest of his quota was achieved through the draft; William Whitely, Caroline County, to Lee, Sept. 1, 1794, Md. State Papers, box 76, item 6; Brigadier General Forrest, Georgetown, to Lee, Aug. 22, 1794, Md. State Papers, box 76, item 7, Md HR, had no problem getting "respectable volunteers to the full number required," but finding enough enlisted men to follow the

officers west was a problem; T. M. Forman, Cecil County, to Lee, Aug. 29, 1794, Md. State Papers, box 76, item 20, Md HR; Md. State Papers, box 76, items 11a, 15, 17a, 23; Md. State Papers, box 77, pt. 1, items 1–50.

21. Lemuel Corke, Surry County, to General [James] Bradley, Sept. 12, 1794, Executive Papers, box 87, VSL; H. Lee to the Secretary of War, Sept. 17, 1794, Executive Letterbook, VSL; Lee to Bradley, Sept. 17, 1794, Executive Letterbook, VSL; Joseph James, Dinwiddie County, to James Wood, Sept. 29, 1794, Executive Department, Governor's Office, Militia Commission Papers, box 11, VSL; Joseph Jones to [?], Sept. 19, 1794 and Sept. 23, 1794, Militia Commission Papers, box 11; R. [?] Ninnon [?] to Joseph Jones, Sept. 16, 1794, Militia Commission Papers, box 11; James Bradley, Surry, to Lee, Sept. 16, 1794, Executive Papers, box 87; James Bradley to Lee, Sept. 12, 1794, Executive Papers, box 87; Jonathan Clarke, Spotsylvania, to James Wood, Sept. 19, 1794, Executive Papers, box 87, VSL; A. Lewis to [?], Oct. 3, 1794, Executive Papers, box 88, VSL.

There was an attempt at the time, and largely successful for the last 190 years, to hide reluctance of citizens to serve in the Watermelon Army. Governor Henry Lee of Virginia, for example, was embarrassed that his state experienced difficulty meeting its quotas, a fact that he thought would reflect discredit on the Commonwealth and confirm the northern impression that "Antifederalism" was strong in the South. Both state and federal officials feared that word of resistance would aid the cause of the rebels, inspire others with the courage to desert to the enemy, and aid their political foes in Congress and the national press. See, for example, Charles Hay, Clerk of the [Virginia] House of Delegates, Nov. 12, 1794, Executive Papers, box 88, VSL; James A. Bradley to the Council, Oct. 26, 1794, Executive Papers, box 88, VSL; Robert Brooke, Circular to the Brigadier Generals, Dec. 16, 1794, Executive Letterbook, VSL; Gazette of the United States, Sept. 6, 1794, 3. Northampton County and Bucks County, Pennsylvania also failed to meet their quotas of troops, although Philadelphia and Baltimore exceeded theirs. See Alexander James Dallas, "Letters on the Western Insurrection," George Mifflin Dallas Collection, box 18, folder 18, 9, HSP.

22. Findley, History, 148–156. The character of this army was not remarkably different from that of the Continental Army in the Revolution. See, for example, Charles Royster, A Revolutionary People at War: The Continental Army and American Character 1775–1783 (Chapel Hill, 1979); John C. Dann, ed., The Revolution Remembered: Eyewitness Accounts of the War for Independence (Chicago, 1980).

23. General Orders and Official Documents for the Direction and Government of the Army in the suppression of Western Insurrection 1794, Am. 661, HSP; Findley, History, 148–156; Captain Jonas Smith, Diary, NJHS; John Hugg Clunn, Diary, printed as "March on Pittsburgh, 1794," PMHB, LXXI (1947): 44–67; Leland D. Baldwin, ed., "Orders Issued by General Henry Lee During the Campaign Against the Whiskey Insurrectionists," WPHM, XIX (1936): 88–89. The army kept no systematic records of desertions, so conclusions are based on correspondence, journals, and orders issued by senior officers. William Irvine, Journal of an Expedition Against the Western Insurgents, Am. 690, HSP; General Orders, Nov. 19 and 22, 1794, Am. 690, HSP; George Gale to [T. S. Lee?], [n. p., n. d.], Md. State Papers, box 77, pt. 2, item 51, Md HR.

24. Diary of Robert Wellford, Mss. 1 W4599a1, VHS; Baldwin, ed., "Orders Issued by General Henry Lee," 86; H. Frank Eshleman, ed., "Autobiography of William Michael: Part II," Papers Read Before the Lancaster County Historical Society, XXV (1921): 70; H. Lee to Dr. [Robert] Wellford, Dec. 17, 1794, Executive Papers, box 87, VSL; Dr. Edward Cutbush to Dr. William Bache, Dec. 20, 1794, APS. The army kept no systematic records of daily troop strength so conclusions about illness among the soldiers are based on physicians' records, diaries, and correspondence.

25. *PA* ser. 2, IV, 429; Ford, "Journal"; [Halifax] *North Carolina Journal,* Oct. 27, 1794.
26. G. W., *Diary,* IV, 212–216; *Papers of A. H.,* XVII, 320–321; G. W. to Randolph, Oct. 11, 1794, *Writings of G. W.,* XXXIV, 1–2; G. W. to Randolph, Oct. 16, 1794, ibid., 2–4.
27. G. W. to Henry Lee, Oct. 20, 1794, *Writings of G. W.,* XXXIV, 5–7; G. W. to A. H., Oct. 21, 1794, ibid., 7–8; G. W. to A. H., Oct. 26, 1794, ibid., 8–9; G. W. to A. H., Oct. 31, 1794, ibid., 9–11.

Seventy-three-year-old Herman Husband was among the first group of four "rebels" arrested in Bedford County during October. He was an itinerant preacher and pamphleteer who also had been associated with the Regulator movement in North Carolina twenty years earlier. Husband had a millenarian, utopian vision of the society in which he now lived, and expected a "New Jerusalem" to flourish in the western country during the immediate future. In fact, he played a rather minor role in the Rebellion. Local tradition associates him with the raising of a liberty pole at Brunerstown, and he was a delegate to the Parkinson's Ferry and Redstone meetings during August 1794. He advocated a moderate course, but Gallatin termed him the "Pennsylvania madman" for his speaking style and biblical allusions on political reform. Husband favored an end to violence accompanied by a petitioning campaign for repeal of the excise law and democratizing amendments to the Constitution. The old man languished in the Philadelphia jail from late October through the end of May 1795, when charges against him were dismissed. His health was ruined, however, and he died shortly thereafter, somewhere on the road back to Bedford. See Mark Haddon Jones, "Herman Husband: Millenarian, Carolina Regulator, and Whiskey Rebel," Ph. D. diss., Northern Illinois University, 1983; Fennell, "From Rebelliousness to Revolution," ch. 6.

28. Eshleman, ed., "Autobiography of William Michael: Part II," 71; Clunn, Diary, 60; A. H. to Samuel Hodgdon, Oct. 7, 1794, *Papers of A. H.,* XVII, 309; A. H. to Henry Knox, Oct. 8, 1794, ibid., 312–313; G. W. to A. H., Oct. 26, 1794, ibid., 343–344; *Maryland Gazette,* Nov. 6, 1794, 2; A. H. to Thomas Mifflin, Oct. 17, 1794, ibid., 372; "A Journal of Major Spear's Battalion of Maryland Militia on the Western Expedition to the Frontier Counties of Pennsylvania for the Support of our Laws, Liberty, and Society," HSP; Virginia Militia Records, Sept. 26–Oct. 7, 1794, Mss 12: 1794: 1, VHS; Col. Thomas Newton to James Wood, Oct. 7, 1794, Executive Papers, box 88, VSL; General Matthews to James Wood, Oct. 6, 1794, ibid.; Samuel Hodgdon Papers, William R. Perkins Library, Duke University.
29. See references in note 28 above.
30. "Journal of Major William Gould of the New Jersey Infantry, During an Expedition into Pennsylvania in 1794," *Proceedings of the New Jersey Historical Society* ser. 1, III (1848–1849): 173–191; Captain Jonas Smith, Diary; Diary of Robert Wellford; Alexander James Dallas, "Letters on the Western Insurrection"; Diary of Captain David Ford, HSP; William Irvine, Journal of an Expedition Against the Western Insurgents, Am. 690, HSP; Charles Smith to Jasper Yeates, Nov. 12, 1794, HSP; James Ten Eyk, Diary of the Whiskey Rebellion Expedition, 1794, Ten Eyk Family Papers, Special Collections, Rutgers University Alexander Library, New Brunswick, N. J.; A. H. to G. W., Oct. 25, 1794, *Papers of A. H.,* XVII, 342–343; Christopher Rockafellow to Major Leddell, Sept. 27, 1794, Leddell Papers, NJHS; Jacob Wolcott to Major Leddle [*sic*], Sept. 29, 1794, ibid.; R. D. Howell to Major Leddell, Nov. 12, 1794, ibid.; Major Leddell to Brigadier General White, Dec. 13, 1794. Officers were surprised by the same frontier phenomena that had shocked eastern visitors for decades. See, for example, Journal of Jacob Ashmead, Am. 009, HSP; *Gazette of the United States,* Nov. 17, 1794, 3.
31. Diary of Captain David Ford, Sept. 19, 20, 21, 23, 1794; *The Poetical and Miscellaneous Works of James Elliot, Citizen of Guilford, Vermont, and Late a Noncommis-*

sioned Officer in the Legion of the United States (Greenfield, Mass., 1798), NYPL, rare books.

32. Findley, *History*, 200–214; Brackenridge, *Incidents*, 31–33; William Leddel papers, diary, NJHS; [Annapolis] *Maryland Gazette*, Nov. 27, 1794, 2; Craig to Neville, Oct. 20, 1794, White, ed., "Correspondence of Craig," 238; Craig to Knox, Oct. 24, 1794, ibid., 239; Neville to Craig, Oct. 28, 1794, ibid., 239–240; Craig to Samuel Hodgdon, Nov. 21, 1794, ibid., 240.

33. Brackenridge, *Incidents*; R. Howe to John Ross, Aug. 9, 1794, Breck Mss., LCP (on eastern rumors implicating HHB); *Papers of A. H.*, XVII, 382–387; *Worcester Intelligencer*, Dec. 2, 1794, 3; A. H. to G. W., Nov. 11, 1794, *Papers of A. H.*, XVII, 366–367; A. H. to G. W., Nov. 15, 1794, *Papers of A. H.*, XVII, 372–373.

Brackenridge paid a price for his moderating efforts in any event. Few of his neighbors on either side of the affray were pleased by his actions, and fewer still trusted his judgment. Brackenridge's law practice suffered as a result, and his *Modern Chivalry* is a testament to the amount of free time he had after the Rebellion. He never again held an elected office in the region, although in 1799 he was appointed to the state supreme court.

34. Fennell, "From Rebelliousness to Insurrection," 155, 169–170, 171.

35. Henry D. Biddle, ed., *Extracts from the Journal of Elizabeth Drinker* (Philadelphia, 1889); *Maryland Journal*, Dec. 26, 1794; Journal of Jacob Ashmead, 1794, in Capt Jacob Ashmead Scrap Book, HSP, Am. 009; Papers of Brigadier General William Irvine, XII, HSP.

36. Criminal Case Files of the U. S. Circuit Court for the Eastern District of Pennsylvania, 1791–1840, reel 1; A. J. Dallas, *Reports of Cases Ruled and Adjudged in the Courts of Pennsylvania*, I (New York, 1882), 334–358; Francis Wharton, *State Trials of the United State During the Administrations of Washington and Adams* (New York, 1849), 102–184; Richard A. Ifft, "Treason in the Early Republic: The Federal Courts, Popular Protest, and Federalism During the Whiskey Insurrection," in Boyd, ed., *Whiskey Rebellion*, 165–182.

37. *Maryland Journal*, Dec. 12, 1794, 2; Brackenridge, *Incidents*, III, 31–33; Edmund Randolph to Alexander Addison, March 25, 1795, VSL.

38. *Maryland Journal*, Dec. 16, 1794, 2; Edward Carrington to A. H., Dec. 12, 1794, *Papers of A. H.*, XVII, 438–441; Benjamin Rush to James Currie, Nov. 30, 1794, in L. H. Butterfield, ed., "Further Letters of Benjamin Rush," *PMHB*, LXVIII (1954), 33–34; General Orders and Official Documents for the Direction and Government of the Army in the Suppression of the Western Insurgents 1794, Am. 661, HSP; William Winans, "Recollections of Boyhood Years in Southwestern Pennsylvania, 1788–1804," *WPHM*, XXII (1939): 19–46.

39. G. W. to John Jay, Nov. 1 [–5], 1794, *Writings of G. W.*, XXXIV, 15–19; G. W., Sixth Annual Address to Congress, Nov. 19, 1794, ibid., 28–37; G. W. to Edmund Randolph, Oct. 16, 1794, ibid., 2–4; G. W. to Henry Lee, Oct. 20, 1794, ibid., 5–7; G. W. to A. H., Oct. 21, 1794, ibid., 7–8.

40. James Madison to James Monroe, Dec. 4, 1794, *Writings of Madison*, VI, 219–227. In this letter Madison also expressed his fear that the consequences of the Rebellion would be even more damaging to the cause of liberty than Shays's Rebellion had been. "You will know the general tendency of insurrections to increase the momentum of power," Madison wrote. "You will recollect the particular effect of what happened some years ago in Massachusetts. Precisely the same calamity was to be dreaded on a larger scale in this case. There were enough, as you might imagine, ready to give the same turn to the crisis, and to propagate the same impressions from it." See also, Thomas Jefferson to James Madison, Dec. 28, 1794, Merrill D. Peterson, ed., *Thomas Jefferson: Writings* (New York, 1984), 1015–1017.

CONCLUSION

1. Edmund Jennings Randolph, *A Vindication of Mr. Randolph's Resignation* (Philadelphia, 1795).

2. G. W. to John Jay, Nov. 1 [-5], 1794, *Writings of G. W.*, XXXIV, 15-19; G. W., Sixth Annual Address to Congress, Nov. 19, 1794, ibid., 28-37; G. W. to Israel Shreve, Jan. 14, 1795, ibid., 87-88; G. W. to James Ross, Jan. 15, 1795, ibid., 89-91; G. W. to Charles Morgan, Jan. 17, 1795; ibid., 94; G. W. to Edmund Pendleton, Jan. 22, 1795, ibid., 98-101; G. W. to James Ross, March 14, 1795, ibid., 142-143; G. W. to J. Savary, March 25, 1795, ibid., 155-157; G. W. to Daniel Morgan, March 27, 1795, ibid., 159-160.

3. Charles A. Beard, *An Economic Interpretation of the Constitution of the United States* (New York, 1923); Beard, *The Economic Basis of Politics* (New York, 1945); Frederick Jackson Turner, *The Frontier in American History* (New York, 1920).

4. James M. Banner, Jr., *To the Hartford Convention: The Federalists and the Origins of Party Politics in Massachusetts, 1789-1815* (New York, 1970).

5. Thomas P. Slaughter, "Liberty and Taxes: The Early National Contest," *This Constitution,* no. 7 (1985): 11-16.

6. John Neville letterbook, Carnegie Public Library, Pittsburgh; Felton, "General John Neville," 69.

7. Alexis de Tocqueville, *Democracy in America*, Henry Reeve, trans., 2 vols. (New York, 1898), I, 294.

8. For an account of whiskey excise-tax resistance in America up to our own time, see Joseph Earl Dabney, *Mountain Spirits: A Chronicle of Corn Whiskey from King James' Ulster Plantation to America's Appalachians and the Moonshine Life* (New York, 1974), xiv.

INDEX